DISTRIBUTED SYSTEMS
AND COMPUTER NETWORKS

Jane.

1/87
Imperial College.

Prentice-Hall International
Series in Computer Science

C.A.R. Hoare, Series Editor

BACKHOUSE, R.C., *Program Construction and Verification*
BACKHOUSE, R.C., *Syntax of Programming Languages, Theory and Practice*
de BAKKER, J.W., *Mathematical Theory of Program Correctness*
BJÖRNER, C., and JONES, C.B., *Formal Specification and Software Development*
BORNAT, R., *Programming from First Principles*
CLARK, K.L., and McCABE, F.G., *micro-PROLOG: Programming in Logic*
DROMEY, R.G., *How to Solve it by Computer*
DUNCAN, F., *Microprocessor Programming and Software Development*
ELDER, J., *Construction of Data Processing Software*
GOLDSCHLAGER, L., and LISTER, A., *Computer Science: A Modern Introduction*
HAYES, I., (Editor), *Specification Case Studies*
HEHNER, E.C.R., *The Logic of Programming*
HENDERSON, P., *Functional Programming: Application and Implementation*
HOARE, C.A.R., *Communicating Sequential Processes*
HOARE, C.A.R., and SHEPHERDSON, J.C., (Editors), *Mathematical Logic and Programming Languages*
INMOS LTD, *Occam Programming Manual*
JACKSON, M.A., *System Development*
JOHNSTON, H., *Learning to Program*
JONES, C.B., *Systematic Software Development Using VDM*
JONES, G., *Programming in Occam*
JOSEPH, M., PRASAD, V.R., and NATARAJAN, N., *Multiprocessor Operating System*
LEW, A., *Computer Science: A Mathematical Introduction*
MacCALLUM, I., *Pascal for the Apple*
MacCALLUM, I., *UCSD Pascal for the IBM PC*
MARTIN, J.J., *Data Types and Data Structures*
POMBERGER, G., *Software Engineering and Modula-2*
REYNOLDS, J.C., *The Craft of Programming*
SLOMAN, M., and KRAMER, J., *Distributed Systems and Computer Networks*
TENNENT, R.D., *Principles of Programming Languages*
WELSH, J., and ELDER, J., *Introduction to Pascal, 2nd Edition*
WELSH, J., ELDER, J., and BUSTARD, D., *Sequential Program Structures*
WELSH, J., and HAY, A., *A Model Implementation of Standard Pascal*
WELSH, J., and McKEAG, M., *Structured System Programming*

DISTRIBUTED SYSTEMS AND COMPUTER NETWORKS

Morris Sloman
Jeff Kramer

Department of Computing,
Imperial College, London

Prentice/Hall
International

Englewood Cliffs, NJ London Mexico New Delhi
Rio de Janeiro Singapore Sydney Tokyo Toronto

Library of Congress Cataloging in Publication Data

Sloman, Morris.
  Distributed systems and computer networks.
  (Prentice-Hall International series in computer
  science)
  Includes index.
  1. Electronic data processing—Distributed processing.
  2. Computer networks. I. Kramer, Jeff. II. Title.
  III. Series.
  QA76.9.D5S56   1987   004′.36   86-9443
  ISBN 0-13-215864-7

British Library Cataloguing in Publication Data

Sloman, Morris
  Distributed systems and computer networks.
  — (Prentice-Hall International series in computer
  science)
  1. Electronic data processing —
  Distributed processing
  I. Title   II. Kramer, Jeff
  004′.36   QA76.9.D5
  ISBN 0-13-215864-7
  ISBN 0-13-215849-3 Pbk

© 1987 Prentice-Hall International (UK) Ltd

Prentice-Hall Inc., Englewood Cliffs, New Jersey
Prentice-Hall International (UK) Ltd, London
Prentice-Hall of Australia Pty Ltd, Sydney
Prentice-Hall Canada Inc., Toronto
Prentice-Hall Hispanoamericana S.A., Mexico
Prentice-Hall of India Private Ltd, New Delhi
Prentice-Hall of Japan Inc., Tokyo
Prentice-Hall of Southeast Asia Pte Ltd, Singapore
Editora Prentice-Hall do Brasil Ltda, Rio de Janeiro

Printed and bound in Great Britain for
Prentice-Hall International (UK) Ltd,
66 Wood Lane End, Hemel Hempstead, Hertfordshire, HP2 4RG
by A. Wheaton & Co. Ltd, Exeter.
Typeset by Mathematical Composition Setters Ltd, Salisbury.

1 2 3 4 5 90 89 88 87 86

ISBN 0-13-215864-7
ISBN 0-13-215849-3 PBK

To Ruth and Nitza

Contents

10 TRANSPORT AND SESSION LAYERS   234

11 PRESENTATION LAYER   260

Preface

This book provides an overview of the principles and concepts of distributed systems, giving details of the software architecture and communications support required. It can be roughly divided into three parts. The first part justifies the need for distributed systems, and describes the overall architecture. The second part describes the facilities required in modern programming languages for constructing distributed systems. The third and largest part describes the networking and communication facilities needed to support distributed systems. Case studies are used throughout to illustrate the particular topics.

The book is intended for use in the final year of an undergraduate course or early in a postgraduate programme. It is also intended to provide those in industry with a comprehensive description of the software and communications support required for distributed systems. It provides an introduction to the concepts and terminology which will enable computing personnel to understand and evaluate detailed specifications of standards and commercial systems.

Perspective

In the design and construction of a distributed system, we are faced with a number of confusing issues and choices. As in all system design, we aim at providing simple yet powerful and efficient solutions; but in practice we are forced to compromise between these aims. This book provides an insight into the main issues and tries to indicate what viable choices we have in solving them. The implications of each choice, or design decision, are discussed. An overview of the book can be presented as a progression through the choices available to the system designer.

The first choice is what should be distributed. Chapter 1 discusses and describes the advantages of distribution and provides case studies to illustrate some typical environments. However, it is usually impractical to completely distribute or replicate all components and most distributed systems provide for some resource sharing. Expensive resources, such as laser printers, plotters and large file stores are often provided from a shared pool of resources. A balance between resource sharing and distribution is required. Chapter 2 describes the overall software architecture required to support the distribution and sharing, and introduces the main issues which then require consideration.

Chapters 3 and 4 provide a high-level programming language view of the software for distributed systems. Once a decision has been made to distribute a particular application, it must be decomposed into suitable components. The form of components and their interconnection structures are discussed in Chapter 3. For instance, the choice of whether the system should be static or should allow dynamic change of its constituent components depends on the flexibility requirements. Although the latter may be desirable, a static system requires a simpler run-time support system. Component connections are determined by the naming scheme used for identifying communicating partners. Indirect naming and name passing provide more flexibility than direct or static naming but can introduce some overheads. Another important design decision is the type of interprocess communication primitives to be used. Chapter 4 compares the various primitives – synchronous and asynchronous sends, request–reply and remote procedure calls – and indicates the implications of use with respect to both usefulness and implementation cost. Implementation support for a system structured as a set of communicating components is provided by a number of existing or proposed languages for concurrent and distributed systems. Examples from some of these are used in Chapters 3 and 4. However, if no such language is available to a designer, the selected primitives can be provided as a set of procedure calls for an available (conventional) language such as C, Pascal or Modula 2. This has the disadvantage that the primitives are less secure as they are not part of a language syntax and semantics.

Distribution is dependent on an underlying communication system to support it. Standardization of services and protocols is essential to allow mixing of components from different manufacturers. The ISO reference model divides the communication system into seven layers, providing a framework for standardization and description of communication systems. The layers of the ISO model are used as the basis for structuring discussion of the communication system in this book.

Chapter 5 provides an overview of the communication system and underlying network. The choice of network topology is dependent on the application – whether over a wide area (WAN) or a local area (LAN). Most distributed systems are based on LANs or LANs interconnected by WANs. The choice of the type of network is mostly influenced by availability of suitable network interfaces for the computers being used. For instance, the preference for ring or bus structure, token passing or multiple access

(CSMA/CD) has been hotly debated. Only the lowest layers of the communication system interface to the network – the physical layer and media access portion of the data-link layer (Chapters 6 and 7) – are dependent on these factors.

An important design decision is whether a layer should provide a connection or connectionless service. Most of the standardization work has been oriented to connection services and protocols which usually involve a considerable communication overhead. They are therefore more suited to interconnection of autonomous computers than to closely cooperating computers in a distributed system. Connectionless protocols entail less overhead but do not enhance the reliability of the underlying communication service. The choice of service defines the functions that the protocol must perform with respect to issues such as error control, flow control and segmentation. Chapter 5 discusses the types of connection and connectionless services offered by a layer and explains the relationship between a service and the protocol which implements it. The controversy as to whether the network layer should provide a connection (virtual circuit) or connectionless (datagram) service is further discussed in Chapter 9.

Chapters 8–10 describe the issues related to protocol implementation for the data-link, network and transport layers respectively. Techniques for connection set-up, error control, flow control, and routing are described with examples from case studies.

The overheads of general-purpose standard and proprietary protocols are very high. Therefore many distributed systems which aim to provide close cooperation between components have a station kernel which supports interprocess communication (IPC) within a station and a highly optimized protocol which supports interstation IPC. These protocols correspond roughly to the transport/session layer of the ISO model but are optimized to support the specific IPC primitives available at the application level. Chapter 10 concentrates on this approach to distributed systems and covers three case studies – the CONIC and V-Kernel communications to support message passing and the Xerox Cedar remote procedure call implementation.

Although the book describes a 'bottom-up' view of the communication system, we advocate a 'top-down' approach to design. The choices of communication primitives should identify the services and hence the protocols required from the lower layers. However, the decisions cannot be made purely top down. Choices of protocol functions are also influenced by what service is being provided by the lower layers. For example, provision of a transport-layer service over a comparatively reliable local area network can be simpler than one over interconnected or wide area networks, which may lose, delay or reorder messages. The choices available at a layer and the need to consider decisions made at other layers is discussed throughout the chapters on the communications system.

If nonhomogeneous computers or different languages are used, the functions relating to the presentation layer, described in Chapter 11, must be included. This covers strategies for representing the primitive and constructed types found in most programming languages. The issues relating to maintaining structural information when transferring complex data structures are also discussed.

In the final chapter we describe two example applications services – virtual file and terminal service – which would be needed by many distributed applications.

Acknowledgements

We wish to thank our colleagues and students who have provided many useful suggestions for improving the book. In particular, our colleagues on the CONIC project – Jeff Magee, Kevin Twidle and Neranker Dulay – have helped to provide a stimulating environment for our work on distributed systems. David Robinson and Xenophon Andriopoulos also provided many helpful comments on the manuscript. Finally we would like to thank the Department of Computing at Imperial College for the use of Departmental facilities during the preparation of this book.

One

DISTRIBUTED SYSTEMS

What? Why? and Where?

In recent years there has been a dramatic fall in the cost of hardware processors and memory, combined with similar cost reductions and technological advances in the communications field. The result has been to make computer networks and interconnected computer systems a viable and cost-effective solution in many environments. Users have recognized the advantages of interconnecting what were independent computer systems to permit interaction, cooperation and sharing of facilities. The feasibility of cooperating distributed computers opens the door to new and more demanding applications.

It is therefore not surprising that the field of distributed computer systems has gained in popularity over the past ten years especially as such systems can offer many additional advantages over centralized systems. Reduced incremental cost, better reliability, extensibility, better response and performance are just some of the potential advantages.

But **what** exactly is a distributed system? What are its attributes? **Why** is it capable of offering such attractive benefits? What are the problems? This chapter will attempt to answer these questions, and to give some examples of **where** distributed systems have been used. The rest of the book will attempt to answer the major question:

How can one construct a distributed system?

What are the main issues to be solved and the current approaches available?

1.1 Definition of a Distributed System (WHAT?)

Distributed processing is a relatively new field and there is as yet no agreed definition. There is rather a spectrum of systems which progress from centralized systems through to a set of diverse, physically dispersed, autonomous computer systems which are interconnected by communications networks to permit the exchange of information. We are mainly concerned with the latter integration of autonomous computer systems to form a cooperative collection of computing components which together combine to achieve some common goal. This is a 'distributed' system. This intuitive description can be refined by taking each of the main components of a computer system and examining the meaning of distribution.

The major components which combine to form a complete system are:

System = hardware
     + system software (control + data)
     + application software (control + data).

However, in many systems the distinction between system software and application software is blurred. For instance in embedded real-time systems the application is often involved in device access and control, and process scheduling (for real-time constraints), both of which are usually the domain of system software. In large data-processing systems the data-management aspects are often integrated into the system software to provide efficient access and control. The distinction can then be made between control and data rather than between system and application. Distributed systems can then be examined using these three dimensions of **hardware**, **control** and **data**:

Distributed system = distributed hardware
      and/or distributed control
      and/or distributed data.

1. **Processing hardware**

    A distributed system must contain two or more computers, each with their own local memory and processors. This aspect of physical distribution is the most important factor in defining a distributed system. In order for the distributed computers to cooperate they must be interconnected: hence the need for some form of communications network. The distribution of the computers can reflect the physical distribution of the application or the functional decomposition of the system, where different computers provide different functions in the system (cf. special-purpose processors).

2. **Control**

    Systems contain both physical resources in the form of processors, terminals, devices etc. and logical resources in the form of processes, files etc. There must be some form of control provided to manage the resources and coordinate activities running on the individual processors. The strategy used to manage the resources of the system could be centralized, hierarchical or allow complete autonomy of the individual processors over local resources. This last approach requires loose coupling between the system components. In many cases an attempt is made to provide transparency in the sense that the system appears as a single uniform system, hiding the physical distribution and heterogeneity of its components.

3. **Data**

   One of the major resources requiring control by both the system and the application software is data. The data being processed can itself be distributed by replication (multiple copies at different locations) or partitioning (parts of the data kept at different locations). Data distribution is often used to enhance tolerance to failures and to provide improved performance by locating the data close to where it is generated and/or used.

The question is whether **all three** dimensions have to be distributed to classify a system as distributed, or is **one** sufficient?

1.1.1 Enslow's Model [Enslow, 1978]

One extreme is represented by Enslow's model, which demands that all three dimensions have the required degree of decentralization in order for a system to be classified as distributed. Enslow also requires that distribution is transparent and users of the system should be unaware that the system actually consists of multiple processors. A simplified form of Enslow's cube model is given in Fig. 1.1.

Each axis of the model contains a number of points, in order of increasing decentralization. A system is classified as fully distributed if all three categories are fully decentralized. Each axis is briefly discussed below.

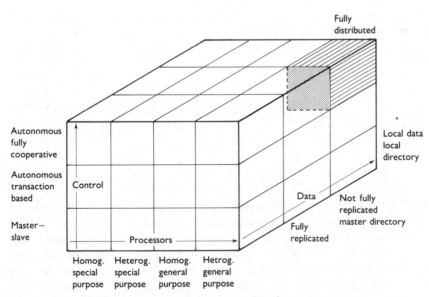

Figure 1.1 Enslow's model of distributed system types

1. **Hardware decentralization**

   Systems which contain a single control unit do not qualify, even if they have multiple specialized processors for functions such as input/output, vector or floating-point arithmetic (e.g. CDC 7600). Systems containing multiple control units do qualify. This includes both closely coupled multiprocessors, which may share a single coordinated input/output system, and fully separate computers.

2. **Control decentralization**

   In order to qualify control must be provided by multiple units, cooperating with each other rather than in a master–slave relationship.

3. **Database decentralization**

   Data must be partitioned and/or replicated, each part with its own local directory.

Enslow's model does provide some criteria for examining the relative decentralization of different systems. However, the strict definition rules out most systems described as 'distributed' in the literature. Also, rather than comparing the relative decentralization of systems, we are more interested in identifying those attributes which characterize a distributed system and the benefits and issues which such systems raise.

1.1.2 Our Model

We will use a more liberal definition:

> *A distributed processing system is one in which several autonomous processors and data stores supporting processes and/or databases interact in order to cooperate to achieve an overall goal. The processes coordinate their activities and exchange information by means of information transferred over a communications network.*

Closely coupled systems which communicate via shared memory or crossbar switches, and so **must** be physically close together, are thus not considered as distributed. Loosely coupled collections of totally autonomous computer systems which may, for example, be capable of transferring files between each other but do not cooperate to achieve some common goal, are also not considered as true distributed systems. Both classes of system are excluded as they do not raise many of the issues nor possess many of the advantages which we associate with true distributed systems.

The following are the attributes required of a distributed system:

1. **Arbitrary number of system and application processes (logical resources)**

   It should be possible to support these processes and accept (within limits) arbitrary increases and decreases in their number. This is essential for system flexibility and availability. In some case the system distribution and implementation structure should be transparent.

2. **Modular physical architecture (physical resources)**

   The system can consist of multiple interconnected and special-purpose processing elements. These can be physically distributed and may also vary in number during the system lifetime, e.g. system extension or component failures.

3. **Communication by message passing using a shared communications system**
   This provides for the transfer of messages in a cooperative (rather than master–slave) manner. It may support higher-level protocols, such as procedure calls, to remote process components. We exclude communication based solely on shared memory or shared address spaces.

4. **Some system-wide control**
   This is necessary to integrate the autonomous distributed processing elements into a 'single' coherent system. A common policy is provided to indicate how the system is used, facilities provided, access control, protection etc. The actual control provided depends on the overall goal of the system, but it usually includes transparent resource access and fault tolerance by loose coupling between the elements of the system.

One of the fundamental characteristics of distributed systems is that inter-process message transit is subject to **variable delays** and **failure**. There is a non-negligible time between the occurrence of an event and its availability for observation at some remote site. It is not possible to build up a consistent and complete view of the state of the system. Rather, the state information is partitioned and distributed. The executive in charge of system-wide control must make decisions using only partial (and possibly inconsistent) information. The possible loss of messages exacerbates this problem. This characteristic of indeterminate message delay and loss identifies the main difficulty in the design and construction of distributed systems.

1.2 The Objectives of Distribution (WHY?)

1.2.1 Motivation

As mentioned at the start of this chapter, there are two main stimuli for the current interest in distributed systems: technological change and user needs [LeLann, 1981].

Technological changes. The growth in microelectronics, VLSI etc., has changed the price–performance ratio to favor multiple low-performance processors rather than single high-performance processors. Also, the interconnection and communication costs have fallen dramatically in the past few years. Buses, packet-switched networks, local area networks etc. are now readily available and cost effective.

User needs. The general growth in the use of computing has led to demands for more sophisticated facilities (faster, extensible, reliable, . . .).

At the same time there is pressure for more economic solutions which reduce unnecessary communications and provide computer power where it is needed. In many cases this is supported by a managerial desire to decentralize.

1.2.2 Objectives

The potential benefits of distribution are many. The main objectives in moving to a distributed system are described below.

Reduced costs
As mentioned, the advent of low-cost micro- and minicomputers with a high performance–cost ratio has been the main impetus for providing distributed processing. However, the cost of peripheral devices has not declined as dramatically. The sharing of expensive resources (laser printers, databases, special-purpose processors, . . .) is another major objective for distributed systems.

In process-control applications, in particular, there can be a large saving of wiring costs by placing processing power adjacent to the plant. This results in the replacement of parallel wiring with serial twisted pair or coaxial cable. In many applications it is possible to use local intelligence to reduce communication costs by reducing the volume of traffic. This can be achieved by

- increased local processing;
- using data compression techniques;
- using memory as a buffer for smoothing 'bursty' traffic; and/or
- use of more efficient communication protocols.

Modularity and simpler software
Distributed systems must be constructed in a very modular fashion, where each component provides well-defined interfaces or services to the rest of the system. The enforced modularity leads to simpler system design, installation and maintenance, and allows analytical verification techniques to be used, at least at the component level.

The reduction in hardware costs has made it feasible to under-utilize a processor and dedicate it to a particular function or task. Where feasible, this functional allocation of tasks to processors has obviated the need for a complex multipurpose operating system at every computer station.

Flexibility and extensibility
As mentioned, distributed systems enforce modularity and the use of very clear interfaces, both for the hardware and the software. This discipline has the added advantage of facilitating modification or extension of a system to adapt to a changing environment without disrupting its operation. Hardware flexibility is provided by the replacement or addition of processing elements and communications connections; similar flexibility can be provided for the software without affecting the other components in the system. It is

therefore possible to start with a small configuration, and provide functional or performance upgrades by adding additional computers at low cost increments.

By using standardized communication protocols, it is possible to incorporate equipment from different manufacturers into a network, reducing reliance on any one manufacturer.

Delivery time of mini- or microcomputers is usually much less than for larger computers, making it easier to plan upgrades.

Availability and integrity

Distributed systems have the potential ability to continue operation if a failure occurs in the hardware or software. The use of multiple processors means that the failure of one processor need not cause the whole system to fail. Critical resources can be replicated. Using mutual inspection, faults can be detected and recovery effected by reconfiguration of the system to use the redundant resource. This is sometimes difficult to achieve in practice (e.g. if a processor is connected to a device, it is not possible for another processor to take over its function unless it is also connected to that device). The autonomous nature of the system components does facilitate graceful degradation of the available services.

In general, the decrease in complexity of each of the software components in a distributed system leads to improved reliability. Also, the loose coupling between processors (no shared memory) can help to provide protection from corruption by a rogue process.

The use of multiple low-cost computers makes it feasible to keep one or two as spares i.e. to provide say 10–20% redundancy in processors. With large single computers the only possible redundancy is to duplicate the entire machine, i.e. provide 100% redundancy. This can be very expensive.

The physical distribution of a computing facility at different geographical locations makes it less susceptible to damage from fire, flood or earthquakes, or from sabotage.

Performance

Performance is generally defined in terms of response time and throughput. Response time can be reduced particularly if most processing is done locally. The parallelism of multiple processors reduces the processing bottlenecks and can provide improved all-round performance.

Local intelligence can also be used to pre-process data by data reduction and formatting before transmitting it to a remote site. This helps to increase throughput.

Local control

Local sovereignty over data and processing can make the system more responsive to local needs. It may also result in increased motivation and involvement of local personnel.

1.2.3   Advantages of Centralization (**WHY NOT** Distribution)

There are still advantages which centralization can offer, particularly as the potential advantages of distribution are not always easy to realize. The new problems introduced by distribution can overwhelm the inexperienced designer.

Economy of scale
For some time, the rule was that the cost of a computer is proportional to the square root of its processing power (known as Grosch's law). This meant that it was cheaper to double the power of a large-scale centralized computer than to buy a second computer of similar power. With the advent of LSI technology and the decline in cost of computer hardware, this is no longer true. However, it does still apply to secondary storage such as disks. Resource sharing in a distributed system provides a possible alternative.

More powerful capabilities
A large centralized computer center can provide a far wider range of services, in terms of operating system software, and compilers which are not generally available for small computers. Also, some scientific programs are just too large: they require vast amounts of memory and processing power, and so must be run on large computers.

Again, these special facilities could be provided at a central site within a resource-sharing network.

Operating costs
The cost of personnel required to support a computing system is less if they can be centralized. It would not be possible to support operators, maintenance engineers, specialized programmers at every site in a distributed system. This obviously does not apply to a distributed system which is local to a single site; here the personnel could still be centralized and shared.

Computer installation management, such as security, provision of a 24-hour service and of an air-conditioned environment, is simpler for a centralized system.

Staff satisfaction
Highly skilled professional computer staff prefer to work in an environment where they can interact with colleagues having similar interests. Staff may feel isolated if assigned to remote sites. Again, this applies to geographical distribution and is not applicable to distribution within a local site.

Local programming and development
There is a negative side to local autonomy:

● It is more difficult to enforce standards when programming personnel are dispersed.

- Separate groups may end up duplicating many facilities and producing incompatible modules.
- If a local computer is small it may not be possible to attract experienced staff, which can result in incompetent design and implementation.

Once a local computer has been installed, possibly for a specialized purpose, additional functions and applications are often added without consideration for the overall goal of the system. Also, the true development cost of these additional applications is often hidden. The programming costs may not be taken into account as the personnel may be officially employed in another function.

Thus a distributed processing system will require some centralized management and very strict enforcement of standards. Alternatively all programming can be done centrally.

Communication subsystem
The complexity of the communications subsystem is often underestimated, particularly for local distributed systems. Any savings in the complexity of the operating system may be offset by the additional complexity of providing reliable communications. In practice, the communications system is replicated in all processors in the distributed system, and should be stable once developed. However, the overhead of supporting a communications system should not be underestimated.

Stretching the state of the art
The main difficulty is that distributed systems are relatively new and hence are not as well understood. The benefits provided by multiple interconnected components (modularity, availability, flexibility, etc.) should be balanced against the problems associated with concurrency and communication delays and failures. As mentioned above, nondeterminacy and the lack of a coherent system state make distributed systems difficult to construct and validate. This certainly deters industry and commerce who do not wish to get involved in research and development projects.

1.3 Distributed Processing Applications Overview (WHERE?)

This section describes various distributed processing applications. Some of these would not be classified as 'distributed' according to our definition given above, but they are often associated with distributed processing applications in the literature since they include many of the elements (e.g. network and communications system) which are necessary for distribution. They also give some feeling for the evolution of systems to full distribution. Three more detailed case studies are also presented.

1.3.1 Data Communication

A number of computers can be interconnected to form a network which is used to switch messages or packets of information between different geographical sites – sometimes between continents. Communication is between terminals and computers or between computers themselves. The computers connected to the network may or may not form a distributed processing system themselves, depending on whether there exists some overall goal for the connected computers together with some system-wide control. However, the data communication subsystem itself can be considered as a distributed system. It is physically distributed, its components cooperate to provide a common service, and it is controlled by a network-management system. Typical examples of such networks are the public packet-switched networks such as Arpanet, Transpac, Telenet and Datapac.

A more constrained use of data communication is in data collection and point of sales terminals which collect data on items being produced or sold. This information is transmitted to a remote computer for automatic stock control, credit checks, discount calculation etc. In this case the terminals can usually operate independently in case the remote computer fails.

1.3.2 Resource Sharing

A number of resources, such as computers, peripherals, special-purpose processors, programs, databases etc. are interconnected by a communication system in order to allow the sharing of resources. Often these are local networks within an office block, research or industrial establishment.

Office automation is one of the fastest-growing applications of resource sharing. As well as the use of intelligent terminals for word processing, accounting, some graphics etc., office automation systems provide some communal services, such as electronic mail, document filing, conferencing, and resource sharing, such as laser printers and databases.

The Cambridge Distributed Computer System (presented below as a case study) and DLCN (Distributed Loop Computer Network) at Ohio State University are examples of resource sharing systems provided on a university campus. It is argued that a resource-sharing system must have an overall common operating system to be considered a true distributed processing system; so large systems such as the ARPA network do not qualify.

Case Study: The Cambridge Distributed Computer System [Needham, 1982]
The system was designed to provide the services usually associated with a large conventional 'time-sharing' system, except that it would employ

- small, self-contained personal computers and terminals for user access, and
- **servers** for those shared facilities which still possess an economy of scale

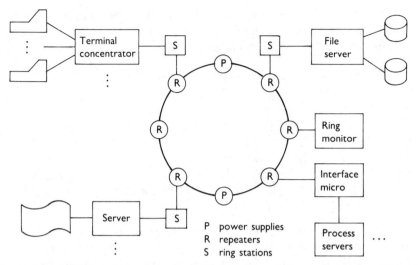

Figure 1.2 Outline structure of the Cambridge Distributed Computer System. Adapted from R. M. Needham and A. J. Herbert, *The Cambridge Distributed Computing System*, Addison Wesley, 1982, p. 28.

and for the more expensive resources (e.g. disks, printers, large memory and processing power).

Figure 1.2 gives an outline of the system.

Objectives
The objectives were to provide a high-performance system at low cost. The loose coupling between the system components would contribute to system flexibility and resilience to failures. The system would consist of heterogeneous components, usually dedicated to performing a particular function as a service to the rest of the system. Finally, as far as possible the distributed nature of the system should be transparent.

The physical system has the following main components:

- About fifty heterogeneous machines in the system.
- Terminals connected via concentrators to the network.
- Use of a 1 km Cambridge ring for communication. This provides a train of fixed-size message slots endlessly circulating around the ring (see Chapters 5 and 7).

The software structure is based on the use of servers:
As mentioned above the services of the system are provided by servers each performing a particular function. For instance,

File server: This provides a uniform interface accessible from all the different machine subsystems. It has a basic naming structure using unique identifiers which prevents unauthorized access but allows different directory structures to be superimposed. All the required functions are provided, such as disk management and integrity, atomic updates and interlocks for shared access.

Processing servers (processor bank): For work which is too demanding for a user's local machine, requests can be made to the processing servers. According to the requirements, allocation will be made to one of the heterogeneous collection of minicomputers which also support different operating systems. It is even possible to run concurrent programs by the allocation of multiple machines.

Resource manager: This server keeps account of what has been allocated, to whom, and for how long. It is essentially responsible for allocating and reclaiming resources.

Some of the other servers which exist in the system are the user authentication server (yields unforgeable tokens to prevent resource usage by an unauthorized user), boot server (loads server code at initialization), a time server (time of day) and a name server (gives the location of a named service or machine).

Issues
Some of the main issues raised by construction of the system were related to the desire for transparent distribution. In order to hide the location of resources and users, a uniform **naming/identification** scheme had to be adopted which was managed by the name server. Also the heterogeneous nature of the system was hidden by providing, as far as possible, uniform **representation** and access mechanisms. User authentication and **protection** was essential to prevent unauthorized access. Also access control to resources (**resource management**) is essential to prevent unwanted interference between users. Finally the efficiency of the **message intercommunication** must be able to provide adequate user response and system performance. These issues are further discussed in Chapter 2.

1.3.3 Process Control and Laboratory Automation

The advent of small, cheap microcomputers has made it possible to place them physically close to a device or plant being controlled. This had led to the use of multiple microcomputers performing the local monitoring and control. These are interconnected (often via a master computer) to coordinate their actions. Eventually, all devices which contain some electronics are likely to include one or more microprocessors. A device station would thus include the device (a sensor, actuator or mechanism controller) directly interfaced to a processor and provided with a communications interface for direct connection onto a network. If the control operation is likely to be time critical or complex, another closely-coupled processor could be incorporated into the station to handle communication functions. Each device station communicates with other stations, and possibly a central computer, to cooperate in the overall control of the plant.

As mentioned in Section 1.2.2, some of the advantages of the use of local processors are:

1. **Reduction in wiring costs**
    Industrial sites usually extend over distances of up to 1000 m, and all wiring for control systems have to be specially laid. Wiring can often account for a substantial proportion of the cost of a control system. Serial transmission lines can be used rather than the traditional use of large numbers of parallel lines linking instruments with a central computer.

2. **Faster response**
    Response time is one of the most important factors in the design of the control system. A local processor can be dedicated to a device and so respond very quickly. In fact the communication system for process control application differs from that for other applications in that low delays and response times are far more important than high throughput.

3. **Easier development and maintenance**
    This is aided by the enforced modularity of the software, which must be distributable. Also, the local intelligence in the device means it can be isolated from the rest of the plant for development or maintenance purposes. Degraded operation is also possible: local processing can continue to provide some level of control even when the central control station has failed. ⟋ 5/1/87

Case Study: Distributed system for underground monitoring and control in coal mines [Sloman et al., 1980; Kramer, 1984]
There are a large number of diverse activities in a coal mine which would greatly benefit from computer monitoring and control: coal cutting and extraction, coal transport, power consumption, monitoring of the environment and control of fans and water drainage. The functions required vary from simple remote monitoring to full automatic control. Not only would this provide more cost-effective operation, but also provide a safer environment by more comprehensive monitoring and enabling personnel to be removed or remote from some of the dangerous and unhealthy activities.

The main characteristics of such a system are that it would be very large (perhaps hundreds of computer stations), physically distributed (up to 20 km), and real-time. An outline of the system structure is given in Fig. 1.3.

Overall physical system

*   Computer stations interface to the local devices and provide local intelligence for fast response and isolated (degraded?) operation.
*   Communication network to provide interstation communication for cooperation and connection to operator consoles and the surface for commands, status reporting, logging, alarms, etc.

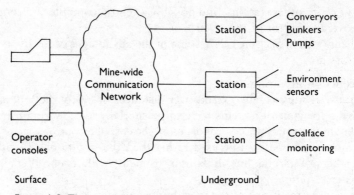

Figure 1.3 The structure of a distributed system for use in mines

The software structure

This is discussed in Chapters 3 and 4, where the software architecture of
a system, called CONIC, is used as a detailed case study. This system was
aimed at large distributed embedded applications, and much of the work was
funded by the British National Coal Board.

Issues

Safety and reliability: In an environment where human life is at risk, the
system must be resistant to failures and provide continuous operation as far
as possible. It must have very low undetected error rates and be designed
to be fail-safe. **Error control** and **synchronization** of actions, despite failures,
are issues of major concern.

Performance: The system must be able to give guaranteed, predictable
response times, even in failure situations. Since efficiency and throughput are
not important in this environment, the most common approach is to over-
dimension the system (**resource management**).

Flexibility and extension: The system is configured (interconnection structure) to match the environment. Although this is essentially static, parts of
the system are shut down and new ones created from time to time as old
coal faces are closed and new ones are opened and extended. Since it is
required that the rest of the system should continue operating normally, the
software must be constructed so as to permit on-line modification and
extension.

Maintenance and diagnostics: Stations should be capable of running
remote diagnostics. Self-diagnostics would help to warn of possible future
faults which could then be corrected during routine maintenance rather than
waiting for failure.

The overall system is under the management and control of a single authority and does not have a community of diverse users (cf. Cambridge system).
Hence the problems of protection, access and user authentication are rather

Table 1.1   Outline characteristics of each control level

Control level	Response times	Transfer rates (bits/s)	Units of information	Distances (m)
direct	ms to s	< 20k	words, raw data	1–100
subsystem	ms to s	100–1k	messages < 100 bytes	100–1000
site-wide	s to mins	10k–300k	messages, files	1000–10 km
management	mins to days	2k–10k	messages, files	

different. Operators must only be given the right to issue certain control commands and to perform certain system changes, but this protection can be provided by conventional password mechanisms at the system interface and need not be embedded in the system. Transparency of distribution and uniform access are again less stringent as the system is often required to reflect the (distributed) structure of the application.

Process-control systems are often structured as a hierarchy with direct control at the lowest level, then subsystem control, site-wide control and finally the management level. Each of the levels of the hierarchy can be roughly characterized with respect to the response times expected, the information transfer rates, units of information transfer and distances involved. A summary is given in Table 1.1.

1.3.4   Distributed Data Bases

A distributed data base is a physical partitioning of a database over a number of computing facilities while providing an integrated access to the data. The justification for distributing the data is as follows:

- Many application environments require the sharing of data among diverse users with different computing facilities.
- Partitioning can improve access time if local data is stored locally. Delays due to transmission time for queries and responses can be reduced by keeping the data close to the users. Also individual databases can be reduced in size. This results in less contention for access from many users.
- Control of the data can be retained where local responsibility lies, e.g. bank accounts.
- Reliability can be improved by maintaining multiple copies at different locations. This provides security against natural disasters such as fire or flood, but it can lead to updating problems (consistency).

Case Study: The Bank of America distributed system [Foster, 1976a,b]
In 1976 the Bank of America in California operated a very large database consisting of information on their customer's accounts – 10 million of them! The bank had over 1000 community offices and two main centers, one in Los Angeles and one in San Francisco. During office hours an estimated peak

of 50 account enquiries per second per center were made. The overnight hours were used to perform the total of approximately 4 million transactions, transits and clearing items to other banks. A courier service was used to bring the entries from the community offices to the centers, they were processed in overnight batch and the results returned by courier in the early morning. In order to provide better information access and remove the need for the courier service, new system architectures were proposed.

An initial proposal was to provide two super computers and databases at the centers and have multidrop communication lines to the community offices and a communication line between the centers (Fig. 1.4).

However this approach raised a number of doubts concerning the architecture adopted at each center:

—reliability   What if the central computer goes down? Standby computers would be too expensive.
—performance?   Would the response for queries and throughput for batch be sufficient? Even if it would be adequate now, what about the future? Hence...
—extensibility?   New larger central computer?
—maintenance?   Of both the hardware and software? Insufficient redundancy in the system.

As a result a different approach was taken. At each center, both the processing system and the database were partitioned into a number of modules (Fig. 1.5). Each module would specialize on a particular group of accounts or on a particular function. This would act to reduce message traffic as the users of the data could be connected to their partition of the database. Also, the functional specialization could help to simplify the processing required by each module. Within a module, a large amount of redundancy was provided not only to provide for failures, but also to improve throughput

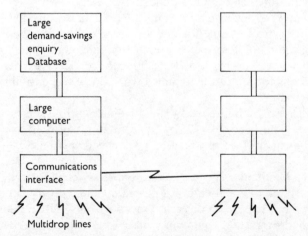

Figure 1.4 Initial proposal: two 'centralized' data-processing centers

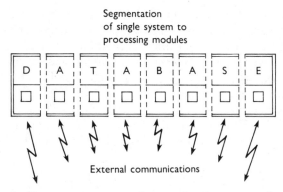

Segmentation
of single system to
processing modules

External communications

Figure 1.5 Database/system segmentation. Reprinted with permission from J. D. Foster, *The Development of a Concept for Distributive Processing*. Compton 1976, Copyright IEEE.

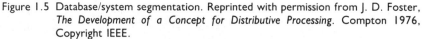

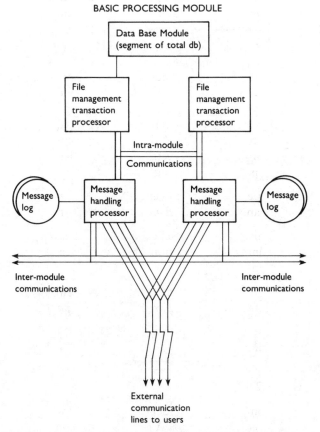

BASIC PROCESSING MODULE

Figure 1.6 The structure of a data base/system segment. Reprinted with permission of *Datamation* magazine, Copyright by Technical Publishing Company—1976 all rights reserved.

and response (Fig. 1.6). The database itself used replicated files on four spindles, and the file-management system, message logger, message-handling processor and intra- and inter-module communications systems were all duplicated. Hence each center constituted a distributed system giving the required reliability, performance, extensibility and opportunity for simpler software and hardware maintenance (Fig. 1.7).

It is interesting to note that the bank still operated (and, to our knowledge, continues to operate) queries only during the day. All transactions were logged for overnight processing and data base update. They thereby avoided many

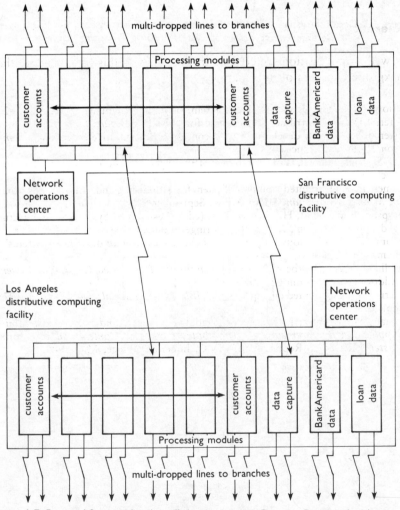

Figure 1.7 Proposal 2: two 'distributed' data-processing Centers. Reprinted with permission of *Datamation* magazine, Copyright by Technical Publishing Company—1976 all rights reserved.

of the difficult problems of consistency in replicated data bases in an environment of concurrent, real-time access and update. This would have required sophisticated locking and the use of atomic (indivisible and recoverable) updates. The current Bank of America system is implemented using one of the general purpose systems which are available from some manufacturers to support transaction processing between autonomous computer systems. In this case it is a data base management system (IMS, Information Management System) which coordinates transactions dealing with data base enquiries and updates, and integrates with a system for interprogram communication (SNA, Systems Network Architecture), both products of IBM [IBM, 1983].

References

As well as publications referenced in the chapter, this list includes other background sources of information.

Enslow, P.H., What is a 'distributed' system?, *Computer*, January 1978, pp. 13–21.

Foster, J.D., (a) 'Distributive Processing for Banking', *Datamation*, July 1976.

Foster, J.D., (b) 'The development of a concept for distributive processing', *Compcon 1976*, San Francisco, California.

IBM Systems Journal, Vol. 22, no. 4, 1983, special issue on 'Systems Network Architecture, SNA'.

Kramer, J., 'A Distributed Computer System for Monitoring and Control', *Electronics in Mining Symposium*, South Africa, September 1984.

Lampson, B.W., Paul, H., Siegert, H.J. (eds), 'Distributed Systems – Architecture and Implementation', *LNCS 105*, Springer Verlag, 1981.

LeLann, G., 'Motivations, objectives and characterization of distributed systems' in Lampson [1981].

Needham, R.M., Herbert, A.J., *The Cambridge Distributed Computing System*, Addison-Wesley, London, 1982.

Scherr, A.L., 'Distributed data processing', *IBM System Journal*, Vol. 17, no. 4, 1978, pp. 324–343.

Sloman, M., Kramer, J., Magee, J., Saadat, S., *Present and Future Coal Mining Application Requirements, for Distributed Computer Control and Monitoring Systems*, Research Report 80/15, DoC, Imperial College, May 1980.

Two

DISTRIBUTED SYSTEM ARCHITECTURE

The last chapter provided some of the motivation for using distributed systems. This chapter gives an overview of **how** distributed systems are constructed, and the issues which must be considered.

The first half of this chapter gives an overview of the structure and composition of a distributed system. In practice there are a wide variety of structures and components which can be used; however, it is our intention to provide a general understanding before discussing any particular system component in detail. The structure presented should therefore be considered as a simplified model of a distributed system architecture.

There are a number of general issues that are common to most of the components of a distributed system [Kramer, 1983]. Unfortunately it is usually not possible to solve each issue independently in each component part of the system. It is necessary to adopt common policies and solutions if an efficient and integrated system is to be produced. These issues are presented and briefly discussed in the second half of the chapter.

Much of the discussion in this chapter is based on the work of Watson [1981(a)].

2.1 Overall Structure

The simplest overview of the structure of a distributed system is that it consists of a set of physically distributed computer stations interconnected by some communications network. Each station has the capability for processing and storing data, and may have connections to external devices such as terminals, printers, process control plant, or even another system. The com-

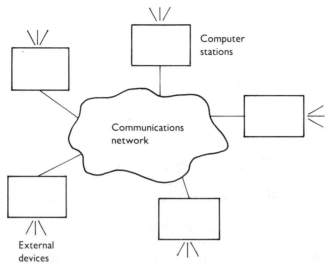

Figure 2.1 Overall structure of a distributed system

munication system is responsible for supporting communication between stations in the distributed system. It allows any station to communicate with any other connected to the communications network (Fig. 2.1).

We now examine the structure at a station in more detail. Consider the structure of the hardware and software at each station roughly as a set of local layers (Fig. 2.2).

The following summary is presented to provide an impression of the functions performed by each layer in a typical distribution system:

Layer	Examples of functions
Application software	Monitoring and control modules, funds transfer, information retrieval, electronic mail.
Utilities	File transfer, device handlers (e.g. virtual terminals), printer servers.
Local management	Software process management (creation/destruction, etc.), local resource control.
Kernel	Multitasking (processor management), I/O drivers, local IPC, memory management, protection.
Hardware	processor(s), memory, I/O, devices.
Communication system	Virtual circuits, datagrams, network routing, addressing, flow control, error control.

This local layered structure is the first step in understanding how a distributed system is constructed. It provides a basis for describing the functions performed and services offered at a station. The communication system is responsible for interstation communication and is considered as orthogonal

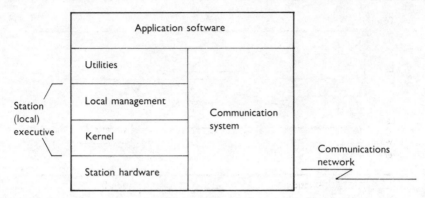

Figure 2.2 Layered architecture at a station in a distributed system

to the system software. Although the communications system uses the system facilities provided by the station executive (it generally runs on 'top' of the kernel), it is also used by both the application software and the local system software, and often includes firmware (software/hardware) for accessing the communications network directly; hence the structure in Fig. 2.2.

If the physical distribution into stations is transparent (i.e. not apparent), then the distributed system as a whole can be viewed as a set of similar functional layers independent of **where** the services are actually offered, i.e. the partitioning into stations is transparent. This integration of the physically distributed system into a single (layered) logical entity is usually the role of the **distributed operating system (DOS)**. It coordinates and unifies the distributed stations into a single system and is usually constructed as follows:

DOS = global executive (not shown)
    + utilities
    + station executives.

The global executive can be considered as part of the application and/or part of the utilities, but is usually a separate layer of software which runs on some stations and makes use of the local management services at each station. As mentioned in Chapter 1, the distinction between system software and application software is often blurred. Hence the dividing lines between application software, utilities and local management is often fuzzy. Also, system and application processes are often treated uniformly. They communicate and provide access to their services by message passing to provide uniform local and remote access. In almost all cases software processes implement their services in terms of those provided by others.

The next section discusses layering further and gives some of the reasons why a layered structure is used. Each of the layers is then discussed in more detail. Finally we discuss some of the main issues which are faced at all levels.

2.1.1 Layers, Protocols and Interfaces

Modular and layered designs have been widely accepted in operating systems

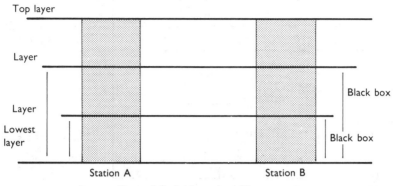

Figure 2.3 A hierarchy of layers

and application programming as good software engineering practice. Distributed systems are complex and so are usually organized in a hierarchy of layers. The basic idea of layering is that, irrespective of station boundaries, each **layer** adds value to the services provided by the set of lower layers. Thus the highest layer is offered the set of services needed to run distributed applications. Viewed from above, a particular layer and the ones below it may be considered to be a 'black box' which implements a set of functions in order to provide a service (Fig. 2.3). For example, the communication system provides a relatively error-free logical link service between processes on top of an error-prone physical link between the stations.

Each individual station (or network node) is logically composed of a succession of layers (Fig. 2.2). A layer may be implemented by a number of **entities** which are analogous to hardware or software processes. Entities in the same layer, and usually in different stations, are called **peer entities**. Peer entities cooperate to provide the services of that layer to the layer above.

A **protocol** is the set of rules governing communication between the entities which constitute a particular layer (Fig. 2.4). That is it defines how the entities at a particular level in one station exchange information with corresponding peer entities in other stations. The protocol defines the format and ordering of the information exchange and any actions to be performed on receipt of the information.

An **interface** between two layers local to a station defines the means by which one local layer makes use of the services provided by the lower layer (Fig. 2.5). It defines the rules and formats for exchanging information across the boundary between adjacent layers within a single station. The interface may be specified in terms of its mechanical, electrical, timing or software characteristics, i.e. the interface may be physical or logical.

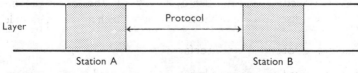

Figure 2.4 A protocol

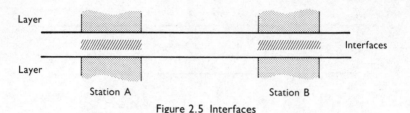

Figure 2.5 Interfaces

Reasons for Layered Structure:

- *Independence between layers*: A layer makes no assumptions about how the one below it is implemented, but only has knowledge of the service provided through the interface. This is associated with the concept of modularity and information hiding.
- *Flexibility*: A change at any one layer, for instance due to a change in technology, should not affect the layers above or below it provided the interfaces are preserved. Also alternative services can be offered at a layer, or the layer can be completely omitted if its services are not required.
- *Physical separation*: The layers can be implemented using the most appropriate technology e.g. software package in an application processor, microprocessor software or LSI hardware. It has proved advantageous in many networks to implement the layers within a station using a minimum of two or three processors.
- *Simpler implementation and maintenance*: This structure makes the implementation and testing of a complex system manageable because it decomposes the overall services into easily comprehensible sections.
- *Promotes standardization*: Precise specification of the functions, services offered and interfaces of a layer permits standard layers to be developed (see Section 2.3).

2.2 The Architecture Layers

2.2.1 Application Layer

As in centralized systems the functions performed by the software at the applications layer varies widely. The needs of the application will define the services required from the DOS layer. Process management, communication, information management, virtual I/O, clocks, accounting and authentication are the usual services required. These services are usually dressed up as a set of mechanisms available in the application programming language.

Some of the issues faced at the applications level are briefly raised below:

- *Decomposition of functions into distributable processes*: The application is a configuration of interconnected, communicating processes. Processes provide a modular software component from which to build the system. The criteria used for deciding where in the distributed system a particular process should run is usually for functional, geographical or performance reasons, i.e. functionally associated processes can be grouped together, or a process is allocated to a station close to where it is used, or it is allocated to a station which is under-utilized (load sharing). The kinds of process components and their interconnections are described in Chapter 3. Another consideration in the decomposition and allocation of components is fault tolerance. Different or redundant components can be allocated to different stations in case of failures.

- *Management of application processes*: The overall management and control of the application can be organized in either a distributed or centralized manner. Centralized control has the advantage that it is much simpler. All major decisions are taken at a single site (cf. a dictator). The disadvantages are that this can be too slow (the manager is a bottleneck) and is vulnerable to failures. Distributed management is more robust but requires that the distributed managers cooperate in the control of the application (cf. a committee). This is more complex [LeLann, 1981]. Hence, as in most companies and countries, hierarchical management is often used as a compromise.

- *Distribution of data*: The data in the system can be partitioned and distributed to different parts of the system. However, this can lead to slow response if the data is remote, and loss if a part of the system fails. Data replication can be used to locate data close to its use. Furthermore this provides redundancy in case of failure. However, the price that must be paid is similar to the use of distributed control. Support must be provided to retain consistency between the replicated copies. This can be very complex [Ceri, 1985].

- *Interprocess communication*: The application processes communicate in order to cooperate and synchronize their activities. The forms of communication and the behaviour of the processes in the event of communication delays or failures is the subject of discussion in Chapter 4.

Chapters 3 and 4 discuss the features which should be supported by languages for distributed programming.

2.2.2 The Distributed Operating System (DOS)

The DOS is required in order to coordinate the use of resources and to provide system-wide services, such as remote program execution, file servers, electronic mail, etc. The services provided are the conjunction of the services provided by its distributed servers in the utilities and local management layers. It must turn a collection of distributed hardware/software resources into a coherent set of resources. The DOS must support naming, sharing, protection, synchronization, intercommunication, and recovery of resources to be accessed by many distributed processes.

Watson [1981(a)] aptly characterizes a DOS as follows:

> One of the major design goals of a DOS is to provide processes with access to real and abstract objects or resources in which the distributed nature of their implementation is hidden as far as practical, and in which all objects (system or user defined) are names, communicated with, shared and protected uniformly. Real objects are entities such as processors, secondary storage, I/O, devices etc. DOS abstract objects or resources are entities such as processes, file directories, virtual I/O devices, databases, clocks etc. which are a useful set of basic building blocks for creating higher level objects.

The objects which Watson refers to can be specified by
- a set of data structures visible at the interface, and
- a set of operations or functions and associated parameters that can be performed on the object.

The manner in which the DOS must provide system wide facilities can be summarized by the following requirements:

1. to provide a basis for extensibility, i.e. easily creating, in a modular fashion, new resources and services out of existing ones, and facilitate inclusion of these network-shareable resources without facing anew all the issues associated with distributed systems;
2. to provide naming and access conventions or interfaces to make heterogeneity transparent, i.e. provide a user with a uniform, coherent view of the system;
3. to provide administrative and accounting procedures;
4. to support both stream (e.g. pipelining) and transaction (e.g. customer–server) oriented systems;
5. to support security and prevent unauthorized access; and
6. to be capable of an efficient implementation.

Although distributed operating systems are not separately described in this book, many of the issues raised are discussed in Section 2.4, and the characteristic mechanisms are described in the chapters on software structure (3 and 4) and the higher layers of the communication system (11 and 12). Other particular systems of interest are Medusa [Ousterhout, 1980], StarOS [Jones, 1979], System Network Architecture, SNA [IBM, 1983] and the use of servers in the Cambridge system [Needham, 1982], described in the case study in Chapter 1. Many current systems consist of one or more function-oriented protocol layers (e.g. virtual terminal, file transfer, database transaction system, ...) built on top of a communication system.

2.2.3. Local Management

This provides the local facilities within a station to support the overall DOS. These facilities include process management (creation/destruction, stop/start) local protection, error control and local resource management (allocation and access). The facilities provided are those of a conventional operating system, except that its facilities can also be accessed remotely. A message-passing interface is often provided so that both local and remote access is uniform. This interface is then used by the DOS.

2.2.4 Kernel

This layer supports the local IPC (interprocess communication) and provides the minimum software necessary for process creation, memory and I/O access, protection and multitasking. In some cases, the kernel is responsible for creating a message-oriented interface to I/O components.

2.2.5 Hardware Environment

This set of components provides a station or node within the distributed system. It typically consists of:

- one or more processors;
- memory (shared or disjoint)
- I/O to devices; and
- communications network interface.

The hardware should support fast context switching (saving/restoring CPU state when suspending/resuming processes), interrupts with low latency and traps for error detection. In addition there is a need for hardware support for efficient communications interfaces, for mechanisms for privacy, access control and protection, and for fault detection and diagnosis. Hardware may in the future also be able to support the distribution and synchronization of state information. Finally we foresee that in the case of special-purpose devices, the inclusion of more intelligence will permit connection directly to the network, e.g. the 'intelligent' sensor or printer which includes a network interface.

2.2.6 Communication System

The communication system local to a station is responsible for transporting system and application messages to/from the station. It accepts messages from the station software, and prepares and multiplexes them (i.e. multiple logical communication paths) for transmission via the shared network interface. It also receives messages from the network and prepares and demultiplexes them for receipt by the station software.

In addition, the communications system provides:

- error control – detection and correction (usually by retransmission);
- flow control – to prevent excessive use of the communications system by a process; and
- routing – to direct messages to their intended destination.

Like the DOS, the individual local communication systems cooperate using agreed protocols to provide the system-wide communications facilities.

The communication system is a crucial component of a distributed system and is itself complex. Hence it too consists of a number of layers. A common reference model for the layered structure of the communication system is now widely accepted and used. This model, the seven-layered ISO Reference model, is outlined in Section 2.3.

2.3   The Communication System Structure: The ISO Reference Model

The evolution of proprietary incompatible communication systems led to the realization that standards were needed to allow interaction between computers of different manufacturers. In 1977 the International Standard Organization (ISO) started working on a Reference Model for Open System Interconnection. The term 'open' means that systems which conform to standards within this model will be open to other systems which obey the same standards.

The purpose of the ISO model [ISO, 1983] is to provide a common basis for the coordination of communication system standards development and to allow existing standards to be placed into perspective. The model does not specify services and protocols as it is not an implementation specification. It is merely a reference model which can be used as a conceptual and functional framework for describing existing communication systems and for development of protocol specifications.

The ISO model defines the seven layers shown in Fig. 2.6. The emphasis of the ISO work is to allow interconnection of independent mainframes rather than distributed processing. The current version of the model only considers

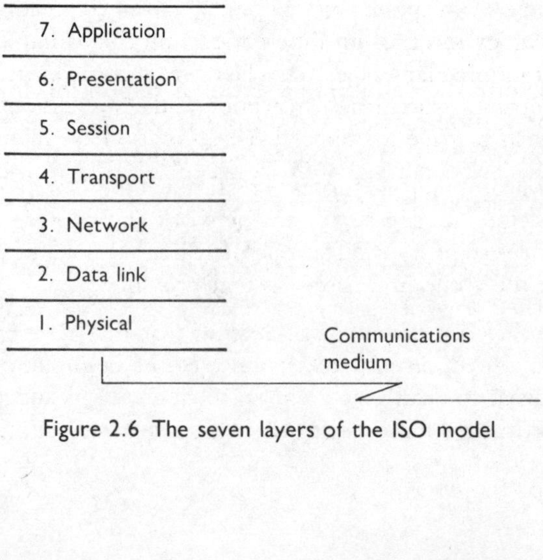

7. Application

6. Presentation

5. Session

4. Transport

3. Network

2. Data link

1. Physical

Communications medium

Figure 2.6 The seven layers of the ISO model

point-to-point connections between two peer entities (see Chapter 5). Extensions for connectionless transactions and multidestination information transfer are being incorporated. These extensions are particularly important for distributed processing applications, and in the rest of this book we have assumed these extensions. Later in this book (from Chapter 5 onwards) we will discuss each layer in detail, but we now give an overview of the communication system layers defined in the ISO model.

Application layer
This is the highest layer defined in the model. In the ISO view only those application entities which are involved in inter-station communication are part of an open system. Those application entities performing local activities are not considered part of the model. A distributed system would not make this distinction as any entity can potentially communicate with local or remote peer entities. As mentioned in Section 2.2 and further discussed in Chapter 4, there is often no distinction between local and remote interprocess communication. Hence this layer corresponds with the application layer discussed in Section 2.2.1.

In our view the application layer includes all entities which represent human users or devices, or perform an application function. Examples are a process controlling a printer, visual display, interacting with a user at a banking terminal, a file-server component or a process performing a compilation.

The application layer may itself be layered. Thus there may be application entities which interact by means of an application protocol to provide a service for other application entities. Examples of these application-oriented protocols include: virtual file and terminal protocols, electronic mail, electronic funds transfer. Chapter 12 discusses some of these application-oriented services.

Presentation layer
The purpose of the presentation layer is to resolve differences in information representation between application entities. It allows communication between application entities running on different computers or implemented using different programming languages. This layer is concerned with data transformation, formatting, structuring, encryption and compression. For example, it is necessary to provide a standard representation for integers, reals and character codes for communication between heterogeneous computers. It would also be responsible for mapping more complex data structures such as lists, trees and structures employing pointers for transfer between computers. Many of these functions are application dependent and are often performed by high-level language compilers, so the borderline between presentation and application layers is not clear.

Chapters 11 and 12 discuss these functions and shows how abstract data types can be used to define information representation and the operations to be performed on the information.

Session layer

This layer provides the facilities to support and maintain sessions (associations) between two (or more) application entities. Sessions may span a long time interval involving many message interactions or be very short involving one or two messages. Typical sessions would be a terminal logged into a remote computer and using the editor, or a transaction between a banking terminal and the bank's computer. In the case of loss of a communication connection, the session layer may provide checkpointing, to allow recovery to a known state. It may also provide facilities for controlling dialogue, e.g. two-way simultaneous and two-way alternate modes of working.

In most distributed systems the session layer is minimal and is often incorporated within the transport or application layer. It is briefly covered in Chapter 10.

Transport layer

The transport layer is the boundary between what are considered the application-oriented layers and the communication-oriented layers. This is the lowest layer using an end-station-to-end-station protocol. It isolates higher layers from concern as to how reliable and cost-effective transfer of data is actually achieved. It optimizes the use of communications resources to provide required performance at minimum cost. An association between two entities at the application layer would be mapped by the presentation and session layers onto a connection provided by the transport service.

The functions performed depend on services provided by lower layers. The transport layer usually provides multiplexing, end-to-end error and flow control, fragmenting and reassembly of large messages into network packets and mapping of transport-layer identifiers onto network addresses. However, if the network layer also offers a reliable service (as is the case with most public networks) then the functions performed could be to merely map a transport connection onto a network one.

In many distributed systems, the remote interprocess communication protocols are implemented by a combined transport/session layer above a simple network layer service as described in the case studies in Chapter 10.

Network layer

The network layer isolates the higher layers from routing and switching considerations. The network layer masks the transport layer from all the peculiarities of the actual transfer medium: whether a point-to-point link, packet-switched network, LAN or even interconnected networks. It is the network layer's responsibility to get a message from a source station to the destination station across an arbitrary network topology. The network layer has been divided into three sublayers to cope with interconnected networks:

Internet sublayer: provides routing, switching and relaying functions across the concatenated subnets.

Subnet enhancement sublayer: enhances the level of service provided by a particular subnet to that expected by the transport layer. This may involve error, flow and sequence control functions.
Subnet access sublayer: the functions needed to transfer data across the subnet.

The network layer is really concerned with addressing networks and stations, whereas the transport layer addresses eventually map onto processes. The network layer is discussed in Chapter 9.

Data-link layer
The task of this layer is to take the raw physical circuit and convert it into a point-to-point link that appears relatively error free to the network layer. It usually entails error and flow control but many local are networks (LANs) have low intrinsic error rates and so do not include error correction. However, error detection is nearly always provided in the data-link layer. The layer also provides access control for LANs and half-duplex channels which have a shared transmission medium. Another function sometimes performed is block synchronization, i.e. the data-link layer provides a message transfer service, whereas the physical layer transfers bits.

In local area networks this layer is divided into two sublayers:

Logical link sublayer: concerned with error detection and possibly error correction, flow control etc. (see Chapter 8);
Medium access: controlling access to a shared transmission medium (Chapter 7).

Physical layer
This layer is concerned with transmission of bits over a physical circuit. It performs all functions associated with signalling, modulation and bit synchronization. It may perform error detection by signal quality monitoring. The mechanical and electrical specification of the plugs and sockets of a physical interface to the network are considered part of this layer (see Chapter 6).

Relationship of the ISO model to the station executive
The ISO model is very unclear as to the relationship between the communication system and the station executive or kernel. In many distributed systems, the application entities use the same communication primitives for both local and remote interprocess communication (IPC). The former is supported by the kernel and the latter by the communication system. The communication system itself is implemented as a set of application processes which are supported by the kernel and use the kernel-provided IPC facilities. The executive in each station manages the resources for both communication and application components. The network operating system manages resources on a network-wide basis, i.e. there is no distinction made between the communication system and the application system. The executive/operating system

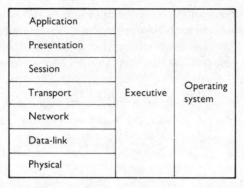

Figure 2.7 Independent operating and communications system hierarchies

hierarchy is thus independent of the communication system hierarchy, as shown in Fig. 2.7.

2.4 Issues Common to All Layers

The purpose of this section is to present an overview of some of the main issues [Watson, 1981(a)] which are faced in the provision of a distributed system. They are as follows:

Naming: identification of objects/resources;
Synchronization: control in an environment with unpredictable delay and failures;
Resource management: efficient control of the use of resources;
Error control: error detection and recovery;
Protection: authorization of access;
Representation: encoding and translation to deal with heterogeneity; and
Flexibility: support for change in a system.

Some of these issues have been briefly introduced in Chapter 1, particularly in the case studies presented there, and in Section 2.2.2 of the DOS. Other issues can be reduced to problems in the above list. For instance, the handling of heterogeneity involves solving naming, resource management and representation issues; availability is subsumed in error control and resource management; and providing transparency involves almost all of the above issues. Intercommunication is often integrated with simple synchronization and hence their interaction must be considered. How the sources and destinations are identified depends on the naming approach. Since message passing is subject to delays and failures, error control must also be carefully considered. Interprocess communication (IPC) is considered in detail in Chapter 4.

Although one may isolate a particular layer and deal with each of the issues at that layer, in many cases they also span all the layers. Discussion of these issues crops up throughout the book when discussing language support for software components or a particular communication layer. In this section we discuss the issues in isolation. However, since they are themselves interrelated, the issues must also be considered in some global (and optimal?) manner, and some coherent, efficient strategy must be adopted. Of course, the solutions adopted must also consider the cost constraints, both in terms of finances for hardware and software construction and also in terms of the effect on system performance.

2.4.1 Naming

The **name** of a resource indicates *what* we seek,
an **address** indicates *where* it is, and
a **route** tells us *how to get there*. [Shoch, 1978]

Identification is an area at the heart of all computer-system design, both distributed and centralized [Watson, 1981 (b)]. Identifiers are used for a wide variety of purposes such as protection, error control, resource management, locating and sharing resources. For instance, possession of a resource name may give a process the right to access that resource (cf. capability). Identifiers exist at all levels of a system architecture, from high-level names to low-level addresses, and in different forms from human-oriented names to machine-oriented addresses.

Important issues are:

1. uniqueness at some level;
2. number of levels of identifiers and interlevel mapping mechanisms;
3. size and structure of identifiers at each level.

In addition an important characteristic is the relation between names and addresses [Su, 1983]. A name can be entirely location independent (such as an individual's name) or it can be location dependent (such as a telephone number). Address-independent names are more flexible as they allow reference to an object or resource without knowledge of its location. The later that names are resolved into addresses (**binding**) the greater the flexibility. However, late binding imposes a greater overhead as it must then be performed at execution time. In general, a compromise is used and names are chosen to have some location-dependent information which gives a hint as to where they might be found. The area code in a telephone number is a good example of such use; a station number within a network might similarly form part of a resource name.

The name space is the set of names or addresses used to identify entities. The **context** in which a name is used is important. The following types of name spaces are found:

Global: A single name space is used throughout the system and this has the same meaning in every context. There is a one-to-one mapping between names and entities, so that any one entity is known by the same name to

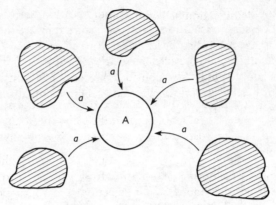

Figure 2.8 Global Naming

all other entities, as shown in Fig. 2.8. It is both simple and efficient. The disadvantage of this scheme is that it is unmanageable and inflexible for very large networks as the name space becomes too large. If the network is reconfigured all stations must be informed of the change.

Local: A particular name may identify different entities in a different context. Different names could identify the same entity (Fig. 2.9) or the same names could identify different entities, depending on the **context**. The context of a particular name space could vary with time i.e. names are reused when entities are removed from the system. Context-dependent naming implies some overhead in mapping between contexts. For instance, the communication system usually maps a local name onto a global address.

Hierarchical: Names of the form *A.B.C.D...* (e.g. *country.network. station.process.entry*) provide global uniqueness for the full name but context-dependent abbreviations. Each subname applies to a different layer. Local names can be used within the lower layers, e.g. *process.entry* need be unique only within a station, but the full name is globally unique. This technique is commonly used in large networks or interconnected networks and is a good compromise between pure local or global name spaces. It is also widely used to attach some location-dependent information to a locally unique name.

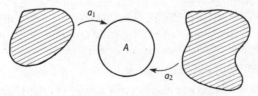

Figure 2.9 Local Naming

The choice of identification scheme affects

- sharing of objects/resources;
- relocation of objects/resources without changing references;
- inclusion of objects/resources without identifier conflicts;
- replication of objects/resources;
- application and DOS view of resource or object access;
- the system is seen as a space of identified objects (logical view) rather than as a space of host stations containing objects (physical view).

Related to the mapping of identifiers from one level into those at another level is the process of *routing* information from one object to another. This is discussed further in Chapter 9 in connection with routing of messages in a network.

2.4.2   Synchronization

A system consists of objects and resources such as files, devices, processes, communication links, etc. It is expected to meet some external specification at all times while ensuring efficient resource utilization, good performance, data consistency and lack of deadlock. In order to do this, control decisions must be made based on the current state of the system. In a non-distributed system, the problem is relatively straightforward as all processes have the same view of the system state. However, in a distributed system this is almost always not the case.

The problem in a distributed system is that the state information is usually distributed in space and time. State information is distributed among the physical stations which perform the processing; and it is also often out of date due to arbitrary communication delays when updating or reporting state changes. Synchronization of distributed state information is further aggravated by the possibility of errors and node failures. Since a complete, global view of the system is generally not possible, we seek to provide partial views which are consistent. Synchronization mechanisms are used for these purposes and ensure that cooperating processes share a consistent view of the system state. Cooperating processes use synchronization mechanisms to coordinate access to share resources or to ensure that events occur in some specific order.

One approach is to enforce sequentiality, i.e. to ensure that operations are executed one after another in a strictly sequential fashion. However, this is very inefficient and may degrade performance of a system to an unacceptable level. Many systems now aim to provide **atomic** operations as a means of preserving system consistency. If an operation consists of a number of actions, then atomicity guarantees that

- either all actions are completed or no action is taken, and
- intermediate states are not visible to any other operation.

Non-interfering actions can occur in parallel, while conflicting actions will (at least, conceptually) occur sequentially. Atomicity ensures that no control decision need be taken based on inconsistent information. However provision of atomic operations in a distributed system is complex and costly (time and space). Some of the required mechanisms are the provision of concurrency control, stable storage, and the two-phase commit protocol [Gray, 1979].

Other distributed strategies for allocation and mutual exclusion synchronization involve the use of

- local logical clocks [Lamport, 1978] to time-stamp messages and select the process with the earliest request, and
- use of a circulating token in a logical ring [LeLann, 1978].

None provide an easy solution to this difficult problem. A more comprehensive discussion of synchronization problems in a distributed environment is given by LeLann [1981], Gray [1979] and Kohler [1981].

2.4.3 Error Control

This is concerned with error detection and recovery. As mentioned, this is particularly acute due to the inherent delays and likelihood of failures during message communication. No single approach is appropriate for all levels, and hence mechanisms must be developed around a knowledge of the types and frequencies of errors that occur at a particular level. Also, if error control is applied at lower levels, then the probability of undetected or uncorrected errors at higher levels may be sufficiently low that additional error control is unnecessary. Alternatively, the lower levels may not need to provide error control if the higher levels provide sufficient coverage (probability that the system will recover from a failure). A more detailed discussion of the problems of error control in connection with the communication system is given in Chapters 8–10.

The complexity of the error-control mechanism varies according to the requirements. For instance, it is very much simpler if the operations on a resource are such that duplicated messages will not cause harm and omissions are covered by information in later messages (e.g. a display). More complex mechanisms such as atomic transactions (discussed in Section 2.4.2 on synchronization) are necessary to ensure consistent update of multiple replicated data files. However, the inherent modularity of the distributed system can be used to provide defensible interfaces and aid error containment.

Error-control mechanisms at any layer are complicated by the fact that information needed for error control uses the same error-prone environment, and so is subject to

- delays and failures in message transmission;
- difficulties in maintaining consistent distributed state and error-control information; and

- reuse of an identifer to refer to a new object when reference to the old (deleted) object still exists (see Section 2.4.1)

A more comprehensive discussion of these issues is given by Anderson and Lee [Anderson, 1981].

2.4.4 Resource Management

There are a wide variety of resources which require management and are local to a station and/or local to a layer, e.g. buffer space, processor, devices, communication channels, etc. Allocating and scheduling resources is usually based on local decisions at a station as this makes each station more autonomous and is very much easier than global management. However, optimization and coordination of the use of resources which are distributed inevitably requires some global control, either by a centralized manager or by special protocols between the distributed managers.

The aim is to provide allocation on demand with

- **low delay** (i.e. fast response time) for transaction oriented systems, and
- **high throughput** (i.e. fast processing) for stream-oriented systems.

For instance, when interacting with a resource, each message exchange can either be self-contained (i.e. contain the context of the conversation) or require conversation set-up and close-down messages at the start and end of the conversation. In the former, the longer messages reduce throughput, but in the latter, the set-up messages can cause high delay. In order to try to achieve both low delay and high throughput, one is usually forced to provide relatively long-term retention of state information and resource allocation. This unfortunately reduces autonomy and makes error control more difficult.

It is also the responsibility of resource managers to ensure that no deadlocks occur, and that no single component monopolizes use of the resource nor suffers starvation (cf. conventional processor scheduling). The communication system is responsible for flow control (regulating information flow between a specific pair of components) and congestion control (preventing global or partial communication system overload).

2.4.5 Protection

The main role of the protection mechanisms is to ensure that only authorized entities can access a resource, and that there is no interference by unauthorized entities.

One approach is to make a station a single protection domain where all the local processes trust one another. The problem is then one of interconnecting mutually suspicious protection domains.

Another approach is where processes only access each other and each others' resources via well-defined and defensible interfaces such as provided by an IPC mechanism. The local executive (kernel) can be responsible for checking access credentials or, even better, each server can protect its resources itself. User processes would be required to present some token (cf. a capability, or protected identifier) possession of which constitutes proof of right of access. In order to prevent forging of these tokens, they can have passwords embedded. Copying can be prevented by encryption [Needham, 1978]. Encryption requires that each party have a matching encryption key or pair of keys. The problem is then one of distributing these keys in a safe, secure manner. Access control and protection is discussed in more detail by Davies [1981].

2.4.6   Representation

Many different objects will be defined in a system and passed across layers and between stations. These objects may be files, directories, or user-defined data structures. These objects may be transmitted in an environment which contains heterogeneous networks, computers, operating systems and source languages. In order to cope with such an environment, the representation and encoding of objects must be specified. Usually **type** information is encoded with the object to permit automatic translation when necessary. A header is provided which contains the control information for translation, and the body contains the data structured as typed data elements. In the communications system, it is the presentation layer which is responsible for handling differences in representation (see Section 2.3 and Chapter 11).

2.4.7   Flexibility

Large computer systems are expected to have a long lifetime. However, they do not remain static during their operational life, but **evolve** as human needs change, the application environment changes and as new technology is incorporated. In fact the introduction of the computer system itself tends to act as a stimulus for change in the application environment, and so the services provided by the system must evolve.

In addition to **evolutionary change**, distributed systems must cater for **operational changes**. Components may have to be physically relocated in response to either personnel or installation changes. After failures of parts of the system, continued, possibly degraded, operation should be possible by manual or automatic reorganization. Distributed systems should also cater for redimensioning: extension by addition of existing components or removal of superfluous ones (see Sections 1.1.2 and 1.2.2).

A system must exhibit the property of **flexibility** in order to adapt to the above evolutionary and operational changes. A classification of the flexibility requirements for distributed systems [Sloman et al., 1984] is given below.

1. **Functional flexibility**

   This is the ability to modify a system to perform different or new functions. This can be achieved by the replacement of existing components or the addition of completely new ones. An important aspect of a system's functional flexibility is the ease with which one can identify the implications of a change, i.e. which other existing modules will be affected by the change.

2. **Implementation flexibility**

   This allows for reimplementation without a change in function. This could be for operational reasons, such as to improve performance, reduce running or maintenance costs, or increase reliability.

3. **Topology flexibility**

   The topology is the structure of the components (hardware, software) of the system. There are three aspects to be considered:

   (a) **Physical** topology flexibility allows hardware components such as computers or transmission lines to be positioned or easily changed to meet the needs of the application. Typical changes are to move a user's workstation from one office to another or to increase the number of workstations. There are always fundamental limitations on the physical topology (e.g. the maximum number of stations on a serial bus or the maximum distance between two stations on the bus). However, one should avoid making any artificial limitations such as system dependence on a specific network topology (see Chapter 5).

   (b) **Logical** topology flexibility in a system allows for any arbitrary communication patterns (between the software components) which meet the application requirements. The logical topology should be independent of the physical topology (see Chapter 3).

   (c) **Mapping** flexibility is needed for the mapping of software components and data onto the physical topology. Software components may be moved from one processor to another to optimize performance or to recover from failures.

4. **Time-domain flexibility**

   This is an indication of when a system can be changed. A **static** system must be completely shut down in order to change any component. It may be necessary to wait for a time when it is quiescent such as during a maintenance period. **Dynamic** systems are flexible in that they allow functional, implementation or topology changes to a running system with no service interruption. In practice the disruption caused by a component change is dependent on whether it is being used by other components.

Flexibility with respect to the software structure of a system is discussed in Chapter 3; flexibility of the communications system is discussed in Chapter 5.

References

Anderson, T., Lee, P.A., *Fault Tolerance: Principles and Practice*, Prentice-Hall, 1981.

Davies, D.W. 'Protection' in Lampson [1981].

Gray, J.N., 'Notes on database operating systems', in Seegmuller G. (ed.), *Operating Systems – an advanced course*, Springer Verlag, 1979, pp. 393–481.

IBM Systems Journal, Vol. 22, no. 4, 1983, special issue on 'Systems Network Architecture, SNA'.

ISO, *Basic Reference Model for Open Systems Interconnection*, ISO 7498, 1983. See also *ACM Computer Comms. Review*, April 1981 pp. 15–65.

Jones, A.K., Chansler, R.J., Durham, I., Schwans, K., Vegdahl, S.R., 'StarOS, a multiprocessor operating system for the support of task forces', *Operating Systems Review*, Vol. 13, no. 5, December 1979, pp. 117–127.

Kohler, W.H., 'A survey of techniques for synchronisation and recovery in decentralised computer systems', *Computer Surveys*, Vol. 13, no. 2, June 1981, pp. 149–184.

Kramer, J. 'Distributed computer systems: two views', in *Specification and Design of Software Systems*, LNCS 152, Springer, Verlag, 1983.

Lamport, L., 'Time, clocks and the ordering of events in a distributed system', *Communications of the ACM*, Vol. 21, no. 7, July 1978, pp. 558–565.

Lampson, B.W., Paul, M., Siegert, H.J., (eds.) *Distributed Systems – Architecture and Implementation*, LNCS 105, Springer Verlag, 1981.

LeLann, G. 'Synchronisation', in Lampson [1981].

LeLann, G. 'Algorithms for distributed data sharing systems which use tickets', *Proc. of 3rd Berkley Workshop*, August 1978.

Needham, R.M., Schroeder, M.D., 'Using encryption for authentication in large networks of computers', *Communications of the ACM*, Vol. 21, no. 12, December 1978, pp. 993–998.

Needham, R.M., Herbert, A.J., *The Cambridge Distributed Computing System*, Addison Wesley, 1982.

Ousterhout, J.K., Scelza, D.A., Sindhu, P.S., 'Medusa: an experiment in distributed operating system structure', *Communications of the ACM*, Vol. 23, no. 5, February 1980, pp. 18–30.

Shoch, J.F., 'Inter-network naming, addressing, and routing', *Compcon 78*, Spring 1978, pp. 72–79.

Sloman, M., Magee, J., Kramer, J., 'Building flexible distributed systems in CONIC' in Duce, D.A. (ed.), *Distributed Computing Systems Programme*, Peter Peregrinus, September 1984.

Su, Z.S., 'Identification in computer networks', *Proceedings of the 8th Data Communications Symposium, ACM Computer Comms Review*, Vol. 13, no. 4, October, 1983.

Watson, R.W., (a), 'Distributed system architecture model', in Lampson [1981].

Watson, R.W., (b), 'Identifiers (naming) in distributed systems', in Lampson [1981].

Three

SOFTWARE STRUCTURE
Components and their interconnection

As we have seen, distributed computer systems have a number of potential advantages over large centralized systems. However, some of the complexities involved can threaten and overwhelm all of these benefits. Concurrency, communication and synchronization of distributed components can increase the complexity rather than provide a panacea if they are not well structured and controlled.

In this and the next chapters we discuss some of the mechanisms required in order to provide manageable application and system software. Software modularity is an essential property. Distributed systems are written as cooperating software components where each component is often merely a simple sequential process. We first describe the various structures and characteristics of the (distributable) components themselves and then discuss how software components can be interconnected to form systems: component interfaces, interconnection patterns, and naming issues. Given that our interconnected components must communicate in order to cooperate, the next chapter concentrates on the interprocess communication (IPC) primitives which can be used in programming a component and describes how each affects the component's behavior.

In these chapters we have taken a **high-level-language view** of the software constructs required for programming distributed systems. They provide a useful framework for describing the concepts involved and the mechanisms required for constructing systems in a type-secure manner. Examples are taken from some existing and proposed languages for concurrent and distributed systems: Ada™ (Ada is a trademark of the US Government – Ada Joint Programming Office) [USA, 1980], ARGUS [Liskov, 1983], CSP [Hoare, 1978], CONIC [Kramer, 1983, Sloman, 1985], and SR [Andrews, 1981].

This approach is in contrast to some of the current, commercially available systems which support general communication transactions across machines. The facilities provided are more akin to operating/communications system facilities which are used to access remote resources by software packages such as database management systems. They provide interprogram communication and it is advocated that they should be incorporated into high-level languages (e.g. interprogram communication facilities of SNA, the System Network Architecture of IBM [Gray, 1983]). The details of such systems can be easily understood and evaluated once the concepts and facilities described in this and the next chapter have been grasped.

3.1　Software Components

3.1.1　Overview of System Structure

A distributed system is constructed from a number of interconnected software **components**. In order to cooperate and coordinate their actions, components communicate by message passing (discussed in Chapter 4). Each component provides an **interface** through which it communicates with other (connected) components. The **logical structure** of the system can therefore be thought of as a network of components where the connections indicate communication paths between components. An example of a simple batch-processing system of three components – READER, EXECUTOR and PRINTER – is given in Fig. 3.1.

A component is indivisible in the sense that it cannot be further decomposed to allow part to run on one physical computer and part on another. It must reside in a single (hardware) computer station. Thus, these software components are the smallest units of distribution. However, as in most multiprogramming systems, more than one component may share a physical computer station. **Allocation** is the process of assigning the software components to physical computers. The **physical structure** of the system is a network of interconnected computers. This must support the desired software component allocation and logical interconnection structure. An example of a mapping for the batch system to a two-station network is given in Fig. 3.2.

Each component encapsulates some function or resource, usually in the form of data or a device. For instance, a component may be responsible for driving a local terminal, performing some control actions on a device, or for managing a database. Hence components may be considered as performing some particular function in the system or providing some service, usually

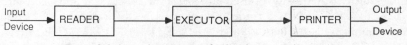

Figure 3.1 Logical structure of a batch-processing system

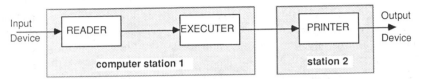

Figure 3.2 Logical-to-physical mapping of a batch-processing system

to other components. However, since components may reside on different physical computers it is essential that they are independent and do **not** share global data. We adopt the view that any shared data or resource should itself be encapsulated in a separate component and accessed via its interface.

Components are analogous to abstract data types and modules in conventional sequential programming, and processes and monitors in concurrent programming.

3.1.2 Structure of a Component

The essential characteristics of a distributable software component are:

- that it is the unit of software modularity in a distributed system;
- that it provides an interface for communication with other components;
- that it encapsulates and acts as a protection domain for some local resource or data – all interaction with non-local resources is via the component interface; and
- that it is capable of processing data, either sequentially or concurrently.

Sequential Execution

In its simplest form, a component is a sequential process. It may be further broken down into a number of actions or procedures but the essential characteristic of a process is that these actions execute sequentially. CSP provides sequential **processes**, Ada and CONIC provide **tasks** (tasks and processes are synonymous). For example,

CSP: x::[{*local data and actions*}]

CONIC: *TASK MODULE x;*
             {*interface definition*}
             {*local data and actions*}
          END.

Ada: *TASK x IS*
             {*interface definition*}
          END;
          TASK BODY x IS
             {*local data and procedures*}
          BEGIN
             {*task actions*}
          END x;

Unlike CONIC and Ada, the CSP process interface is not explicit. In Ada the task interface is separately defined from the body which gives the encapsulated data and actions. Note that although Ada is used as an example, it is debatable whether it is suitable for distributed systems. One of the reasons is that it does not enforce the independence required for distributable components since Ada tasks may access global data. There are other reasons, some of which will be discussed below and in Chapter 4.

Concurrent execution

More complex components can be provided in order to support more powerful or flexible component-structuring mechanisms. These components can encapsulate multiple processes which execute concurrently. They usually also permit local data and procedures to be declared and shared by the processes. Initialization code can be used to ensure that the data is initialized to some valid state. The encapsulated processes communicate by message passing or via the shared data.

For example, Ada also provides the 'package' construct which may have multiple tasks within it. SR provides 'resources' which also provide processes and encapsulate some shared resources (usually in the form of data), ARGUS provides 'guardians', and CONIC provides 'segment' or 'group modules' as a means of collecting together associated task modules. The processes are grouped into a single component since they perform closely related functions (e.g. management of a database or control of a terminal) and are better structured as a number of small processes rather than as a large sequential, and often multithreaded process. This encourages one to mirror in the component the natural parallelism in the application and also increases the amount of parallelism which can be permitted. For instance, it is easier to program the case of multiple readers to a database and to separate the keyboard-handling process from the display-handling process for a terminal. The shared data can also be used to improve efficiency. Since a component must reside in a single station, the constituent processes can also communicate via the shared data rather than pay the overhead of message passing.

An outline example of a resource in SR which provides transactions on a database is given below:

```
RESOURCE transactions;
   DEFINE {interface};
   {local data and initialization statements}
   PROCESS r[1..m];                  {m read processes}
      {actions to perform read operations}
   PROCESS w [1..n];                 {n write processes}
      {actions to perform write operations}
   PROCESS allocator;
      {actions to enforce access constraints}
END transactions
```

3.1.3 Process vs Resource Components (clients and servers)

Process components <u>actively perform some function</u> whereas <u>resource com</u>-ponents (or servers) <u>provide services</u> which are used by processors (cf. monitors). As mentioned above, it is possible to handle a shared resource such as a data structure by encapsulating the resource, together with the code for accessing it, in a process component. The code provides mutual exclusion and defines the operations which can be performed on the resource. Other processes access the resource by sending messages to the encapsulating task. This is very similar to the monitor concept, except that the encapsulating process is active rather than passive. The users of the resource are often referred to as **clients**, and the active resource component as a **server**. Note, however, that assigning a critical resource to a single component could lead to reliability problems in a distributed system.

Most systems provide a single mechanism for both abstractions, usually with a leaning towards one or the other. CSP provides processes, SR provides resources which encapsulate the resource and processes. Ada provides both tasks and packages. ARGUS guardians are similar to SR resources except that they also include mechanisms for resource recovery and concurrency control. CONIC task modules are used to provide active components, but a group of modules can also be formed which is similar to an SR resource.

3.1.4 Component Types and Instances

In order that software components can be separately designed, constructed, compiled and tested, they should be as independent as possible from the rest of the system. In this way components which are reusable in many system environments can be produced. This approach is greatly aided by the ability to define software component **types**. The actual system is then constructed by instantiating (creating **instances**) from the predefined types. Ada supports the definition of task types but unfortunately not of packages. ARGUS defines guardians as types from which instances can be created. CONIC provides for the definition of types at all levels: individual task modules and group modules. CONIC and ARGUS additionally provide for simple module parameters to tailor instances to specific contexts. However, neither CSP nor SR provide component types but rather allow for a limited form of replication by the definition of some fixed array (or range) of components at component definition time. (Most later versions of CSP have introduced the notion of process types in some form or another.)

> *Type definitions and instance declaration:*
> Ada: *TASK TYPE keyboard IS . . . END*
>   *teletype: keyboard*
> CONIC: *TASK MODULE resource (limit:INTEGER); . . . END*
>   *CREATE controller:resource(10);*

Replicated instances definitions
CSP: *buffer (b*:1 . . *max)* :: [. . .]
SR: *RESOURCE transactions* [1 . . *max*]; . . .
            END transactions

Component instances (objects) can be created statically at system configuration or initialization. For instance, an SR system consists of a constant number of components specified in the program and created at initialization time. A CONIC system consists of static collection of modules defined in a separate configuration language. In addition to static creation, it may be possible to instantiate components dynamically during execution of the system. Ada supports dynamic task creation but not for packages; in CSP one can define subprocesses. Dynamic structures are discussed further in the next section.

3.1.5 Nesting and Dynamic Structures

Some languages permit nesting of components in some hierarchical structure. This is usually provided as a means of controlling name scope visibility. As discussed in Section 2.3.1, nesting can be used with hierarchical naming to provide unique local naming in a restricted local context but the ability to identify non-local entities by the use of longer names with global uniqueness. Names are further discussed in Section 3.2.4 with respect to connecting components.

The ability to dynamically vary the level of nesting can be accomplished by permitting components to be created and destroyed dynamically. For instance, process spawning can be useful for handling an indeterminate number of transactions such as creating a process to handle each telephone call in a telephone exchange or each query in a database. Both CSP and Ada provide such nesting and permit one process to spawn other (sub)processes.

CSP uses a parallel command, ||, to provide a 'fork and join' form of parallelism. All subprocesses start simultaneously and the parallel command terminates successfully if and when all subprocesses have successfully terminated. It is possible to spawn a single process or arrays of processes.

CSP: [. . . [*reader*:: [. . .] || *executor*:: [. . .] || *pr(i*:O..3):: [. . .]]
        . . .]

This creates one subprocess named *reader*, one named *executor*, and four printer subprocesses named *pr(*0) to *pr(*3). The outer or parent process continues execution when all the subprocesses have terminated. It can therefore be used for system initialization before subprocess creation and system finalization after subprocess termination. It can also be used simply to provide parallel execution of some commands within a process.

Ada provides a more versatile form of task creation than 'fork and join' by permitting continued execution of the parent. Tasks can be created by declaration on entry to a block. Although the termination rules are more complex than CSP, it is possible for the subprocess to continue execution even after the block in which it was created has terminated.

Ada: *BEGIN*
                 input:keyboard;   {(*declares a task which is created*
                            . . .   *when the block is entered*}

In ARGUS it is possible to define creator operations with each guardian type. Any guardian can then execute the creator operation which will create an instance of a particular guardian type at any specified computer station in the system. For example, given that a guardian type named *spooler*, with parameter of type *printer*, has the creator operation of the form

ARGUS: *instance = CREATOR (dev:printer) RETURNS (spooler)*
then   *spooler$instance(pdev) @ home*

will create an instance of spooler at *home* and return the name of the instance. Here creation and allocation are performed at the same time.

One of the major problems associated with dynamic structures are exhaustion of resources at component creation. The *create* operation can therefore fail and should do so without causing any other failures, such as overwriting existing, active components. Another difficulty is that of identifying and deleting components which no longer serve a purpose or can no longer be referenced. These are referred to as **orphans**. This can require fairly complex identification algorithms, followed by deletion of any outstanding references to the orphan, and then by garbage collection. The component should also not have any outstanding message transactions or resources allocated to it. This can be an extremely complicated process, but provided the system has been designed such that operations may fail (such as sending a message to a nonexistent destination), component destruction should not lead to too many problems.

CONIC does not provide for dynamically varying degrees of task nesting or parallelism from within the task module programming language. No CONIC task can spawn subtasks by the execution of some command or entry to a block. This greatly simplifies the facilities required to support task modules. Using a separate configuration language, the system can be configured from a predefined set of modules, each of which has predefined (static) resource requirements, such as memory. This is similar to building a system from a set of interlocking blocks. However, the system can also be reconfigured by the addition/deletion/replacement of modules, including module (re)connection to provide the communication paths. Since this may be performed without recreating or stopping the system, it provides a mechanism for dynamic incremental change to a system. Also, nested groups of modules for subsystems are provided. Hence some form of both nesting and dynamic component creation are provided at the **configuration level**. This is further discussed in Section 3.5.

All the above examples of dynamic creation have implied creation of instances of existing component types, known at system compile time. However, in many practical systems there is a need to support the introduction of component instances of **new** types as well. This can be supported by facilities for separate component compilation and for dynamic instance creation. Both ARGUS and CONIC provide these facilities. The difficulties lie in the interconnection of new and existing components. This is discussed in Sections 3.2.2 and 3.2.5.

3.2　Connecting Components

We have discussed the basic structure of the software components themselves and indicated how systems consisting of multiple components can be defined. In this section we examine how components are connected in order to form systems which permit communication. A connection is the association of the sender(s) of information with the receiver(s) of that information. How this is achieved depends on the component interfaces, the connection patterns, and the naming conventions which determine how components refer to one another.

The actual communication primitives used by the software components to communicate with each other are discussed in Chapter 4. At this stage it is sufficient to make the simplifying assumption that this communication is a message which is sent by a source component via a connection and received by the connected destination component(s). This is unidirectional communication. Bidirectional communication permits a reply to be sent in response to a message received.

    i.e.   *SEND message (RECEIVE reply)*
    and   *RECEIVE message (SEND reply)*

This message model can also be dressed up as a procedure call for bidirectional communication with the source as caller (or client) and the destination as server.

    i.e.   *CALL server.entry(actual parameters)*
    and   *entry(IN parameters OUT parameters)*

The discussion below is independent of the details of the communication primitives.

3.2.1　Interfaces

Components are independent entities which interact with other components by communication. A fully specified component interface can at best describe the form of the messages which can be sent and received and the potential sources and destinations of these messages. All recent languages which provide intercomponent communication, associate a **data type** with the message. This type provides the structural information on how the message should be interpreted. Messages sent and messages received must be type compatible. The interface to a component is therefore given by the types of messages which can be sent and received and the names of the connected recipient(s) or source(s) of the messages. Equally, the interface to a component using procedure-like calls can be given by the types of parameters (value and result) and the names of the connected callers and servers. The issues of component connection and naming are the subjects of the next sections.

A component may also interface to some device or other part of an embedded system. This too forms part of the component interface but is not considered further here. If data is shared between components, then the independence of the component is compromised, the interface is obviously more difficult to define and distribution of the components is restricted. As mentioned before, some attempt should rather be made to encapsulate the data in a separate component. We consider only loosely coupled components without shared data.

3.2.2 Connection Patterns

The association between senders and receivers for the purpose of communication is called a **connection**. This is a logical link between **all** the possible correspondents in a communication, each connection providing a potential communication path from sender(s) to receiver(s). For example,

SEND message TO ??	specifies a connection to one or more receivers
RECEIVE message FROM ??	specifies a connection from one or more senders

In CSP a send in a source process can address only a single-destination process; and a receive in a destination can address only a single-source process. Each connection in CSP is thus termed *one-to-one*. However, in Ada and CONIC, a destination *entry(port)* can be called or sent to by any number of sources. This connection is thus termed 'many-to-one'. In fact only a single pair of sender and receiver will be engaged in a communication transaction (see below) at a time. The connection therefore indicates only the **potential** correspondents. The possible connection patterns are as shown in Fig. 3.3.

In general, the use of only 1–1 and 1–n connections simplifies synchronization and protection problems as there is only one possible source. However, this restriction makes the provision of servers (e.g. a library component) difficult. For this the m–1 connection is appropriate. If a single send in a source can address multiple destinations, and if the corresponding receive can address multiple sources, then the connection is m–n. The implementations of both 1–n and m–n are best supported by a communications system using a broadcast medium (Chapter 5).

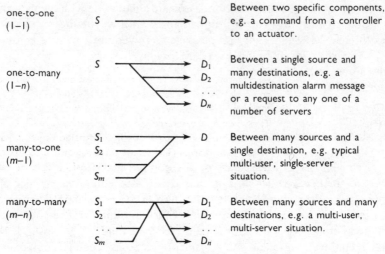

Figure 3.3 Connection patterns

Connections may be *static* or *dynamic*. Static connections are set up at compile or load time and cannot be changed. This is the case for CSP and to a lesser extent, Ada. Dynamic connections can be created, modified and deleted at run time. This can be provided 'internally' to the component by allowing component names to be passed in a message and used by the receiver to provide a new connection (i.e. a new potential destination). For instance, a user could request a printer service from an administrator who in turn provides him with the name of a currently available printer server. ARGUS supports such an approach. The introduction of new types of servers is then supported by the servers offering their services (their names) to known administrators or clients; or in the case of new clients, requesting service from known servers. Name passing is discussed in Section 3.2.5. An alternative is to provide dynamic connections 'externally' by a third party changing the connection between source(s) and destination(s). This is provided in the CONIC configuration language by the ability to change configurations at run time. Static and dynamic connections are related to direct and indirect naming issues discussed in Section 3.2.4.

3.2.3 Transaction Patterns

The communication **transaction** determines the actual correspondents involved in communicating on a connection. The transaction pattern defines the number of sources and receivers involved in a *single* use of the communication primitives. For unidirectional communication, a single use of the communication primitives is a single *SEND* of an application message and a single *RECEIVE*. For bidirectional communication this includes an additional response message in the opposite direction. For procedure-like communication, this is a single call.

Table 3.1   Transaction patterns

Transaction	Connections	
1–1	all	One sender and one receiver are involved in a particular message transaction. This is the simplest and most common and is used with all connection patterns and all primitives.
1–n	1–n	Many receivers are involved in the same message transaction.
	m–n	This is commonly referred to as multidestination communication and can be used to distribute information such as status or alarm messages. (This is not usually provided for bidirectional message passing as the meaning of multiple replies is unclear.)
m–1	m–1	Many senders and only one receiver. This is very unusual but
	m–n	can be used to provide redundant sources of information for fault-tolerant systems, i.e. collect information from multiple sources at exactly the same time. Very difficult to implement without global time.
m–n	m–n	Many sources and receivers. Similar to m–1 but even less used and more difficult to provide.

The possible transaction patterns are listed in Table 3.1. Obviously the actual transaction pattern is dependent on there being a suitable, available connection.

All of $1-n$, $m-1$ and $m-n$ can be simulated by the use of multiple $1-1$ transactions, but the protocols can become fairly complex. The different types of communications primitives and their relation to transaction patterns are fully discussed in Chapter 4.

3.2.4   Naming

Naming refers here to the technique for identifying the recipient(s) and source(s) involved in communication. It is the means by which connections are established. Naming can be either **direct** or **indirect** as well as being **symmetric** or **asymmetric**. Note that the naming conventions discussed below can be used with any of the communication primitives, both uni- and bidirectional. Also, names must be sufficient to identify each component uniquely. Names are translated into addresses which are used in the communication system for message transmission. Addressing in the communication system is discussed in Chapters 8–10.

Direct naming

In this case, a component names the other connected component(s) explicitly in the communication primitives. Connections are therefore specified by directly naming the source(s) or destination(s) of messages. For instance, a process wishing to send a message to one or more other processes explicitly names those processes:

i.e. *SEND Message* **TO Process_P**

Direct naming of the recipient applies to both Ada and CSP. Similarly the recipient may have to name the sender from which it wishes to receive a message:

i.e. *RECEIVE Message* **FROM Process_Q.**

CSP uses such symmetric naming but Ada does not. We discuss these two approaches to naming below.

CSP is **symmetric**, in that the sender process has to name the recipient in the output command and the recipient must name the sender in the input command:

CSP: ⟨*output command*⟩ ::= ⟨*destination process*⟩ ! ⟨*expression*⟩
       ⟨*input command*⟩ ::= ⟨*source process*⟩ ? ⟨*target variable*⟩
e.g. *reader*::[. . . *executer*!(3*a + b*) . . .]   {i.e. *SEND* (3*a + b*)
                                                            TO executor}

      executor::[. . . *reader*? i   . . .]   {i.e. *RECEIVE i*
                                                            FROM reader}

Although it is the simplest approach, use of symmetric, direct naming has a number of severe disadvantages. It hides and disperses the component interface and communication connections. The message types which are sent and received and the destination/source names of those messages are embedded in the component code. Also, since the connections are part of the component definition, components are dependent on their contexts and hence not reusable. For instance, it is not possible to define server components which can receive requests for service from any of a number of clients (many-to-one connections) without the server explicitly naming, in the input command, all of the potential clients (many one-to-one connections)!

CSP: . . . [c1?req → . . .□c2?req → . . .□. . .□cn?req → . . .] . . .
i.e.   Receive c1 request or receive c2 request or . . .

At best, if all the client processes are identical, and an array C(1..n) of the client processes was used, then this can be contracted to

      . . . [(i:1..n)C(i)? → . . .] . . .

Direct naming of the recipient seems also to imply that there can be only a single connection from a source to the named recipient. Since servers often provide many different types of service this is unduly restrictive. Hence most languages try to provide for multiple connections. In CSP an input command only succeeds if the received message also matches the target variable type. In those cases where the message is merely a synchronization signal (i.e. no message type) different connections can be distinguished by using name tags, e.g. *P* and *V* in *semaphore!P*() and *semaphore!V*() respectively. This effectively allows a process to offer multiple different connections by having different target variable types or tags.

In order to overcome some of these problems, a compromise naming scheme can be used. The sender explicitly names the recipient task, but the recipient does not name the sender, i.e. the naming is **asymmetric and partly indirect**. In Ada the sender (caller) actually identifies an entry in the destination:

Ada: *dest.e(request,response)*
                                    {*source task calls entry e in task 'dest'*}

        TASK dest;
               ENTRY e (m:IN message; r:OUT reply)
                      {*Recipient task declares an entry*}

                · · ·

               ACCEPT e (m:IN message: r:OUT reply) DO · · ·
                      {*Receive the request message*}

        · · ·

Multiple clients can use the same entry to a server task (many-to-one connections). In order to provide many different connections, an Ada task can have multiple entries. A source makes calls to a particular entry of a task. As shown above, Ada uses a hierarchical naming scheme to identify the particular entry in the destination task, e.g. *dest.e*. Hence entry names need only be unique in a task. This provides a partially explicit interface as the entry names are given; however, like CSP, the calls made by a task are again hidden within the task code. Hence the connections are also hidden.

A further problem with direct naming is that any change to the constituent processes or interconnection structure (hence involving name changes) may require recompiling and/or relinking of all processes that communicate with (i.e. have connections to) the changed process(es). There is also the added problem of finding which processes are affected: this may require a search of all the other processes to find the connections hidden in the code. Hence separate compilation and system extension are more difficult in Ada and CSP since the caller must name the recipient. As mentioned, this lack of modularity makes the provision of servers, utilities, library programs etc. particularly difficult in CSP since the recipient must also name the sender.

Dynamic connections can be provided if the communication primitives permit the use of process variables and the passing of process and entry names in messages. A source could then send to a changeable set of recipients. Since for symmetrical direct naming the destination must also name the source, this would still be difficult to use and is not provided in CSP. It is partially provided in Ada by the use of access variables to tasks. A task access variable is a typed reference to which tasks of the same type can be assigned. Hence they can be used to refer to different task instances. Name passing is further discussed in Section 3.2.5.

Indirect naming

Instead of directly naming the recipient or sender, a local name of a port is used as a name holder. A message is sent to a local exitport in the sending task and is received from a local entryport in the recipient task (cf. entry in ADA). The binding of local name holders to actual source or destination names is performed separately (Fig. 3.4). This approach is used in CONIC:

Source task: *SEND message* **TO exitp**
                                    {*exitp is a local exitport*}
Destination task: *RECEIVE message* **FROM entryp**
                                    {*entryp is a local entryport*}
Configuration: **LINK source.exitp TO destination.entryp**

This is very flexible in that the programmer writing a component need not be aware of the actual source or destination. The association (linking) between exit and entryports can occur at a later stage, during system generation or at run time, thereby providing dynamic connections. Like entries, ports can be typed allowing compile-time checking that messages sent or received on a port correspond to the port type. There can be a similar check for type matching performed when linking entry and exitports. The interface is explicitly provided by the ports and their associated data types, and the connections are explicitly provided by the linkage commands. These linkage commands can be maintained in a file to give the logical interconnection structure of the system.

The main disadvantage is the additional levels of naming indirection involved in the message transaction. The extra port names required by indirect naming can lead to a proliferation of names. Although this presents a conceptual overhead (more names for the designer/configurator), it need not present any run-time overhead as the names can be resolved into addresses at configuration time.

A comparison of direct and indirect naming is given in Table 3.2.

Other mechanisms for providing indirection include the use of a local pseudonym for the sender or recipient, or identifying a named intermediate object such as a buffer or channel. These intermediate objects are also sometimes referred to as **mailboxes** and are discussed below. One of their main advantages is that they support all communication patterns, and in particular provide convenient support for many-to-many connections with one-to-one transactions (one of multiple users being serviced by any one of multiple servers).

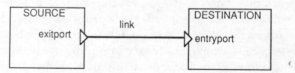

Figure 3.4 Binding by linking indirect names

Table 3.2 Comparison of direct and indirect naming

Direct naming	Indirect naming
Changing a process name requires searching for references to that name and recompiling.	References are to local names, so very modular.
Relationships between processes must be defined at compile time.	Links between exit and entryports can be made at any time – very flexible.
Logical interconnection structure is implicit.	Logical interconnection structure is explicit, in terms of linkages between entry and exitports.
Essentially single path communication between processes.	Multipath communication as entries can be related to message source or type.
Difficult to write server processes which can receive a message from any process (CSP).	Easy to write server processes which do not know where their next request will come from.
No additional names other than task names needed.	Leads to a proliferation of names as tasks and ports must be identified.
Separate compilation requires compiler access to names in rest of the system.	Compiler needs message type definitions only. Linker needs system configuration information.

Mailboxes (channels)

Some systems provide a typed communication object, called a mailbox (or channel), independent of the sender or receiver. Mailboxes must have global or uniquely identifiable names. Source components send messages to named mailboxes and destination components receive messages from named mailboxes.

> e.g.   *SEND message* **TO mailbox_X**
> *RECEIVE message* **FROM mailbox_X**
> or   *CALL* **mailbox_X** *(parameters)*
> *ACCEPT* **mailbox_X** *(IN parameters OUT parameters)*

Systems then consist of software components **and** mailboxes, connections being indicated by a shared use of the same mailboxes. This approach is less flexible than pure indirect naming as the sources and recipients both name the same object and are thus connected, in the code, via that object. However, each component is more independent of other components than with direct naming. Mailboxes are therefore more restrictive than indirect naming but less so than direct. Like indirect naming, mailboxes lead to a proliferation of names. In addition, they may also be less efficient as they introduce additional levels of indirection in the execution of a message transaction. The message must be transmitted via the mailbox. It is even possible for the mailbox to reside on a different computer station from either the source or destination.

One of the main advantages of mailboxes is that they conveniently support many-to-many connections, i.e. multiple senders and receivers can be permitted to use the same mailbox. This is very useful for implementing multiservers where any one of a number of servers can handle a request from any one of a number of users (one-to-one transaction). Another variation of this is to permit receivers to take a copy of the message, leaving the original in the mailbox (one-to-many transaction). This is sometimes called a noticeboard and is similar to reading from a shared memory. The mailbox is then usually restricted to having only a single sender.

An example of the system structure for multiple clients and multiple servers is given in Fig. 3.5. Whenever a client process requires a record to be logged on a printer, it sends the record to mailbox P. Whenever a server process is free to print a record it receives a record from P. The mailbox matches a client message with a server receive, i.e. although the mailbox provides a many-to-one connection, the communication transaction is one-to-one.

3.2.5 Component Name Passing

Some systems allow the passing of component, entry, mailbox or port names in messages. This is a very powerful facility which forms the basis for provision of **dynamic connections** and **third-party service**. For instance, in a system with asymmetric direct naming, a component can receive a destination component name in a message, and use it in a subsequent transaction

e.g.   *RECEIVE process_id;*
        SEND message TO process-id;

Note that it is also necessary to be able to declare component **name variables** to hold component names. The values actually passed by the system and assigned to the variables are the current addresses of the named components.

A common requirement is for a server to enter into a prolonged conversa-

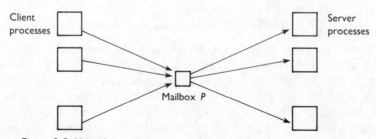

Figure 3.5 Use of a mailbox to match waiting clients to free servers

tion (a number of transactions) with a client. The server needs to receive and set up a connection with that particular client. This can be done using, for example, the THOTH [Cheriton, 1979] operating system primitives (later to become V-Kernel [Cheriton, 1984], Chapter 10) as follows:

THOTH: *id* := . *RECEIVE(request)* {*receive a request from any client and set id to the client identifer*

  id := . *SEND(response,id)* {*send response to client id*}

  id := . *RECEIVE(message,id)* {*receive message from client id*}

An example of third party service is shown in Fig. 3.6. Component A sends a request to component B, which is unable to deal with it. B passes the request on to component C. Unless B can also pass the name of the original component, C will not be able to communicate the results directly with A.

In systems which communicate via mailboxes, one would send mailbox names in messages and store these names in mailbox variables.

A system based on ports or entries must pass both the name of the component and of the entry(port) within the component. The component wishing to use the received name must either have an existing connection (from its exitport) to the remote entry (entryport) or it must be able to create one. In ADA, as for all direct communication, this connection is available by virtue of knowing the name of the destination task and entry. In CONIC links must be set up prior to message transactions. Although there is no link command in the component programming language, a link can be set up by sending a link request to a system service, the link manager. In fact CONIC does not support name passing since this would violate its ability to retain a configuration description giving the current components and their connections (Section 3.4) [Kramer, 1985].

For bidirectional communcation, the ability of the destination to obtain and store the source identity when the request message is received can also be very useful. For instance, in the example above, if *A* had used a request-reply (see Section 4.4.1) and *B* was able to pass the identity of *A* to *C*, then

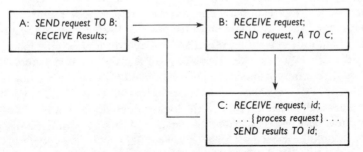

Figure 3.6 Third party service using name passing

C could perform the reply! This is provided in CONIC where a request can be *FORWARD*ed to another component for processing and reply directly to *A*. As before, it also frees component *B* from involvement in the transaction once the request has been forwarded. The V-Kernel [Cheriton, 1984] provides a similar facility (Section 10.11).

Storing the source identity is also useful if a request cannot be handled immediately and requires a later reply (e.g. scheduling). In any case, knowledge of the source can be useful for performing validity checks such as access rights. One of the original criticisms of ADA is that the destination task could not find out the identity of the source task. This has been somewhat corrected by the provision of access variables (task references) which can be sent in messages. THOTH (V-Kernel) supports all of the above facilities.

Uncontrolled passing of names can lead to difficulty in verifying that a system is correct, of keeping track of the connection structure and to problems of clearing up after a component is destroyed. It is difficult to ensure that no other component still retains the name of (and hence a connection to) a terminated or aborted component.

3.3 Installation of Software Components of a System

This section describes a possible scenario for the installation of software components in a system. It is based on the approach used to provide a CONIC system.

The first stage in software production is compilation of the software component to produce relocatable object code for the component type. It is obviously essential in a distributed system that separate compilation of the components be supported. For languages which use indirect naming this is easy, provided that agreed data type definitions are available. Direct naming (and even mailboxes) implies that a component must be compiled in the context of the current system in order to access existing component names (or mailboxes) and message types. This is sometimes referred to as an 'eternal compiler' as it must keep track of the components (and mailboxes) in the system at any time.

One approach to installation (Fig. 3.8) is to load the component type code at a station and to create named instances of that type as required. This is the mapping of the logical system of software components onto the physical system of stations. The component code need not be downline loaded if it is already held locally at the station (e.g. in ROM). If indirect naming had been used, the components must then be linked together to provide the interconnections. Type checking must be performed to ensure compatibility. Linking completes the mapping of the logical interconnection structure onto the physical network of stations. In the case of direct naming the interconnections would have been set up at compile time. Finally, the system (or parts thereof) can be started. The actual order in which these operations are per-

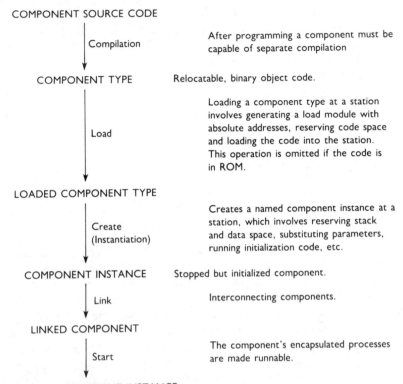

COMPONENT SOURCE CODE

Compilation — After programming a component must be capable of separate compilation

COMPONENT TYPE — Relocatable, binary object code.

Load — Loading a component type at a station involves generating a load module with absolute addresses, reserving code space and loading the code into the station. This operation is omitted if the code is in ROM.

LOADED COMPONENT TYPE

Create (Instantiation) — Creates a named component instance at a station, which involves reserving stack and data space, substituting parameters, running initialization code, etc.

COMPONENT INSTANCE — Stopped but initialized component.

Link — Interconnecting components.

LINKED COMPONENT

Start — The component's encapsulated processes are made runnable.

RUNNABLE COMPONENT INSTANCE

Figure 3.7 Stages in installing a software component at a station

formed may vary in some systems (e.g. creation and linking for a single station can be done before loading) but the operations which are performed remain essentially the same.

In case of component failure or system modification or extension, it should be possible to allow any of the installation stages (including stopping, unlinking and deleting of components) to be carried out while the rest of the system is operational. Extension of the system by the addition of component instances of new types then consists of compiling, loading and creating the new components. They are then linked to existing components and started. As mentioned in Section 3.2.2, if the new components are clients using existing services, or new servers providing service via some administrator, then the linking can be performed by translating the server or administrator names (respectively) to the appropriate addresses. This can even be performed before loading.

System installation and maintenance could be greatly enhanced if a database were provided in which data and component type definitions, logical and physical configurations, and name to address translation information were maintained. The type definitions of components could be maintained for use by the loader. Message types would be used by the compiler (for component type definition) and the linker (for checking connection links). The logical configuration information would provide an up-to-date picture of the component instances and the interconnections. The physical configuration would provide descriptions and status information of stations and subnetworks (see Chapter 5). Together they would provide a logical and physical picture of the current system, and a means of logical translation from name to physical address.

3.4   Case Study: CONIC

The CONIC software architecture was designed to be used for the production of large, distributed embedded systems. In particular CONIC provides the necessary **flexibility** for a system to evolve and change to meet changing requirements and conditions. It can easily incorporate new functionality in response to evolutionary changes and allows reorganization of existing components in response to operational changes [Kramer, 1985].

The CONIC system originated from a research project funded by the British National Coal Board to investigate the use of distributed microcomputers for underground monitoring and control in coal mines. The requirements for such a system have been discussed in the case study in Section 1.3.4 as an example of a process-control environment. The large size, physical distribution and real-time requirements have been mentioned. In particular the need for flexibility was paramount. It was felt that fault tolerance could be approached by using the mechanisms which support the flexibility. Performance was obtained by the use of simple techniques wherever more powerful but costly approaches were considered unnecessary. The result is a well-integrated system which provides all the facilities for the efficient implementation and maintenance of large, distributed real-time systems.

As mentioned before, it is obvious that in order to build large software systems, it is necessary to decompose the system into components which can be separately programmed, compiled and tested. The system is then constructed as a configuration of these software components. The separate activities of component programming and system building (configuration) have been referred to as 'programming-in-the-small' and 'programming-in-the-large' respectively [DeRemer, 1975]. In CONIC this is reflected in separate component programming and configuration languages [Kramer, 1983, Magee, 1984]. In the rest of this section, based on [Sloman, 1984], we show how CONIC can be used to provide a distributed system in which configuration management is used to satisfy the flexibility requirements discussed in Chapter 2.

In Section 3.4.1 we explain how the CONIC module programming language provides the necessary modularity characteristics (functional and implementation flexibility). The message primitives employ indirect naming and provide transparency between local and remote communication. They are described in detail in Chapter 4. In Section 3.4.2 we describe the CONIC configuration language and briefly indicate low logical configurations are mapped onto the physical topology of interconnected networks (topology flexibility). The facilities for structuring configurations to provide abstraction are also covered. Section 3.4.3 explains the use of an on-line configuration manager to achieve dynamic configuration (time-domain flexibility) in a CONIC system. Finally, Section 3.4.4 gives a brief overview of the CONIC distributed operating system.

3.4.1 The CONIC Module Programming Language

Task modules

Modularity is the key property for meeting the flexibility requirements. The CONIC programming language is based on Pascal, which has been extended to support modularity and message-passing primitives.

The language allows the definition of a **task module type**, which is a self-contained, sequential task (process). A task module type is written and compiled independently from the particular configuration in which it will run, i.e. it provides **configuration independence** in that all references are to local objects and there is no direct naming of other modules or communication entities. This means there is no configuration information embedded in the programming language and so no recompilation is needed for configuration changes as is the case with other languages such as CSP and Ada.

At configuration time, **module instances** are created from these module types. Module instances exchange messages and perform a particular function in the system such as controlling a device or managing a resource. Multiple instances of a module type can be created on the same or different stations and a station can contain many different modules. This meets the requirements for mapping flexibility.

CONIC modules have a **well-defined interface** which specifies all the information required to use the module in a system. This is essential to provide implementation abstraction. The interconnections and information exchanged by modules is specified in terms of **ports**. An **exitport** denotes the interface at which message transactions can be initiated and specifies a local name and message type in place of the destination name and type. An **entryport** denotes the interface at which message transactions can be received and specifies a local name and type in place of the source name and type. The binding of an exitport to an entryport is part of the configuration specification and cannot be performed within the task module programming language. Simple parameters (e.g. integers, reals, booleans) may also be used at the interface to a task module type. Parameter values may then be passed to a module instance when it is created. This can be used to tailor a module type for a particular environment, for example to pass a device address to a device driver.

```
TASK MODULE bound;
ENTRYPORT putchar : char REPLY signaltype;
              getchar : signaltype REPLY char;
CONST poolsize = 100;
VAR inp,outp,contents : integer;
      buf:ARRAY[1 . . maxsize] OF char;
BEGIN
   inp : = 1;  outp : = 1;  contents : = 0;
   LOOP
   {receive and handle characters to store and requests for characters}

   END
END.
```

Figure 3.8 Bounded buffer task module

Figure 3.8 is an outline example of a simple bounded buffer task module.
There are two classes of ports which correspond to the message transactions classes described in Chapter 4. **Request-reply ports** are bidirectional as they declare the types of values to be used for both a request message and the corresponding reply. **Notify ports** are unidirectional, i.e. they have no reply port. For convenience, it is possible to define families (arrays) of identical ports. The following are examples of port definitions:

EXITPORT getch : *chr REPLY signaltype*;
         alarm : *boolean*;
         datalinks [1..3] : *message*;
ENTRYPORT print : *line REPLY status*;
         message : *msgtype*;
         callsin [1..n] : *printrequest REPLY printertype*;

Ports define all the information required to use a module and so it is very simple to replace a module with a new or different version with the same operational interface. This provides the implementation and functional flexibility identified in Chapter 2. The indirect naming used by the communication primitives (refer to local port names) provide complete configuration independence for a task module.

The CONIC communications primitives are described in Chapter 4.

3.4.2 CONIC Configuration Language

One of the key elements in the provision of flexibility is the need to separate the programming of individual software components (task module types) from the building of a system from instances of modules. This has led to the development of the CONIC configuration language which can be used to specify both the initial system and subsequent changes as described below. The following sections describe the essential properties which must be supported by a configuration language.

Context definition
The context definition identifies the set of module types from which the system
is constructed, and is provided by a **use** construct, e.g.

USE bound, serial_output;

Modules communicate by typed messages so it is necessary for data type
definitions to be shared between modules. Having to redefine types wherever
they are used would make type checking more difficult, more error prone
and require redundant effort by the programmer. CONIC allows common
data types and constants to be defined in separate **definition** units. (Data
variables, functions and procedures can also be included in these definition
units.) These are imported to make them accessible from both the programming and configuration languages, e.g:

FROM commstypes USE datatype, acktype, buffer_size;

Instantiation
The **create** construct declares the named instances of module types to be
created in the system. Instantiation parameters can be used to pass information such as device or interrupt vector addresses to device drivers. In order
to cut down proliferation of names we allow the type identifer name to be
overloaded and used as an instance name where only one instance of a type
exists in a (sub)system.

CREATE serial_output (177560 # 8, 100 # 8);
         datalink1, datalink2: CRdriver (retries);

Families (cf. arrays) of module instances can be created by specifying a
'range':

CREATE FAMILY k: [1..maxcalls]
         caller [k] : call_handler (k);

Interconnection
The **link** construct specifies the interconnection of module instances by binding a module exitport to a module entryport. Both type and operation compatibility are checked so an exitport can only be linked to an entryport of
the same data and transaction type. Multiple exitports can be linked to a
single entryport, which is particularly useful for connecting clients to servers
(e.g. a file server). A single notify exitport can be linked to multiple entryports,
which provides multidestination message transactions. Multidestination is
not provided for request–reply ports because the semantics of dealing with
multiple replies to a single request are unclear.

LINK mod1.xp TO mod2.ep;
         manager.errorout TO logger1.errorin, operator.reports;

Families of modules and/or families of ports can be linked by defining range identifiers and associated ranges. This is merely a shorthand to save on repetitive link statements. The repetitions can be nested and are then performed in an analogous way to nested for-loops in Pascal:

> *LINK FAMILY k*: [1..*maxcalls*]
>   *caller* [*k*].*in TO manager.requests*;

Mapping onto physical topology

The only constraint imposed by the configuration level on the interconnection of module exit and entryports is that they are compatible in terms of type and operation. The logical interconnection is completely independent of the physical configuration of the hardware components on which the system is to be run. The same logical configuration can be mapped onto a single computer, a closely coupled multiprocessor station or distributed stations connected via an arbitrary network. It is thus important to separate the specification of a logical configuration from its mapping onto a physical configuration. Currently this mapping is performed by using an **at** clause in the create construct to specify a particular station or co-location with some other module. For example,

> *CREATE filer* : *file_ server AT NODE(7,2)*;
>   *dir*: *directory AT filer*;

creates an instance of filer at station 7 on network 2, and dir at the same station as filer.

The physical topology supported by a CONIC system consists of local area networks (LANs) interconnected by store-and-forward gateways. A station can communicate with any other station, if necessary via a gateway. This topology is fully described in Chapter 5.

Structuring configuration specifications

The modules in a distributed system often exhibit a hierarchical relationship. For example, a database subsystem makes use of file servers, which may themselves consist of directory servers, record access servers and disk drivers. This structure can be represented by nesting software components at the configuration level by means of **group modules**. A group module type is a configuration specification and identifies a collection of module types, instances of those types and their interconnection. The constituent modules may be the primitive task modules containing a single process, described in Section 3.5.1, or group modules. The group modules also have an interface defined in terms of exit- and entryports, as well as formal parameters. This structuring of the specification is essential for large systems with many module instances, otherwise the name space would become unmanageable and the configuration specification unreadable.

As mentioned, group modules provide configuration abstraction. The structure of a group module is defined by the **use, create,** and **link** constructs described previously. The interface to the module is also defined in terms of exit- and entryports and so from the outside it is not possible to distinguish between a task and a group module. The group interface ports are bound to the ports of component module instances using link statements within the group module specification. These links are exitport-to-exitport or entryport-to-entryport, e.g.

> *LINK groupentry TO mod1.entry1;*
>   *mod1.exit1 TO groupexit;*

This linking is merely a name mapping and does not entail any run-time overheads; i.e. there is no copying or queueing of messages at interface ports to group modules. The interface port name is global within the group specification and must be unique, whereas ports on different module instances can have the same name. The combined *module_name.port_name* must be unique within its scope (the group specification).

An example of a configuration description for a simple system which echoes characters at a terminal and uses a buffer and an inverter is shown in Fig. 3.9. (*Invert* is a simple module which takes the front character from the bounded buffer and makes it available at its exitport *outchar*.) The configuration is shown diagrammatically in Fig. 3.10.

A **segment module** is a restricted form of group module in that the constituent module instances share an address space and so must be in a single station. The components of a segment module may share procedures and pass pointer values in messages. However, there is no global data within a

```
GROUP MODULE buffer;
    ENTRYPORT inchar: char REPLY signaltype;
    EXITPORT outchar: char REPLY signaltype;

    USE bound, invert;
    CREATE bound;
          invert;
    LINK invert.getchar TO bound.getchar;
         inchar TO bound.putchar;
         invert.outchar TO outchar;

END.

GROUP MODULE echo;
    CONST status = 177560 # 8;
          vector = 100 # 8;
    USE serial-input, serial-output, buffer;
    CREATE Rx: serial-input(status, vector);
           Tx: serial-output(status + 4, vector + 4);
           B: buffer;
    LINK Rx.input TO B. inchar;
         B. outchar TO Tx.output;
END.
```

Figure 3.9 Configuration description

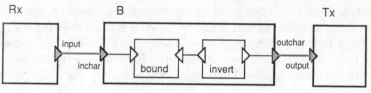

Figure 3.10 Configuration diagram

segment module. Any shared data must be encapsulated within a task module and references explicitly passed by messages. The only synchronization primitives available for control of access to shared objects in a segment module are the message primitives. For example the CONIC modules which implement the various layers of the communication system within a station pass pointers to message buffers in order to reduce the overheads of copying messages between these modules.

Also a group of tasks may be required to provide parallelism within a particular function. The terminal driver is an example of a set of closely related tasks which are grouped to form a segment module (i.e. input from a terminal keyboard and output to its screen). This capability for parallelism at the task level encourages simpler cooperating sequential tasks rather than multi-threaded ones. The concept of a segment module is similar to that of a resource in SR and a guardian in ARGUS.

3.4.3 Dynamic Configuration

The configuration specifications described so far are essentially static. A host development environment is used to produce load images which are down-line loaded into target distributed stations or put into ROM memory for embedded systems. In a CONIC distributed system, where the operating and communication system is itself implemented as CONIC modules, this static configuration is essential to provide the basic support for dynamic configuration in each station.

Dynamic configuration is necessary to provide the time-domain flexibility mentioned in Chapter 2. For many applications, it is too costly or unsafe to shut down a complete distributed system in order to change a component. A CONIC system allows arbitrary, unpredicted modification and extensions to an existing system without rebuilding the entire system [Kramer, 1985]. It should be possible to perform incremental changes on the system without stopping the unaffected parts of the system. Changes which can be performed on a running system include:

Installation and removal of module types;
Creation and deletion of module instances;
Changes to the interconnections between modules.

These changes are performed by submitting a change specification to an **on-line configuration manager** which validates the change (ensuring type security) and produces a new system specification incorporating the changes. It also generates the necessary commands to the operating system to perform the changes. Deleting a component would obviously affect other modules using it but changing the interconnections can often be performed without affecting other modules.

Change specifications

The change specification uses the configuration constructs described in Section 3.4.2, but must also specify the inverse functions, namely:

unlink: disconnects a module exitport from an entryport.

delete: deletes the named module instances from the system. This can be performed only after all its ports have been unlinked.

remove: removes knowledge of the type from the configuration specification, and is valid only after all instances have been deleted.

For example, to remove the buffer from the example of Fig. 3.4 the change specification outlined in Fig. 3.11 would be submitted to the configuration manager.

Configuration Manager

A change specification is submitted to a configuration manager which validates the specification, translates it into commands to the distributed operating system to execute the reconfiguration operations and produces the new system configuration specification. The configuration manager requires information on the current state of the system (e.g. is a component type already in station or will it have to be downloaded?) and must also have access to information necessary to perform validity checks. Some of this information can be obtained by querying the system to check its current state but type information is not maintained in stations and so must be held in an online database. A single change may result in a number of commands to the system (e.g. create component instance => query resources, load type, instantiate).

The configuration manager currently being designed consists of three parts: a database describing the current system, specification translator and a command executor (Fig. 3.12). The initial version of the configuration manager will be centralized but later versions will be decentralized.

```
CHANGE echo;
    UNLINK Rx.input FROM B.inchar;
            B.outchar FROM Tx.output;
    DELETE B;
    REMOVE buffer;
    LINK Rx.input TO Tx.output;
END.
```

Figure 3.11 Change specification

Change specification

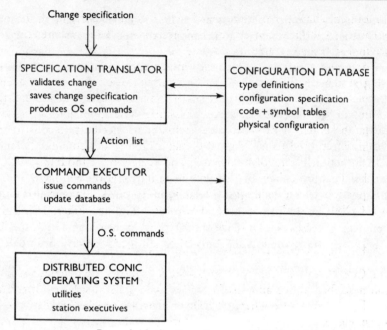

Figure 3.12 Configuration management

Configuration database.   This holds the following information:

Task module types: The code generated by the module compiler, together with symbol tables for port names etc. These will be held in an intermediate machine-independent target language called EM [Tanenbaum, 1983] and the final target code generated when the type is loaded into a particular processor.

Type definitions: These are the definitions files of port and message types.

Configuration specification: The updated current specification of the system configuration together with a history of all change specifications in time order.

Physical system configuration: Information on the subnets such as type, stations connected and current status. Also descriptions of the physical stations, including their resources such as memory and devices.

Specification translator.   This validates the change specification with respect to availability of resources (e.g. memory or I/O devices) as well as type operational compatibility for interconnections. The specification is translated into a sequence of simple commands to the operating system which are passed to the command executor. The translator uses the database to map the names in the specification into system address, e.g. a port address is specified by *subnet_id.station_id.module_id.port_id*.

The change specification effectively produces a new system configuration but the change specification is kept in order to provide a history of changes.

If required, changes can be reversed, which is particularly useful for testing purposes. A module can be installed, tested and the system restored to its original state by a single command.

Command executor. This performs operations on the distributed operating system by means of CONIC communication primitives. A change specification is translated into a series of commands called an **action list**. The command executor is responsible for issuing these commands and updating the database. In order to keep the system and its specification consistent, the system is returned to its original configuration if any commands fail.

If an action list involves deleting and recreating a module (possibly in another location), then any internal state information will have been lost. It is possible to use redundancy techniques to mask configuration changes in a CONIC system, as described elsewhere [Loques-Filho, 1984].

3.4.4 The CONIC Distributed Operating System

The CONIC distributed operating system supports the dynamic configuration described above and also provides some general services. It conforms to a layered structure where each layer provides services used by the layer above (Fig. 3.13). The distributed operating system consists of a set of utilities which are *not* replicated in every station and an executive which is in every station (see Chapter 2).

The main influences on the design of the CONIC distributed operating system [Magee, 1984] were that the station executive should be small and efficient so that dynamic configuration could be provided on small microprocessor systems without backing store. This led to the principle of

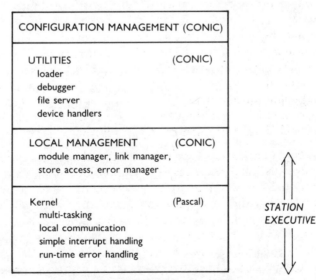

Figure 3.13 Conic distributed operating system

providing minimal functionality in the executive present in every station and rather implementing as much as possible remotely by utility modules. The executive should itself be configurable so that smaller ROM stations could omit the dynamic configuration support. This was accomplished by implementing most of the station operating system components as a set of CONIC modules which can be configured using the static configuration facilities. The flexibility of the CONIC module structure has been exploited in allowing distribution of the operating system components.

Station executive

The executive is the set of CONIC modules which together with the kernel manage the resources within a station. Unlike most operating stystems, the executive does **not** include device drivers. These are considered application utilities. Since flexibility is regarded as more important than performance the executive was mostly written as Conic modules, with the kernel being implemented in Pascal.

Station kernel.   This is implemented in Pascal and provides multitasking and the primitives used by the executive's local management modules for task execution control and port linkage. It also provides the run-time support for the language extensions to Pascal, i.e. inter-task message communication within a station, timing primitives, and a simple interrupt mechanism.

Local management.   This is a set of four CONIC modules the **module-manager** deals with the loading of task types and creating instances; the **linkmanager** handles requests to link exitports of task instances within the station to either local or remote entryports; **storeaccess** allows remote reading or writing of blocks of memory and is used for both down-line loading and remote debug; **errormanager** receives run-time error messages detected by the kernel or issued by a module and reports them to a selected destination.

Utilities

The utilities provide the shared services traditionally found in operating systems. These utilities are implemented as normal CONIC group modules and may themselves be distributed, but they are not found in every station.

File Server: This consists of a group of modules which perform the functions of file access (reading or writing blocks of a file), directory lookup (translates symbolic file names into file identifiers), management facilities (creating, deleting and renaming files) and disk drivers (reads or writes disk blocks).

Loader: This downline loads module type code into target stations. It obtains the type code from the file server and performs the final translation into the machine-specific target code. It also relocates code to absolute memory addresses for processors with no memory management hardware. The memory instance address is obtained from the station's module manager.

Debugger: This allows a remote module to be tested via its message passing interface or by examining its memory space. The debugger provides the capability to construct test messages to send to a module's entryports and to decode and display messages received from exitports. It can also use the store-access manager of a (remote) station to read or write to the test module's memory space. The debugger operates on record-structured objects, messages and variables. It obtains information on record structures from symbol table information stored on the file server.

Device handlers: These have been implemented for a number of network interfaces, terminals, disks, etc. Our experience has been that these are comparatively simple to implement and integrate into the system as they are written in a high-level language using a mechanism which makes interrupts available at the language level.

Configuration system

The operating system utilities, together with the local station executives, cooperate to implement dynamic configuration operations for **load**ing and **unload**ing module types, **creating** and **deleting** module instances, **linking** and **unlink**ing ports, **starting** and **stopping** module instances, and **querying** the state of the module instances in a station.

Communicating system

This consists of a set of modules to support inter-station message passing. An exitport linked to a remote entryport is actually linked to a local communication module which formats a message by adding station addresses etc. and sends the message over the network to the remote station. At the remote station a communication module receives the message, strips off headers and then uses standard local CONIC communication primitives to deliver the message. The communication system thus acts as a surrogate local source or destination for remote communication. The CONIC communication system is described in more detail in Chapter 10.

3.5 Software Structure: An Example in CONIC

As an example of the decomposition of a simple system into software components, we present an example of a simplified pump control system for the mining environment [Kramer, 1983].

3.5.1 Description of a Pump System for Mine Drainage

The diagram in Fig. 3.14 is the schematic of a very simplified pump installation. It is used to pump mine-water collected in a sump at shaft bottom to the surface.

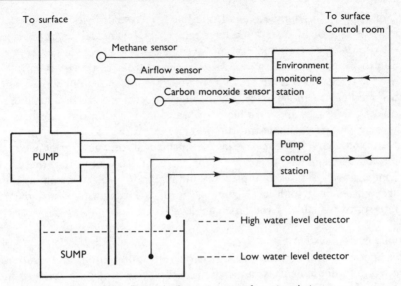

Figure 3.14 Control of a main pump for mine drainage

The required control of the pump is such that once **start** has been enabled by a command from the surface, the pump runs automatically, controlled by the water level as sensed by the high- and low-level detectors. Detection of high level causes the pump to run until low level is indicated. The surface operator may also **stop** the pump, and query its current **status**.

The pump is situated underground in a coal mine, and so for safety reasons it must not be started or continue running when the percentage of methane in the atmosphere exceeds a set safety limit. The pump controller obtains information on methane level by communicating with a nearby environmental monitoring station. As well as methane this station monitors carbon monoxide level and airflow velocity. The environment monitoring station provides information to the surface and other plant controllers as well as to the pump controller.

3.5.2 Software Structure

The decomposition of the system into three main components is easy in this example as it follows the physical structure of the system. A brief outline of the function of each component, its interface in terms of the message types it sends and receives, and the interconnection configuration, should be given. This is similar to the general design approaches advocated in data-flow design methods [Yourdon, 1975] and more recently and methodically by Jackson's system design method [Jackson, 1983].

CONIC is used to briefly describe the software structure for some of the component modules.

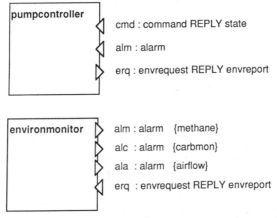

Figure 3.15 Pump-controller and environment-monitor modules

Module and port types

The group module definitions for the pump controller and the environment monitor are shown in Fig. 3.15. The message type definitions for the ports are stored in a definitions unit called *pumpdefns*:

DEFINE pumpdefns;
TYPE command = *(start, stop, status);*
state = *(running, ready, stopped, lowstop, methanestop);*
sensor = *(methane, carbmon, airflow);*
envreport = *RECORD reading* : *REAL* ; *sn* : *sensor END;*
envrequest = *sensor;*
alarm = *(signaltype);*
END.

System configuration

{*Module creation from predefined types*}
    CREATE pump1 (177562 # 8):pumpcontroller AT node(2);
    CREATE surface:operatormod AT node(1);
    CREATE env1:environmonitor AT node(3);
{*Port linkage with type validation*}
    LINK surface.out TO pump1.cmd;   {*one–one connection*}
    LINK pump1.erq TO env1.erq;   {*one of many–one connection*}
    LINK env1.alm TO pump1.alm,surface.alm;
                                   {*one–many connection*}

. . . . . .
{*Initiation of this configuration*}
    START pump1, surface, env1 ;

The relevant part of the configuration is shown diagrammatically in Fig. 3.16.

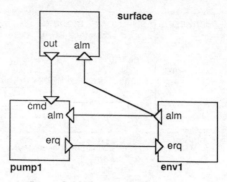

Figure 3.16 System configuration

Software structure of the pump controller

For the sake of brevity only the group module pump controller is described in detail. Its internal structure is shown in Fig. 3.17.

The pump controller is a group module and consists of the included type definitions, pumpdefns, and the three task modules, control, pump and level. Level is a simple task which periodically scans the water level sensors and sends the level reading to the control task via an internal link from port W to WL. *Pump* merely receives commands from the control to start or stop the pump. The control task performs the required pump control.

```
GROUP MODULE pumpcontroller (sensoraddr:integer);
    USE controltask, pumptask, leveltask;
    USE pumpdefns: command, state, envreport, envrequest, alarm;
    ENTRYPORT
            cmd:command REPLY state;
            alm:alarm;
    EXITPORT erq:envrequest REPLY envreport;
                                        {Module interface}
    CREATE control:controltask;
    pump: pumptask;
    level:   leveltask(sensoraddr:integer);
                                        {Internal components}
    LINK level.W TO control.WL;
    control.PC TO pump.C
                                        {Internal links}
    LINK cmd TO control.cmd;
    alm TO control.alm;
    control.erq TO erq;                {Interface links}
END.
```

The CONIC programs which constitute the control, pump and level tasks are given as examples in Section 4.7.4 after discussing communication primitives and related software issues.

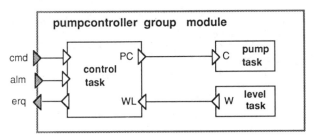

Figure 3.17 Structure of the pump controller group module

References

Andrews, G.R., 'The distributed programming language SR – mechanisms, design and implementation', *Software Practice and Experience*, Vol. 12, 1982, pp. 719–753.

Cheriton, D.R., Malcolm, M.A., Melen, L.S., Sager, G.R., 'Thoth, a portable real-time operating system', *Communications of the ACM*, Vol. 22, no. 2, February 1979, pp. 105–115.

Cheriton, D.R., 'The V-Kernel: a software base for distributed systems', *IEEE Software*, Vol. 1, no. 2, April 1984, pp. 19–43.

DeRemer, F., Kron, H., 'Programming-in-the-large versus programming-in-the-small', *Proc. of Conference on Reliable Software*, 1975, pp. 114–121.

Dulay, N., Kramer, J., Magee, J., Sloman, M., Twidle, K.P., *The Conic Configuration Language: version 1.3*, Imperial College Research Report, DOC 84/20, November 1984.

Gray, J.P., Hansen, P.J., Homan, P., Lerner, M.A., Pozefsky, M., 'Advanced program-to-program communication in SNA', *IBM Systems Journal*, Vol. 22, no.4, 1983, pp. 298–318.

Hoare, C.A.R. 'Communicating sequential processes', *Communications of the ACM*, Vol. 21, no. 8, August 1978, pp. 666–677.

Jackson, M., *System Development*, Prentice-Hall, 1983.

Kramer, J., Magee, J., Sloman, M., Lister, A., CONIC: an Integrated Approach to Distributed Computer Control Systems', *IEE Proceedings*, Part E, Vol. 130, no. 1, January 1983, pp. 1–10.

Kramer, J., Magee, J., Sloman, M., Twidle, K.P., Dulay, N., *The Conic Programming Language: version 2.4*, Imperial College Research Report, DOC 84/19, October 1984.

Kramer, J., Magee, J., 'Dynamic configuration for distributed systems', *IEEE Trans. on Software Engineering*, Vol. SE-11 no. 4, April 1985.

Liskov, B., Sheifler, R., 'Guardians and actions: linguistic support for robust-distributed programs', *ACM TOPLAS*, Vol. 5, no. 3, July 1983, pp. 381–404.

Loques-Filho, O., *A Fault Tolerant Distributed Computer Control System*, Ph.D Thesis, Imperial College, February 1984.

Magee, J., *Provision of Flexibility in Distributed Systems*, Ph.D. Thesis, Imperial College, April 1984.

Sloman, M., Magee, J., Kramer, J., 'Building flexible distributed systems in Conic', in Duce, D.A. (ed.), *Distributed Computing Systems Programme*, Peter Peregrinus, September 1984.

Sloman, M., Kramer, J., Magee, J., 'The Conic toolkit for building distributed systems', *Proc. of 6th IFAC Workshop on Distributed Computer Control Systems*, California, May, 1985, Pergamon Press.

USA Department of Defense, *Reference Manual for the Ada Programming Language*, Proposed Standard Document, July 1980.

Tanenbaum, A., van Staveren, H., Keizer, E., Stevenson, J., 'A practical tool kit for making portable compilers', *Comm. ACM*, Vol. 26, Sept. 1983, pp. 654–662.

Yourdon, E., Constantine, L.L., *Structured Design*, Yourdon Press, New York, 1975.

Four

COMMUNICATION PRIMITIVES
AND RELATED SOFTWARE ISSUES

As we have seen in the previous chapter, distributed systems are composed from a number of software components which communicate in order to cooperate. We have examined the structure of the components and the connections between them. In this chapter we concentrate on the communication transactions between components. In particular we describe and compare the various communications primitives which can be used in programming a component and describe how each affects the component's behavior. As in Chapter 3, we take a **high-level language view** of the communication primitives for programming distributed systems.

4.1 Introduction: Communication and Synchronization

Components in a distributed system execute concurrently, each performing some required function. It is the synchronization and communication primitives which provide the means of coordination and cooperation between these components.

1. **Synchronization**
   This involves the coordination of actions, with respect to time, of two or more software components. Synchronization might be used to prevent interference when the components access a shared resource (mutual exclusion), or to make sure actions on a shared resource are performed in a particular order.
2. **Communication**
   This is the exchange of information between components and does not necessarily imply synchronization.

These two aspects are very closely related. In a closely coupled system communicating via shared memory, software components must synchronize access to the shared memory in order to communicate safely. Synchronization mechanisms such as semaphores or monitors are used. Information is passed using shared variables and/or parameters to monitor procedures.

In a loosely coupled system, interconnected by communication lines, communication primitives such as message passing must be used to implement both synchronization and information passing. A communication system is responsible for actually transporting a message from one station to another. A detailed description of the types of service offered by a communication system is given in Chapter 5. For our purposes in this chapter, we will assume that it usually includes mechanisms for restricting a component from monopolizing the use of the communication system (**flow control**), and a means of **error reporting** (such as failure to deliver a message). The class of service provided can roughly be divided into three categories:

1. very reliable, but expensive – usually involves some connection state information and protocol overhead (e.g. virtual circuits);
2. best efforts, with notification if the communication system fails to deliver the message (e.g. reliable datagrams); and
3. unreliable, with no notification of failure (e.g. datagrams).

We will discuss the relationship between the various communications primitives and these rough classes of communications service.

In the same way as data **types** are associated with shared variables or procedure parameters, so all recent message-passing languages associate a data type with a message. This provides the (structural) information on how the message should be interpreted. A message which does not contain any data is called a **signal** and is used for synchronization only (ADA and SR use an empty parameter list to indicate a null message).

The rest of this chapter concentrates on message-passing mechanisms for loosely coupled systems, as mechanisms for closely coupled systems are well described in most operating-system text books. We concentrate on one-to-one transactions as these are the most commonly used. The primitives for receiving messages are discussed first followed by those for sending messages. In both these cases the flow of information is **unidirectional** from the sender to the receiver. Together a send and a receive form a single message transaction. The different synchronization options provided by the primitives is emphasized. The request–reply, rendezvous and remote procedure call primitives are then presented. These provide **bidirectional** flow of information: a communication transaction includes a return message (and synchronization) in response to the initial request or call. In all cases we briefly examine the implementation overheads and indicate the reliability which is expected from the communication system. As in the previous chapter, examples will be taken from CSP [Hoare, 1978], Ada [USA, 1980],CONIC [Kramer, 1983,

Sloman, 1985], SR [Andrews, 1981], ARGUS [Liskov, 1983] and others as appropriate. A full discussion on interprocess communication is given by [Cashin, 1980] and [Fukuoka, 1982].

4.2 Message Receipt

4.2.1 The Basic Receive Primitive

In most systems the recipient must explicitly execute a receive instruction to accept an incoming message. The recipient names the sender, mailbox, or a local entry(port) upon which the message can be received (naming was discussed in Section 3.2.4). For instance,

Ada:	*ACCEPT store(msg:IN data)*	
		{*accept msg from entry store*}
SR:	*IN store(msg:data)*	{*accept msg from operation store*}
CSP:	*producer? msg*	{*accept msg from process producer*}
CONIC:	*RECEIVE msg FROM store*	
		{*accept msg from entryport store*}

The message is copied into the target variable or data structure specified in the receive, i.e. *msg* in the examples above. In Ada and SR the target variable is declared in the form of a formal parameter to the receive primitive as in procedures. This means that if the message is to be retained in the component (such as in a buffer) it must be copied, e.g. *buffer(i) := msg*. In CSP and CONIC the target is any local variable in the component and hence the message can be received directly into the required variable, e.g. *producer? buffer(i)*.

In some systems messages are identified by a type or tag rather than by the source or entry. The receive then indicates the message identifiers it will accept. This is used in CSP to distinguish between different types of message from the same source. Selection of messages from different sources and/or of different types is discussed later in Section 4.2.3.

If no message is outstanding, the recipient is normally delayed (**blocked**) until a message arrives. This blocking provides the synchronization element of message receipt. However, if no messages arrive the recipient process could be blocked indefinitely and so there are a number of variations of this receive statement in order to allow a component to withdraw from the commitment to receive a message and to wait on a number of different possible messages.

4.2.2 Extensions to the Basic Receive Primitive

Conditional receive
The component receives a message if one is outstanding; otherwise it receives an indication of no message and the component is **not blocked** but is allowed

to continue processing (cf. if–then–else statement):

e.g.   *RECEIVE msg FROM store* =⟩ ...
                                   {*process message*}
       ELSE   =⟩ ...
                                   {*continue processing if no message*};

   This is useful for polling to see if a message has arrived and is often justified by the argument that the blocked receive will inhibit parallelism (i.e. concurrent execution of components). However, polling can lead to inefficient programming such as a 'busy wait' for a particular message. It also tends to be used in the programming of multithreaded processes. When a number of functions have to be performed (e.g. polling a sensor, controlling a device and receiving commands from an operator) it is usually better to try to structure this as a number of separate processes rather than as a single (error-prone?), interleaved process. Where a component is required to accept a number of different messages which can arrive in some non-deterministic order, we advocate waiting on all selected messages (see selective receive below) rather than polling. Finally, if no blocking is inherent in the receive, some additional mechanism will be needed for synchronization when it is required. For these reasons the unblocked receive is not provided as a primitive in most modern languages for distributed systems. Where it is provided as an option, it should be carefully used.

Timeout on receive

The component associates a time period with the receive and waits until a message arrives or the timeout expires. A timeout of zero is equivalent to the conditional receive:

e.g.   *RECEIVE msg FROM store* =⟩ ...
                                   {*process message*}
       ELSE timeout(period)   =⟩ ...
                                   {*process after period if no message*}

   A limit on the waiting time is required in real-time environments. For instance, the timeout can be used to initiate some corrective action should a device have failed to respond within the timeout period. However, for the reasons described above associated with the conditional receive, the timeout period should not normally be very short (approaching zero). Also small delays can make the component behavior dependent on small variations in the communication service. Timeouts should only be used as a back stop in case of communication failure or failure of a communicating component. Failures and exception handling are discussed in Section 4.5.

Selective receive

The component names the set of message sources or entries from which it is prepared to accept a message. The select is similar in concept to a case statement in the sense that execution of the statements associated with a particular receive branch is dependent on satisfaction of the receive i.e. if a messsage is available. Also only one branch may be selected. If more than one message is available, the choice of which message is received is usually non-deterministic (discussed below):

e.g. *SELECT*

$$RECEIVE \ m_1 \ FROM \ e_1 \ =\rangle ... \ \{process \ m_1\}$$
$$OR \ RECEIVE \ m_2 \ FROM \ e_2 \ =\rangle ... \ \{process \ m_2\}$$
$$OR \ RECEIVE \ m_3 \ FROM \ e_3 \ =\rangle ... \ \{process \ m_3\}$$

END

This is very useful for programming a component in which the message arrival pattern is non-deterministic, e.g. a component which monitors messages from a number of sources or a resource component which may receive different types of request.

A variation of the select is acceptance of **any** message, e.g.

RECEIVE mess FROM any

Since any of the messages is to be received into the same target variable, all messages must then be of the same data type or be typeless. Hence this last facility is often provided as a basic receive primitive in typeless languages.

Guarded, selective receive

This is a more powerful form of selective receive. A receive can be preceded by a guard or boolean condition. A receive branch is eligible for selection only if the guard is satisfied. If no message is available, then the component waits for the first message on an eligible receive branch:

e.g. *SELECT*

$$WHEN \ g_1 \ RECEIVE \ m_1 \ FROM \ e_1 \ =\rangle ...$$
$$\{process \ m_1\}$$
$$OR \ WHEN \ g_2 \ RECEIVE \ m_2 \ FROM \ e_2 \ =\rangle ...$$
$$\{process \ m_2\}$$
$$OR \ WHEN \ g_3 \ RECEIVE \ m_3 \ FROM \ e_3 \ =\rangle ...$$
$$\{process \ m_3\}$$

END

The guards are useful for tailoring a select according to the current state of the component, e.g. a buffering process can block messages from producers when the buffer is full.

If no shared variables are used in the guards or there is no parallelism within the component, the values of the guards cannot change while the component waits for messages. Hence the guards need only be evaluated once. However, in some language proposals the receipt can even be conditional on the contents of the message itself! For example:

SELECT
    RECEIVE m_1 WHEN $m1.temp > 100$
      DO . . . {process message with temp > 100}
  OR RECEIVE m_2 WHEN $m_2.press > 15$}
      DO . . . {process message with press > 15}
END

This means that the underlying system must interpret the contents of the message before the receiver is prepared to accept it. This reduces the independence between the system software and the application since the system must then be capable of interpreting and manipulating typed application messages.

Both CSP and SR provide selective receipt of messages in a form based on guarded commands of Dijkstra [1975]. Guarded commands provide for the selective execution of a statement depending on the value of a boolean guard. In CSP the guards may or may not include a receive primitive: hence the *select* is not restricted to just selection between different messages:

e.g. CSP:
  ☐ $g_1; p_1?m_1 - \rangle$ . . .   {*provided g_1 is true,*
               receive m_1 from p_1 and . . .}
  ☐ $g_2; p_2?m_2 - \rangle$. . . {*or provided g_2 is true,*
             receive m_2 from p_2 and . . .}
  ☐ g_3 $- \rangle$. . . {*or provided g_3 is true, . . .*}
  ☐

This is similar to a combination of the select and conditional receives, except that branch selection in CSP is non-deterministic (see Section 4.2.3). Hence, if g_3 were satisfied in the example above, that branch **might** be selected even though g_1 were true and m_1 were available.

Some currently proposed languages (Pascal-m [Abramsky, 1983]) and some suggestions for extensions to CSP [Bernstein, 1980] specify that a guard may include a primitive to send a message ('guarded send'). This provides the additional option of mixing guarded sends with guarded receives. This is very useful, e.g. a bounded buffer can offer to receive the next message from a producer or to send the next buffered message to a consumer. However, it is extremely difficult and expensive to implement in a general distributed system as it involves matching offers to send with offers to receive in an environment with delays (see Section 4.6.3).

Both Ada and CONIC provide a form of selective receive which can be used in all cases: conditional, timeout, selective and guarded receipt:

e.g. Ada: *SELECT*
      WHEN $g_1 =\rangle$ ACCEPT e_1 (m_1: IN message)
      DO . . . END; . . .

OR   *WHEN* g_2 =⟩ *ACCEPT* e_2 (m_2: IN *message*) DO
            ...END;...

OR   *WHEN* g_n =⟩ *DELAY(period)*;...

ELSE ...

END

In fact it does not make sense to have both a timeout (delay part) and conditional receipt (else part) in the same select statement, as the timeout would never be selected.

4.2.3   Message Selection

There are two forms of message selection which can occur at a component: selection between entries (or sources) and selection between messages waiting at an entry. We discuss each in turn.

Selection between different entries or sources
If multiple message reception conditions are satisfied (the guard is true and there is a message waiting), then the choice of which is selected could be:

1. **Arbitrary**
   This implies a random or unspecified selection method. Components should be written such that they do not rely on a specific order of selection. CSP, SR and Ada provide such a selection, except that CSP infers some form of non-deterministic fairness (or at least lack of starvation) while Ada and SR make no such guarantee. Implementation of fairness in CSP would incur some overheads while in Ada and SR it would leave the implementation free to choose any policy.

2. **Fixed**
   Selection follows some fixed, predefined policy, such as the overall order of message arrival. The order in which messages arrive at a component, no matter to which entry, is maintained and the most recent message in a particular select is selected. This provides a relatively fair method but does imply some implementation overhead.

3. **User controlled**
   The application can control the order in which it wishes to receive messages, perhaps by message priority or by the lexical order in which the branches of the select are written. This latter approach is a possible solution for real-time applications as it is simple to implement and does not introduce additional non-determinism into the programs. For instance, urgent messages such as alarms could be treated first. A flood of such messages could, however, prevent others from being received, i.e. there is a real danger of starvation for less urgent messages. CONIC has adopted this approach.

Example.   Although Ada provides for arbitrary selection, a programmer can still control the order of selection between entries. For instance consider a task which services normal requests but must also be prepared to receive and react immediately to a 'stop' message, i.e. it must give preference to stop messages. Let us develop such a program segment:

```
SELECT
      ACCEPT stop( );
      EXIT;
ELSE
      ACCEPT service(. . .);
      . . .
END SELECT;
```

This first tries to accept a stop message if available, but if no messages are available the task blocks waiting for a service request **only**. This can be overcome by replacing the second accept by a nested select which has both stop and service entries.

Ada also provides an alternative method for achieving a similar end using a *COUNT* attribute of entries. The *COUNT* attribute (referred to using *entry*, COUNT) gives the current number of calling tasks (messages) waiting at an entry. (SR provides a similar attribute.) The examples can then be programmed as follows:

```
SELECT
      ACCEPT stop( );
      EXIT;
OR
      WHEN stop'COUNT = 0  =>ACCEPT service(. . .);
END SELECT;
```

The guard will ensure that the service entry is only accepted if no stop call is waiting. This example can obviously be easily programmed in CONIC using a select with the *stop* entryport as the first branch.

Selection at an entry
If a number of messages are waiting at an entry, then there is also the need to decide which of these should be accepted. This selection is usually according to a fixed policy, but it can be user controlled.

1. **Fixed**
   Messages are usually queued at the receiver and accepted in arrival (FIFO) order. This is the simplest most popular approach. Other fixed policies, such as selection according to message priority, are also possible but less frequently provided. Messages at the same entry are usually of the same data type and priority.
2. **Controlled**
   The receiver may be able to control the selection of messages. For instance, as described in the guarded receive above, the receiver might select

according to the value of some field condition in the message itself. SR provides such a mechanism to facilitate scheduling of requests, such as shortest job next or disk access nearest current head position. A 'BY integer-expression' can be included in an *IN* statement and priority is given to the request with the smallest expression value, e.g.

SR: *IN request(amount:integer)* **BY amount** $-\rangle$ . . .
     NI

will accept request with the smallest amounts first.
(Another proposed language, PLITS [Feldman, 1979], provides a simpler selection mechanism by specifying acceptance of a message if it contains a specific transaction key, a special field of the message itself.

PLITS: *RECEIVE request ABOUT key*;

This is actually used more as a means of associating messages which belong to the same transaction, where a transaction may consist of a long sequence of messages or protocol.)

In general the scheduling of message reception is best left as some simple and efficient fixed policy. Providing controlled selection by the applications programmer introduces overheads for the sake of the few cases in which it is useful. Messages can usually be received by a front-end process and scheduled internally where necessary.

4.3 Unidirectional Message Transmission

The complementary primitive to the explicit receive is the explicit send instruction which initiates the sending of a message. In this section we deal with unidirectional message transmission. A message transaction consists of a message being transferred in a single direction from source to destination or to many destinations in the case of one-to-many transactions (multidestination).

4.3.1 Asynchronous SEND

The asynchronous (or unblocked) send does not block the sender but allows the component to continue processing as soon as the message has been saved (copied out of the sender) or transmitted. This is useful for real-time applications where the component may be performing a time-critical activity and cannot wait for confirmation that the message has reached or been received by the destination. Alternatively, the sender may be repeatedly performing some local activity and sending messages, and may not care whether every message is received, e.g. display update or logging. Asynchronous sends are also useful for event signalling.

Both CONIC and SR provide an asynchronous send primitive, but CONIC uses indirect naming (an exitport) while SR uses direct naming of the destination.

CONIC: *SEND reading TO readout*
                           {*send reading via exitport READOUT*}
S R :   *SEND display.sensor(reading)*
                           {*send reading to display*}

The main problems associated with the asynchronous send are concerned with buffering. Since the source process is permitted to continue processing after the send, it must be prevented from accessing or altering the message contents before or while it is actually being transmitted, or while it is waiting to be received by the destination. This requires that the message (value) is copied from the source process address space and placed in a system buffer. Buffering may occur at the source or destination stations or both. Buffer exhaustion (no more available buffers) may occur. If the system runs out of buffers, the sender process must either be blocked, which is contrary to the original definition of the primitive, or the send operation must fail. Since some failures may only be detected after the sender has continued processing (no available buffers at the destination) it may be difficult to inform the sender, who is perhaps performing some other actions. Error reports on individual messages can be handled as exceptions or interrupts but there is then the difficulty of matching error reports to particular send operations. Hence in many systems the asynchronous send is considered 'unreliable' and is supported by an unreliable communication service with no error reporting. Support by a more reliable communication service is desirable, but error reporting to the sender is still omitted. Implementation and exceptions are further discussed later in this chapter.

An alternative approach to the buffer exhaustion problem is to adopt a policy for discarding messages. In CONIC, a user-defined amount of buffering is provided at the entryports associated with asynchronous (notify) transactions. Should this allocation be insufficient, the oldest message is overwritten. Although this implies a loss of information, it seems preferable to any attempt to halt the sender or abort the transaction, and can be very efficiently implemented as it requires only local actions at the receiver. The use of a known policy of information discarding can be used by programmers. For instance, it is useful for periodic operations such as display updating, where loss of an old display message is quite acceptable. Another use is for signals that some event has occurred. In this case a single buffer (*unibuffer*) is sufficient. Other fixed policies (discard most recent message) or user-defined policies (discard smallest or largest message value) are also possible.

Another problem associated with buffering is that design and verification of the correctness of the overall distributed system is complicated as it no longer depends only on the states of the application processes, but the contents of the system buffers must also be considered.

Although the asynchronous send primitive may make reasoning about distributed programs more difficult, it results in very loose coupling between the sender and receiver. This means that there can be more parallelism in the system as processing components are not delayed. Also it permits more autonomy of the individual processes. It can be used as a simple, basic (efficient but possibly unreliable) primitive to implement more sophisticated ones. It is particularly suited to multidestination messages. For example CONIC permits notify exitports (i.e. those used for asynchronous messages) to be linked to any number of destination entryports. Finally, asynchronous communication is also used where buffering within the system is important to increase throughput and optimize the use of communication resources, e.g. file transfers.

4.3.2 Synchronous SEND

In the synchronous (blocked) send the source process is blocked until the destination process actually receives (i.e. accepts) the message. Similarly the destination process is suspended until the source has executed the send. The sender and receiver are thus synchronized.

CSP provides the synchronous send. In fact, Hoare has described synchronous communication as an interprocess assignment. This can be very useful for synchronizing distributed processes and as a means of confirming to the source that the message has indeed been received by the destination. The logical clarity of CSP with its synchronous communication also makes it useful as a system specification language.

CSP: ⟨*output command*⟩ ::= ⟨*destination process*⟩ ! ⟨*expression*⟩
      {*the value of the expression is sent to the destination process*}
      ⟨*input command*⟩ ::= ⟨*source process*⟩ ? ⟨*target variable*⟩
      {*the value of the message is assigned to the target variable*}
e.g. *buffer*! *msg*   "*send msg to buffer*"
      producer?*buf*   "*accept msg in buf from producer*"

This tight coupling means that a delay at the receiver could delay the sender, and if the receiver (or the communication system) fails, the sender could be held up indefinitely. A mechanism for withdrawing from a send (e.g. a timeout) seems necessary; however, no such mechanism has been provided in the original CSP proposal. Thus CSP seems to require that the underlying system (including the communication system) is reliable and that a failure in one component implies failure of the distributed system.

For looser coupling, a message-buffering process can be explicitly programmed (see CSP example in Section 4.7) to decouple the source from the destination and vice versa. Another similar approach is for the source process to delegate the send to a subprocess which the source creates for that purpose. Multiple unreciprocated sends would then result in a multiplicity of subprocesses. Hence one of the criticisms of this approach is that it can result in a proliferation of processes.

A powerful extension to the synchronous send is the guarded (or selected) send. This is analogous to the selected receive except that it permits a source process to offer to **send** to one of a selection of destinations. When combined with the selective receive it is extremely useful. For instance, in CSP, the buffering process described in Section 4.7 waits for characters to be stored in the buffer by the producer or for requests for characters from the consumer. In the latter case, the consumer must first request a character using the signal, *more()*, and the buffer process will then send it, i.e.

CSP: [*producer? buffer(inp)* $-\rangle$ ...
        $\Box$ *consumer?more()* $-\rangle$ *consumer! buffer(outp)*; ...
        ]

With guarded sends, the buffer process could offer to both send a character to the consumer and receive a character from the producer, i.e.

CSP: [*producer? buffer(inp)* $-\rangle$ ...
        $\Box$ *consumer! buffer(outp)* $-\rangle$ ...
        ]

However, the implementation of the combination of selected send and selected receive is extremely difficult in general. It requires the matching of offers of sending with offers of receiving in a distributed environment with delays and failures. Hence it is not provided in CSP. (A prototype implementation of Pascal-m, which does have both selective sends and receives, does exist. Hoever, the proposed protocols for matching sends and receives were both complex and costly, and had a small possibility that matching would be 'indefinitely prolonged' [Abramsky, 1983].)

There is no multidestination synchronous send in CSP, although one can imagine that it might be desirable to synchronize and communicate with more than one process at a time. This would be equivalent to a parallel assignment ($receiver_1 := receiver_2 := \ldots := receiver_n := message$). There is an implementation overhead in synchronizing a number of distributed processes.

4.4 Bidirectional Transactions

This form of communication provides for bidirectional information flow. A transaction consists of a message or call, with value parameters, from the source component and a reply message or return parameters from the destination component. In all cases the transaction is one-to-one and the source is synchronized with the destination.

Bidirectional transactions are an essential form of communication for programming client–server relationships. In conventional sequential programming, the procedure provides a means of encapsulating some service, actions or function which can then be invoked. Similarly, the bidirectional transaction permits a client component to request some service, actions or function to be performed by some (remote) server component. The client then waits until the results of that request (if any) are returned.

Bidirectional transactions can be provided in a message oriented notation; perhaps consisting of a **request** message and an associated **reply** message, as in CONIC. Another approach is to provide them in the guise of procedure calls in which the server may be remote, i.e. **remote procedure calls (RPC)**. A superficial difference lies in the syntax, but the essential differences are apparent in the semantics in the event of any failures. We discuss these two approaches below.

4.4.1   Message-oriented Communication: Request–Reply

The source
CONIC provides a request–reply transaction in which the source sends the request message and waits for the reply. For instance, a consumer task may send a signal request to a buffer (via exitport *input*) and receive the next character as the reply message (see CONIC example in Section 4.7):

CONIC: *SEND signal TO input WAIT nextchar*

Since the source task is delayed until the reply is received, it is possible for the source to be blocked indefinitely. This may be due to a communication failure, failure of the (remote) destination or merely that the destination task is too busy or cannot generate the reply in a reasonable time. For these reasons, a mechanism is provided – similar to that provided for receives – to allow the sender to withdraw from the commitment to wait for the reply. In CONIC this takes the form of an alternative fail part with which an optional timeout can be associated. The fail part is selected if the time period (if specified) expires or if the system or destination detects some failure and aborts the transaction.

CONIC: *SEND request TO server*
           WAIT results =⟩ ...   {process results}
           FAIL period   =⟩ ...   {handle aborted transaction}
         END

The destination
In the buffer example, the buffer task module can associate a reply with a message received on a request–reply entryport, i.e. the receive primitives discussed in Section 4.2 can be extended to include a reply part.

CONIC: *RECEIVE signal FROM getchar REPLY nextchar*

DSCN–D*

In order to permit the destination task to perform some processing of the request before replying, the reply part can be decoupled from the receive.

CONIC: *RECEIVE request FROM clientport*;
         ... {process request to produce results}
         REPLY results TO clientport;

Explicit naming of the entryport, clientport, in the delayed reply ensures that the reply message, *results*, is sent to the source of the last request. It is not permitted in CONIC to receive more than one request at an entryport and to reply in any arbitrary order. Each request should be given a reply before the next is received. (An operating system, the V-Kernel [Cheriton, 1984] described in Chapter 10, does support such reordering.) This means that scheduling of the requests is not provided by the CONIC system, but we believe that where required scheduling can be explicitly provided by a front-end administrator. In CONIC, a *FORWARD* instruction can be used in place of a *REPLY* to forward a request on to another task for processing. This frees the task to handle other requests, and the reply is returned directly from the eventual destination to the original source (see Section 3.2.5). Also, if the destination cannot handle the request, then the transaction can be ABORTed, which causes the sender to execute its fail branch. Both of these alternatives to the *REPLY* are further described later in Section 4.7.4.

As mentioned, CONIC provides the sender with the option to set a timeout when waiting for a request–reply transaction to complete. If no reply has been received by the time the timeout expires, then the fail branch is selected. This does not guarantee that the receiver has not received the request message even if the sender times out. However, any replies to cancelled requests are automatically discarded. This possible side-effect at the receiver must be handled by the programmer at the application level, but at least he can rely on the autonomy of the sender to withdraw at the specified time, i.e. the timeout is a local decision. In any case, as in the receive primitive, the timeout should only be used as a backstop in case of undue delay or failure. Other major reasons for this approach are that it is much simpler to implement and does not require the reliable communication required by other approaches, such as the Ada rendezvous (see below).

There is no multidestination request–reply since the semantics of such a transaction are unclear (would the source then receive multiple replies?) and it would also be difficult to implement. The request–reply transaction synchronizes a single sender with a single receiver. There is no implicit buffering and so, as with the synchronous send, it can limit parallelism. It too can result in a proliferation of processes for buffering or waiting for a message.

Finally it is worth noting that, in the implementation, the reply can be returned either by a synchronous send or by an asynchronous send. In the first case the receiver is delayed until receipt of the reply is confirmed; in the latter case the receiver continues immediately after sending the reply. Although the asynchronous approach does not delay the receiver, it does mean that the receiver cannot be sure that the reply was actually received. Reporting such a failure has all the problems discussed above in connection with communications failures in an environment using asynchronous communication. Again because of its inherent simplicity, CONIC uses the asynchronous approach.

4.4.2 Procedure-oriented Communication: Remote Procedure Call (RPC)

As mentioned above, the bidirectional transaction can be provided in much the same way as are procedures, except that the invoked 'procedure' may be a separate processing component and that it may reside in a remote computer station. One of the main advantages is that the programmer need not be aware whether the call is invoking a local or a remote procedure or process. This means that programmers may not need to learn new primitives in order to cope with the distributed and concurrent environment. However, if the programmer is to take advantage of the transparency of location, this also means that the behavior (semantics) must be the same in both cases. This can be costly and difficult to achieve, especially in the face of failures.

Another advantage of the RPC is that it provides marshalling of the parameters for message transmission, i.e. the list of parameters is collected together by the system to form a message. In conventional message-passing environments, the programmer must explicitly assign all the required values into the fields of the message before transmission.

In this section we first discuss an example of a transaction which can loosely be considered as an RPC – the Ada rendezvous. It is really a mixture of the request–reply and the genuine RPC. A more general discussion of the structure and semantices of RPCs is given afterwards.

The Ada Rendezvous
The Ada rendezvous is so named since, as in the request–reply, the caller (source) and called (destination) tasks synchronize during the transaction, i.e. they rendezvous for the duration of the call and thereafter continue processing in parallel. The syntax of an entry call is similar to that of a procedure call, and in fact an entry call can be replaced (using renaming) by a procedure. The form of a call is:

Ada: *Destination.Entry (IN parameters OUT parameters)*

The *IN* parameters are analogous to a request message and the *OUT* parameters to the reply. When the receiver accepts the call the *IN* parameters are received by the called task which executes the code associated with the entry and returns the *OUT* parameters.

Like CONIC, Ada also permits the caller to initiate a timeout to prevent being blocked indefinitely waiting to rendezvous. However, this timeout is cancelled when the receiver **accepts** the rendezvous rather than when the reply is returned. This ensures that a sender timeout can be transparent to the receiver, who need never be aware of the call at all. However, it is more difficult to implement in a distributed system and does not cater for delays or failure of the receiver while servicing the call. Exception mechanisms are used in the failure case but no mechanism exists for releasing the caller if the receiver delays completion of the rendezvous (e.g. loops indefinitely). Hence, whereas the timeout in CONIC is an absolute (local) limit on the waiting time of the source to receive the reply, the Ada timeout is a limit on the time to acceptance of the call by the receiving task [Kramer, 1981].

Ada: SELECT
               bounded buffer.write(. . .);
        OR
               DELAY (period); . . .
        END SELECT

RPC: The structure of the 'procedure'

We now examine RPCs more generally. In particular, the differences from the procedure call in conventional sequential programming are apparent when one remembers that the environment may consist of many possible callers all executing in parallel and that the environment is subject to delays and failure. We examine the structure at the receiving end of the so-called 'procedure' and the semantics of the call.

In general the invoked 'procedure' takes the form of a process. There are two main cases here:

1. **The process exists before the call**

    The process is structured as a loop which repeatedly waits for and processes each call. This means that multiple calls are executed sequentially and that mutual exclusion between the calls is inherent. This can be useful to prevent interference but it does also restrict parallelism. SR supports this form of RPC in calls made to the processes which are encapsulated in each resource. However, in order to allow more parallelism where desired, SR does support different processes in the same resource which can share data and execute in parallel. These processes may then need to synchronize their access to shared data if they are to avoid interference.

    The Ada rendezvous is similar to this case except that the called tasks do not exist essentially as remote procedures but are active entities (see the discussion in Section 3.1.3 on process vs. resource components). The call is accepted and serviced only when the called task chooses to wait at the called entry and not at any time the caller chooses. They therefore only act as remote procedures for the duration of the rendezvous. Also Ada tasks (and SR and others) can provide more than one entry in a selective receive, and hence, unlike conventional procedures, may provide more than one entry and type of service.

2. **The process is created to handle the call**

   In this case multiple calls result in the creation of a process to handle each call, all of which may execute in parallel. If these multiple instances access shared data, they may need to synchronize such access. The handlers in ARGUS guardians [Liskov, 1983] are provided in this way. ARGUS thus provides a form of abstract data structure (the guardian) with operations defined by the handlers which can execute concurrently.

Distributed processes (DP) [Brinch-Hansen, 1978] is an interesting combination of these two forms. A DP process has its own variables and execution code, but also offers procedures which can be called from remote processes. Execution of the process code and the procedures are interleaved in that a procedure can only be executed if the process code is waiting on some condition. Execution of a procedure may change the condition and allow the process to continue. Thus, procedures and process code exclude each other. The DP process is a combination of the conventional process and the abstract data structure, but they do not execute concurrently.

RPC: Call semantics

Provided that there are no failures or undue delays, the RPC (and the request–reply for that matter) can provide either of two accepted semantices:

1. **Exactly-once semantics**

   The call should be serviced exactly once at the receiver and terminates only when the return (out) parameters have been correctly received by the caller.

2. **At-least-once semantics**

   Normal termination of the call implies one or more executions of the call at the receiver.

The former is obviously the preferred behavior. The latter is sometimes provided as it allows the underlying communication system to retransmit messages without the restriction that all duplicates must be eliminated. We advocate providing the necessary filtering to enforce exactly-once semantics.

The above descriptions discuss only successful termination. What should the semantics be if failures occur? The call or reply message may be lost, or the server may crash during execution of the procedure. Two main approaches exist: 'last-one' and 'at-most-once' semantics.

3. **Last-one semantics**

   Termination of the call implies one or more executions of the call at the server, but the lasting effect is of the last call.

Nelson [1981] argues that, if the aim is to provide transparency – the same behavior whether the procedure is local or remote – then we must aim to provide the same behavior as in the case of a failure in a local procedure call. In a local environment, a failure usually implies failure of both the caller and the procedure. Either the entire program will be restarted or, if checkpoints are provided, then the program will restart from the previous checkpoint. In either case the call is repeated until it terminates successfully. The results and side-effects that are used by the program are therefore those of the **last call**, although the side-effects of the intermediate unsuccessful calls may influence the results of the last one: hence **last-one** semantics.

Thus the semantics even in the local case are not simple. The objective is to provide last one semantics for the remote case as well. Here the failure usually leaves one or both parties running rather than both failed. This can lead to an inconsistent system. For instance failure of the caller can leave a remote procedure executing without any caller. This execution is called an 'orphan' and leads to some interesting problems quaintly referred to as 'orphan killing' [Shrivastava, 1983]. In order not to spend the rest of the chapter on this one topic, it suffices to say that the provision of the 'ideal' semantics is difficult and costly. A full discussion and description of a viable approach is described by Nelson.

4. **At most once semantics**
   Exactly once semantics for the case where the transaction completes successfully, and no effect otherwise.

A number of other approaches argue that the possibility of long delays and failures cannot and should not be masked. For instance ARGUS adopts **at-most-once** semantics defined above. This all-or-nothing approach of the RPC is associated with the provision of atomic transactions in ARGUS. This seems more practical and attractive in that, if the caller is also informed of failures, he is then free to try some alternative approach of his choosing. The atomicity provided at the receiver ensures that if the transaction does not complete satisfactorily (commit), then the effects of the call are discarded. Atomicity and exceptions are further discussed in the next section. Note, however, that atomicity does impose high implementation overheads.

4.5 Exceptions

Distributed systems can provide a more robust environment by virtue of the loose coupling between the components and the provision of redundant hardware and software. However, as we have seen, there are also further problems to be considered. The underlying communication system is subject to delays and failures and the software components themselves can fail. For instance, during a procedure call one expects centralized systems to execute successfully or to fail totally. However, distributed systems usually produce partial failures where the caller or called process continues processing after the failure of the partner. This degraded operation offers more opportunity to construct robust systems provided that the system behavior can still be controlled. Control in the face of failures requires the provision of exception handling facilities.

We concentrate on those exception mechanisms provided in association with the communication primitives. Since neither CSP nor SR provides any such mechanisms, we refer to Ada, CONIC and ARGUS for examples.

Causes of exceptions

Although most of the transmission errors in the communication system can be masked, there are some which are not recoverable. Partitioning of the underlying network can lead to total communications failure between two components in different subnetworks. Also the recipient of a message may have failed or refuse to receive the message, perhaps due to invalid access rights or buffer overflow. Deadlock may occur if process calls form a cycle in which each waits for the other to service its call. In all cases the failure must be detected and some recovery or compensatory action taken.

Detection and reception of exceptions

Many exceptions are detected by the underlying communication or run-time systems. Examples of these types of errors is the failure of the communication system to deliver a message and exhaustion of the available system message buffers. Components can be informed of these system-detected failures either simply by the return of an error code, perhaps in place of the normal reply, or by raising an exception. The former are generally synchronous events which cause an alternative piece of code to be executed in place of the normal. The latter are asynchronous in that they cause an interrupt in the current execution and a branch to the execution of some handler. Asynchronous events can be handled in a synchronous manner by transforming exceptions into system messages. The application component must then indicate its readiness to receive such a message from some predetermined entry. This can be conveniently used with a select to provide receipt of both normal and exception messages.

In both CONIC and ARGUS alternative branches are provided to handle transaction failures. It is also possible for the receiver to abort the current transaction and return some form of error indication. This is then handled by the *FAIL* clause in the CONIC send–wait, and in ARGUS by the *EXCEPT* clause:

```
ARGUS:   spooler.write(. . .)              {normal execution}
             EXCEPT WHEN busy: . . .        {exceptions}
                WHEN terminated: . . .
             END
```

Ada has fairly comprehensive exception definition, handling and propagation facilities. It provides facilities for both system and user-defined exceptions and for specifying exception handlers. These handlers are associated with a block:

Ada: *BEGIN*
             . . .
             EXCEPTION
                 WHEN overflow =⟩ . . .;
             END

There are also rules for the propagation of exceptions if a local handler is not provided. During a rendezvous, an exception can be propagated to the caller if the called task has terminated or terminates (say by the execution of an *ABORT* instruction) during the rendezvous. In addition, Ada (and CONIC) support timeout facilities.

A common approach which puts the onus for detection at the application level is the use of a timeout. The component specifies the longest time it is prepared to wait for completion of the transaction and the actions it wishes to take in the event of exceeding the time limit. This approach is popular in real-time systems and has the advantage that the decision can be based on purely local status and timing. The source of a communiction transaction can prescribe local conditions for withdrawing from the transaction: compare the CONIC send–wait, with its timeout to completion, with the Ada rendezvous, with its timeout to acceptance (described in Section 4.4). However there are arguments against the use of the timeout mechanism. The extra syntax can clutter a program, hiding the normal execution. Also, time can be considered as a poorly defined, implementation-dependent quantity. On the other hand, provided it is only used as a backstop, it can and has been used to ensure real-time behavior.

Exception handling
The decision of what action to take after a detected failure is difficult. In general the best action is very application dependent. Non-critical exceptions can be ignored; others should lead to the abortion of the component. In some circumstances retrying the action may seem the best policy. This is usually true for low-level applications, such as retries to read from an input device. In most cases, however, retries have already been performed by the underlying system (communication retries) and the exception is an indication that a retry is useless. In some cases it may merely have been a reply that was lost and the retry may cause re-execution of the action and result in undesirable side-effects. If an alternative component offers the required service then, if time permits, that component could be used instead.

One of the main difficulties is that failure may imply partial execution of the transaction and result in side-effects. This involves the added encumbrance of backtracking, if possible, or attempting to compensate for the side-effects. Both can be extremely difficult.

The most uniform approach is to provide atomic transactions. This provides an all-or-nothing execution in that all the actions which constitute the transaction either complete satisfactorily or there is no effect at all (failure atomicity). In addition the rest of the system never sees partial executions, the transaction is executed indivisibly (synchronization atomicity). Provision of these facilities requires provision of some form of 'stable storage', a place where checkpointed information can be stored and which survives crashes. Also commit protocols must be used to ensure that correspondents in a communication transaction agree about when a transaction has completed successfully and the results should be committed to stable storage and made visible. If the transaction fails to commit, no changes to the stable storage will be made, and its state is that before the transaction. In order to ensure that all participants in a transaction agree to commit, a two-phase commit protocol is necessary. A coordinator first sends 'request commit' messages to the participants. If there are any 'no' or missing replies, then the transaction must be aborted. If all answer 'yes', the coordinator records this fact and instructs all the participants to commit their results to stable store. More detailed discussions of atomicity, and two-phase commit protocols can be found in Lampson [1981] and Gray [1978].

ARGUS provides stable data objects, which are kept on stable storage, and atomic actions for local data and atomic transactions for calls to remote guardians. Nested atomic transactions are also provided so that failure of a higher-level transaction may still cause lower-level nested transactions to be undone despite the fact that they had previously 'committed'. This approach is very appealing, particularly for applications which require secure data and transactions rather than guaranteed response. There is, however, a price to be paid in the form of communication and system overheads. (A distributed, prototype implementation of the ARGUS system has only recently been achieved in late 1985, and it is still too early to assess its performance and applicability.) The decision of what to do in the *EXCEPT* clauses is still left to the application programmer, although he can rely on the consistency of the system.

4.6 Implementation Overview for the Communication Primitives

In order to obtain some feeling for the underlying support required to implement the various communication primitives, we must first outline the responsibilities of the software layers. For convenience, we view these in terms of three layers: the application, the operating system and the communications system (Fig. 4.1).

A **simplified** view of a connection between a source and a destination

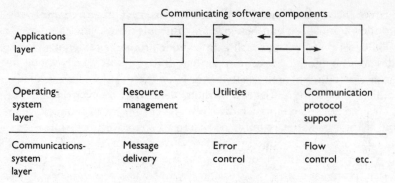

Figure 4.1 Outline layers in a distributed system

component can be considered as shown in Fig. 4.2. The local operating system provides a **conceptual** 'process' which supports the communication protocol on behalf of the source. Using this protocol, the operating system provides the application with its view of the communication primitives and uses the communication system service to transfer messages to the destination. The communications system is then merely responsible for transferring messages as best it can, masking any errors if possible. If a message cannot be delivered, it must report the failure to the operating system, which may then inform the application if so defined by the communication primitives. (In practice, the operating system 'process' is often combined with the communication system, as described in Chapter 10.)

In the rest of this chapter we discuss the associated functions performed by the operating system and outline the protocol required to provide the various communication primitives. In many cases this is a simplified view, **disregarding failures**, but it is intended to provide some feeling for the overhead required when using the primitives.

4.6.1 The Destination: Message Receipt

In most cases queuing of messages at the destination is provided by the system. If the source component is blocked until the receiver has accepted the message (synchronous communication) then the source identity must also be queued so that the system knows where to send the acknowledgement of message acceptance. The source can then be allowed to continue processing.

Alternatively, source buffering can be used for synchronous communication, i.e. the message is held in the source until the destination requests the message. Only the source identity need be queued at the destination to indicate an offer to send. In general destination buffering is simpler to implement but can consume more space. Source buffering is usually slower and

Source ──────▶ OS ──────▶ Communication system ──────▶ OS ──────▶ Destination

Figure 4.2 The path from source to destination

more complex, requiring more protocol. However, it can be used with synchronous communication, particularly in the face of source failures and timeouts. This is discussed with the synchronous send and the request– reply primitives.

4.6.2 Unidirectional Communication: the Asynchronous Send

Since the sender should be allowed to continue processing after execution of the send, some form of message buffering must be provided. Queuing of message buffers is usually provided by the local operating system at the destination. For local communication (source and destination in the same station) the message must be copied from the source to an intermediate system buffer and then to the destination when it is ready to receive. This can be optimized to a copy directly into the receiver if the receiver is waiting when the source sends. For remote communication the above copy are in addition to those required by the communication system.

As can be seen in Fig. 4.3, there is a one-to-one correspondence between messages that the application sends and those carried by the communication system. The asynchronous send can be supported by any class of communication service, from unreliable to reliable. As discussed in Section 4.3.1, it is not sensible to provide error reporting on a per-message basis as the source will have continued processing and may well not be able to identify which message failed to reach its destination. For this reason the asynchronous send is often considered cheap and unreliable and associated with an unreliable communication service. Support by a reliable communication service will of course improve the chances of message delivery but does not make use of the error reporting usually provided with that service.

4.6.3 Unidirectional Communication: the Synchronous Send

Since the sender and receiver are synchronized there is no need for system buffers. For local communication the message can be transferred directly from the sender to the receiver's address space. For remote communication the message (and the source identification) could be buffered at the destination for the receiver if it were not already waiting (Fig. 4.4). Note that the CLEAR message is part of the protocol and is not visible to the application.

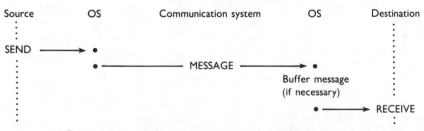

Figure 4.3 A possible implementation of asynchronous send

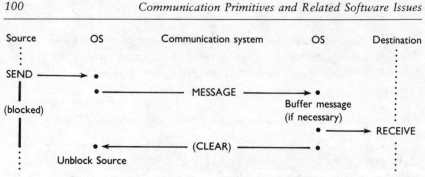

Figure 4.4 A possible implementation of synchronous send

The problem is that synchronizing sender and receiver is time consuming and can fail in a loosely coupled distributed system. Also, if a timeout were provided with the synchronous send, the implementation in Fig. 4.4 would still leave the message at the destination waiting for the receiver. In order to prevent this a more complex protocol must be used. An example, using source buffering is shown in Fig. 4.5, i.e. the message is kept at the source until the destination has indicated its readiness to receive the message.

If the sender has timed out when the receiver accepts the offer, then the source sends a CANCEL in place of the message. The receiver can then accept another pending offer or, if none, it must wait for further offers. As can be seen, the implementation becomes rather complicated but the send timeout is transparent to the receiver. Destination buffering could also be used in a similar protocol shown in Fig. 4.6. If the source has timed out when the ACCEPT? query is received, then the (NO) reply is sent. Source buffering saves buffering at the destination and allows the message to be held in the sender until acceptance.

Another approach relies on the use of global time in the distributed system. A validity time equal to the sender's timeout is attached to the message. The message can then be discarded if it times out and has not yet been received. Although this protocol is simpler to implement, it relies on global time, which is rarely provided.

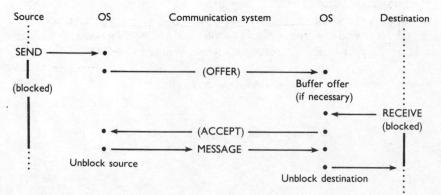

Figure 4.5 Source buffering implementation of synchronous send with timeout

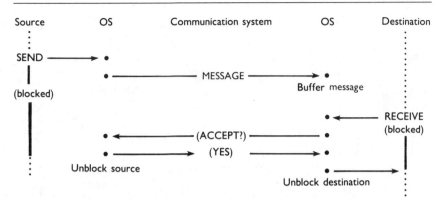

Figure 4.6 Destination buffering implementation of synchronous send with timeout

Loss of any of the protocol messages can cause indefinite blocking for the sender or receiver or both! It is for this reason that the synchronous send tends to be associated with a very reliable communication service.

4.6.4 Bidirectional Communication: Request–Reply / RPC

Implementation of the request–reply is very similar to the synchronous send except that there is a reply message which must be returned to the source process. We deal with the simpler (CONIC) approach first (Fig. 4.7).

The source and destination are again synchronized. For local communication the request message can be transferred directly to the destination and the reply message returned directly to the waiting source (or discarded if it is no longer waiting). For remote communication destination buffering can again be used if necessary (see Fig. 4.4). The CLEAR message of Fig. 4.4 is now a REPLY message. Again, if the sender has timed out, the reply

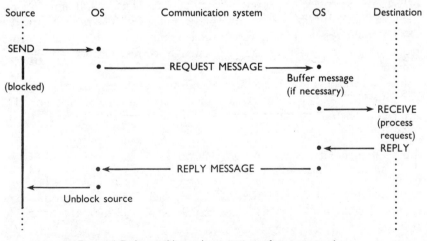

Figure 4.7 A possible implementation of request–reply

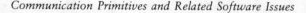

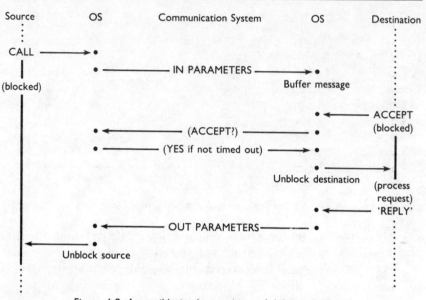

Figure 4.8 A possible implementation of Ada rendezvous

timeout
to
Completion

message can be discarded. An <u>unreliable communication service</u> would be satisfactory to support this implementation as the <u>reply confirms receipt of</u> <u>the request</u> and <u>no failure can</u> leave either the sender or receiver <u>blocked</u> indefinitely.

timeout
to
acceptance

In Ada a source <u>timeout before acceptance</u> by the destination <u>must not</u> <u>leave the request message at the destination.</u> As before, this can be prevented either by the <u>use of global time</u> (rarely provided in distributed systems) or by a more complex protocol. A destination buffering protocol similar to the one discussed in Section 4.6.3 is shown in Fig. 4.8. The <u>CLEAR message</u> of Fig. 4.4 is <u>replaced by a query whether acceptance is still appropriate,</u> i.e. is the offer still open or has the source timed out? The reply is now the OUT parameters in Ada. A <u>very reliable communication</u> service is again required since any <u>loss of messages can</u> cause the correspondents to be <u>blocked</u> indefinitely.

Implementation of the full RPC mechanisms must take account of failures and orphans. A detailed discussion of the possible implementations for RPC is given in Section 10.10.

4.6.5 Implementation when using Mailboxes

Mailboxes provide an intermediate naming entity for connections between senders and receivers (see Section 3.2.4). Message queuing and protocol execution can be associated with the mailbox, controlled by the operating system.

For use with asynchronous communication, the sender sends the message and continues. The mailbox is then a queue either of messages awaiting receivers or of receivers awaiting messages, but not both simultaneously. For synchronous communication a sender sends its name and the message to the mailbox and is suspended until a receiver is ready to receive the message. When the receiver accepts the message the named source is cleared to allow it to continue processing. If the receiver requests a message and there are no messages, the receiver is suspended in the queue. The mailbox is then a queue of either senders (and messages) or receivers, but not both. If there is only a single receiver and a single sender (1–1 connection), then the implementation is identical to the synchronous send of CSP.

4.7 Examples

An example is given in each of the languages, Ada, SR, CSP and CONIC. To aid comparison, the same simple application, a **bounded buffer**, has been selected for all four cases. It provides a rough indication of the differing styles, conciseness and capabilities of the languages. More detailed comparisons of the various constructs have been given in the text of Chapters 3 and 4. CONIC is used as a longer case study at the end of the section, together with descriptions for some of the tasks of the pump-control system of Section 3.5.

The **bounded buffer** examples:
A bounded buffering process can be used to smooth variations between the speed of output of a producing process and the speed of input of a consuming process. It contains an internal pool of characters processed in a round-robin fashion. The buffer pool has two indices, *inp* denoting the space for the next input character and *outp* denoting the space for the next output character.

4.7.1 ADA™ [USA, 1980]

(Ada is a trademark of the US Government – Ada Joint Programming Office)

Summary
Ada is essentially a block-structured language with scope rules for the visibility of and access to variables. Therefore, although it provides tasks (processing components) and packages (resource components), they may also have shared global data. For this reason (among others) Ada is not actually suitable for distributed systems. There have been a number of suggestions either restricting its use to avoid any global data [Downes, 1980] or extending the language to provide package types.

Ada supports both one-to-one and many-to-one connections but only one-to-one transactions. Naming is partially indirect: the source names the destination but not the reverse. A limited form of name passing is supported by the use of task access variables.

Bidirectional communication is provided by the rendezvous, together with most options in the selective receipt of calls. Timeout at both the source and/or destination are also supported, together with a fairly comprehensive support for exceptions and their propagation.

Example The buffering task provides two entries at its interface, one to put a character and one to get a character.

```
TASK bounded_buffer IS
   ENTRY getchar (c : OUT character);
   ENTRY putchar (c: IN character);
END;

TASK BODY bounded_buffer IS
   poolsize    : CONSTANT INTEGER := 100;
   pool        : ARRAY (1 .. poolsize) OF CHARACTER;
   count       : INTEGER RANGE 0 .. poolsize := 0;
   inp, outp : INTEGER RANGE 1 .. poolsize := 1;

BEGIN
   LOOP
      SELECT
            WHEN count < poolsize =>
                    ACCEPT putchar (c : IN CHARACTER) DO
                                                   pool (inp) := c;
                    END;
                    inp := (inp MOD poolsize) + 1;
                    count := count + 1;
         OR  WHEN count > 0 =>
                    ACCEPT getchar (c : OUT CHARACTER) DO
                                                   c := pool (outp);
                    END;
                    outp := (outp MOD poolsize) + 1;
                    count := count - 1;
         OR
                    TERMINATE
      END SELECT;
   END LOOP;
END buffer;
```

Since a task executes sequentially, each call to get or put will exclude all others, i.e. gets and puts execute sequentially. Note however that the rendezvous with the producing or consuming task ends at the end of the accept before the buffer task updates the index and count. In order to allow as much concurrency in the system as possible, a rendezvous should be kept short. (The *TERMINATE* branch is selected to terminate the task if the surrounding block terminates.)

The producing task may contain the statements

```
LOOP
    ...{produce the next character CHAR}
    bounded_buffer.put(char);
    EXIT WHEN char = end_of_transmission;
END LOOP;
```

and the consuming task may contain the statements

```
LOOP
    bounded buffer.ger(char);
    ...{consume the character CHAR}
    EXIT WHEN char = end_of_transmission;
END LOOP;
```

4.7.2 Communicating Sequential Processes (CSP) [Hoare, 1978]

Summary [Cashin, 1980]
CSP uses input and output as basic primitives of program communication and uses parallel composition of communicating sequential processes as a fundamental program-structuring method. There are no process types, but an array (family) of processes can be declared.

Communication is synchronous with direct naming.

e.g.   [$X :: i{:}integer;$ $Y!i$ $\|$ $Y :: j{:}integer;$ $X?j$]

This concise notation names two processes X and Y which are to run in parallel. Process X sends process Y information i via the statement $Y!i$. Process Y receives this with the input statement $X?j$. All connections and transactions are one-to-one.

Guarded commands are used to control non-determinism. A guarded command has the form:

$G \rightarrow S$

the statement S is evaluated only if G, the guard, is executed without failure. A guard fails if a boolean expression in the guards is evaluated as false, or when an input command is not matched by an outstanding output command from the designated process. This can be used to provide a form of selected receipt of messages. There are no timeout or exception mechanisms.

The notation

* [$G_1 \rightarrow S_1$ $\square$ $G_2 \rightarrow S_2$]

allows the repetition, *, of a set of guarded commands. The $\square$ denotes an alternative guard; if neither guard G_1 nor guard G_2 fails then statement S_1 or statement S_2 is selected at random.

Example   The bounded-buffer example can now be presented as follows:

> *boundedbuffer* : :
>   [*pool* : (1..100) *char*;
>   *inp, outp* : 1..100; *count* : 0..100;
>   *inp*:= 1; *outp*:= 1; *count*:= 0;
>   * [*count* < 100; *producer*   ? *pool(inp)*   −〉
>   *inp*:= (*inp* MOD 100) + 1
>   ☐ *count* > 0   ; *consumer* ? *more* ( )   −〉
>   ; *consumer* ! *pool(outp)*;
>   *outp*:= (*outp* MOD 100) + 1
>   ]
>   ]

The producing process may contain the statements

> * [... {*produce the next character C*}
>   *boundedbuffer* ! *C* ...
>]

and the consuming process may contain the statements

> * [...
>   *boundedbuffer* ! *more( )* ; *boundedbuffer* ? *C*
>   {*consume the next character C*} ...
>]

Notice the need for a double call protocol with the consumer. The need for this is the unidirectional message passing and is discussed in Section 4.3.2.

4.7.3 SR [Andrews, 1982]

Summary
SR provides self-contained resource components which contain a number of processes to provide access to and to manipulate the resource. A system is constructed as a number of distributed resources which use other resources essentially by means of remote procedure calls. Although, like CSP, it is not possible to define resource types, ranges (or families) of resources can be declared.

As in Ada, connections are one-to-one and many-to-one, and transactions are one-to-one. Naming is also partially indirect. Both a bidirectional RPC and a unidirectional asynchronous send are provided. Almost all the selective receipt options are provided except that there is no timeout and no exceptions mechanisms.

> *RESOURCE boundedbuffer*;
>   *DEFINE getchar, putchar* {*call*};
>   *VAR pool* : ARRAY [1 .. 100] OF CHAR;
>   *inp, outp, count* : INTEGER

```
inp:= 1; outp:= 1; count:= 0;

PROCESS service;
   DO TRUE -〉
     IN putchar (C:char) AND count < 100 -〉
           pool[inp] := C;
           inp:= (inp MOD 100) + 1;
           count:= count + 1
     □  getchar (VAR C:char) AND count > 0 -〉
           C:= pool[outp];
           outp:= (outp MOD 100) + 1;
           count:= count − 1
     NI
   OD
END service
END boundedbuffer
```

Since SR provides for more than one process in a resource, it is possible to allow concurrent access. Provided it is not the same character, one process may be storing a character in the buffer while another is removing one. In order to provide exclusion when incrementing and decrementing the count variable (to prevent interference), a third process is provided.

```
RESOURCE concurrent boundedbuffer;
   DEFINE getchar, putchar {call};
   VAR pool : ARRAY [ 1 .. 100 ] OF CHAR;
     inp, outp , count : INTEGER;
   inp:= 1; outp:= 1; count:= 0;

PROCESS deposit;
   DO TRUE -〉
     IN putchar(C:char) AND count < 100 -〉
       pool[inp] := C;
       inp:= (inp MOD 100) + 1;
       increment_count
     NI
   OD
END deposit

PROCESS receive;
   DO TRUE -〉
     IN getchar (VAR C:char) AND count > 0 -〉
       C:= pool[outp];
       outp:= (outp MOD 100) + 1;
       decrement_count
     NI
   OD
END receive
```

```
PROCESS counter;
   DO TRUE ->
      IN increment_count ->
         count:= count + 1
      □ decrement_count ->
         count:= count - 1
      NI
   OD
   END counter
END concurrent-boundedbuffer
```

4.7.4 CONIC [Kramer, 1983, Sloman, 1984, 1985]

Summary

CONIC provides task modules as the processing components. These are parameterized component types written in CONIC/P, the programming language [Kramer, 1984]. This is an extension to Pascal providing message passing and modules. The separate configuration language, CONIC/C [Dulay, 1984] is used to define subsystems and systems. Subsystems are built by creating instances of these types and linking them together to form interconnected components. Subsystems are called group modules and can themselves be nested within other group modules. All modules have a well-defined interface given by their message-passing ports.

Connections in CONIC can be one-to-one, one-to-many and many-to-one, while transactions can be one-to-one or one-to-many. Naming is indirect using ports which are subsequently linked together at the configuration level at build or run time.

Communications primitives

The communications primitives are designed to provide **transparency** – the same behavior (with some inevitable time differences) for local and remote communication. This allows modules to be allocated either to the same or different stations, which can be particularly useful during the development of embedded systems in that modules can be fully tested together in a large computer with support facilities and then later distributed into target stations.

Communication primitives are provided to **send** a message to an exitport or **receive** one from an entryport. The message types must correspond to the port types. There are two classes of message transactions:

1. Notify

A notify transaction provides unidirectional, potentially multi-destination (one-to-many transaction) message passing (Fig. 4.9). The send operation is asynchronous and does not block the sender, although the receiver may block waiting for a message. There is a (dimensionable)

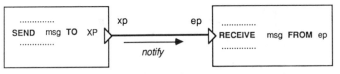

Figure 4.9 The notify transaction

fixed size queue of messages associated with each entryport. Messages are held in order of arrival at the entryport. When no more buffers are available the oldest message in the queue is overwritten. The *notify* can be used for time-critical tasks such as within the communication system, with the queue size corresponding to a flow-control window.

2. **Request reply**

This provides bidirectional synchronous message passing (Fig. 4.10). The sender is blocked until the reply is received from the receiver. A fail clause allows the sender to withdraw from the transaction on expiry of a timeout or if the transaction fails. The receiver may block waiting for a request. On receipt of a request, the receiver may perform some processing and return a reply message. In place of a normal reply, the receiver may either **forward** the request to another receiver or he may **abort** the transaction. The forward primitive is particularly useful for the construction of 'switch' tasks which can redirect requests. The forwarding task is then free to handle further requests. The reply from the ultimate handler of the request is returned directly to the original source of the request. The abort primitive can be used at the application level to indicate to the source task that the transaction cannot complete successfully. It forces the source task to execute its fail clause.

3. **Selective receive**

Any of the receive, receive–reply, receive–forward, or receive–abort primitives can be combined in a select statment (Fig. 4.11). This enables a task to wait on messages from any number of potential entryports. An optional guard can precede each receive to further define conditions upon which messages should be received. A timeout can be used to limit the time spent waiting in the select statement.

Example. As can be seen, the CONIC bounded buffer is very similar to that described in the Ada example except that Ada communication (rendez-vous) resembles a procedure call and CONIC communication is explicit

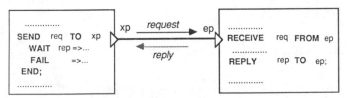

Figure 4.10 The request–reply transaction

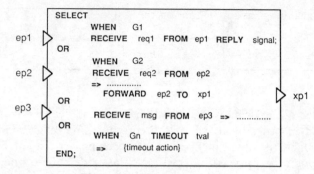

Figure 4.11 The selective receive

message passing. Also, the users of the buffer use indirect naming of their exitports rather than naming the buffer entries directly. Finally notice that there is no need to reassign the messages to local variables (as with parameters) as they can be received and sent directly.

```
TASK MODULE bounded_buffer;
  ENTRYPORT putchar : char REPLY signaltype;
              getchar : signaltype REPLY char;
  CONST poolsize = 100;
  VAR inp,outp : 1 .. poolsize;
    count : 0 .. poolsize;
    pool : ARRAY [1..poolsize] OF char;
BEGIN
  inp:= 1; outp:= 1; count:= 0;
  LOOP
    SELECT
            WHEN (count < poolsize)            {buffer not full}
            RECEIVE pool[inp] FROM putchar REPLY signal =>
              inp:= (inp MOD poolsize) + 1;
              count:= count + 1;
      OR
            WHEN (count > 0)                   {buffer not empty}
            RECEIVE signal FROM getchar REPLY pool [outp] =>
              outp:= (outp MOD poolsize) + 1;
              count:= count - 1;
      END
    END
END.
```

A producing task may contain the statements

```
LOOP
        ... {produce the next character CHAR}
      SEND char TO out WAIT signal;
END
```

and the consuming task may contain the statements

```
LOOP
      SEND signal TO in WAIT char;
      ...{consume the character CHAR}
END
```

The association between ports is performed at the configuration level by the following link statements, where *buff* is the instance of the *bounded buffer* task module type.

```
LINK producer.out TO buff.putchar;
      consumer.in TO buff.getchar
```

Another simple example is a splitter task which accepts an input message and sends copies on each of its two output ports.

```
TASK MODULE splitter;
   ENTRYPORT input:string REPLY signaltype;
   EXITPORT   output1:string REPLY signaltype;
              output2:string REPLY signaltype;

   CONST waitperiod = 150; { 3 seconds}
   VAR buffer:string;
   BEGIN
      LOOP
        RECEIVE buffer FROM input REPLY signal =>
          SEND buffer TO output1
             WAIT signal
             TIMEOUT waitperiod => {do nothing}
          END;
          SEND buffer TO output2
             WAIT signal
             TIMEOUT waitperiod => {do nothing}
          END;
      END;
END.
```

The pump control system

We now return to the pump control system whose software structure was described in Section 3.5. For the sake of brevity only the group module pump controller is described in detail. Its internal structure is shown diagrammatically in Fig. 4.12.

The *pump controller* is a group module and consists of the included type definitions, *pumpdefns,* and the three task modules, *control, pump* and *level.* Level is a simple task which periodically scans the water level sensors and sends the level reading to the control task via an internal link from port *W* to *WL. Pump* merely receives commands from the control to start or stop

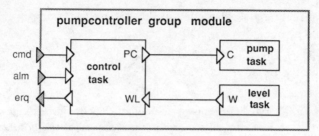

Figure 4.12 Structure of the pump-controller group module

the pump. The control task performs the required pump control. Programs for *pumpcontroller* are given below.

```
GROUP MODULE pumpcontroller (sensoraddr:integer);
    USE controltask, pumptask, leveltask;
    USE pumpdefns: command, state, envreport, envrequest, alarm;
    ENTRYPORT cmd:command REPLY state;
                alm:alarm;
    EXITPORT    erq:envrequest REPLY envreport;
                                            {Module interface}
    CREATE control:controltask;
            pump: pumptask;
            level: leveltask(sensoraddr:integer);
                                            {Internal components}
    LINK level.W TO control.WL;
        control.PC TO pump.C
                                            {Internal links}
    LINK cmd TO control.cmd;
        alm TO control.alm;
        control.erq TO erq;                 {Interface links}
END.


DEFINE pumptypes;
    TYPE waterlevel    = ( low,high,normal );
        pumpcontrol = ( start,stop );
END.
```

———————— ◇ ◇ ◇ ————————

```
TASK MODULE leveltask(sensoraddr:integer);
USE pumptypes:waterlevel;
EXITPORT W:waterlevel;
    CONST period = 10;
    VAR    wlevel : waterlevel;
    BEGIN    {*periodically send water level reading*}
    LOOP
        – – – –scan waterlevel sensors at module parameter address
            sensoraddr and put result in wlevel.
```

```
            SEND    wlevel TO W;
            delay(period) ;
        END;
    END.


TASK MODULE controltask ;
   USE pumpdefns: command, state, sensor, envreport, envrequest,
                                                      alarm;
   USE pumptypes: waterlevel, pumpcontrol;
   ENTRYPORT cmd:command REPLY state;
               alm : alarm;
               WL : waterlevel;
   EXITPORT erq:envrequest REPLY envreport;
            PC:pumpcontrol;
      CONST safetylimit = 1.25; period = 100;
      VAR pstate:state; palarm:alarm;
              plevel:waterlevel; pcommand:command;

   FUNCTION startcheck:state; { * request and check methane level * }
      VAR request:envrequest; report:envreport;
      BEGIN request:= methane;
        SEND request TO erq
          WAIT report => IF report.reading<safetylimit
                             THEN startcheck:= ready
                             ELSE   startcheck:= methanestop
             FAIL period => writeln(error, 'Environment request failure')
                             startcheck:= methanestop;
        END;
      END;
                    ——————  ◇   ◇   ◇  ——————
BEGIN pstate:= stopped;
   LOOP
      SELECT { * process a command * }
             RECEIVE pcommand FROM cmd =>
             CASE pcommand OF
                 stop:BEGIN
                     IF pstate = running THEN SEND stop
                                               TO PC;
                     pstate:= stopped;
                     END;
                 start:IF pstate< >running THEN
                                              pstate:= ready;
                 status: ;
             END;
             REPLY pstate
```

```
OR    { *process an alarm * }
         RECEIVE palarm FROM alm =>
            IF pstate = running THEN SEND stop TO PC;
            pstate:= methanestop;
OR    { *process waterlevel* }
         RECEIVE plevel FROM WL =>
         CASE plevel OF
                high:IF pstate = ready OR pstate = lowstop
                     THEN BEGIN
                        pstate:= startcheck;
                        IF pstate = ready THEN BEGIN
                        SEND start TO PC;
                        pstate:= running END
                     END;
                low: IF pstate = running THEN BEGIN
                     SEND stop TO PC;
                     pstate:= lowstop   END ;
                normal: ;
            END;
      END;
   END;
END.
```

———————————— ◇ ◇ ◇ ————————————

```
TASK MODULE pumptask;
   USE pumptypes:pumpcontrol;
   ENTRYPORT C:pumpcontrol;
   VAR command: pumpcontrol;
   BEGIN
      LOOP
      RECEIVE command FROM C;
      CASE command OF start: ——start the pump;
                       stop: —— stop the pump
      END;
      END;
   END.
```

References

Abramsky, S., Bornat, R., 'Pascal-m: a Language for Loosely Coupled Distributed Systems', in Paker, Y. and Verjus, J.P. (eds.), *Distributed Computing Systems – Synchronization, Control and Communication*, Academic Press, 1983, pp. 163–190.

Andrews, G.R. 'The distributed programming language SR – mechanisms, design and implementation', *Software Practice and Experience*, Vol. 12, 1982, pp. 719–753.

Bernstein, A.J., 'Output guards and non-determinism in 'Communicating sequential processes', *ACM TOPLAS*, Vol. 2, no. 2, April 1980, pp. 234–238.

Brinch-Hansen, P., 'Distributed processes: a concurrent programming concept', *Communication of the ACM*, Vol. 21, no. 11, November 1978, pp. 934–941.

Cashin, P.M., 'Inter-process communication', *Bell-Northern Research Report*, May 1980.

Cheriton, D.R., Malcolm, M.A., Melen, L.S., Sager, G.R., 'Thoth, a portable real-time operating system', *Communications of the ACM*, Vol. 22, no. 2, February 1979, pp. 105–115.

Cheriton, D., 'The V-kernel: a software base for distributed systems', *IEEE Software*, Vol. 1, no. 2, April 1984, pp. 19–43.

Dijkstra, E.W., 'Guarded commands, nondeterminacy and formal derivation of programs', *Communications of the ACM*, Vol. 18, no. 8, 1975.

Downes, V.A., Goldsack, S.J., 'The use of the Ada language for programming a distributed system', *Real Time Programming Workshop*, Graz, April 1980.

Dulay, N., Kramer, J., Magee, J., Sloman, M., Twidle, K.P., 'The Conic configuration language: Version 1.3', *Imperial College Research Report*, DOC 84/20, November 1984.

Gray, J.N., 'Notes on Database Operating Systems', in Seegmuller, G. (ed.), *Operating Systems: an Advanced Course*, Springer Verlag, 1979, pp. 393–481.

Feldman, J.A., 'High level programming for distributed computing', *Communications of the ACM*, Vol. 22, no. 1, June 1979, pp. 353–368.

Fukuoka, H., 'Interprocess communication facilities for distributed systems: a taxonomy and a survey', *Research Report, Georgia Institute of Technology*, GIT-ICS-82/06, February 1982.

Hoare, C.A.R., 'Communicating sequential processes', *Communications of the ACM*, Vol. 21, no. 8, August 1978, pp. 666–677.

Kramer, J., Magee, J., Sloman, M., 'Intertask communication primitives for distributed computer control systems', *Proc. 2nd Int. Conf. on Distributed Computing Systems*, April 1981, pp. 404–411.

Kramer, J., Magee, J., Sloman, M., Lister, A., 'CONIC: an integrated approach to distributed computer control systems', *IEE Proceedings*, Part E, Vol. 130, no. 1, January 1983, pp. 1–10.

Kramer, J., Magee, J., Sloman, M., Twidle, K.P, Dulay, N., 'The Conic programming language: Version 2.4', *Imperial College Research Report*, DOC 84/19, October 1984.

Kramer, J., Magee, J., 'Dynamic configuration for distributed systems', *IEEE Trans. on Software Engineering*, SE-11, no. 4, April 1985.

Lampson, B.W., 'Atomic transactions', in Lampson, B.W., Paul, M., *Distributed Systems – Architecture and Implementation*, H.J. Siegert (ed), LNCS 195, Springer Verlag, 1981, pp. 246–265.

Liskov, B., Sheifler, R., 'Guardians and actions: linguistic support for robust distributed programs', *ACM TOPLAS*, Vol. 5, no. 3, July 1983, pp. 381–404.

Nelson, B.J. 'Remote Procedure Call', *Tech. Rep. CSL-81-9*, Xerox Palo Alto Research Center, Calif., 1981.

Shrivastava, S.K., 'On the treatment of orphans in a distributed system', *Proc. of 3rd Symp. on Reliability in Distributed Software and Database Systems*, IEEE Computer Society, Florida, October 1983, pp. 155–162.

Sloman, M., Magee, J., Kramer, J., 'Building flexible distributed systems in Conic', in Duce, D.A. (ed.), *Distributed Computing Systems Programme*, Peter Peregrinus, September 1984.

Sloman, M., Kramer, J., Magee, J., The Conic toolkit for building distributed systems, *Proc. of 6th IFAC Workshop on Distributed Computer Control Systems*, California, May 1985, Pergamon Press.

USA Department of Defense, *Reference Manual for the Ada Programming Language'*, Proposed Standard Document, July 1980.

Five

COMMUNICATION SYSTEM

In the preceding chapters we have examined what constitutes a software component in a distributed system, how these components name each other and the communication primitives used. The mechanisms described could apply to software components within a single computer system or to components in physically distributed computers. This distribution introduces problems due to errors, delays and the uncertainty of the state of the communicating partner. The communication system is responsible for transferring information between physically distributed stations and overcoming these problems. It is an important part of a distributed system as without communication there cannot be distribution. In the next few chapters we will examine interstation communication techniques in detail.

5.1 Evolution of Communication System Architectures

In early computer systems, each application designed its own communication interface, as shown in Fig. 5.1. The communication support was usually designed into the application programs and was not usable by any other application. This evolved into shared communication support which was provided by the operating system and so was specific to particular computer systems (Fig. 5.2). A number of research networks had been developed in the 1970s to interconnect computers from different manufacturers (Arpanet in USA, NPL network in UK and Cyclades in France). In the 1970s computer manufacturers announced their network architectures to provide common communication techniques across their own range of computers. Typical examples were IBM's SNA [Cypser, 1978] and Digital's DNA [Wecker, 1980]. The objective of these Network Architectures was to allow the interconnection of different computers from the

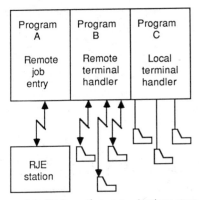

Figure 5.1 Dedicated communications support

manufacturer's range and to create a single integrated communication mechanism. This allowed exchange of information, sharing data, access to remote devices, message passing between processes and use of diverse physical transmission facilities. All these architectures were based on hierarchically layered models which defined the functions performed by the network, the allowed topologies, network interface and communication protocols.

These proprietary communication system architectures were incompatible. It was realized that agreed international standards were needed to allow interworking of computers from different manufacturers in order to overcome differences in information representation, communication techniques and operating systems. In 1972 the Consultative Committee for International Telegraph and Telephones (CCITT) started working on standards for public packet-switched networks. It soon became clear that standards were needed at many levels, so in 1977 the International Stan-

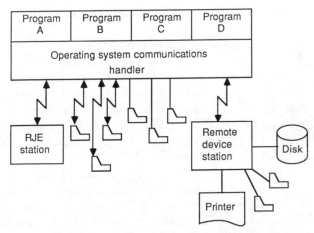

Figure 5.2 Shared communications support

dards Organization (ISO) formed subcommittee 16 to develop an architecture for Open Systems Interconnection [*Proc. IEEE*, 1983, Zimmerman, 1980, International Standards Organization, 1983] which could serve as a framework for the definition of standards. This is known as the ISO Open Systems Interconnection Reference Model. The term 'open' means that by conforming to these standards a system is open to all other systems which obey the same standards. An overview of the ISO model has been given in Chapter 2 and we will cover the ISO terminology in more detail in Section 5.4. The ISO model is used in this book as the framework in which to describe the communication system.

In this chapter we give an overview of the functions performed by the communication system followed by a discussion of issues related to networks – their topologies, a comparison of local area and wide area networks and the switching techniques used. After an introduction to ISO terminology we give a classification of communication services and protocols. Finally the architecture of four distributed systems are examined as case studies.

5.2 Communication System Functions

The **communication system** is the collection of hardware and software which supports interprocess communication between software components in distributed stations. The stations are interconnected by a **network** (Fig. 5.3) which provides a bit serial transfer path between stations. A direct connection between two or more computers which does not involve intermediate computers is called a **link**. The processor performing application functions is sometimes called a **host**. Host computers can be directly connected by point-to-point links to form a simple network (Fig. 5.4) as is often the case with mini- or microcomputers.

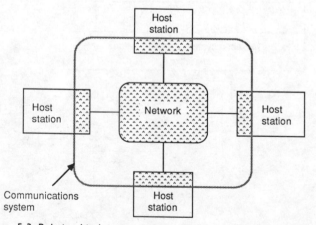

Figure 5.3 Relationship between communication system and network

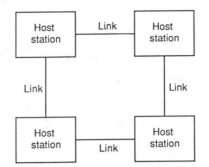

Figure 5.4 Directly connected network of host computers

Alternatively the host computers can be interconnected via an independent public network (Fig. 5.5), which is a complex topology of **switching nodes** and links. The nodes switch data between computers which are not directly connected. Postal Telegraph and Telecommunications Authorities (PTTs), such as British Telecom, provide public networks.

Figure 5.6 illustrates a typical resource-sharing application involving remote communication, which will be used as an example for this discussion of the functions performed by the communication system. A user sits at a workstation (station A) connected to a local network. He wishes to transfer a program, which has been stored in his local file server (station B), to a remote computer (station C) which has the necessary processing power. The program will be compiled and run at station C with the output being returned for printing at a local printer (station P). Assume station C is hundreds of miles away and is accessed via a public network.

Naming and addressing

The distinction between a name, address and route were discussed in Chapter 2. To summarize:

a **name** of an object indicates **what** we seek,
an **address** indicates **where** it is and
a **route** tells us **how to get there.**

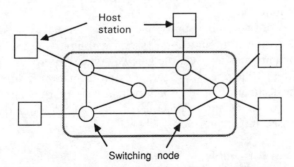

Figure 5.5 A public network with internal switching nodes

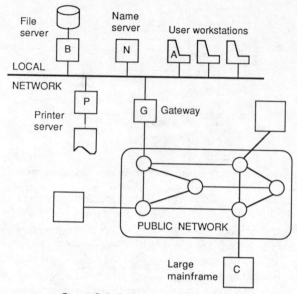

Figure 5.6 A resource-sharing example

The user will supply a name in symbolic form such as 'Daresbury Cray' for the remote large computer (station C in Fig. 5.6) and 'LP' for the line printer (station P). The communication system will use binary integer addresses and so names have to be translated into addresses. This is accomplished by means of a local **name-server** which is similar to the directory enquiry service provided in the telephone system. Of course the address of the name server must be well known, so that the user's workstation can communicate with it in order to find out the addresses of the other resources.

The communication system has to manipulate names for objects such as processes, ports, mailboxes, subnets, stations or even sessions between users. Name-mapping functions are needed in many layers to map a name used at one level onto an entity which it identifies at another level. The communication system must maintain the necessary tables (directories) to perform this function.

The address of the remote station C will indicate that it is on a different network and so the communication system will have to know how to get there, i.e. to route messages via the gateway which interconnects the local network to the public one. Routing is related to mapping. In routing, the address of the destination object is mapped onto an intermediate object such as the gateway or next station along the path to the final destination. Routing will be discussed in Chapter 9.

Segmenting and reassembly
In the above example, the program and the output generated may be very

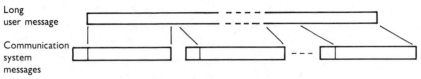

Figure 5.7 Segmentation

long files (e.g. >1 Mbyte). These files are too long to be transmitted as a single message and so they will have to be segmented (fragmented) into smaller packets for transfer by the communication system (Fig. 5.7). Segmentation may occur at many levels within the communication system for the following reasons:

- Internal buffers used within various layers of the communication system will have a finite size.
- Very long messsages monopolize the use of shared resources, particularly a shared transmission medium, thus increasing access delay for other users.
- Breaking a long message into smaller packets for transmission allows the use of multiple data links, present in some networks, to be used in parallel to decrease overall delay.
- If the error rate is high, improved efficiency can be obtained with shorter messages.
- The transmission path may traverse more than 1 network with different message size. For example, the local network and public network in Fig. 5.6 may support different maximum message lengths.

When the communication system segments a long message it should re-assemble it before delivery to the user. It must therefore preserve the identity of a logical unit being segmented and the segments must be reassembled in their original order.

Blocking

There are considerable protocol overheads involved in transferring each message and so some protocols combine messages from different users into a single message for transfer. This can improve the efficiency of the layer and is known as blocking. For example, if a number of users were using an editor on the remote station C in Fig. 5.6, it would be more efficient to combine short blocks of characters from different users into a long message for forwarding over the public network as shown in Fig. 5.8.

Figure 5.8 Blocking

Connections and multiplexing

Sessions or connections are needed to provide an association in which multiple messages can be transferred. They maintain state information to allow recovery from errors, in-sequence delivery, segmentation and reassembly etc. A connection can thus be considered a message stream between two communicating entities. In Fig. 5.6, connections will be needed between the following stations:

A–B, A–C to control the file transfer and initiate the job.
B–C to transfer the file,
C–P to print the file.

In addition short sessions (transactions) are needed between the various stations and the name server (N) to translate names to addresses. Section 5.5 presents a detailed discussion of the various types of connections and transaction services provided by a layer.

Larger servers such as station C will have multiple simultaneous remote users and hence must support simultaneous connections. Stations will probably have only a single physical interface to the network, so multiplexing of different logical connections onto a single physical one must be performed within the communication system. This mapping of multiple higher-layer connections onto a lower-layer connection is called **upward multiplexing** (see Fig. 5.9(a)). It can also be used within a layer to make more economic use of the lower layer service e.g. if connection costs are very high.

Multiplexing does entail overheads. Each message must contain a connection identifier so that it can be demultiplexed at the remote end. Also the layer must ensure that too many messages on one connection do not use all the communication resources.

Downward multiplexing (**splitting**) entails the support of a single connection by multiple lower-level connections (Fig. 5.9(b)). It can be used to increase reliability by using redundant physical circuits. Traffic can be split over multiple $N - 1$ connections to increase the capacity for the N-layer connection. There may also be cost advantages in using multiple low-speed links instead of a single high-speed link. Sequence numbering of the messages will be needed so that they can be reordered at the remote end.

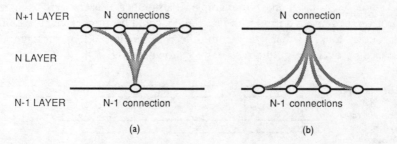

Figure 5.9 Multiplexing: (a) upward; (b) downward

Error control

One of the prime objectives of the protocols in the communication system is to provide reliable communication. There are three aspects to this – detection, correction and recovery from errors. Typical problems which occur in communication systems are noise on the transmission line, corruption of data within intermediate switching nodes, node or link failures. Many protocols implement error recovery by automatic retransmissions if no acknowledgement is received within a timeout period. In some networks messages can take different routes to a destination or be delayed in intermediate nodes. These result in the following errors which must be catered for by the layer protocols:

- information corruption – bit errors;
- loss of a message;
- duplication of a message;
- messages out of sequence.

The communication system must provide recovery from these errors on an end-station to end-station basis. However, if one particular hop is error prone (e.g. the link connecting the gateway to the public network), relying on end-to-end error control can result in long delays and a waste of communication resources in transmitting corrupted messages. Point-to-point error control is also needed over each hop where errors may be introduced.

Information corruption is detected by including redundant information with a message. Sequence errors are detected by giving messages a unique identifier (sequence number). The sequence range must be large enough to prevent identifiers being reused when old messages with the same identifier are still in the network, as these could be accepted as new ones. Most layers use some form of retransmission to correct errors, although error-correcting codes can be used in some circumstances. A more detailed discussion on error control is given in Chapter 8.

There are some error situations which may occur which cannot be recovered by the above methods. The only recovery technique available may be to reinitialize one or more protocol layers to a state of common agreement or to backtrack to the last known error-free state.

Congestion and flow control

Many network systems, such as roads, telephones and data communications are designed (for economic reasons) to share limited resources amongst many users on the assumption that not all users will be active at the same time. In a data-communication network consisting of independent stations, this design strategy may result in the offered traffic exceeding the capacity of the network resources. Traffic is allowed to form queues in order to smooth bursts of activity and maximize the use of resources. Figure 5.10 shows typical characteristics of the type of interlinked queues found in most networks. As the network becomes overloaded, congestion occurs with

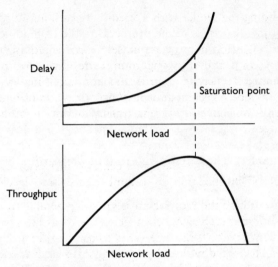

Figure 5.10 Delay and throughput characteristics for network congestion

queues filling up. The result is that stations are unable to receive messages due to lack of buffers and so the messages are not acknowledged and are retransmitted. This causes an increase in offered traffic but a decrease in total network throughput. In the worst case, the delays can tend to infinity and the throughput drops to zero, i.e. a 'traffic jam' or deadlock situation occurs. Congestion control aims to prevent the network reaching saturation by limiting the amount of traffic entering the network.

Congestion control can be defined as the set of mechanisms used to prevent congestion or deadlock and to manage shared network resources in order to optimize performance. That is, the network resources of line capacity, buffers, processor time, table space, etc., must be shared between all users so as to minimize delay and maximize throughput. This is needed wherever multiple data streams are multiplexed onto a shared resource. Most congestion-control mechanisms are based on reservation of resources (e.g. buffers) or discarding of messages, as discussed in Chapter 9.

Flow control is used to regulate the flow of information between a pair of communicating entities, to prevent one from sending more information than the partner can handle. Flow control is needed at many levels, between:

- neighboring switching nodes connected by a data link (e.g. within the public network in Fig. 5.6);
- source and destination network access nodes;
- source and destination host stations connected via an arbitrary network (e.g. stations A & C, B & C in Fig. 5.6)
- pairs of communicating processes.

Flow-control mechanisms are usually based on explicit 'stop/go' interactions or providing the sender with a 'credit' allocation as discussed in later chapters.

Flow and congestion control are closely related, although flow-control mechanisms cannot prevent congestion. They are also related to the mechanisms used for error control and routing. Flow and congestion control may thus be considered a complex interaction of many techniques with the overall objective of keeping traffic flowing smoothly.

Synchronization

For communication to take place between two processes over a network there must be synchronization on a number of distinct levels:

Bit synchronization: the receiver must know or be able to determine the start and duration of each signal element as it will have to sample the signal line at regular intervals. If the receiver is faster than the transmitter it will gain extra bits through double sampling, and if slower it will lose some bits. This is the responsibility of the physical layer and will be discussed in Chapter 6.

Byte synchronization: most computer systems interchange information in 8-bit bytes or characters, although multiple bytes may be grouped into blocks (messages) for transmission. The receiver must therefore be able to determine the start and end of a byte, otherwise it will group bits from one byte with those from another, or possibly lose bytes (see Chapter 6).

Block synchronization: it is necessary to determine the start and end of a block of bytes which has logical significance, e.g. the bytes form a message. Information contained within a block often has positional relevance. The first few bytes act as a header containing protocol control information for the layer and must be distinguished from the data part (see Section 5.4).

Synchronization of access to a communication medium: the problems of access to shared transmission media (e.g. serial bus) are discussed in Chapter 7. It is necessary to ensure only one user at a time has access but competing users have fair access.

Protocol synchronization: communicating peer entities which maintain state information (e.g. sequence numbers) must be synchronized at initialization or after a major error has occurred to make sure the state information is consistent, as described in Chapter 8. This type of protocol synchronization will be required at many levels.

Process synchronization: this type of synchronization is needed for access to a shared resource such as common data. The synchronization provided by IPC message primitives is discussed in Chapter 4.

Priority

Priority can be assigned to messages within the communication system to allow preference when competing for resources. In general, high-priority messages can be expected to have lower delays and could overtake earlier messages from the same source. Typical uses would be to signify alarms in process-control applications, to signify an application interrupt (e.g. an attention key on a terminal), or for protocol control messages. Priority may be assigned statically to a message source (e.g. station priority for gaining access to a serial bus), or according to message content. The latter is more flexible.

Many protocols provide for two priority levels – normal and expedited. An expedited data unit is generally a short (typically 1 or 2 bytes) message which has priority over normal messages, and may be used for signalling or interrupts. It often bypasses the normal flow-control mechanisms.

5.3 Networks

We have discussed the functions performed by the overall communication system, and we now look at how the stations which form a distributed system are interconnected to form a network.

5.3.1 Network Topology

Network topology defines the interconnection structure of stations and links. In the following, we will be looking at how the interconnection structure influences:

- expansion cost – the incremental cost of adding another station;
- reconfiguration flexibility – the ease of modifying the topology;
- reliability – dependency on a single component for network operation;
- software complexity – the complexity of protocols required;
- performance – in terms of throughput or delays;
- broadcast capability – sending a single message which is received by all other stations.

Network topologies can be classified as either **broadcast** (mostly local area networks) or **store-and-forward** (mostly wide area networks). The former implies that all stations are connected to a common transmission medium and so a single message transmitted by a station will reach all other stations. The latter is a network in which a complete message or packet is received into a buffer in the memory of an intermediate station before being retransmitted on the route to its destination. The stations in a store-and-forward network are interconnected by independent point-to-point transmission lines. More information on network topologies can be found in Weitzman [1980], Anderson [1975], Penney [1979].

Complete interconnection
Each station is connected by a dedicated point-to-point link to every other station (see Fig. 5.11). The multiple links can operate in parallel resulting

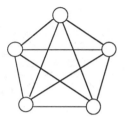

Figure 5.11 Fully connected

in high throughput and the delay is low as there are no intermediate nodes. The communication software can be simple as no routing is needed and links are end-to-end.

A fully connected network can give very high reliability if routing is included to take advantage of the alternative paths available after failure of a link. This then requires store-and-forward transmission via an intermediate station.

The main disadvantage is that the topology is very expensive: n stations require $(n-1)n/2$ links and each station must have $n-1$ interfaces for all the links. Adding the mth station requires $m-1$ additional links and a spare interface in all other stations. Broadcasting a message requires sending it on each link.

Fully connected networks are not very common because of the high cost. They are sometimes used for small local networks or in military applications where redundancy is of prime consideration.

Mesh (partial interconnection)

A mesh has point-to-point links between some stations i.e. all stations are not directly connected (Fig. 5.12). Store-and-forward transmission is required between some pairs of stations.

If each station is connected to at least two others, alternative paths are easily provided in case of failure of a link or station. An additional station requires only two extra links. Mesh networks are commonly used for wide area networks as it is possible to provide high reliability at comparatively low cost. The placing of links and their capacity can be matched to the traffic requirements.

Network delay depends on the number of intermediate stations or switching nodes which can be fairly high for a large network. The communication

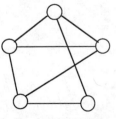

Figure 5.12 Mesh

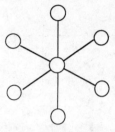

Figure 5.13 Star

system must incorporate routing strategies and generally provides both point-to-point and end-to-end error and flow control, which increases its complexity. The switching nodes are susceptible to queuing delays and traffic congestion. Broadcast communication is not easily implemented as it requires sending a copy of the message to every station.

Star

All stations are connected via a single link to a central switching node (Fig. 5.13) which results in a low expansion cost, simple table lookup routing in the switching node and a maximum delay of only one intermediate node. This topology is commonly used for connecting terminals to a central computer.

The main disadvantage is poor reliability, as a failure of a link isolates a station. Failure of the central switch stops all communication so redundancy is sometimes provided at the switch. Throughput is limited by that of the central switch, which may be a bottleneck. The network is usually not homogeneous in that the central switch is different from the remote stations, i.e. all stations are not interchangeable.

Tree or hierarchical network

This is really an extension of the star topology and so has very similar characteristics. It is often used for terminal networks, where the top level is a central computer, the intermediate level consists of remote multiplexors and the lowest level is terminals. It is also used for process control as it reflects the hierarchical organization of the control system, but a single failure can isolate part of the network.

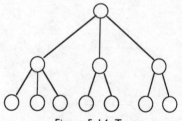

Figure 5.14 Tree

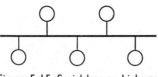

Figure 5.15 Serial bus or highway

Serial bus or highway

A bus (Fig. 5.15) is intrinsically broadcast as the shared transmission medium (twisted pair or coaxial cable) interconnects all the stations. Simultaneous transmission by multiple stations results in interference, and so a media access control mechanism is needed to prevent or resolve contention for the transmission medium. This can be quite complex (see Chapter 7).

A single transmission line links all stations, which minimizes the length of wire and hence the installation cost. It is simple to tap into the transmission line at any point, without affecting other stations. Only a single interface is needed to connect a station, resulting in low expansion costs and easy reconfiguration. The communication software is comparatively simple as no routing is needed. Error and flow controls are end-to-end. The transmission medium can be completely passive and so be inherently reliable. The above reasons make the serial bus very attractive for local area networks for resource sharing, office automation and process control.

All communication fails if the transmission medium is cut, so redundant transmission lines may be required. It can be difficult to determine the failure point. The single transmission line means it must be high capacity to cater for the sum of all the communication within the network and will only support half-duplex transmission. The overall length of the bus is limited to 1 or 2 km unless repeaters are used, in which case the bus is no longer passive.

Radio network

This is conceptually identical to a highway but uses radio rather than wires or cables (see Fig. 5.16). The stations may transmit directly to each other or via a repeater, e.g. a satellite for greater coverage. Most of the characteristics of highways apply to radio networks, but there is no cable to lay or to be cut. The stations can therefore be mobile. Receivers and transmitters are comparatively expensive.

Ring or loop

Each station is linked to its neighbor by a unidirectional link and so communication is only in one direction round the loop (see Fig. 5.17). The ring interface regenerates the signal and contains a few bits of buffering

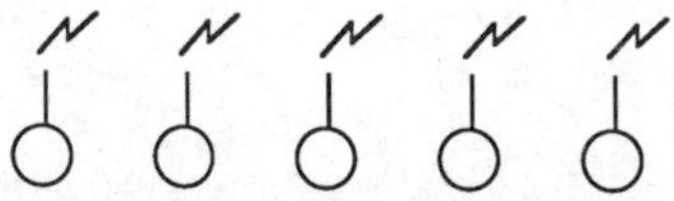

Figure 5.16 Radio network

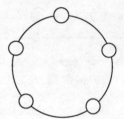

Figure 5.17 Ring or loop

Table 5.1   A comparison of broadcast and store-and-forward topologies

Broadcast	Store and forward
Mostly LANs, e.g. highways, some loops and radio networks.	Generally used in WANs – mesh, star, tree and some loops.
Simpler software as no routing and all error control is end-to-end	Routing techniques can be very complex. Two levels of controls are needed: point-to-point for efficiency and end-to-end to cater for intermediate node failures.
The destination address must be recognized before a message can be received by a station. So the address must be one of the first fields in the header.	The information coming in on a point-to-point line is first received, then the destination address can be checked at a later time to decide whether the message has reached its destination or should be routed on.
A single transmission medium must support the sum of all the communication within the network; thus high-speed lines (usually >1 Mbit/s) are required.	Multiple transmission lines can operate in parallel, and so lower speed lines (2–50 k bits/s) can be used.
The main delay is waiting for acccess to the shared transmission medium (contention delay).	The main delays are due to transmission times over multiple hops.
Transmission path can be completely passive and hence be more reliable.	Transmission path includes switching nodes so is less reliable.
Redundant transmission lines and duplicate network interfaces will be required for some applications in case a line is cut.	Redundancy is inherent in mesh networks with connectivity >2, but other topologies will require redundant lines and interfaces.
Low wiring costs. A simple system can be built with a single interface per station.	More wiring required and mesh networks require at least two interfaces per station.
Complex VLSI network interfaces for highways and loops are becoming available.	Cheap LSI interfaces which provide some error control facilities are available.
May not be compatible with PTT lines.	Compatible with PTT lines.

(1–16 bits). Transmission can be broadcast in that a message goes all round the ring and is removed by the source. Alternatively the transmission may be point-to-point, with the message removed by the destination. A media access mechanism is also needed (see Chapter 7).

Only one additional link is required for an additional station, and the communication software is also simple as no routing is required and controls are end-to-end. Delays are small provided the buffer in the ring interface is small.

The signal is regenerated at each loop interface, which means the transmission line is not passive, i.e. consists of multiple point-to-point links. The overall length of the ring is not limited by line-driving capability as in buses, but power failure at a station causes loop failure unless the interface is designed to bypass a station or some form of redundancy is included. Cutting any link also causes complete failure and so double or braided loops are used where reliability is important.

A comparison of broadcast and store-and-forward topologies

In general, the broadcast topologies require simpler protocols but the hardware required to access the transmission line is more complex. They are commonly used in local area networks. Most wide area networks are store-and-forward and require multiple layers of protocol for routing and error control. Table 5.1 compares the two classes.

5.3.2 Wide Area and Local Area Networks

Most early networks, such as Arpanet, spanned countries and were used to interconnect mainframes or for terminal access to remote computers. These are known as Wide Area Networks (WAN) or long-haul networks. These are generally based on transmission lines interconnecting switching nodes. Public networks fit into this category.

Cheap microprocessors have resulted in the proliferation of computers in a single site such as a university campus, factory or office. Local Area Networks (LAN) have been developed to interconnect them for resource sharing and distributed processing. A LAN is thus confined to a moderately sized geographic area such as a single building or groups of buildings.

Table 5.2 compares the characteristics of wide area and local networks. WANs are often based on store-and-forward switching nodes connected by error-prone links, whereas LANs are based on rings and highways which constitute a single data link. The error rates on LANs are usually less than in WANs. The routing mechanisms used in WANs may result in out-of-sequence message delivery, but most LANs do not reorder messages. There is no sharp distinction between LANs and WANs. A LAN in a mine may span distances of 20 km and a private network which interconnects the offices of a single organization would be considered a WAN. Even the differences in data rates are no longer that distinct. Cheap low-speed LANs are emerging

Table 5.2   Characteristics of WAN and LAN

Wide area networks (WAN)	Local area networks (LAN)
Distances up to thousands of kilometres	Within a site of up to 2 km
Typical data rates (up to 100 k.bits/s.)	High bandwidth (> 1M. bit/s.)
Complex protocols	Simpler protocols
Interconnect autonomous computer systems	Interconnect cooperating computers in distributed processing applications
May be managed by organizations independent of users, e.g. telecommunications authority (PTT)	Usually operated by the same organization which operates the computers it interconnects
Often use analogue circuits from the telephone system	Generally digital signalling over private cables
Higher error rates (1 in 10^5)	Lower error rates (1 in 10^9)
Generally use point-to-point links	Can broadcast a single message to multiple destinations
Common topologies – mesh or star	Common topologies – bus or ring

to interconnect very simple home computers and megabit capacity data links (e.g. British Telecom's Megastream) are becoming available. Most of the networking techniques discussed in this book apply to both.

There is a new class of networks emerging, known as metropolitan networks. These provide LAN-like characteristics over distances found within a city and are based on broad-band communication mechanisms (see Chapter 7).

As indicated in the example in Section 5.1, a typical communication system may consist of a number of interconnected LANs and WANs.

5.3.3   Network-switching Techniques

The network topologies discussed above show that not all stations connected by a network have a direct physical link between them. The network must switch data between links or even subnetworks to provide an end-to-end path between some stations. ISO refers to this as a **relay** function.

In this section we will explain the two main switching techniques used in modern networks – circuit and packet switching. A more detailed discussion can be found elsewhere [Davies, 1979, Chapter 2; Tanenbaum, 1981a, p. 114].

Circuit switching
A circuit-switching network establishes a dedicated channel or circuit between two stations, as in the telephone network. Switching nodes are only involved in setting up a circuit and once the circuit is established they are no longer in the data path (see Fig. 5.18). The network does not provide any processing or storage of the data which it transfers, so communicating

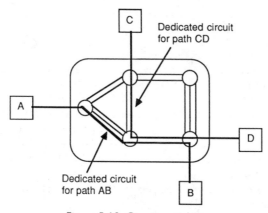

Figure 5.18 Circuit switching

stations must have complete code, speed and format compatibility. The network can be compatible with a digital telephone system. The digital voice/data circuits usually have a capacity of about 60 kbits/s. However, most telephone networks use analog voice circuits which only have a bandwidth of about 3 kHz. The guaranteed bandwidth of switched circuits is best suited to high-throughput applications such as fascimile transmission and file transfers.

The network may be inefficient in the utilization of circuits, as no sharing is possible with other 'conversations', i.e. this technique does not suit applications with 'bursty' traffic characteristics. Circuit switching is used where it is possible to take advantage of the installed wiring and switching capability provided for voice.

Packet switching

As mentioned previously long messages are usually segmented into shorter packets (of 100–2000 bytes in length) for transfer over a network. It is these packets which are switched by internal switching nodes or gateways. Packets from different sources are multiplexed onto individual circuits (see Fig. 5.19) which can increase the utilization of expensive circuits. If the destination is not available, the network does not store packets for later delivery but discards them. Each packet usually contains addressing and control information in a header, and error-detection codes in a trailer. These protocol overheads may account for a sizeable proportion of the line capacity particularly if the maximum packet length is quite short. Packet switching favors those applications in which the traffic characteristics are bursty, e.g. transaction processing, interactive computing and process control.

A LAN such as a ring or bus assigns the shared transmission medium to a station for the time it takes to transmit a single packet. This has some similarity to the demand multiplexing of circuits which occurs in packet-switched networks.

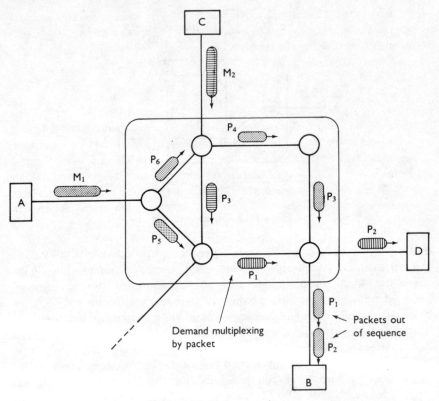

Figure 5.19 Packet switching

The cost of communication has not been decreasing as fast as the cost of processing power. This has favored the development of packet switching and LAN access techniques which allow the transmission facilities to be shared by a number of users. We shall concentrate on these types of networks in this book as they appear to be the most suitable for distributed processing applications.

Message switching is often discussed in the literature as an alternative technique to circuit and packet switching. It involves storing any size message (including long files) on backing store in switching nodes until the destination host wishes to receive the message. Messages can be stored for hours or even days. Modern packet switching systems implement this type of service as an electronic mail application rather than as the basic communication service.

5.4 ISO Terminology

As mentioned previously the need for communication between computers from different manufacturers has led to the development of communication standards for distributed systems. The ISO Open System Interconnection Reference model was defined as a framework for the development of communication standards. The work on this model also resulted in the definition of new terminology which we shall cover in this section.

5.4.1 Layering

As discussed in Chapter 2, layering is a structuring technique used in operating systems and programming. A communication network can be extremely complex and so it is organized in a hierarchy of layers which divides the total problem into smaller pieces. Each **layer** adds value to services provided by the set of lower layers so that the highest layer is offered the set of services needed to run distributed applications. Because of their importance, we will briefly review the seven layers defined in the ISO model (Fig. 5.20).

Application: all application-specific processing;
Presentation: responsible for information representation and transformation;
Session: maintains the association between application entities and performs dialogue control;
Transport: end-station to end-station error and flow control. In LAN based distributed systems the IPC protocols described in the previous chapter are considered part of this layer;
Network: routing, switching and internetwork considerations;
Data-link: error and flow control across a single data link, as well as media access;
Physical: bit transfer and signalling.

A layer may be implemented by a number of **entities** which perform the functions of the layer and are analogous to hardware or software processes.

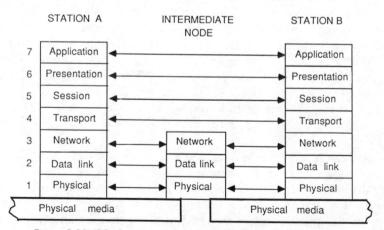

Figure 5.20 ISO Open systems interconnection reference model

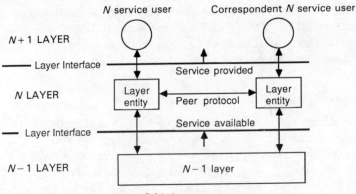

Figure 5.21 Layer concepts

Entities in the same layer which interact are called **peer entities**. A layer is referred to as the N layer while the next lower and higher are referred to as $N-1$ layer and $N+1$ layer respectively (Fig. 5.21). In the ISO model layer 1 is the physical layer and layer 7 is the application layer. The terms layer and level are often used interchangeably in the literature.

An actual network implementation may merge the functions of two or more layers into a single layer. Generally this is for efficiency purposes but some functions may not be required in a particular network. For example, serial bus protocols are always end-to-end, so the routing function of a network layer is not needed. Also the provision of error and flow control at both the transport and data-link layers is redundant.

Protocol: the set of rules (semantic and syntactic) governing communication between the entities which constitute a particular layer (Fig. 5.21). That is, the N protocol defines how an entity at the N level in one system exchanges information with its corresponding peer entities in other stations in order to provide the N level service. The syntactic protocol rules define the format of the information exchanged. For instance the third byte in a message may represent the sequence number. The semantic rules define the operations to be performed by sender and receiver, e.g. under what conditions data must be retransmitted, acknowledged, or rejected. The physical media provides the only physical path between sender and receiver. All peer protocol communication must pass through lower layers within the system to reach the physical circuit, but the peer protocol can be viewed as a **logical link** between peer entities.

Service: the N layer provides an N service to the $N+1$ layer and may use the $N-1$ layer's services to do so, i.e. it adds value to the service available from the lower layer. An example is the provision of a relatively error-free logical link on top of an error-prone physical link. A layer may provide more than one class of service (see Section 5.5). Note that not all the functions performed within a layer are visible as services from the layer above and the

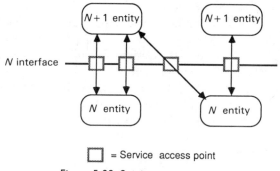

[ ] = Service access point

Figure 5.22 Service access points

service specification does not say how a service is provided. For example, two implementations may offer the same service although one performs error control and the other does not. The relationship between classes of service and the protocols which implement them is further discussed in Section 5.5. Service quality is defined in terms of delay, throughput, reliability etc. When a user requests a service from a layer the quality of service required may be passed as a parameter to the layer.

Service access point (SAP): the point at which entities in adjacent layers in the same station interact. There may be multiple SAPs between two layers in a station, corresponding to the classes of service offered (see Fig. 5.22). When an N layer entity in station A communicates with a peer entity in station B, it may address a message to an $N - 1$ layer SAP in station B. Thus an entity in one station may name SAPs in other stations. In a CONIC system the SAP would correspond to a port and in Berkley Unix a SAP is called a socket. In the postal service a SAP is a postbox.

Internal interface: defines the rules and formats for exchanging information across the boundary between adjacent layers within a single station. The interface may be specified in terms of its mechanical, electrical, timing or software characteristics, i.e. the interface may be physical or logical. The OSI standards do not define internal station interfaces as they do not affect remote communication. For example two application processes in different stations can communicate according to OSI standards although the transport

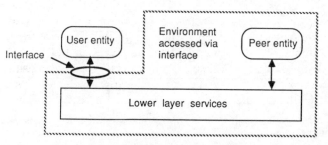

Figure 5.23 External interface

service is accessed via a hardware interface in one station and via a software interface in the other. An interface interaction may result in remote communication and so the interface operations are related to protocol operations. **External interface:** specifies the relationship between an entity and its environment (see Fig. 5.23). This involves interaction with peer entities as well as lower-level service providers and so is a candidate for standardization. Examples are the X.25 interface specification for accessing public networks (see Chapter 10) and the communication primitives discussed in Chapter 4.

5.4.2 Units of Information Transfer

We now define the ISO terminology for units of information transfer with respect to the protocol, internal interfaces and service.

Protocol data unit (PDU): the fixed or variable length unit of information exchanged between peer entities in different stations as part of the protocol. This corresponds to what is commonly called a message, packet or frame. It contains protocol control information (PCI), usually in the form of a header and possibly a trailer and may contain user data (Fig. 5.24). In order to transfer an N layer PDU it must be passed to an $N - 1$ layer entity via an $N - 1$ service access point. The $N - 1$ entity sees the N protocol data unit as user data which must be transferred to its remote peer entity.

Interface data unit (IDU): the unit of information passed across the interface in a single interaction. It also consists of control and data components. The N layer protocol data unit has to be passed across the $N - 1$ interface but may not correspond exactly to an $N - 1$ IDU. For example a 1000 byte protocol data unit would have to be transferred a byte at a time across a byte parallel interface and would need timing control signals to synchronize the transfer. Another example of control information would be quality of service parameters requesting a particular reliability.

Service data unit (SDU): the interface data whose identity is preserved between peer N entities, i.e. the logical data unit transferred by the service. If the $N - 1$ layer does not perform any fragmentation then an $N - 1$ SDU corresponds to a N PDU. The $N - 1$ layer may fragment a long N IDU into small $N - 1$

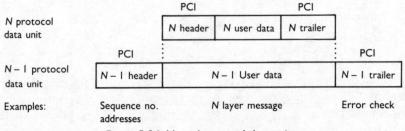

Figure 5.24 Nested protocol data units

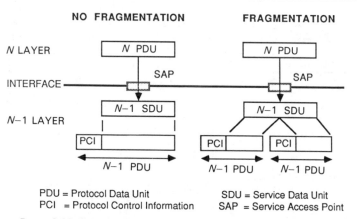

Figure 5.25 Relationship between protocol and service data units

PDUs which are transferred to the remote station and then reassembled for delivery to the remote N layer (see Fig. 5.25).

The above terminology is rather cumbersome and so we use the term message or packet to correspond to a PDU.

5.5 Classification of Communication Services and Protocols

We will now examine the types of communication service that are typically offered to the user of a layer. A service offered by a layer may be directly mapped onto a service provided by a lower layer. Alternatively the layer protocol may perform some functions (e.g. error control) to enhance the lower layer service. The user of the service should be unaware of the functions being performed by the layer, i.e. the user views the layer and the underlying lower layers as a 'black box' (Fig. 5.21). In the next few sections we will classify both services offered at the interface to a layer and the protocol within the layer which provides the service. We will then show the relationship between a service and the protocol which provides the service.

Figure 5.26 illustrates the notation that will be used in this section. User A and User B are in different stations and use the communication services of a layer to exchange information. The communication layer providing the service can be considered a 'black box' which encapsulates all lower layers as discussed in Chapter 2. Each user accesses the service via a service access point (SAP). A transaction is initiated by means of a **request** (e.g. data request to send a message) and the destination gets an **indication** of a transaction (e.g. a message is received by means of a data indication). The remote peer user may send back a **response** which is received by the initiator as a **confirmation**. A **confirmation** could be generated by the service provider, rather than by the peer user, to indicate whether the transaction completed successfully or failed.

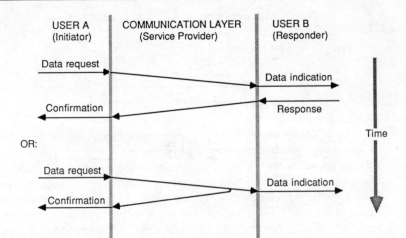

Figure 5.26 Notation for classification of communication services

The communication service is **connectionless** if each message transaction is independent of previous or subsequent ones [Chapin, 1982; 1983]. A **connection-oriented** service provides a relationship between the sequence of units of information transferred by the layer. In the following we refine this broad categorization of services. In practice, a communication layer may provide a service which is a mixture of the various types described below.

5.5.1 Connectionless Services

Connectionless services [Chapin, 1982] are simple to implement in that the layer does very little to enhance the underlying service. The layer does not prevent the loss, duplication or out-of-sequence delivery of messages. In fact, the layer may itself discard messages in some circumstances. Each message transaction initiated at an SAP is a single, self-contained operation, independent of previous message transactions. A sequence of transactions could be to different destinations and hence each transaction must provide the full address of the destination. The service request may also indicate other parameters such as quality of service or error options.

Datagram
This is the simplest type of service. The user is not provided with any form of response to a transaction (see Fig. 5.27). The service is sometimes called 'send and pray' as the user relies on the inherent reliability of the communication system and is not told whether or not a particular message was delivered. A datagram service often provides broadcast or multidestination message transmission.

A datagram service is often provided at the data-link layer over an LAN. This is inherently reliable with no duplicate or out-of-sequence messages.

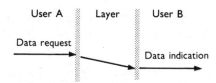

Figure 5.27 Datagram service

There may be an <u>occasional loss</u> of a message due to a receiver not being ready or corruption, but the error <u>rates</u> are <u>usually low</u>.

A datagram service is sometimes <u>provided at the network layer in store-and-forward networks</u> and <u>over interconnected subnets</u> (see Chapter 9). These network layers often <u>use adaptive routing techniques</u> which can result in out-of-sequence messages. Data-link or network-layer retransmissions can result in duplicate messages being generated and messages may be discarded because they have been corrupted or because buffers are full. For the above reasons a WAN datagram service is considered unreliable.

A datagram service is thus a simple, <u>basic service with low overheads</u>, from which more complex but reliable connection services can be built at higher levels. The asynchronous send IPC primitive discussed in Chapter 4 also provides a datagram service at the application level. A datagram service is particularly suited to applications which involve a high level of data redundancy and have critical real-time requirements, e.g. digitized voice.

Confirmation of delivery

The layer provides a response for each message sent by the user. This confirms that the message was successfully delivered to the remote station, the layer was unable to send the message, or the layer does not know whether the message was delivered or not. A confirmation of delivery may mean that the message was received by the remote user or merely that it was received within the remote station. The latter occurs in some LANs (e.g. Omninet and Cambridge Ring). The synchronous send primitive described in Chapter 4 has an implicit confirmation of delivery.

<u>Confirmation of delivery service</u> is sometimes called a **reliable datagram** because the layer <u>may enhance the reliability of the underlying service</u>. The confirmation received by User A does not contain any data from User B, as it is generated by the layer and not by the user (see Fig. 5.28). Although the

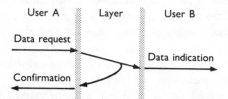

Figure 5.28 Confirmation of delivery service

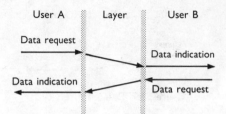

Figure 5.29 Request–reply service

sender will be informed that a message may have been lost the service does not prevent loss, duplication or out-of-sequence messages with respect to the receiver.

Request reply
The transaction consists of two messages, a request from User A to User B, and the response (reply) from User B to User A. The reply is received by A as a confirmation to the request. The initiator may get an error indication instead of the reply if the transaction is not completed successfully. This transaction generally has 'at least once' semantics. This means that a reply indicates that at least one request was received by User B, but more than one may have been received. An error reply means zero or more requests were received by User B, i.e. the request or the reply may have been lost.

This service is suited to applications involving short, idempotent message transactions such as querying the state of a component or performing a name-to-address translation at a name server.

5.5.2 Connection-oriented Services

A connection is an association between two or more entities for conveying data. Connection-oriented services are far more complex than connectionless ones. They represent relationship between two user entities which exist over more than one message transaction [Chapin, 1983]. For example, a terminal session to a remote computer or the association between a controller and a particular sensor in a process control system. The CCITT X.25 interface to public packet-switched networks is an example of a network layer connection service.

Most connection services have 3 phases of operation as shown in Fig. 5.30. The connection must be established before data transfer takes place, and it must be terminated afterwards. Usually either side or even the layer can initiate the termination of a connection. A third party (i.e. a manager entity), rather than the users, may be responsible for establishing and terminating connections. The CONIC configuration system described in Chapter 3 is an example of the use of third party connections.

The full address of the destination user must be given when a connection is established. Thereafter a connection identifier (e.g. a local index which

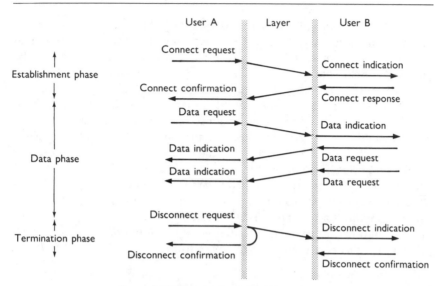

Figure 5.30 Connection-oriented services

can be much shorter than an address) is all that is needed to identify the remote user when transferring data.

The establishment phase can be used to negotiate quality of service or options. The address of the source is provided with the connect indication, so user B can decide whether to refuse the connection. An unsuccessful connection establishment is shown in Fig. 5.31.

Reliable message sequence service

This is the most common form of connection service. It is considered reliable because it enhances the underlying communication service and reduces the probability of lost, duplicate or out-of-sequence messages. After connection establishment, either user can transmit variable-length messages (up to a fixed maximum length) which are delivered in-sequence to the remote user. Any errors from which the layer cannot automatically recover are indicated by a connection failure to the users. Often the user can send a single short (1 or 2 bytes of data) message which bypasses the message sequence. This is called **expedited data** and can be used to transfer interrupts or out-of-band signals.

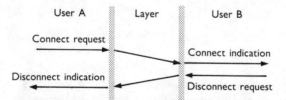

Figure 5.31 Unsuccessful connection establishment

The characteristics of the three phases: establishment, data transfer and termination, together with the in-sequence delivery of messages are similar to those of a circuit-switched network. Hence this service is often called a **virtual circuit service**.

This service is suited to applications in which a transaction involves a number of messages to the same destination over a period of time. For instance file transfers and terminal sessions. The time overheads of the connection establishment and termination phase make it impractical for applications in which a transaction involves a single message or a request–reply pair of messages. Most implementations restrict the number of simultaneous connections because of the space needed to maintain connection state information. These implementation limitations may prevent the service from being used for applications which have simultaneous associations with large numbers of other entities. An example would be a monitoring station which periodically checks hundreds of remote sensors.

Byte stream service
This is similar to the message stream service, but the service supports a sequenced stream of bytes. This is analogous to the virtual input/output provided in many operating systems and is generally used for character transfer. Logical boundaries (e.g. end of line) can be marked with special byte values and the service usually supports-out-of-band interrupt signals. The layer is responsible for buffering the byte stream into messages for transfer within the communication system.

This service is particularly suited to connecting dumb devices to a network or for incorporating a communication service into an existing operating system which supports byte stream I/O.

Unreliable connection
It is also possible to have an unreliable connection service. The connect request binds a destination address to a datagram type SAP. All messages sent on the SAP will be delivered to the same destination, without the user needing to specify a destination for each message. This type of connection could be used with datagram, confirmation of delivery and request reply services. It is not a very common type of service but it is an option in Berkley Unix and is the basic service provided in CONIC (see Chapter 4). In CONIC the user does not perform the binding as it is done by a third party.

5.5.3 Protocols

Protocols which implement the services described above will have a similar classification, but the mapping between service and protocol is not one-to-one, as explained in the next section.

1. **Stateless or datagram protocol**
   This is the simplest form of protocol as it maintains no state information. Each message must be self-contained with full destination and source address. This can entail greater overheads than a connection identifier. The protocol may provide error detection in the form of checking for information corruption (see Chapter 9), but there is no retransmission of lost messages. Corrupted messages are merely discarded. Messages may also be discarded for other reasons, such as lack of buffers. Because no state information is maintained the protocol cannot detect lost, duplicate or out-of-sequence messages.

2. **Acknowledged datagram**
   This includes acknowledgements and retransmissions to recover from corrupted or lost messages. The only state information is usually at the sender which holds a message until an acknowledgement is received or a time limit is exceeded (see Chapter 8). The receiver cannot detect an out-of-sequence or duplicate message. It is used in many ring local area networks and in some buses.

3. **Request reply**
   This is similar to the reliable datagram, but transfers data in both directions. It is most commonly used to implement interprocess communication as described in Chapter 4. The protocol must match replies to requests so a transaction identifier must be maintained at the source during a transaction, and be carried in messages. Some implementations perform automatic retransmission of the request if a reply is not received before a timeout [Xerox, 1981a]. Duplicate detection is not usually performed at the receiver.

4. **Connection protocol**
   These are protocols with the three phases of establishment, data transfer and termination. Connection protocols maintain various types of state information – unacknowledged messages, remote entity address, message sequence numbers and flow-control information. The establishment phase is needed to synchronize this state information. The termination phase releases resources. A connection protocol corrects errors which may have been generated within the underlying service and performs flow control. It is commonly used over error-prone transmission lines, for communication over public networks and as a transport-layer protocol.

5. **Timer-based protocols**
   These have similar characteristics to connection protocols in that they prevent loss, duplication or out of sequence delivery, but they do not explicitly establish and terminate connections. They rely on messages having a defined maximum lifetime. A new message establishes a connection (i.e. state information) if none exists. A timer set to a time greater than the maximum packet lifetime is associated with a connection and the timer is reset each time a message is received or transmitted. When the timer expires the connection is considered closed (see Chapter 10).

5.5.4   Relationship between Services and Protocols

The service provided by a layer specifies the behavior characteristics as seen by the users. The protocol specifies how a service is provided, i.e. implementation characteristics. A particular class of service can be implemented by different protocol classes within a layer. Table 5.3 shows which protocol classes can provide a particular service class. The relationship between service and protocol can be very confusing, and it can be difficult to classify a protocol. For example Arpanet provides a connection service to host computers but at first sight appears to use a stateless (datagram) protocol within the network [Tanenbaum, 1981a, p. 196]. In fact there are sublayers within the network layer. There is a sublayer protocol between access nodes to which the hosts are connected. This implements a connection protocol above the datagram sublayer which performs switching.

A datagram service can be implemented by any of the protocols but the connection protocols are 'overkill' and hence reduce performance. Consider the scenario of a datagram service being provided by a transport-layer connection protocol. When the user sends a message addressed to a process on a remote station (e.g. by means of an asynchronous send) the message is copied into a transport-layer buffer. The transport entity then checks its state information to see whether it already has a connection set up for this user to the destination process. If not, a connection request is transmitted. When connection confirmation is received, the user's message is transmitted. The transport entity waits for an acknowledgement and if necessary performs retransmissions. When the message has been received by the remote transport entity the connection is disconnected. Alternatively the transport layer may delay disconnection on the assumption that the user will send another message to the same destination. The user is not informed if the message is not

Table 5.3 Relationship between layer service provided and protocol used

SERVICE PROVIDED		PROTOCOL USED IN LAYER TO PROVIDE SERVICE				
		Stateless	Acked. datagram	Request-reply	Connection	Timer based
CONNECTION-LESS	Datagram	Good match			OK, but high overheads	
	Confirmed delivery	No	Good match		OK, but high overheads	
	Request-reply	OK, but no retrans-mission	OK	Good match	Needed for exactly once semantics	
CONNECTION ORIENTED	Message & byte stream	Cannot provide a reliable, sequenced service			Good match	
	Unreliable connection	Good match			OK, but high overheads	

delivered for any reason (see Chapter 4). Obviously a number of transport layer messages are needed to transmit one user message. This results in increased overheads and reduced performance.

It is not possible to confirm delivery unless a protocol which performs acknowledgements is used. A request-reply service can be implemented using a stateless protocol, but no retransmissions are provided. If the request–reply service guarantees that only one request is ever received at the destination, then it must use a connection or timer protocol, which maintains state information beyond the current transaction. A connection protocol can be used to implement a request–reply service by including the request data in a connect request. The receiver sends back an immediate disconnect request which contains reply data. This is very similar to a request–reply protocol. A message or byte stream type of service can be implemented using a connectionless protocol, if the underlying service is reliable and does not generate duplicates or re-order messages. If the underlying service is not reliable, then a connection or timer protocol should be used.

In general there is a better match if the service and protocol are both connectionless or both connection oriented. A connectionless service can be implemented using a connection protocol, but the overheads reduce performance.

5.6 Implementation Considerations

5.6.1 Hardware

We have discussed the functions performed within the communication system, network topologies and the classes of service and protocol provided by the layers within the communication system. We will now briefly examine some of the tradeoffs that can be made by implementing the communication system using special hardware or front-end processors.

Direct

The network could be implemented by using transmission lines to interconnect RS 232 or V.24 terminal ports on stations (see Fig. 5.4). The host computer then performs both application and communication functions. These terminal ports perform simple error detection (e.g. parity) and work at speeds up to 19.2 k.bits/s. There is minimal hardware support so all the communication software including switching and error control must be implemented in the host computer. Higher-speed transmission can be obtained by using special-purpose communication ports. Typical topologies which can be implemented are star, tree, mesh and store-and-forward loop.

Independent network

This offloads all the switching and routing functions into switching nodes which form an independent packet-switched network, as shown in Fig. 5.5.

This approach is used for connecting to WANs, particularly public networks. The network performs point-to-point error and flow control between switching nodes and may even perform error and flow control on an end-access node to end-access node basis. Host computers are usually connected into the nearest access/switching node using a communication port and leased line. Error and flow control must still be performed over the link between the host computer and the access node.

Communications processor

With the decrease in cost of microprocessors it has become feasible to off-load more of the communications processing into a special-purpose processor which is closely coupled to the host computer. This is responsible for many of the communication functions such as end-to-end error control and fragmentation of large messages into smaller packets. The interface with the host computer could be via a shared memory or DMA (see Fig. 5.32). Large mainframe computers have had front-end communications processors for some time, but it has now become feasible to use this approach for connecting comparatively small microcomputers into a network. The host computer is still responsible for protocols pertaining to the application, presentation, session and possibly some transport-layer functions.

LAN interface

Special-purpose sophisticated VLSI circuits are available to connect microcomputers to LANs. They often contain multiple processors and are mainly concerned with media access control and low-level synchronization, although some also perform error control. These circuits perform mostly data-link layer functions, although they could be combined with a communications processor as under 'Communications processor' above, to offload most of the high-level functions.

   LANs are themselves increasingly being used as a means of connecting a number of computers into a public WAN. A gateway computer interconnects the LAN and public network as in Fig. 5.6. The complex protocols needed to access the public network can be offloaded into the gateway which is shared by many host computers on the LAN. Simpler protocols can then be used between the host computers and the gateway.

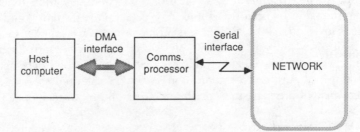

Figure 5.32 Use of a front-end communications processor

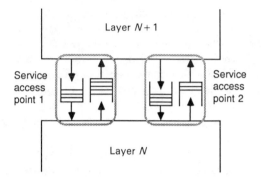

Figure 5.33 Message queues between layers

5.6.2 Software

The software in a station which implements a layer of the ISO model could be implemented as one or more processes (tasks) supported by a multitasking station kernel [Ellis, 1983]. The interface between layers can be characterized by two queues of messages per service access point – one queue for incoming and one for outgoing messages (see Fig. 5.33). The queues could be implemented by monitors or directly by the kernel if it supports message passing.

There are two design considerations which can affect performance of a communication system implementation:

- copying of messages within the communication system;
- overheads of task switching.

Copying overheads can be minimized by passing pointers within the communication system. This is only feasible if the communication tasks can share memory. Task-switching overheads can be reduced by combining the implementation of multiple layers into a single process. Essentially layer functions are implemented by procedure calls rather than interprocess communication [Belanger, 1980]. Various implementation approaches are illustrated in Chapter 10.

5.7 Case Studies

We now examine four communication-system architectures which have been designed for distributed applications, and we will relate these to the ISO model:

Xerox PUP Internetwork Architecture;
Lawrence Livermore Laboratory LINCS Architecture;
CONIC communication system for distributed embedded applications;
General Motors Manufacturing Automation Protocol.

5.7.1   Xerox Pup Internetwork Architecture

Xerox provide an open-ended set of internetwork packet transport protocols [Xerox, 1981a], used across a variety of communication media, computers and office automation applications. The framework is based on the PUP architecture [Boggs, 1980] developed at Xerox Parc. The topology assumed is a collection of heterogeneous LANs and WANs interconnected by store-and-forward gateways, but the protocols are simple enough to be used over a single LAN.

The basic concept is to provide a single internetwork datagram protocol which can be used to transfer packets over any subnet and acts as the unifying factor in the set of protocols (see Fig. 5.34). Note that the layers of Fig. 5.34 do not correspond to the ISO model. The source generates the Internet datagram packet with headers and trailers. Individual subnets are treated as data links by gateways. They encapsulate the internet datagram packets with the subnet specific headers and trailers (see Chapter 9).

There are four Levels defined in Fig. 5.34, but there may be many protocols at a level:

Level 4: **Application:** The users of level 3 protocols.

Level 3: **Application-oriented protocols:** These provide conventions for data structuring and interaction between particular application classes. They correspond to the ISO application, presentation and to a lesser extent session layers.

    Courier: A remote procedure call which transforms the representation of parameters to allow them to be transferred across the network. It performs segmentation and reassembly of long data structures into packets for transfer and makes use of the sequenced packet service from level 2.

    Various protocols for accessing servers are also defined at level 3 e.g. printing, filing, time of day, clearinghouse (name server).

Level 2: **Interprocess communication:** This set of protocols provides different combinations of reliability, throughput, delay, and complexity. Both connectionless and connection protocols are provided at this level, which corresponds roughly to the ISO transport layer. Examples of these protocols are:

    Echo: This is a simple request–reply protocol which can be used to check the existence of a destination host or for maintenance purposes. The information sent as the request is returned as the reply.

    Error: The destination or an intermediate node may generate an error message (as defined in this protocol) to the source if it cannot deliver a packet. It is an optional protocol and is meant as a diagnostic tool.

    Sequenced packet: This is a connection protocol providing a

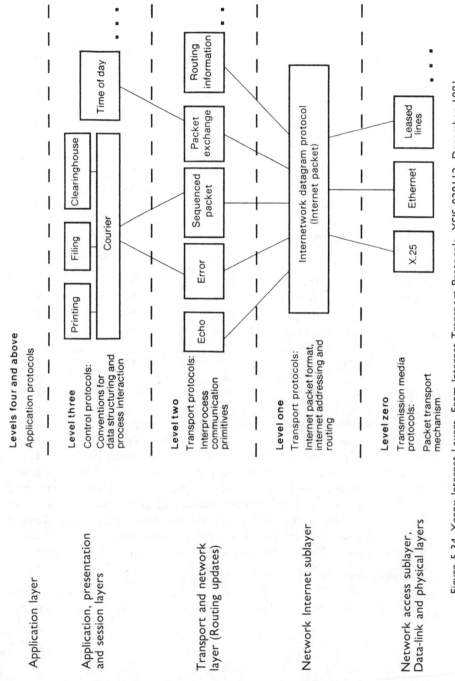

Figure 5.34 Xerox Internet Layers. From Internet Transport Protocols, XSIS 028112, December 1981.

message stream service which performs error control, flow control and provides in-sequence delivery of packets.

Packet exchange: This is a request–reply protocol which performs retransmissions if the reply is not received within a timeout period. The timeout depends on the destination and is obtained from the router. The protocol does not perform duplicate filtering.

Routing information: This defines how routing tables are updated in gateways and really corresponds to an ISO Network Layer protocol, but routing information is sent as a standard internet (level 1) packet.

Level 1: Internet packet transfer: This is responsible for transferring the internet packet (message) across arbitrary interconnected subnets and delivering it at the destination station. It provides a uniform interface to the higher layers which is independent of the types of networks used at level 0. It provides a datagram service and performs routing and error detection. Broadcast and multidestination addressing are supported. A packet may be discarded if it is corrupted or for other reasons such as lack of buffers. Level 1 defines a standard internet packet format (see Chapter 10) and corresponds to the network layer of the ISO model.

Level 0: Subnet packet transfer: These are the protocols responsible for getting a packet across a single subnet or leased line, and are dependent on the type of subnet used. They correspond to the physical, data-link and the subnet access sublayer of the network layer in the ISO reference model.

5.7.2 LINCS architecture

LINCS is a communication system to support resource sharing and process cooperation amongst stations which can range from microcomputers to super-computers at Lawrence Livermore Laboratory in California [Fletcher, 1982]. Like the Xerox system, LINCS also supports a variety of interconnected subnets and point-to-point links. LINCS is a part of a distributed operating system which is implemented on top of the host-operating system of individual stations. LINCS is unusual in that the basic interaction mechanism between application processes is based on a simplex (unidirectional) channel called a **monologue**. LINCS is structured to correspond to the ISO model.

Application/Service Layer: this defines application-oriented services common to classes of applications, e.g. terminal handling, filing, accounting, user authentication. There are a number of sublayers used by these services, e.g.

Dialogue protocol provides a request–reply service by combining two monologues.

Data server protocol for accessing printer or file servers.

Resource model defines naming and protection mechanisms for accessing resources (files, shared data, etc.).

Presentation layer: defines network standard representation for data types and provides transformations between local and the standard representations. The presentation layer provides a 'shared data' model for communication via a monologue and specifies the syntax and format of control and data exchanged. A typed data structure similar to a Pascal record can be defined at the receiver. The sender can insert data into fields in this structure and the receiver can read data from these fields. The receiving presentation layer merely places information into the relevant field in the data structure, but does not interpret or act on it. The sender can explicitly 'wake up' the receiver when particular data is to be acted upon.

Other types of presentation protocols include an array data monologue which allow a possibly infinite array (stream) of typed data elements to be transferred and a virtual terminal protocol.

Session layer: provides a simplex monologue (connection) between a sending and receiving process port. It allows the transfer of begin, end, wakeup or data symbols and so provides data transfer and synchronization.

Transport layer: transfers data from sender to receiver port buffers, performing error and flow control. It is a time-based protocol (see Chapter 10), which provides a connection-like service without explicit connection establishment and termination phases. The transport-layer connection is bidirectional although it supports a unidirectional session because the session requires control information in the reverse direction.

Network layer: provides a datagram internet service similar to that of Xerox level 1, but includes a protection service, i.e. matches the user's security protection level specified in a packet with those of a station or a link. A high protection level packet will only be routed through secure nodes or links (i.e. those which are cannot be accessed by outside users). It also enforces maximum packet lifetime within the network.

Data-link layer: supports a variety of protocols ranging from simple acknowledged datagram type to standard connection protocols (e.g. HDLC).

Physical layer: performs standard ISO physical layer functions except a channel could be a virtual circuit across a packet-switched network.

5.7.3 CONIC

The CONIC software architecture has been described in Chapter 3 and the Conic message communication primitives in Chapter 4. We now describe the CONIC communication system [Sloman, 1986]. It supports a topology of independent subnets (LANs) interconnected by store-and-forward gateways to form a mesh (see Fig. 5.35). This structure is extensible both by adding stations within a subnet, or by adding new subnets. A mesh topology allows multiple gateways between subnets and so provides redundant paths. A subnet could be a ring, serial bus or even a point-to-point link.

The configuration flexibility of CONIC has been exploited in the design of the communication system. It provides a basic unreliable connection service

DSCN–F*

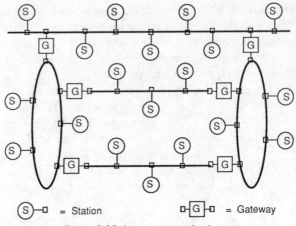

Figure 5.35 Interconnected subnets

between an exitport and remote entryport. This minimal functionality can be enhanced at configuration time to provide routing and reliable sequenced packet connections (virtual circuits).

The layers in the CONIC communication system are:

Application: performs application-dependent processing.

Presentation: not currently implemented but would be needed for nonhomogeneous computers.

Session: the association between and exitport and entryport. It is considered part of the operating system rather than communication system. One-to-one, one-to-many and many-to-one connections are supported.

Transport: implements the unreliable connection service between remote exit and entryports for notify and request–reply transactions. The notify is implemented by a stateless protocol and the request reply by a request–reply protocol which discards duplicate replies. There is no fragmentation or error control performed. An optional reliable connection protocol which performs error and sequence control of messages can be provided as a configuration option.

Network: implements routing and provides a datagram internet service similar to that of Xerox level 1.

Data link and physical: uses commercially available LAN hardware and different types of LANs can be supported, e.g. Cambridge Ring, Ethernet, Omninet.

5.7.4 General Motors Manufacturing Automation Protocol (MAP)

The MAP architecture has been developed to support factory automation systems, e.g. for the automobile industry [General Motors, 1984]. MAP is a set of specific recommendations from available international standards for each layer of the ISO reference model. It is designed to allow the integration of computers from different vendors to form a distributed system in a LAN environment. It assumes interconnected subnetworks and that sites will be interconnected via WANs.

Application layer: This is still being defined, but will include network management services, a directory service to allow name-to-address mapping, virtual terminal and virtual file service. MAP differs from the previous case studies in that it assumes only a connection service will be provided [Fong, 1985].

Presentation layer: No standards have yet been adopted but a GM standard message protocol which includes presentation-layer functions is being considered. This is briefly described in Chapter 11.

Session layer: This will probably adopt the ISO session-layer protocol when it has been completed.

Transport layer: This is based on the American National Bureau of Standards protocol which is very similar to the ISO Class 4 Transport Protocol (see Chapter 10). It provides a connection service with full end-to-end error and flow control.

Network layer: This provides a datagram service based on interconnected networks. The main function performed is routing. It is assumed that routing tables will be generated centrally and distributed to gateways. MAP defines the format for routing tables which will be generated centrally and distributed to gateways. A hierarchic addressing structure is also specified.

Data link and physical: This is based on the IEEE 802.4 token passing broadband bus for use within a factory (see Chapter 7).

References

Anderson, G.A., Jensen, E., 'Computer interconnection: taxonomy, characteristics, and examples', *ACM Comp. Surveys*, Vol. 7, no. 4, Dec. 1975, pp. 197–213.

Belanger, P., Hankins, C., Jain, N., 'Performance measurements of a local microcomputer network', in West A. and Janson, P. (eds.), *Local Networks for Computer Communications*, North-Holland, 1980.

Boggs, D., Shoch, J., Taft, E., Metcalfe, R., 'Pup: an internetwork architecture', in IEEE [1980], pp. 612–623.

Chapin, A.L., 'Connectionless data transmission', *ACM computer Comms. Review*, Vol. 12, no. 2, pp. 21–61.

Chapin, A.L., 'Connections and connectionless data transmission', in Proc. IEEE [1983], pp. 1365–1371.

Cypser, R., *Communications Architecture for Distributed Systems*, Addison-Wesley, 1978.

Davies, D., Barber, D., Price, W., Solomonides, C., *Computer Networks and their Protocols*, Wiley, 1979.

Ellis, G., Dillon, S., Stritter, S., Whitnell, J., 'Experiences with a layered approach to LAN design', *IEEE Journal on Selected Areas in Comms.*, SAC Vol. 1, no. 5, November 1983, pp. 857–868.

Fletcher, J., Watson, R., *An Overview of LINCS Architecture*, UCID 19294, Lawrence Livermore Laboratory, Livermore, California, November 1982.

Fong, K., Amarath, P., 'MAP application layer interface and management structure', *ACM Computer Comms. Review*, Vol. 15, no. 2, April 1985, pp. 28–45.

General Motors, *Manufacturing Automation Protocol – April 1984*, available from Manufacturing Engineering and Development, APMES A/MD-39, GM Technical Centre, Warren, MI 48090-9040.

IEEE Trans. Comms., Special Issue on Computer Network Architectures and Protocols, Vol. 28, no. 4, April 1980.

International Standards Organization, *Basic Reference Model for Open Systems Interconnection*, ISO 7498, 1983. See also *ACM Computer Comms. Review*, April 1981, pp. 15–65.

Penney, B., Baghdadi, A., 'Surevey of computer communication loop networks', Part 1 & 2, *Computer Communications*, Vol. 2, nos. 4 & 5, August and October, 1979.

Pouzin, L., Zimmerman, H., 'A tutorial on protocols', in Proc IEEE [1978], pp. 1346–1370.

Proc. IEEE, Special Issue on Packet Communication Networks, Vol. 66, no. 11, November, 1978.

Proc. IEEE, Special Issue on Open Systems Interconnection, Vol. 71, no. 12, December, 1983.

Sloman, M., Kramer, J., Magee, J., 'A Flexible Communication Structure for Distributed Embedded Systems', *IEE Proc. Pt E*, Vol. 133, no. 4, July 1986, pp. 201–211.

Tanenbaum, A. (a), *Computer Networks*, Prentice-Hall, 1981.

Tanenbaum, A., (b), 'Network protocols', *ACM Computing Surveys*, Vol. 13, no. 4, December 1981, pp. 453–489.

Wecker, S., 'DNA: the digital network architecture', in IEEE TC [1980], pp. 510–526.

Weitzman, C., *Distributed Micro/Minicomputer Systems*. Prentice-Hall, 1980.

XEROX CORPORATION (a), *Internet Transport Protocols*, XSIS 028112, Xerox OPD, Network Systems Administration Office, 3333 Coyote Hill Road, Palo Alto, California 94304, December 1981.

XEROX CORPORATION, (b) *Courier: the remote procedure call protocol*. XSIS 038112 (as above), December 1981.

Zimmerman, H., 'OSI reference model', in IEEE TC [1980], pp. 425–432.

Six

PHYSICAL LAYER

The physical layer is responsible for the transmission of bits over a physical circuit. It is concerned with all aspects of signalling and modulation, i.e. the transformation between electrical signals on wires (voltages or currents) and the 1s or 0s representing digital information. In addition the physical layer of the ISO model defines the physical and mechanical means for interconnecting components, i.e. plugs and sockets for connecting components to the communication system [Bertine, 1980].

The physical layer is usually implemented in hardware, but many of the modern VLSI communication circuits also implement the functions of the data-link layer, and so the distinction between the implementation of the functions of these two layers is sometimes rather vague [Taylor, 1983].

This chapter will merely give an overview of the functions of the physical layer, introducing the terminology used, discussing how bit and byte synchronization is achieved and various modulation methods. More detailed information is available elsewhere [NCC, 1982; Davies, 1973; Halsall, 1985; Stallings, 1985]. Some aspects of the physical layer of LANs are covered in the next chapter.

6.1 Data-transmission Components

Figure 6.1 shows the typical components involved in transmitting bits between two network stations.

Transmission line: This is the medium which transfers signals over a distance. It could consist of a twisted pair of wires, coaxial cable, fibre optic cable or radio waves, etc. The distance which the signal can travel along a transmission line depends on the electrical characteristics of the line (impedance), the power of the transmitter and the signal frequency. Long lines may require regeneration or amplification of the signal.

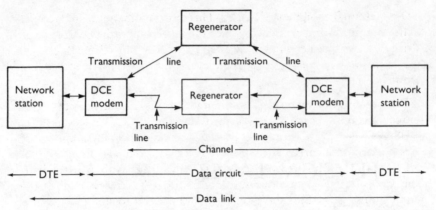

Figure 6.1 Data-transmission components

Regenerator: This is a simple device which allows increased distance between stations. It receives signals and amplifies or regenerates them. It differs from a switching node in that it does not store messages but introduces a delay of typically less than 1 bit.

Modem: Many wide area networks make use of the telephone system which was designed for analogue voice transmission. Some LANs also use analogue signalling as this allows higher data rates and longer transmission lines without regenerators. A modem converts digital information into analogue signals (modulation) for transmission and converts received analogue signals into digital information (demodulation). Modulation techniques will be discussed in more detail in Section 6.4.

Data circuit terminating equipment (DCE): This is the general term for the functional unit which transforms the digital signals seen by the computer into the signals carrying information on the transmission line. It could be a modem, but for a transmission line which is designed for digital signals it could be a line coupler or level converter. Most LANs use digital signals so do not use modems.

Data circuit: This is the data path which includes the transmission line, regenerators and the DCE at each end. It is a means of two-way communication between two or more points.

Data channel: A data circuit can support a number of independent information transfers by a multiplexing technique (see Section 6.5). Each path used for transferring information in a particular direction is called a channel. A multiplexed circuit can thus support multiple channels, but conversely a channel can be distributed over multiple circuits. Note that a channel implies one-way transmission whereas a circuit implies two-way transmission.

Data link: This data path includes a data circuit (i.e. transmission line and DCE) as well as some equipment which controls the circuit and performs error detection and correction functions (see Chapter 9).

Data terminal equipment (DTE): This term is sometimes used to refer to the data-processing equipment which is connected to a data circuit. In practice this could be a computer, front and processor or a terminal. It is rather a confusing term as it can include everything other than the DCE and transmission line (see Fig. 6.1.)

The organizations which provide data transmission facilities to users are known as **common carriers**, e.g. British Telecom, AT&T or Western Union in USA. They provide permanent (leased) or switched circuits. In some countries the common carrier is the Postal Telegraph and Telephone Authority (PTT) and the term PTT is often used synonymously with common carrier. The Consultative Committee for International Telegraph and Telecommunications (CCITT) is the standards organization for the PTTs and produces many data communication and computer network standards.

6.2 Channel Characteristics

Transmission media or channels have the following characteristics:

Bandwidth: This is an electrical characteristic of a transmission line or circuit. It indicates the range of frequencies measured in hertz (cycles per second) which can be successfully transmitted over the line. A typical bandwidth of a voice grade telephone line is 300 to 3300 Hz as shown in Fig. 6.2.

Baud rate: The number of signal elements or condition changes per second. This defines the signalling rate on the transmission line. A signal element is a discrete voltage, phase or frequency value. If the signalling method uses only two distinct voltage levels as in Fig. 6.3(a), then each level can represent a 1 or a 0, i.e. one bit per level. The signal can take one of four discrete voltage levels (or 90% phase changes), as in Fig. 6.3(b). Then each signal element is coded as two binary digits: 00, 01, 10, 11.

Channel capacity: This is the **maximum** rate at which it can carry information without error. For digital information this is measured in bits per second, and

capacity = baud rate × number of bits per signal element.

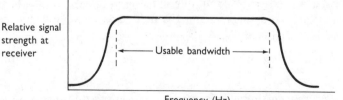

Figure 6.2 Bandwidth of a transmission line

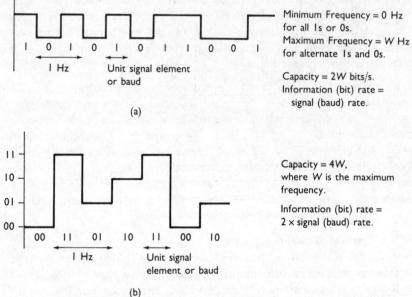

(a)

(b)

Figure 6.3 Relationship between bit and baud rate: (a) signalling using two levels; (b) signalling using four levels

6.3 Transmission Modes

There are a number of characteristics of the transmission mode – whether parallel or serial, full or half duplex, digital or analogue signalling.

Parallel transmission: Although the unit of communication may conceptually be a message containing thousands of bits, it is not practical to transmit all of them in parallel. Messages can be of variable length and so they are usually serialized into 8-bit character streams (see Fig. 6.4a), even for local input/output. For local communication (less than 20 m) it is feasible to provide 8 or even 16 signal channels allowing parallel transmission. An extra clock line is usually included, which indicates to the receiver exactly when to sample the line.

Serial transmission: When the transmission is over a long distance, it is too expensive to provide multiple signal lines (two are required for each channel) and so a single channel is used, and the characters are transmitted bit serial (see Fig. 6.4b).

A communication circuit can be used in one of the following modes (Fig. 6.5):

Simplex transmission: Information is transferred in one direction only and never in the other direction.

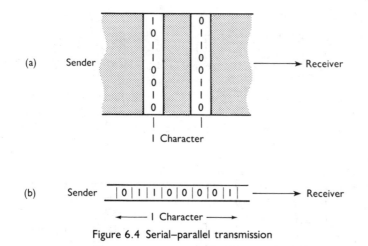

I Character

Figure 6.4 Serial–parallel transmission

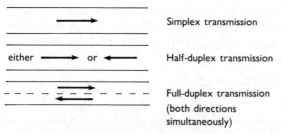

Half-duplex transmission: Information is transferred in either direction but not in both directions simultaneously.

Full-duplex transmission: Information is transferred simultaneously in both directions.

The terms simplex, half-duplex and full-duplex can also be used to describe an intrinsic property of the circuit:

Simplex circuit: A circuit which is capable of transmitting information in one direction only. It may contain amplifiers which will only amplify in one direction.

Half-duplex circuit: A circuit which provides a single transmission path (e.g. two wires) and can transfer information in either direction but not in both directions simultaneously. A half-duplex circuit can also be used in simplex mode.

Full-duplex circuit: One which provides two independent transmission paths (e.g. four wires) and so can allow simultaneous transmission in both directions. A full-duplex circuit can be used in full- or half-duplex mode or even in simplex mode.

Simplex transmission

Half-duplex transmission

Full-duplex transmission
(both directions
simultaneously)

Figure 6.5 Simplex–duplex transmission

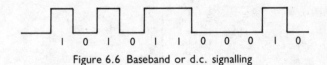

Figure 6.6 Baseband or d.c. signalling

There are frequency-division multiplexing modems which provide full-duplex mode of transmission on two wires. Two frequency bands are used, one for the forward direction and the other for the opposite direction (see Fig. 6.5).

Baseband signalling: The transmission of a digital signal at its original frequency, without modulation, is called baseband signalling (see Fig. 6.6). A long string of 1s or 0s will result in a d.c. signal, so this is also known as d.c. signalling. It is commonly used in LANs.

The capacitive and inductive effect of the wire results in distortion of the signal, as shown in Fig. 6.7. The distortion depends on the length of the transmission medium and the frequency. Baseband signalling is suitable only for local transmission over distances < 1 Km. The actual distance depends on the transmission rate for a given transmission line and given power of a transmitter. For example, a 500 m coaxial cable supporting 100 stations can work at 10 M.bits/s. A twisted pair cable supporting 10 stations can work at about 1 M.bits/s.

Switched or leased lines from public carriers are generally not suitable for baseband transmission. The signals on these lines are amplified by regenerators which do not pass d.c. signals. In addition, these carrier lines are often 'loaded' with an inductance to reduce distortion of analog signals. It is possible to lease an unloaded local line, which does not have any regenerators.

Analogue or broadband transmission: Digital signals are used to **modulate** a carrier signal using one of the modulation methods discussed in Section 6.4. The carrier frequency must be within the bandwidth of the channel. This technique must be used for networks that use voice grade lines which generally have a bandwidth of 300–3300 Hz. It is nearly always used in WANs, but also for some LANs based on cable-television technology (see Chapter 7).

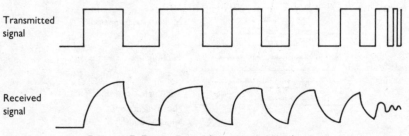

Figure 6.7 Distortion with increasing signal rate

6.4 Modulation Methods

1. **Amplitude modulation**
   Two different amplitudes of a carrier wave (e.g. 1500 Hz) are used to represent a 1 and a 0, as shown in Fig. 6.8.
2. **Frequency modulation**
   This is also called frequency shift keying (FSK). A 0 and a 1 are presented by two different carrier frequencies (e.g. $0 = f_1 = 1300$ Hz, $1 = f_2 = 1700$ Hz).
3. **Phase modulation**
   There are two types of phase modulation:
   (a) A phase shift of $180°$ in the carrier occurs each time a binary 0 is transmitted. No phase change takes place for a binary 1.
   (b) Phase shift keying (PSK) in which a 0 and a 1 are represented by two carrier signals $180°$ out of phase.

The above methods all have two signal levels so each signal element represents 1 bit of information. It is possible to have variations and

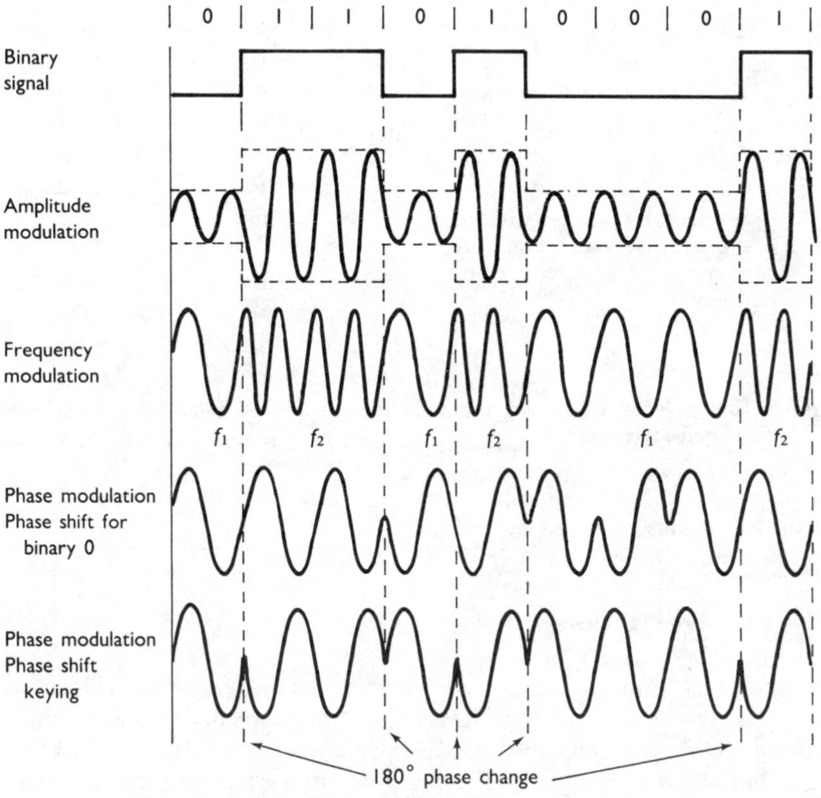

Figure 6.8 Modulation methods

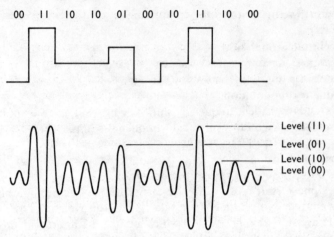

Figure 6.9 Four-level amplitude modulation for dibit transmission

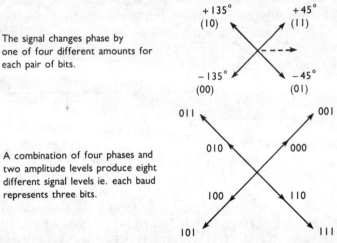

Figure 6.10 Combined phase and amplitude modulation called quadrature amplitude modulation (QAM)

combinations of these techniques which result in more than 1 bit per baud, as shown in Figs. 6.9 and 6.10.

6.5 Synchronization

Bit synchronization involves determining the start and end of individual bits and is a function of the physical layer as it is closely related to the signalling method. Byte synchronization involves determining the start and end of the group of bits forming a byte or character. In parallel transmission, both bit and character synchronization are achieved by the clock line, which indicates when all the bits comprising a character are simultaneously available.

The modems used for analog transmission usually generate bit-clocking signals and so are responsible for bit synchronization. For baseband transmission the digital information is encoded so that there is always a signal transition for each bit transmitted, e.g. using phase encoding (see next chapter).

There are two methods for achieving character synchronization – asynchronous (start/stop) or synchronous transmission.

6.5.1 Asynchronous (Start/Stop) Transmission

Individual characters or bytes are transmitted with variable time intervals between them. It is generally used for traffic to or from terminals which because of human interaction generate characters in short bursts. The availability of these cheap interfaces on most computers has resulted in their use for communication between computers.

The unit of information over which synchronization is achieved is a single byte and asynchronous transmission achieves both bit and byte synchronization. A character is transmitted as a serial group of bits with variable intervals between characters. The receiver must know the bit transmission rate so that it can sample the incoming signal at regular intervals to determine whether it is receiving a 1 or 0. The sample rate is usually 16 × bit rate.

A character is framed by a 'start' (space or 0) and 'stop' element (mark or 1) as shown in Fig. 6.11. This guarantees a transition even if all 1s characters are transmitted as a block with no idle intervals. When the receiver detects a polarity transition from an idle (stop) state, due to a start element, it begins sampling the line at regular intervals, assembling the bits of the character. The stop element has a certain minimum length, usually 1.5 or 2 bits, but no maximum length as there is no fixed interval between characters.

Characters must be fixed length, but there is no limit on the size of a block of characters because the local clock in the receiver which controls the sampling rate is resynchronized for each character. Even if it is slightly faster or slower than the transmitter, it is unlikely to drift enough to cause an error

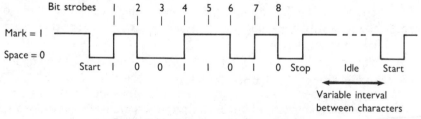

Figure 6.11 Asynchronous transmission

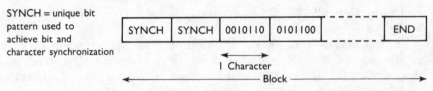

SYNCH = unique bit pattern used to achieve bit and character synchronization

Figure 6.12 Synchronous transmission

within one character time. The start and stop bits reduce the available bandwidth for information transfer. The maximum asynchronous transmission rate is usually less than 19.2 k.bits/s.

6.5.2 Synchronous Transmission

This achieves byte and block synchronization over a whole block of characters (see Fig. 6.12). A constant rate clock (usully within the modem) determines the exact time interval at which bits are transmitted and received. Thus stop and start bits are not required. The receive clock is synchronized with the transmit clock either by means of a separate clock line (very rare) or transitions of the line signal are used to correct a local receive clock. There must be sufficient changes in the line state to enable bit synchronization to be maintained and so special techniques may be required to prevent long sequences of 1s or 0s.

Special synchronization characters (synch) are transmitted at the start of the block (frame) to allow the receiver to determine character boundaries. Characters within a block are received at regular intervals and the receiver relies on a very accurate local clock to maintain byte synchronization, but it cannot be maintained indefinitely. Synch characters must be transmitted at set time intervals, or else in between frames. The latter implies that the frames are then limited in length. The synch characters are removed from the frames by the receiver. Obviously these synch characters must be prevented from occurring in the data. Block synchronization and methods of achieving transparency are discussed in more detail in Chapter 8.

Synchronous transmission is more efficient than asynchronous as it does not require start and stop bits. The fact that the unit of transmission and synchronization is a block implies the network stations must have adequate buffering to hold a block. Also if synchronization is lost, the whole block must be retransmitted. Synchronous transmission is used for higher data rates and for traffic between computers over both LANs and WANs. With the advent of suitable LSI circuits it is becoming the predominant form of transmission as it is more suited to message type traffic rather than traffic generated by terminals.

6.6 Multiplexing and Concentration

Multiplexors and concentrators allow a physical circuit (two wires) to be shared simultaneously by a number of users.

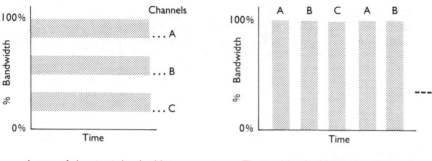

A part of the circuit bandwidth is assigned to each channel all the time.

The total bandwidth is assigned to each channel at regular intervals. The channel assignment time interval could correspond to a character or block of data.

Figure 6.13 Multiplexing: (a) frequency-division multiplexing; (b) time-division multiplexing

Multiplexing

A circuit is statically divided into a number of frequency or time slots to form a number of channels. Each channel is assigned to a particular user, who thus has a guaranteed share of the circuit capacity. If a channel is idle, it is not available for use by the other users.

The two most common techniques are frequency-division (FDM) and time-division multiplexing (TDM) as shown in Fig. 6.13.

Concentration

The channels are shared amongst the users on a demand basis. Bandwidth is assigned to a user only when required. The aggregate input and output bit rates need not be matched in a concentrator, which implies a traffic smoothing effect. The concentrator, which is often an intelligent device such as a packet-switching node, generally provides buffers to smooth input bursts.

A concentrator which connects a number of unintelligent terminals to a packet-switched network is called a Packet Assembler Disassembler (PAD). These are discussed in Chapter 12.

References

Bertine, H.V., 'Physical level protocols' *IEEE Trans. Comms. Com.*, Vol. 28, no. 4, April 1980, pp. 433–444.

Davies, D.W., Barber, D.L., *Communication Networks for Computers*, Wiley, 1973.

Halsall, F., *Introduction to Data Communications and Computer Networks*, Addison-Wesley, 1985.

National Computing Centre, *Handbook of Data Communication*, NCC Publications 1982.

Stallings, W., *Data and Computer Communications*, Macmillan 1985.
Tanenbaum, A.S., *Computer Networks*, Prentice-Hall, 1981.
Taylor, D., Oster, D., Green, L., 'VLSI node processor architecture for Ethernet',
    IEEE Journal on Selected Areas in Comms. SAC, Vol. 1, no. 5, November 1983,
    pp. 733–739.

Seven

LOCAL AREA NETWORKS
Data Link Medium Access Sublayer

7.1 LAN Layers

A data link is a communication path with no intermediate store-and-forward nodes but the path may include signal regenerators, i.e. it is not necessarily a single transmission medium. Thus a serial bus, ring or point-to-point channel would all be data links. The data-link layer is concerned both with controlling access to a shared communication path and the protocols for communication between two stations which are directly connected by a communication path. In LANs these two functions are separated into two sublayers – medium access and logical link control. This division has been reflected in this book by splitting the discussion on the data-link layer into two chapters.

Most of the standarization work on LANs has taken place within the IEEE 802 committee [IEEE Project, 1983]. They have defined a family of standards (see Fig. 7.1) for various ring and bus LANs. There is a separate standard for each type of access control which also covers aspects which are normally considered part of the physical layer. The logical-link sublayer is concerned with protocol issues such as error and flow control between a pair of stations and is independent of the type of medium access control. Note that the IEEE 802.1 standard covers both network architecture and internetworking. Figure 7.1 also shows the relationship of the IEEE sublayers to the ISO reference model.

In this chapter we first cover medium-access mechanisms for rings and then those applicable to serial buses. WANs often use full duplex point-to-point channels, so no mechanisms for sharing are needed. However, multidrop links are sometimes used to connect remote terminals to a central computer.

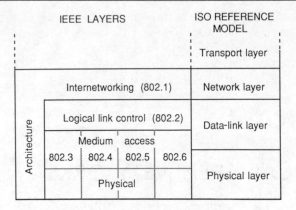

802.3 = Carrier sense multiple access bus with collision detection
802.4 = Token passing bus
802.5 = Token passing ring
802.6 = Metropolitan area network on a broadband bus

Figure 7.1 Relationship between IEEE LAN family and the ISO model

Polling techniques are then used to control access to the shared data link
and the polling messages are defined as part of the logical link control (i.e.
within the data-link layer). Polling will not be discussed in this book as it
is well described in the literature. Further information on LANs can be found
in [Stalling, 1984; IEEE Journal, 1983; Halsall, 1985; IEEE Project, 1983].

7.2   Token Ring

Token passing rings are very popular in proprietary LANs, as they cater for
variable-length messages and can be adapted to allow priority-based access.
Prime and Appollo both market token passing rings as a basis for interconnecting their own machines. IBM appears committed to this type of ring for
their long-term LAN technology. The following description is based on the
IEEE 802.5 token ring.

A token circulates round the ring giving the stations permission to transmit.
Only one station on the ring (the token holder) can be transmitting at any
time. A station can only transmit a message when it receives a token marked
'free'. It changes the token to 'busy' and transmits its message immediately
following the busy token. If the station did not have a message to transmit
it would pass on the free token. The destination station recognizes its address and copies the contents of the message. It also sets response bits (see
below) as the message goes past. The transmitted message circulates round
the ring and is removed by the source. It generates a new 'free token' when
it has completed transmission of its message and after it has received the busy
token which has circulated round the ring (see Fig. 7.2). If the sender receives
a message with a source address other than its own, then more than one free

token must be circulating, so the transmitter does not generate a free token after its message. Each station requires a 1-bit delay in the ring interface to allow it to change bits as they pass by.

When a station transmits a free token, the next station downstream has an opportunity to seize the token and transmit a message. Thus in heavy load conditions, access to the ring is scheduled 'round robin'. Knowing the maximum message length it is possible to calculate maximum delay for access to the ring.

The source station receives and removes its own message and so the message can contain a response from the destination. This allows the sender to determine whether the destination is active or inactive; busy (message not copied);

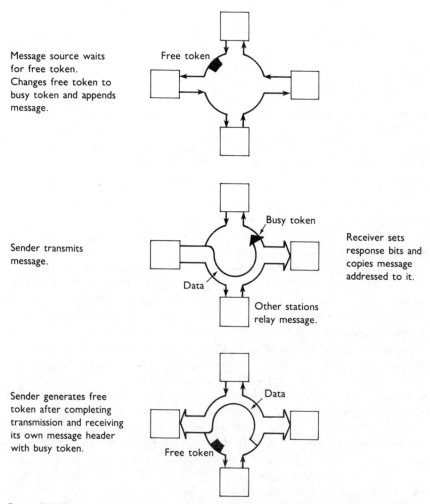

Figure 7.2 Token ring. Based on Figure 5 in Strole [1983]. Copyright 1983 by International Business Machines Corporation; reprinted with permission

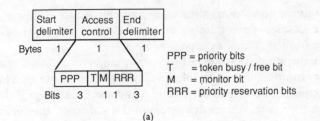

PPP = priority bits
T   = token busy / free bit
M   = monitor bit
RRR = priority reservation bits

(a)

Start Delimiter	Access control	Frame control	Destination address	Source address	Data	FCS	End delimiter	Response bits
Bytes 1	1	1	6	6		4	1	1

Start delimiter: start of message delimiter.
Access control: see token format above.
Frame control: message type - used for token management etc.
Destination address: address of destination station - can specify:
  an individual station,
  broadcast to all stations,
  multicast to a group of stations.
Source address: address of source station.
Data: variable length data field.
FCS: frame check sequence (32-bit cyclic redundancy check).
End delimiter: end of message delimiter - contains a bit field to indicate an error detected by a station.
Response bits: indicate whether address recognized and message copied.

(b)

Figure 7.3 Token ring message formats: (a) token format; (b) data message format

message received correctly; or an error was detected by any station round
the ring.

The token contains a priority indicator. A station with a high-priority
message to transmit can insert its priority level in a busy token. When the
sender generates a free token, this will be at the high-priority level. A station
with a lower-priority message cannot claim the free token and so it will circulate to a station with the high-priority message. When there are no more
messages to transmit, the priority of the token is lowered to its previous
priority by the station which raised the priority.

One station is designated as an active monitor and it is responsible for
detecting loss of the token or a continually circulating busy token. A lost
token is detected by means of a timeout, as the maximum time for a free token
to circulate round the ring is known. If the timeout expires, then the current
active monitor generates a new free token. This mechanism can also be used
to generate the initial free token at start up. The circulating busy token is
detected by the monitor setting a bit in the busy token message to one. If
the monitor sees a busy token with the bit set, it knows the message has
already been round the ring and was not removed correctly by the source.
This is recovered by changing the busy token to a free token. Any station

has the potential of becoming an active monitor. Different timeouts or a contention resolution algorithm can be used to prevent multiple stations assuming the role of active monitor.

The main disadvantage of the token ring is the complex token management required. Also a bypass mechanism is needed in the ring interface to cope with station power failure. The advantage of the token ring is that it caters for variable-length messages and has defined delays. Error reporting can easily isolate faults to a particular station or link between stations.

7.3 Slotted (Cambridge) Ring

Slotted rings based on a design developed at Cambridge University, are marketed by a number of companies in the UK. This description will be based on the Cambridge Ring 82 specification [Cambridge Ring, 1982]. A number of fixed-length (40-bit) slots circulate continuously round the ring. A header bit indicates whether the slot is full or empty. A station wishing to transmit waits for an empty slot, marks it full and inserts 16 bits of data as the slot goes by (Fig. 7.4). Figure 7.5 shows the slot format. The sender also inserts source and destination addresses in the slot. The receiver copies the data out and sets the response bits as described below. When the slot comes back to the source it is marked empty, so it can be used by the next station downstream. The sender is only allowed one slot in flight at a time. It counts passing slots to determine when the slot it transmitted returns and so each station must know the number of slots in the ring.

The receiver can set the ring interface to receive slots from any source, which would normally be the case for a server waiting for a request. Then the interface can be set to receive slots from a particular source to allow the multiple slots forming a single data-link layer message to be received, i.e. a form of connection. The receiver may be physically or logically absent from

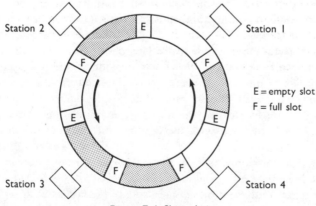

Figure 7.4 Slotted ring

BITS I	I	I	8	8	16	2	2	I
START = I	FULL/ EMPTY	MONITOR	DEST. ADDR.	SOURCE ADDR.	USER DATA	TYPE	RESPONSE	PARITY

START	Start of slot indictor (always I)
FULL/EMPTY	Set and cleared by source station
MONITOR	Used to detect lost full slots
DESTINATION	Address of destination station
SOURCE	Address of source station
USER DATA	16 bits of higher-level data
TYPE	Used to indicate start and end of variable-length blocks of user data
RESPONSE	Set by destination to indicate:
	Destination busy
	Source not selected
	Data copied into destination
	Destination station absent or powered off.
PARITY	Error detection

Figure 7.5 Cambridge Ring slot format

the ring and in this case the response bits will indicate that the slot has been ignored. The receiver can also generate a 'busy' response when unable to process the slot as fast as the transmitter tries to send them. A transmitter seeing the busy response sends the data again in a new slot as often as required. A slot that has been successfully received is marked as 'accepted'. The sender can check a returned slot against that transmitted to detect errors, in which case the response seen by the attached device is 'transmit error', overriding the response within the slot.

Whenever a sender receives a response other than 'accepted' it is not permitted to transmit immediately but must wait for a complete ring cycle. Second and subsequent unsuccessful transmission attempts cause the transmitter to be backed off for 15 ring cycles. This prevents the ring being swamped with useless traffic. Further, the delay is made traffic dependent by requiring that ring cycles are only counted for back-off purposes if they contain an empty slot. The round robin scheduling puts an upper limit on this delay while the variable back-off produces a system in which efficiency improves under load.

Each ring interface inserts a typically 3-bit delay. A central monitor inserts a variable-size shift register into the ring to provide 'padding' so that the ring always contains an integral number of slots (typically 2–4) and a small gap of a few bits to mark a complete cycle. The monitor detects a continuously circulating full slot by clearing the monitor bit (set by the source) in a full slot. If a full slot goes past with the monitor bit cleared then the slot can be marked empty.

The data transmission rate is 10 M.bits/s over twisted-pair cables. Each station has an active repeater which is powered by the cable and so is independent of whether the station is operational. Two pairs of wires are used and the cable transmits data, clock and 50 V d.c. power. It is possible to have redundant power supplies on the ring. Phase modulation is used for signalling as shown in Fig. 7.6.

In addition to the error detection used by transmitters, facilities are included to continually monitor the entire system. Every slot includes a parity bit that is checked and maintained by all stations. A station that detects a parity fault corrects it and also sends a fault message in the next empty slot to destination zero (an error logger station). The fault message contains the address of the sending station and so indicates the section of the ring where the fault occurred. The monitor is able to detect errors that interfere with the permanent slot structure and rapidly reinstate the correct structure in a non-destructive way. Large numbers of errors, perhaps caused by a power dip, cause the monitor to reinitialize the network, resetting its basic frequency. A monitor can also fill empty slots with random addresses and data as they pass and check them as they return if they are still marked empty. In this way the monitor keeps the performance of the ring under continuous surveillance and can give warning of incipient faults.

A station is only allowed to send one slot at a time and it must be passed on marked empty. In addition the immediately following one must be allowed to pass. Thus the maximum slot utilization that a transmitter can achieve is one in every $(n + 2)$ slots for an n-slot ring. Since there are 16 data bits in every 40-bit slot this determines the maximum point-to-point data transmission rate to be $4/(n + 2)$ M.bits/s. For a one slot ring the value is 1.3 M.bits/s. The round robin scheduling means that this rate can be achieved simultaneously by two pairs of communicating stations. Increasing the number of slots slightly decreases the point-to-point bandwidth but increases the number of pairs of stations that may simultaneously achieve the maximum rate. If $m > 1$ stations all wish to transmit simultaneously then each one is still guaranteed access to one in every $m + n$ slots (provided of course it is not backed off by a slow receiver). The bandwidth is effectively shared out with each station achieving at least $4/(m + n)$ M.bits/s unless limited by the maximum value.

The main advantage of the Cambridge Ring is that it can be very simple and gives guaranteed response times and throughput. However the efficiency is low due to the address overheads on each slot, and fragmentation of messages into 16-bit slots is needed. Also it does not allow for broadcast communication as some receivers may be set to receive from particular sources.

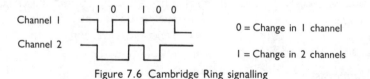

Figure 7.6 Cambridge Ring signalling

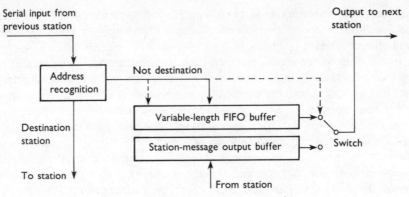

Figure 7.7 Buffer-insertion ring interface

7.4 Buffer Insertion Ring

Most of the work on buffer insertion rings has been performed at Ohio State University [Liu, 1978, Wolf, 1981]. Serial Camac also uses a form of insertion, as does the SILK ring produced by Hasler in Switzerland [Huber, 1983].

A station with nothing to transmit normally relays anything received. When it wishes to transmit its own message, it 'breaks' the ring and inserts a delay buffer to hold any incoming messages while transmitting. The delay buffer can only be inserted at the end of a message or when the ring is idle. As soon as the station finishes transmitting its own message it switches to transmitting from the delay buffer. The inserted buffer can be emptied and removed from the ring when there is a message gap (see Fig. 7.7).

This type of ring allows variable length messages and can have multiple stations transmitting simultaneously. The access time is thus very fast but the propagation time can be rather long if all stations have their buffers inserted. The destination can remove messages or allow them to circulate back to the source. An active monitor detects and removes lost packets from the ring to prevent them for circulating indefinitely. It uses a monitor bit similar to the mechanisms already described for the other rings.

7.5 Carrier Sense Multiple Access (CSMA) Buses

A station wishing to transmit listens to the transmission channel to detect if any other station is transmitting. This usually involves sensing for the presence of a 'carrier' signal. If the channel is idle the station may transmit. Otherwise, the station has to wait for some period of time before trying again. There are three types of algorithm to determine the action of a station when it finds the channel busy:

1. **Nonpersistent**
   The station waits a random time before sensing the channel again. Two

stations waiting to transmit when the medium is busy are likely to back off for varying times and hence avoid a collision. However there is likely to be some wasted idle time after the end of a transmission.

2. **1-Persistent**

The station continues to sense the medium until it is idle, then it transmits. This attempts to reduce the idle time because a station can transmit as soon as the channel goes idle after the end of a transmission. Unfortunately if more than one station is waiting to transmit, there will be a collision with multiple messages being transmitted simultaneously.

3. ***p*-Persistent**

The station continues to sense the channel until it is idle, then it transmits with a probability p. With probability $1 - p$ it waits for a fixed time, then senses the channel again, i.e. repeats the procedure. This is a compromise that attempts to minimize both idle time and collisions.

The problem with all these algorithms is that they do not completely prevent collisions. There is a probability that two stations will detect an idle channel and start transmitting simultaneously. Some systems such as the Corvus Omninet use error-detection mechanisms to detect collisions. The receiver sends an acknowledgement if no collision was detected. In Omninet a waiting station has to delay for a fixed period after the channel becomes idle, before sensing again to give time for an acknowledgement to be transmitted by the receiver. If a collision does occur, the channel is wasted during the time that the colliding messages are being transmitted. Some systems (such as Ethernet described below) detect collisions immediately by monitoring the channel while transmitting and abort the transmission when a collision is detected.

7.6 Ethernet–CSMA/CD Serial Bus

Ethernet is a serial bus LAN developed by Xerox which is now being promoted by Digital, Intel and Xerox [Xerox 80]. It is the basis of the IEEE 802.3 LAN standard, which is being standardized by ISO. Licenses to build Ethernet-compatible products are available for a nominal fee from Xerox. The Ethernet was aimed at office-automation and resource-sharing applications rather than industrial ones. It is named after the historical 'luminiferous ether' through which electromagnetic radiations were alleged to propagate. It uses a coaxial cable with baseband signalling and a data rate of 10 M.bits/s. It can be used to interconnect up to 1024 stations over a maximum distance of 2.5 km. The service provided is a datagram or 'best efforts' delivery. A cyclic redundancy check is used to detect errors and a message may be discarded, so higher layers (above the data-link layer) must be used to provide error recovery.

Although the Ethernet is essentially a broadcast bus, using coaxial cable as a transmission medium, it is possible to have branches off the bus (see

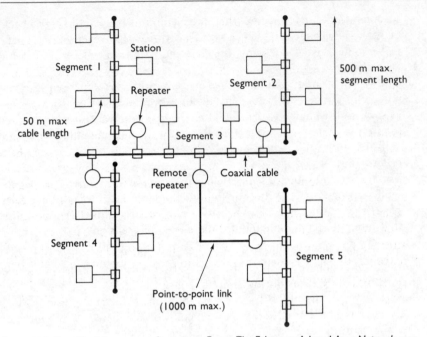

Figure 7.8 Possible Ethernet configuration. From *The Ethernet: A Local Area Network*, version 1.0, Sept. 30th, 1980.

Fig. 7.8). The connection to a branch is via a repeater which does not have any store-and-forward action. There must be only one path between any source and destination so that a signal does not arrive at a destination via paths of different length, as this would result in interference. Thus the Ethernet could be considered as an 'unrooted tree', i.e. the signals propagate over all branches of the tree and the branches cannot be used independently. Using coaxial cable it is possible to tap into the Ethernet at any convenient location. The Ethernet principles could be applied to other transmission mediums, e.g. radio.

Control of access to the transmission medium is completely distributed amongst all stations and is based on 1-persistent CSMA with collision detection. It makes use of the following mechanisms.

Carrier sense: The baseband signalling technique uses phase encoding (Fig. 7.9) which guarantees a signal transition during each bit time and is similar to a carrier signal. Bit clocking can also be derived from these signal transitions. A station, wishing to transmit a message, first listens for the carrier and **defers** transmission until the bus is quiet.

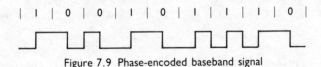

Figure 7.9 Phase-encoded baseband signal

Collision detection: It is possible that two or more stations will find the bus free and so start transmitting simultaneously, i.e. a collision may occur. The station's transceiver receives the signal from the transmission medium while transmitting and compares the received data with that just transmitted. Thus if a collision has occurred the received data will be in error and so the transmission is aborted. This can also be used to detect noise errors without waiting for acknowledgement. When a transmitting station detects interference it momentarily transmits a jamming signal to ensure that all other colliding stations detect the collision and abort their transmission. If this did not happen, two adjacent stations may detect a collision and stop transmitting before their signal had time to propagate to a distant station. The distant station would not detect interference even though the signal received by the destination was corrupted. The **collision window or slot** is the maximum time during which a collision can occur after the line goes quiet. In the worst case, for stations at opposite ends of the bus this time is twice the maximum propagation time (450 bits) plus the signal jamming time (48 bits), i.e. slot time is defined as 512 bit times (51 μs). After detecting interference the colliding stations stop transmitting and timeout for varying (random) periods before trying again.

Exponential back-off: The timeout intervals are multiples of a slot. The algorithm used to calculate the timeout interval uses a random time period which is biased by a count of the number of collisions which have occurred and is seeded with the station address to make sure the algorithms in two stations do not get synchronized. Thus as the Ethernet becomes heavily loaded and collisions occur more frequently the timeout intervals increase. A station must still defer to existing transmissions after the timeout interval. After 16 collisions a station reports an error.

Wait time is random in the range 0 to 2^k slots (45 μs to 45 ms) where k is the number of retries (up to a maximum value of 10).

The format of an Ethernet message is shown in Fig. 7.10. The addresses are defined to be 48 bits so that every Ethernet station will have a unique address which is built into the hardware. Address ranges are assigned by Xerox as part of the licence. Thus a portable workstation could plug into any Ethernet and there would be no possibility of address clashes. Broadcast of a message to all stations and multicast to a group of stations is supported. The type field is reserved for use by higher-level protocols. The preamble is a bit pattern used to synchronize a phase-locked loop in the receiver to give character synchronization. Note that the minimum message size is equivalent to the number of bits transmitted in a slot (512 bits)

PREAMBLE	DEST. ADDR.	SOURCE ADDR.	TYPE	USER DATA	FCS
Bytes: 8	6	6	2	46–1500	4

Figure 7.10 Ethernet packet format

excluding the preamble. The IEEE 802.3 specification defines a slightly different message format. Addresses can be either 16 or 48 bits and a 16-bit length of message field replaces the type field.

The ethernet is very efficient in that the utilization can be between 80% and 95% of the channel capacity, depending on average message length. However, it should not be loaded above 50% as delays increase. Measurements have shown that channel capacity is equally shared by all stations but the probabilistic nature of the operation means that it is not possible to guarantee a finite delay on a particular message as can be done with rings and token buses, when errors are ignored. Errors make the performance of all communication systems probabilistic. When lightly loaded, the probability of collisions becomes comparable to the probability of noise errors. Because the access control mechanism is very fast the probability of transferring a message with a given delay is comparable with, if not better than, most other access mechanisms.

Because the minimum message length is defined by the slot time, CSMA/CD is impractical for very high-speed buses (710 M.bits/s). The requirement to listen while transmitting makes the design of the transceiver rather critical and requires the use of expensive high-quality coaxial cable.

7.7 Token-passing Serial Bus

The IEEE 802.4 standard for a token-passing bus has also been adopted as the preferred media access method for General Motors' Manufacturing Automation Protocol (MAP). The token bus has the advantages of a passive bus but gives deterministic access times for real-time applications.

The stations connected to the bus form a logical ring. The station possessing the token controls access to the channel. The token is passed in an ordered sequence around the stations connected to the bus. Each station has to maintain information on its predecessor and successor in the sequence. Unlike a token ring, the sequence of the stations is independent of their physical position on the bus.

The token holder may transmit messages or request responses from other stations, i.e. it acts as a master station for the time it holds the token. When the station has finished or its time has expired, it passes the token to the next station in the sequence by means of a token transfer control message. The token bus priority message scheme is similar to that of a token ring.

Token management includes the following functions:

Addition to ring: New stations must periodically be given the opportunity to enter the logical ring. A token holder periodically generates a 'solicit successor' message inviting stations with an address between itself and its successor to request entrance. The token holder waits for a period of time equal to the response window (at least twice the end-to-end propagation delay). If there is no request, the token is passed to the successor as usual. If there is one request, the token holder sets the new station as its successor and passes it the token. If more than one station requests access to the ring, then the requests will collide and be garbled. In that case the token holder transmits a 'resolve-contention' message and waits for four response windows. The colliding stations use the first two bits of their address to identify the response window in which to request access. However, if the new station hears anything before its window comes up it does not transmit. If a collision occurs again the colliding stations go through another contention resolution phase based on their second two address bits. This continues until one valid request gets through, or a maximum retry count is exceeded.

Deletion from ring: The station wishing to leave the logical ring sends a 'set-successor' message (containing its successor) to its predecessor when it gets the token. The predecessor changes its successor accordingly.

Duplicate tokens: If a token holder hears another station transmitting it discards its token and reverts to listener mode.

Failed successor: When the token is passed to the successor it must transmit within the response window. The token holder will make another attempt to pass the token before sending a 'who follows?' message to find the successor to the failed station. The token holder should get a 'set-successor' response. It adjusts its successor information and passes on the token. This is repeated one more time and then the token holder generates an 'any successor?' message to try to get any other station as a successor. If it gets no response it assumes it is isolated and reverts to listener mode.

Ring initialization: This occurs at start-up or after a lost token when one or more stations detect no activity for a specified period. When a station's inactivity timeout expires it issues a 'claim token' message and contention is resolved using addresses and response windows as described previously.

The token passing bus has very complex token management, and the performance is worse than CSMA/CD for light loads. However, it is superior in performance under heavy loads. If there are no errors, it is possible to put an upper bound on the delay for a particular message. The bus can be longer than that for CSMA/CD as there is no need to listen while transmitting, and so the electrical constraints are less severe. This allows the use of cheaper cables, and token passing can be used for very high-speed buses (> 50 M.bits/s).

7.8 Broadband Bus

Broadband LANs use radio frequency (e.g. 5–300 MHz) modulation and so can use cable TV components. These allow splitting and joining operations so broadband topologies include both buses and trees. A number of

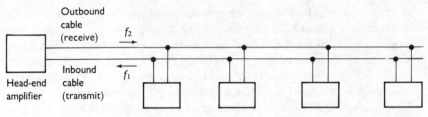

Figure 7.11 Twin-cable broadband LAN

manufacturers offer Broadband LANs, e.g. IBM's PC-net, Wang's network. Broadband is suitable for distances of tens of kilometers if amplifiers are used and so this is the basis of the IEEE 802.6 Metropolitan Network. A metropolitan network could connect tens of thousands of subscribers within a city [Mcgarty, 1983].

The bus taps and amplifiers tend to be unidirectional, so only a station 'downstream' from the transmitter will receive the signal. Two channels are needed with a 'head-end' repeater linking the two. A station transmits on an 'inbound' channel. The signal is received by the head-end which retransmits the signal on the 'outbound' channel. All stations listen to the outbound channel, i.e. it is a broadcast network. The two channels can be implemented by two separate cables, in which case the head end is merely an amplifier joining the two cables (Fig. 7.11). Stations send and receive at the same frequency, but twice as much cable is needed and each station must have two taps onto the cable. Alternatively a single cable can be used, with the two channels being provided by different frequency bands (typically 5–116 MHz and 168–300 MHz). The head end must then act as a frequency converter as it transmits the signals received on the inbound frequency band on the outbound frequency band (see Fig. 7.12). Special bidirectional amplifiers are needed to amplify the channel in each direction. Each station only needs a single tap onto the cable but the radio-frequency modems needed are more complex and hence expensive.

The wide bandwidth of the channels is often further subdivided by frequency-division multiplexing into a number of narrower channels so a single cable can carry voice and video as well as data. There could be one or two high-data-rate (10 M.bit/s) channels allocated by CSMA/CD techniques as well as many lower-data-rate channels (64 k.bits/s or 9.6 k.bits/s) which are allocated permanently or by a controller on a per session basis. A station

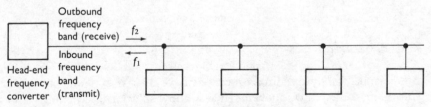

Figure 7.12 Single-cable broad-band LAN

wishing to establish a session sends a request to the controller on a predefined control channel. The controller allocates a channel and tells the destination (using the control channel) to tune to the allocated channel. Rather expensive frequency-agile modems are needed for these multichannel systems, e.g. as in Wangnet.

The main advantage of the broadband network is its capability of mixing video, voice and data on a single cable and hence cutting the cost of laying separate cable networks. In addition the network can cover much greater distances than a baseband network. However, the cost of the physical interfaces is much greater, particularly if frequency-agile modems are needed.

7.9 Summary

One of the design choices in a distributed system is whether it should use a bus or ring LAN topology. The former is a passive transmission medium if no signal regenerators are used, so is inherently more reliable. However, maximum cable length is limited to about 1 km before signal regenerators are needed. Buses seldom use fiber-optic transmission media, as tapping into these is very difficult. A ring regenerates the signal at each interface so can traverse longer distances. Because the station interfaces are active, the ring must include mechanisms to cope with a station being switched off or failing, otherwise all communication over the ring will be prevented. It is easier to locate a fault on a ring as the station immediately 'downstream' will generate an error report. Locating a break in the transmission medium of a bus requires measuring the time it takes for reflections to be returned, so is more difficult.

The choice of access mechanism often depends on whether guaranteed access times are required. CSMA/CD as in Ethernet is the simplest widely available access mechanism which gives the lowest average delays for a lightly loaded LAN. However, the access for a particular message is probabilistic and it does not include any priority mechanisms. Token passing over a ring or bus has a longer average delay but it is deterministic under heavy load conditions, so is favored for real-time applications. Token passing can easily include priority. The token management needed for dealing with installation of new stations is very complex, making it more difficult to manufacture chips to support token passing. CSMA/CD is impractical for very high data rates (> 10 M.bits/s) as the minimum message length (data rate × slot time) is too large.

Both slotted and buffer insertion rings have simpler reconfiguration management than token-passing ones, but slotted rings only cater for fixed-length messages, which is not really appropriate for distributed systems. Buffer insertion rings cope with variable-length messages, but the propagation delay can become quite large if many stations have their buffers inserted.

Broadband LANs are more suited to longer distances and can be used for mixed media (data, voice and vision) networks. However, the modems needed can be quite expensive, particularly if they handle multiple frequencies. A broadband bus has a single failure point – the head-end which can halt all communication.

A more detailed performance comparison of LANs can be found in Stallings [1984]. Additional information on LANs can be found in Franta [1981], Dallas [1984], and Ravasio [1982].

References

Cambridge Ring 1982: Interface Specification, SERC Rutherford Lab., Didcot, OX11 0QX, UK.

Dallas, I., Spratt, B., (eds.), 'Ring technology local area networks', *Proc. IFIP WG 6.4 Workshop*, University of Kent, September, 1983, North-Holland, 1984.

Franta, W., Chlantac, I., *Local Networks*, Lexington Books, 1981.

Halsall, F., *Introduction to Data Communications and Computer Networks*, Addison-Wesley, 1985.

Huber, D., Steinlin, W., Wild, P., 'SILK: an implementation of a buffer insertion ring', in *IEEE Journal* [1983], pp. 766–775.

IEEE Journal on Selected Areas in Communications, Special Issue on Local Area Networks. SAC Vol. 1, no. 5, November, 1983.

IEEE Project 802 Local Area Network Standards, 1983, available from IEEE Press, 345 East 47th Street, New York, NY 10017, USA.

Liu, M., *Distributed Loop Computer Networks*, Advances in Computers, Vol. 17, Academic Press, 1978, pp. 163–221.

Mcgarty, T., Clancy, G., 'Cable based metro area networks', in IEEE Journal [1983], pp. 816–831.

Ravasio, P., Hopkins, G., Naffah, N., (eds), 'Local computer networks', *Proc. Symposium*, Florence, April 1982, North-Holland 1982.

Stallings, W., 'Local area networks', *ACM Computer Surveys*, Vol. 16, no. 1, March 1984, pp. 3–42.

Strole, N., 'A local communications network based on interconnected token-access rings: a tutorial'. *IBM J. of Research and Development*, Vol. 27, no. 5, September 1983, pp. 481–496.

Wolf, J., *A Distributed Double Loop Computer Network (DDLCN)*, UMI Research Press.

Xerox, Digital and Intel, 'The Ethernet, Version 1.0' September 1980, in *ACM Computer Comms. Review*, Vol. 11, no. 2, July 1981, pp. 17–65.

Eight

DATA LINK LAYER
Protocol Sublayer

The data-link layer is responsible for transferring messages (frames) across a physical channel (Fig. 8.1). It transforms an error-prone physical channel into a relatively error-free logical link. In WANs the data-link layer provides a connection service across point-to-point links and performs the functions and procedures necessary to establish, maintain and release these connections between network entities.

Within a store-and-forward network the data-link layer creates error-free paths between switching nodes. These point-to-point paths are used by the higher layers to create an end-to-end path. In a LAN the data link layer itself creates an end-to-end path between multiple stations. Data-link protocols are often used to directly interconnect two computer systems by a serial transmission line. The main functions performed by the data-link layer include message framing, addressing of the stations inter-connected by the data link, error and flow control on a point-to-point basis.

In this chapter, these functions will be related to typical data-link protocols such as ISO's Basic Mode and High-Level Data-Link Control (HDLC);. IBM's Binary Synchronous Communication (BSC) and Synchronous Data-Link Control; and Digital's Data Communication Message Protocol (DDCMP).

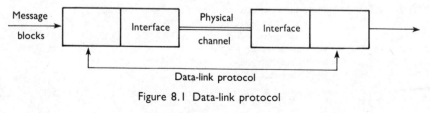

Figure 8.1 Data-link protocol

8.1 Message Framing

A data-link layer protocol data unit is commonly called a 'frame'. Message
framing or block synchronization is the process of locating the start and end
of the information block transmitted over the communication channel. This
is closely related to achieving data transparency. The protocol should allow
the transmission of arbitrary bit patterns (e.g. binary user data), and so this
must not be interpreted as protocol control information. Protocol control
information can either be 'positional', i.e. contained in the header field in
the first few bytes of the message (see Fig. 8.2) or it can be 'position independent', i.e. the protocol uses special control characters which must not occur
in the user data.

Reserved control codes

This method was used in some of the older character-oriented protocols e.g.
ISO's Basic Mode and IBM's BSC [Conrad, 1980]. These protocols were
designed for the transmission of printable text. Certain bit patterns within
the set of characters were reserved as control characters, but as these were
not printing characters, they would not normally occur in the user data.

Typical examples of control characters are:

SOH   (Start of header) – indicates the start of a header within a packet
or message.

ETB   (End of transmission block) – the end of message delimiter.

STX   (Start of text) – indicates the start of the user data field, i.e. text
rather than the header.

ACK   (Acknowledge) – the character used to acknowledge correct
receipt of a packet.

NAK   (Negative acknowledge) – the character transmitted by the
receiver to indicate that the received packet contained errors.

SYN   (Synchronous idle) – the character used to achieve character
synchronization in synchronous communication. It is also transmitted in the absence of any data, to maintain synchronization.

DLE   (Data link escape) – an escape character used to change the meaning of a limited number of contiguously following characters.

SYNC. PATTERN	START	HEADER	USER DATA	BLOCK CHECK	END

SYNC. PATTERN – The bit pattern used to achieve byte synchronization
START   – The start of message indicator
HEADER   – Protocol control information
USER DATA   – Next higher level information
BLOCK CHECK – Error detection and/or correction information
END   – End of message indicator

Figure 8.2 A typical data link frame

Message synchronization is achieved by searching for a number of SYN characters (typically 2–6) followed by an SOH character and the end of the message is indicated by the ETB character. When these protocols are used to transfer binary user data the control characters must be prevented from occurring within the text field. The binary data could either be coded into a hexadecimal format and mapped onto the allowed character set (i.e. 4 bits per character) or a transparent mode could be used. This involves inserting a DLE character before every occurrence of a control character in the text field. The DLE character is removed by the receiver. These methods are cumbersome and inefficient.

Bit insertion (bit stuffing)

This technique is used in bit-oriented protocols, e.g. IBM's SDLC, ISO's HDLC [Carlson, 1980]. A unique sequence of bits (01111110) is defined as a flag and is used as both the start and end message delimiter. The flag character is also used as a sync. character to achieve character synchronization, so it must be prevented from occurring elsewhere in the message.

Transmitter: after transmitting the flag, the bit stream is examined and a '0' bit is inserted after all sequences of 5 contiguous '1' bits.

Receiver: the incoming bit stream is examined and a '0' bit which follows 5 contiguous '1' bits is discarded. If 6 contiguous '1' bits are received, the bit pattern must be a flag or an error.

For example,	First bit								Last bit
Before bit insertion at the transmitter	0	1	1	1	1	1	0	1	0
After bit insertion at the transmitter	0	1	1	1	1	1	0 0	1	0
After bit removal at the receiver	0	1	1	1	1	1	0	1	0

This technique is very inefficient to implement in software, but LSI communication interfaces which perform bit insertion and deletion are available.

Length field

A field within the header contains the length of the message (usually in bytes). Once this length field has been obtained, the receiver can merely count bytes to determine the end of a message and hence the start of a new one if it follows on. This method is used in DEC's DDCMP. It has the advantage that it is not necessary to examine every character in the message looking for message delimiters and so is efficiently implemented in software. The length can also be useful for buffer allocation if variable-length packets are allowed. If the length field is corrupted or part of the message is lost the problem of recovering message synchronization still remains. Some form of start indicator is still required. The length field could be used together with bit insertion.

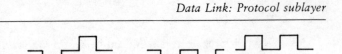

I bit   0 bit   Violations

Figure 8.3 Data and violation signals

Transmission signalling method

Many LANs achieve message synchronization at the physical layer using some form of signal violation technique to detect a start of message. A particular signal which cannot represent data is used to indicate start and end of a message. This allows message synchronization to be achieved in a single bit time and also accomplishes transparency. An example is shown in Fig. 8.3.

8.2 Addressing

Data-link layer addressing is concerned with identifying the source and destination station on a data link which interconnects multiple stations, e.g. multidrop line or LAN. Each message may contain explicit source and destination addresses, or the context of the message may identify by implication the source or destination or both. In a broadcast system, many stations share the same transmission medium. Some form of destination address is needed so that the recipient can identify that a particular message is destined for itself. If any station could have transmitted the message then it must explicitly carry the source address as well so that the recipient can identify where the message came from in order to return a reply or acknowledgement.

Implicit addressing: On a point-to-point line connecting two stations, any information transmitted by one station must be destined for the other, i.e. both source and destination are implicit and so no explicit station addresses are needed at the data-link level. The receiver might not be the final destination but it must still receive the whole message in order to keep it or forward it on. Station addressing is left to higher levels (usually network layer).
Preselection: Some buses use a form of preselection. For instance in the IEEE 488 parallel bus (also known as the Hewlett Packard bus), a controller preselects a source (called a talker) and a destination (called a listener). Then the source can send a defined number of messages to the destination. The messages need not contain any addresses, as no other stations can be active at the same time. This is a form of connection set up between talker and listener, by the controller.
Single master systems: Some multidrop lines have a single master and all communication takes place between the master and the slave stations. The slaves are not allowed to communicate directly with each other. Only a single address is required to identify the destination slave station when the master is transmitting and to identify the source when a slave is transmitting.

Multiple master: A system in which any station can transmit on its own volition requires both source and destination addresses to be explicit in every message. Most LANs fall into this category. An advantage of explicit addresses is that a single station can monitor the traffic and analyse it without keeping track of which station is currently master.

Multicast messages: Multicast addressing is a single message addressed to a group of stations. Broadcast is a special (and most common) case of multicast addressing, whereby a single message is addressed to all stations. Most LANs support broadcasting of messages to all stations. In a loop or highway this is easily done by having a special station address (e.g. all 1s) which is recognized by all stations.

Associative name lookup: In some LANs each station maintains a list of identifiers of current processes in a fast associative memory. This allows a very fast table lookup and is really a hardware implementation of logical to physical name mapping at the data-link level of the message destination. This allows dynamic assignment of processes to processors and the sender need not know where a particular process is currently running.

8.3   Error Control

Physical circuits provided by telecommunication authorities tend to have comparatively high error rates. It is the responsibility of the data-link layer to convert this to a relatively error-free logical link. This may entail both detection and correction of errors. LANs, however, often have lower error rates and so may perform only detection of information corruption at this level and leave error correction to higher levels.

8.3.1   Error Characteristics

Individual bits or groups of bits within a message are likely to be corrupted due to electrical noise, cross-talk, faulty electronic equipment, etc. Typical error rates for voice grade public lines are in the order of 1 bit in 10^3 to 10^6, but errors are more likely to occur in bursts than individual bits, as shown in Fig. 8.4. Information corruption mostly occurs on a transmission line as it is particularly susceptible to electromagnetic interference, but it can also occur in the memory of intermediate switching nodes or when transferring information across any physical interface within a computer system.

The error rate depends on:

- type of line – private cable, public switched or leased;
- transmission media;
- environment through which a line passes;
- time of day (for public lines);
- transmission rate.

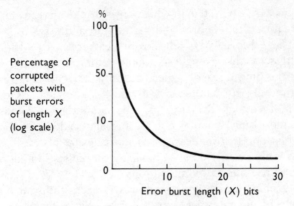

Figure 8.4 Error burst size distribution

The data-link layer does not perform any store-and-forward action and so, in the absence of errors, information will be delivered in the order in which it is transmitted. If a destination address is corrupted a message may not be received, and will be lost. An out-of-sequence message may result from a retransmission mechanism as discussed in Section 8.3.3.

8.3.2 Error-detection Techniques

The mechanisms used to detect corruption are based on including redundant information within a message which allows the receiver to detect errors. In the simplest case data is retransmitted several times and the received data is compared for equivalence. This can be extremely effective but the multiple retransmissions can reduce the throughput to a small fraction of the link's capacity. It can also be extended to provide correction by voting on the contents of an odd number of messages.

Parity check
If the number of 1s in a group of bits is even, the parity bit = 0 for even parity, and parity bit = 1 for odd parity. An extra parity bit is added to each character (vertical parity check) and a longitudinal parity check over corresponding bits of each character is performed by adding a block check character (BCC) at the end of the message as shown in Fig. 8.5.

This is capable of detecting all 1-, 2- and 3-bit errors, all odd number and some even number of bits in error. An even number of bit errors in the same rows and columns will not be detected (as marked with small crosses in the figure).

The percentage redundant information for n characters is $(n + 8)/7n \times 100\%$. For 128 character blocks this works out as 15% redundancy. Parity is used where the error rate is rather low, e.g. the Cambridge ring.

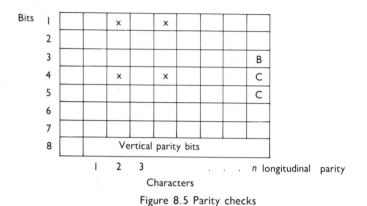

Figure 8.5 Parity checks

Cyclic redundancy check (CRC)

This is more efficient than parity in that it gives better error-detection capabilities with less redundancy. The transmitter treats a message as a binary number (or polynomial) which is divided, using modulo 2 arithmetic, by a suitable binary number (the generator polynomial). The remainder forms the check digits which are appended to the message. This is equivalent to adding in the remainder. At the receiver a similar division is performed using the same generator polynomial. If there are no errors in the incoming data, the remainder will be zero.

A 16-bit generator polynomial gives a 16-bit CRC code which is an overhead of only 1.6% in a 128-character message. A suitable r-bit polynomial gives the following error detection:

all single-bit errors
all 2-bit errors
all odd number of bits in error
all error bursts of less than $r + 1$ bits
$1 - (0.5)^{r-1}$ is the probability of detecting a burst of $r + 1$ bits
$1 - (0.5)^{r}$ is the probability of detecting a burst greater than $r + 1$ bits.

Thus for a 16-bit polynomial, the probability of an undetected error for bursts greater than 17 bits is 1.5×10^{-5}. Although the CRC checks are slow and expensive to perform by software, LSI communication interfaces are available to perform error detection based on CRCs. It is now the most commonly used system for detecting errors at the data-link level.

It should be noted that the bit-insertion framing mechanism, described earlier, can result in a less effective CRC in data-link protocols such as HDLC. A single-bit error can cause a bit pattern such as '1001001' to be corrupted to form a valid flag '1000001'. The bits preceding the flag could form a valid CRC and so a truncated message will be accepted as valid because HDLC does not have a length field. Although higher-level protocols are likely to detect this type of error it reduces the effectiveness of the data-link CRC by about a factor of 1000 [Funk, 1979].

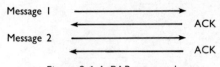

Figure 8.6 A PAR protocol

Loop check

A technique often used in rings is that the destination does not remove the information from the ring, but allows it to loop round to the source station. The source can then check that the received information is identical with that which was transmitted, and if not can retransmit. A similar technique is sometimes used on full duplex point-to-point lines. It has a number of disadvantages in that it reduces the data-link capacity by 50% and it is not possible for the sender to determine whether an error was caused on the outward or return journey.

8.3.3   Error-correction Techniques

It is possible to code the information using redundant bits so that errors can be corrected at the receiver. This is sometimes called **forward error correction**. It is difficult to design codes that are effective for both random and burst errors. The overheads of error-correcting codes are much greater than for error-detecting codes (up to 50%). This can be very wasteful if the error rate is rather low. Error-correcting codes are not as effective at detecting errors as pure error-detecting codes. The resultant undetected error rate is much higher – about 1 in 10^3. Forward error correction is used on high-bandwidth links with long propagation delays (e.g. via satellites).

Most networks, in which the propagation delay is not very long, use the method of detecting errors by CRC check and retransmitting those messages received in error, i.e. those for which no acknowledgement is received. These are called positive acknowledgement retransmit (PAR) protocols.

8.4   A Simple Data-link Protocol

In the PAR protocol, shown in Fig. 8.6, a message may be lost due to any of the following communication faults or errors:

- hardware automatically discarding messages with CRC errors;
- the destination failing or not being in the receiving mode;
- a communication line or communication interface failure;
- in a LAN system, if the destination address is corrupted and so not recognized, the message will not be received;
- insufficient buffer space resulting in the message being discarded by the receiver.

If a message is lost the destination will not send an acknowledgement

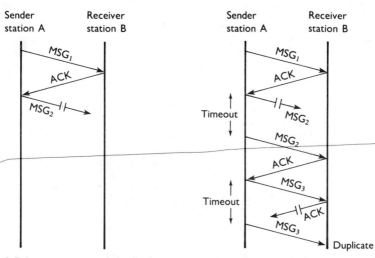

Figure 8.7 Lost message and deadlock

Figure 8.8 Timeout on Ack, but now get duplicate

(ack) and so the source will be deadlocked waiting for one (Fig. 8.7). This can be overcome by a limit on the period a source will wait for an acknowledgement before retransmitting, i.e. **timeout** (Fig. 8.8). Generally a station retransmits a message up to a retry limit (e.g. 3) before giving up and indicating a permanent error.

If an acknowledgement is lost, the transmitter will timeout and retransmit, which will lead to a duplicate message being received at the destination (Fig. 8.8). Message identifiers are needed to enable the receiver to detect

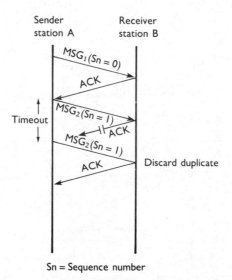

Sn = Sequence number

Figure 8.9 Sequence numbers detect duplicates

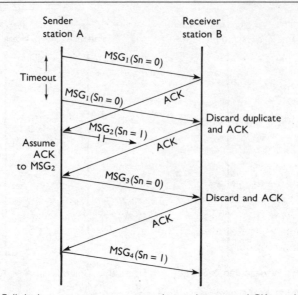

Figure 8.10 Full-duplex operation, no correlation between ACKs and data – lost messages

duplicates and discard them (Fig. 8.9). Duplicates arise not only from lost acknowledgements, but if the receiver is a bit slow and so the sender times out before the acknowledgement is sent. The receiver must always discard a duplicate but send an acknowledgement. The message identifier is usually a **sequence number**. The sequence number range must be necessarily finite, and so identifiers must be reused eventually. Most networks use a cyclic

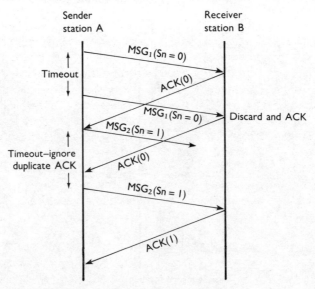

Figure 8.11 Numbered ACKs – complete protocol

number scheme $0 - N$, i.e. modulo $N + 1$. Figure 8.9 shows the use of a 1-bit, modulo 2 sequence number. If both sides can transmit simultaneously and the timeout is a bit short, the sender may accept an acknowledgement for the wrong message and a message could be lost without being detected (Fig. 8.10). It is thus necessary to identify acknowledgements so that they can be correlated with messages transmitted, i.e. acknowledgements should contain the sequence number of the message they are acknowledging (Fig. 8.11).

The timeout period will depend on the round-trip delay, i.e. the total time for a message to reach the destination, be processed and a reply be returned. This depends on transmission rate, packet length, distance between stations, etc. If the timeout period is set too low too many unnecessary retransmissions will take place, and if it is set too high the efficiency will be reduced. An approximate value for the timeout period could be $1 - 2$ times the average round-trip delay.

8.5 Protocol Performance Enhancements

The above protocol is simple, and complete, but a number of additional features are commonly found in data-link protocols to enhance performance.

Pipelining

More than one message is sent before an acknowledgement is received. This increases the throughput of the data link as it can cut down on waiting time and on message-synchronization time. A modulo N message sequence number will allow up to $N - 1$ unacknowledged messages to be outstanding. The number of unacknowledged messages which can be outstanding depends not only on the range of sequence numbers, but also on the buffer space available. All messages must be stored until acknowledged in case they have to be retransmitted. These systems generally allow a single acknowledgement to cover more than one message. For example if message 3 was the last one to be acknowledged and messages 4–7 are transmitted, the receiver can send an ACK for message 6 and at the same time acknowledge 4 and 5. If the sequence number received is less than that expected, it must be a duplicate and so it should be acknowledged and discarded. A received message with a sequence number above that expected is usually rejected but some protocols allow the destination to accept out of sequence messages.

Negative acknowledgement (NAK)

The efficiency of the protocol can be improved by using an explicit message to indicate an error has occurred. In many situations the NAK will be received by the transmitter before a timeout expires and so the retransmis-

sion can be speeded up. It is also useful for the NAK to indicate the reason
for the packet rejection, so that error statistics can be maintained. There are
some cases in which it is necessary to prevent transmission, e.g. there is no
buffer space, the packet is too long or it contains an unknown address, etc.
NAKs on their own are unable to give complete security as they do not
guard against complete loss of a message. They are used when the complete
loss of a message is unlikely, e.g. on a point-to-point line, or where the
probability of an error is very low. This reduces the overheads of sending
ACKs when very few packets are likely to have errors. Two NAK
mechanisms are frequently used:

1. **Pullback NAK**
   In this a NAK for packet *m* means any outstanding packets from *m*
   onwards must be transmitted, e.g. if a station has transmitted messages
   5–7 and a NAK is received for 5, then 5–7 must be retransmitted even
   if 6–7 did not contain errors. This is used in HDLC, X.25, DDCMP.
2. **Selective repeat**
   Only the particular packet which is rejected must be retransmitted. So
   if a NAK is received for packet 5 in the above example, then 6 and 7
   do not also have to be retransmitted. Selective repeats increase the complexity of both the transmitter and receiver, and so this may not be
   worth the slight increase in efficiency obtained.

Piggyback acknowledgements
In many applications there is a two-way flow of information and so the
efficiency of the link can be improved by combining ACKs (or NAKs) with
data messages. For instance station A sends station B a data message and
instead of B returning a special ACK, it is combined with a data message
waiting to go from B to A. This is particularly useful on full duplex paths.
If there is no data to be sent then an acknowledgement must be transmitted.
The message header must then contain two sequence numbers:

1. **Transmit number**
   This is the sequence number of the data message used by the receiver to
   detect any sequence errors.
2. **Response number**
   This is the sequence number of the message being acknowledged. It is
   usually the sequence number of the last correctly received message.

HDLC, DDCMP and SDLC all use protocols which incorporate the
above enhancements. These protocols all guarantee in-sequence message
delivery, without loss or duplication of messages. These are all connection-
oriented protocols and are commonly used in WANs. Many LANs use connectionless protocols which only detect errors and may discard messages,
but are much simpler to implement.

8.6 Protocol Synchronization

Loss of bit or character synchronization usually result in corruption of the data-link layer message and so can be detected by one of the error-detection techniques described previously. Loss of message synchronization could result in user data being interpreted as protocol control information, but should also be detected by the use of block checks. Whenever an error occurs the data-link layer should re-establish bit, character and message synchronization. This is particularly true for protocols which require a number of sync. characters for this type of synchronization. In LANs this type of synchronization is usually inherent in the receipt of a new data-link message.

No system is completely free from errors, which may occur in the hardware or software components of the system. The techniques described in the previous section are, in general, applicable to errors which can be corrected by retransmission or including redundant information. There are some error situations which may occur which cannot be recovered by the above methods. The only recovery technique available might be to reinitialize one or more protocol layers to a state of common agreement or to backtrack to the last known error-free state. Protocol synchronization involves the resetting of state information, e.g. sequence numbers, usually to zero. It may result in the loss of any outstanding messages. It is necessary in the following situations:

Station start-up: whenever a station is powered up it must initialize protocol state information and announce that it is available for communication with its neighbors.

Station failure: If a hardware or software failure has occurred in a station or switching node, resulting in the loss of protocol state information, the protocols will have to be resynchronized. Otherwise incoming messages will be rejected as being out of sequence as the receiver's sequence numbers will be invalid.

Errors detected at other levels: Although the levels within the communication system are meant to be completely independent, an error at one level may result in a reset at another level. If a higher layer detects an error in a lower layer it might request the lower layer to reinitialize.

Protocol control or supervisory messages which differ from the normal information transfer packets are required to implement initialization or resetting of a connection. These control messages should not be subject to the normal sequence checks as they may result in a sequence number reset. They should still be acknowledged so as to prevent loss. In some circumstances it does not matter if they are duplicated as they generally set the receiving station into a known state, e.g. initialized. A simple scheme which allows only 1 outstanding control message is usually adequate for the data-link layer.

8.7 Frame Length

The data-link message is generally both the unit of information for error control and for access to the transmission media. There are a number of conflicting requirements in the choice of a suitable length. The protocol control information (header and block check) is fixed for a given protocol and so the relative overheads of this information is decreased for long messages. An acknowledgement for a long message covers more information and so the proportion of the line capacity wasted on error control overheads is less. That is, long protocol data units increase data link layer efficiency but result in increased delays. A long message increases the access delay for a shared transmission medium and can increase store-and-forward delays as described previously. Buffers must be allocated to cater for the longest messages and so more buffer space is needed.

Typical data-link layer message sizes are 128–1000 bytes. Slotted rings and some time-division multiplexed highways have very short messages (2–4 bytes) and so usually segment a message into minipackets at the data-link level.

8.8 Flow Control

Data-link level flow control prevents overloading the capacity of a particular link, or the overflow of input buffers at the remote end. This may be inherent in the mechanism used to control access to a shared transmission media, as discussed in the Chapter on Medium Access. There are a number of techniques which directly control whether a station is allowed to transmit packets and how many can be transmitted.

Stop and go: The signals controlling the transmission are of a binary nature – 'stop or go'. It is used in most data-link control procedures (e.g. HDLC or BSC). The received signal takes effect immediately or at the earliest opportunity after the current transmission. The effects of transit delay must be taken into consideration in the use of stop and go signals and they are not suited to half-duplex links. On satellite links the propagation delay could be equivalent to the transmission time of several messages. Thus when a receiver sends a 'stop' signal many messages could be transmitted before the signal reaches the sender.

Rate: The sender transmits traffic at a predetermined rate which may be static or adjusted dynamically according to the availability of resources. Time-slot allocation schemes used in loops and some satellite links are examples of this technique.

The error-control mechanism may also have a side effect of throttling the flow of information. Transmission must stop when all unacknowledged messages have used the available sequence number range. A modulo N sequence number will allow $N - 1$ unacknowledged messages to be outstanding if the data-link layer does not accept out of sequence messages. If out-of-sequence messages will be accepted, then $N/2$ messages can be transmitted before waiting for an acknowledgement (see the next chapter for justification of this).

8.9 Protocol Supervisory Messages

Messages which do not carry data are known as protocol supervisory or control messages. The above sections have identified the need for the following types of data-link layer messages which are typically found in many protocols.

Connect – initializes the protocol layer and resets all station information.
Disconnect – used to close down a connection when there is not more information to transfer.
Data – used to transfer user data, so includes a sequence number.
Ack – acknowledges receipt of a data message.
Nack – rejection of a message.
Busy indication – used for flow control, e.g. to indicate a temporary lack of buffers.
Resume – resume transmission after a busy condition
Query – this could be of the form 'who are you?' or 'what is your state information?'. The latter may be used when a timeout occurs.
Mode change – used as a form of initialization command to set the station into a mode of operation.

A very simple protocol will only need the Connect, Disconnect, Data and Ack. All the other message types are enhancements. If there is any possibility of multiple commands arriving out of sequence, e.g. if the order of a 'stop', 'go' sequence is reversed, then the protocol-control messages must be sequence checked. In this case the sequence numbers used for supervisory messages should be different from those for transferring user information. If there can only be one outstanding protocol-control message at a time, as is common in data-link layer protocols, they need not be numbered, but the acknowledgements should indicate the type of protocol-control message received.

We have now covered the principles of framing, error and flow control for a data-link protocol and will examine how these are applied in Digital's Decnet and the IEEE LAN standards. Additional information on data-link protocols can be found in Halsall [1985], Tanenbaum [1981] and Bleazard [1982].

8.10   Case Studies

8.10.1   DDCMP

DEC's Digital Data Communication Message Protocol [Wecker, 1980] is a byte-oriented data-link control protocol which performs error correction by retransmission, and uses both positive and negative acknowledgements. It piggybacks acknowledgements and data and can be used on a variety of channels – serial or parallel, full or half duplex and with synchronous or asynchronous transmission. DDCMP can only be used on point-to-point lines or single master multipoint lines. No direct slave to slave communication is allowed on a multipoint line.

The format of the data messages which carry higher-level information is shown in Fig. 8.12, and that of the unnumbered supervisory or control messages which carry acknowledgements or connection set-up requests etc. is shown in Fig. 8.13.

The types of supervisory messages are:

ACK   – acknowledges correct receipt of a data message when there is no data to return. The data message sequence number is in the RESP field. SUBTYPE and NUM are not used.

NAK   – notifies the transmitter of an error at the receiver which may have resulted in the supervisory message or data message being rejected. SUBTYPE holds the reason for the error, e.g. header

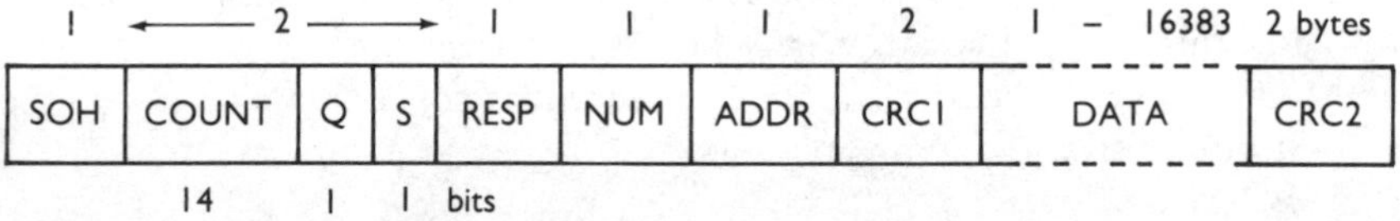

1	← 2 →	1	1	1	2	1	– 16383	2 bytes
SOH	COUNT	Q	S	RESP	NUM	ADDR	CRC1	DATA	CRC2

     14   1   1 bits

SOH   – Identifies the message as a data message (value = 129).
COUNT – The number of bytes in the data field.
Q   – Quick sync. flag, used to inform the receiver that the next message does not abut this one and so the receiver should resynchronize after this message.
S   – Select flag, used only in half-duplex and multipoint lines. It is set in the last message being transmitted by the sender and gives the receiver permission to start transmitting.
RESP   – Response number, used for piggybacking acknowledgements. It contains the sequence number of the last correctly received, in-sequence message and implies acknowledgement of all messages up to and including this number.
NUM   – The transmit sequence number.
ADDR   – The slave station address on multipoint links. It is not used on point-to-point links and is set to the value 1.
CRC1   – The header cyclic redundancy check on SOH through to ADDR.
DATA   – The data field containing between 1 and 16383 8-bit bytes.
CRC2   – The cyclic redundancy check on the data field.

Figure 8.12 DDCMP data frame format

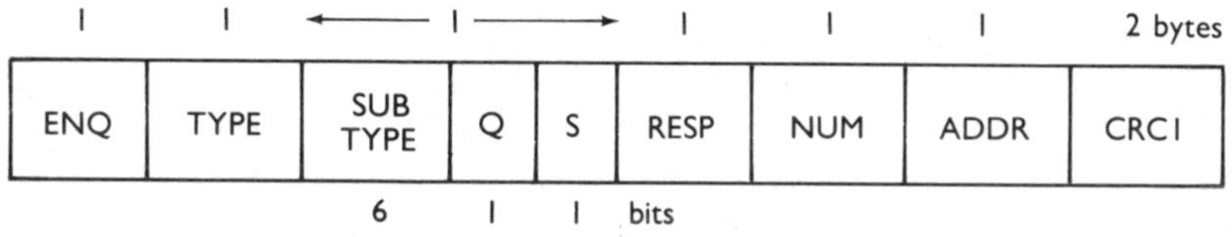

ENQ	TYPE	SUB TYPE	Q	S	RESP	NUM	ADDR	CRCI

6   bits

ENQ — Identifies supervisory messages.
TYPE — The type of supervisory message.
SUBTYPE — Provides additional information for some message types.
Q — Quick sync.⎫ as for data messages.
S — Select ⎬
RESP — Response field, holds the sequence number of the last correctly received, in-sequence message.
NUM — Number field, not used for most supervisory messages (NUM = 0)
ADDR — Slave address as for data messages.
CRCI — The CRC computed over ENQ through ADDR fields.

Figure 8.13 Supervisory message format

> CRC error, data CRC error, buffer temporarily unavailable, receiver overrun, message too long, header format error. A NAK message may also be sent in response to a REP (see below). The RESP field still acknowledges the last correctly received message.

REP — requests the status of the receiving station, and is usually sent after a timeout has occurred. The NUM field indicates the sequence number of the last message transmitted by the sender (i.e. the station which timed out). The response is either ACK or NAK, depending on whether or not all messages have been received.

STRT — This is used to set up a connection or for reinitialization. It resets all sequence numbers to zero, and clears any outstanding messages. Both RESP and NUM = 0.

STACK — This is returned in response to a STRT and indicates the station has initialized and reset sequence numbers.

The connection must be set up in both directions as shown in Fig. 8.14. For multipoint lines a connection must be set up between the master and each slave and the master maintains sequence numbers for each slave. Note that there is no disconnect message, and once set up a connection is expected to last indefinitely.

Data is transferred in numbered data messages starting with transmit sequence number 0, after start-up. Each subsequent data message increments the sequence number by 1. At the receiving station, the data message is checked for CRC errors. If there is an error a NAK message is transmitted, showing the last correctly received message and the reason for the error. The sequence number (NUM) of the received message is compared with expected sequence number. If less, it implies the message is a duplicate and so it is discarded but acknowledged. If greater it is an out-of-sequence message

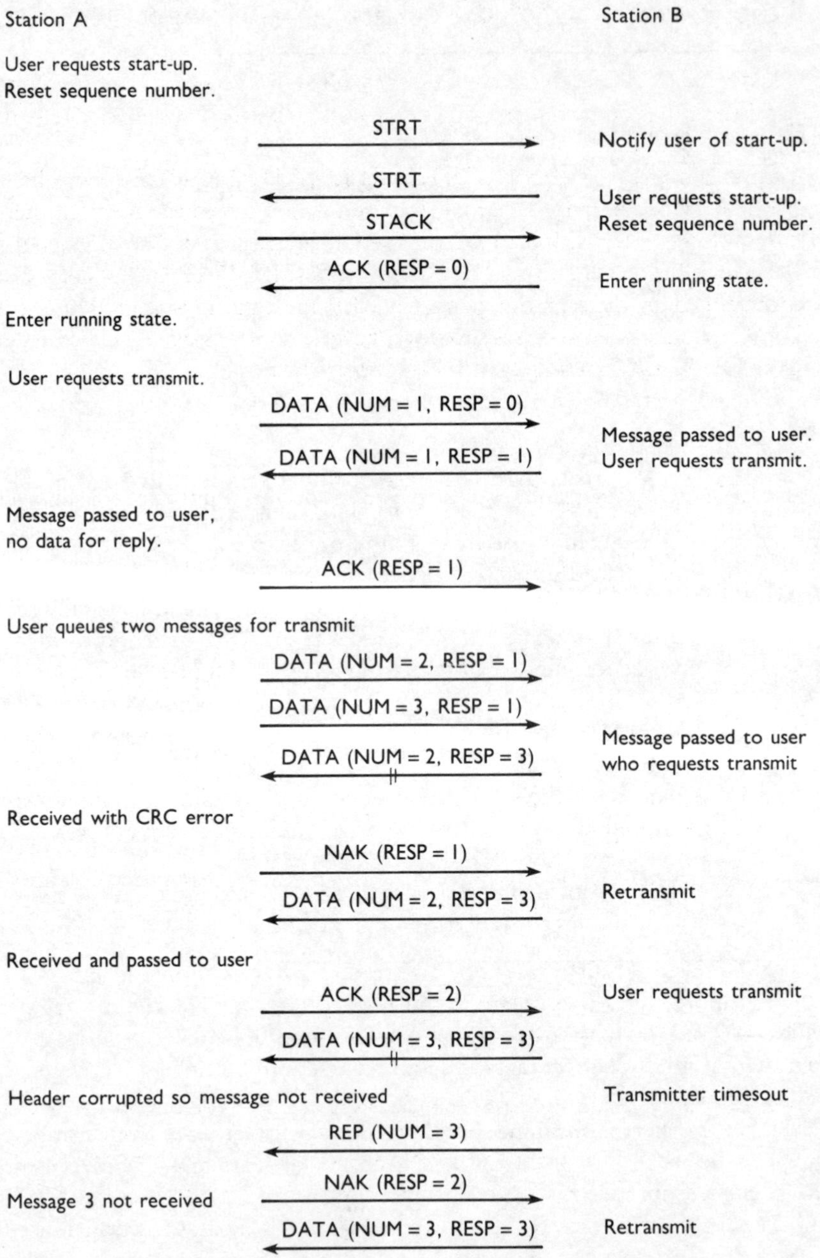

Station A   Station B

User requests start-up.
Reset sequence number.

                    STRT ──────────────▶   Notify user of start-up.

           ◀────────────── STRT
                    STACK ──────────────▶   User requests start-up.
                                                     Reset sequence number.

           ◀────────── ACK (RESP = 0)   Enter running state.

Enter running state.

User requests transmit.

                DATA (NUM = 1, RESP = 0) ──────────▶
           ◀────────── DATA (NUM = 1, RESP = 1)   Message passed to user.
                                                     User requests transmit.

Message passed to user,
no data for reply.

                    ACK (RESP = 1) ──────────────▶

User queues two messages for transmit

                DATA (NUM = 2, RESP = 1) ──────────▶
                DATA (NUM = 3, RESP = 1) ──────────▶
           ◀────────── DATA (NUM = 2, RESP = 3)   Message passed to user
                                                     who requests transmit

Received with CRC error

                    NAK (RESP = 1) ──────────────▶
           ◀────────── DATA (NUM = 2, RESP = 3)   Retransmit

Received and passed to user

                    ACK (RESP = 2) ──────────────▶   User requests transmit
           ◀────────── DATA (NUM = 3, RESP = 3)

Header corrupted so message not received   Transmitter timesout

           ◀────────── REP (NUM = 3)

Message 3 not received   NAK (RESP = 2) ──────────▶
           ◀────────── DATA (NUM = 3, RESP = 3)   Retransmit

Figure 8.14 Example of the use of DDCMP

indicating an error. If the sequence number is correct the message is passed to the user and the expected sequence number incremented. The message is acknowledged by an ACK or DATA message with RESP = received NUM. This may acknowledge multiple messages.

When a NAK is received all messages from RESP + 1 to the last one transmitted must be retransmitted, i.e. a pullback NAK acknowledgement method is used.

A timer is started whenever a STRT, STACK, DATA or REP message is transmitted. This may not be a real clock but rather keyed to selection intervals in multipoint links. If a STRT or STACK message is not acknowledged it is repeated up to a maximum of about 7 times. If a DATA message is not acknowledged in the timeout period a REP message is sent to request a response. The timer must be restarted whenever a new message is acknowledged if there are unacknowledged messages still waiting.

8.10.2 IEEE 802 Logical Link Control

The IEEE 802.2 LAN Standard [IEEE 1983] specifies a link-control sublayer which provides two types of service across a single LAN. There is a connectionless service which provides no acknowledgements but allows point-to-point, multicast or broadcast transfers. A point-to-point connection service provides error and flow control and is based on the HDLC protocol. It is similar in functionality to DDCMP in that it piggybacks acknowledgements with data and implements a 'pull-back' NAK type of error control. It differs from both HDLC and DDCMP in that it allows communication between any stations on the link rather than master–slave interaction.

The logical link sublayer can be used above different media access mechanisms, e.g. token bus, token ring or CSMA/CD.

Figure 8.15 shows the message format. Note that station addresses, CRC checks, length fields, etc. are all part of the media-access sublayer and so

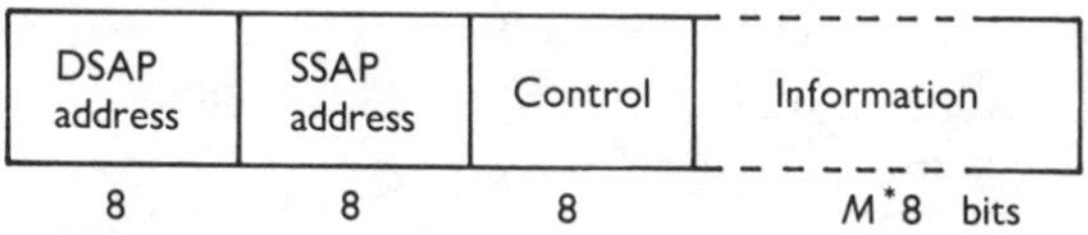

DSAP address	SSAP address	Control	Information
8	8	8	$M*8$ bits

DSAP   destination service access point address field. It is possible to specify a single, a group (multicast address) or all (broadcast) service access points within a station. It is not clear how multicast and broadcast addressing of service access points can be used, although it is obviously a useful feature at the station addressing level.

SSAP   source service access point address field from which the information field was initiated.

Control   this field specifies sequences numbers and types of messages (see below).

Information   variable length data field in multiples of 8-bit bytes.

Figure 8.15 IEEE 802 logical link control frame format

| 1 | 2 | 3 | 4 | 5 | 6 | 7 | 8 | bits |

| 0 | N(S) | P/F | N(R) |

N(S) – Transmit sequence number.
N(R) – Response sequence number, the number of the next expected information message.
It acknowledges receipt of messages up to N(R)–1.
P/F – Poll/final bit. It is used to solicit a response from the receiver. No other messages
will be sent on the connection after transmitting a message with the poll bit set. On
receipt of a message with a poll bit set, the link entity must return a message with
the final bit set.

Figure 8.16 Control field format

are not part of the logical link layer message. The addresses specify service
access points at the network/logical link interface within a station and would
typically be used to distinguish between different network layer protocols,
e.g. connection, connectionless or to address management entities. The
control field in an information message has the format shown in Fig. 8.16.

In addition to the information message there are the following supervisory
messages:

Receive Ready (RR) – used as an acknowledgement when there is no data
    to send and to indicate that the receiver is now ready after a temporary
    busy condition.
Receive Not Ready (RNR) – is used to indicate a busy condition, i.e. a
    temporary inability to receive information messages.
Reject (REJ) – requests the resending of information messages starting
    with N(R), i.e. a form of negative acknowledgement.
Set Asynchronous Balanced Mode (SABM) – initialize a connection. The
    receiver sets sequence numbers to zero.
Disconnect (DISC) – terminates a connection.
Unnumbered Acknowledgement (UA) – acknowledges receipt and
    acceptance of SABM or DISC commands.
Disconnected Mode (DM) – is used in report that a connection has not
    been set up to the addressed service access point.
Exchange Identification (XID) – is used to pass state information such as
    station class and window size.

There is also a Test message which is echoed back by the peer entity but
does not affect sequence numbers or state.

References

Bleazard, G., *Handbook of Data Communications,* NCC Publications, 1982.
Carlson, D., 'Bit-oriented data link control procedures', *IEEE Trans. Comms. COM,*
    Vol. 28, no. 4, April 1980, pp. 455–467.
Conrad, J., 'Character-oriented data link control protocols', *IEEE Trans. Comms.
    COM,* Vol. 28, no. 4, April 1980, pp. 445–454.

Funk, G., *Reliability and Efficiency in Various Standard Protocols*, EUROCOM, Venice, 1979.

Halsall, F., *Introduction to Data Communications and Computer Networks*, Addison-Wesley, 1985.

IEEE 802.2 Local Area Network Standards – Logical Link Control Procedures, 1983. Available from IEEE Press, 345 East 47th Street, New York, NY 100017, USA.

Tanenbaum, A., *Computer Networks*, Prentice-Hall, 1981.

Wecker, S., 'DNA: the digital network architecture', *IEEE Trans. Comms. COM*, Vol. 28, no. 4, April 1980, pp. 510–526.

Nine

NETWORK LAYER

9.1 Interconnected Networks and Gateways

There has been a proliferation of many types of both private and public networks – LANs, packet-switched WANs, circuit-switched, radio and satellite networks. As indicated in the example in Chapter 5 there is a need to interconnect these networks. Interconnection is needed to allow automatic debiting of bank accounts when making payments in shops, for electronic mail between computers connected to different networks or access from a workstation to remote resources on a different network.

A **gateway** is the collection of hardware and software which interconnects two or more networks (see Fig. 9.1). An individual network is called a **subnet** and the collection of subnets is called an **internet**. An internet can be considered a store-and-forward 'supernetwork' with the gateways corresponding to switching nodes and the subnets corresponding to data-links. A subnet could itself be an internet, i.e. subnets can be nested.

The network layer is responsible for transferring messages from a source to a destination station across arbitrary interconnected data links and subnets. It isolates the transport layer from the network topology and the data-transfer technology. It provides independence from routing and switching considerations.

Many of the service and design considerations that apply at the internet level also apply to individual subnets. Each subnet includes a network layer which provides a service to the stations directly connected to the subnet. The network layer can therefore be considered as a series of nested network layers. For example the internet layer provides routing and switching within gateways which interconnect subnets but routing and switching may also be performed within a store-and-forward subnet.

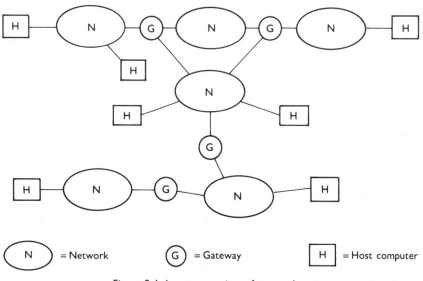

Figure 9.1 Interconnection of networks

In this chapter we discuss the sublayers needed for internetworking and then compare the use of virtual circuits and datagrams for the network layer. The various functions performed by the network layer such as addressing, routing, congestion and flow control are explained. Finally we cover the various approaches to the interconnection of networks, which includes Xerox Internet and CCITT X.25/X.75 as two contrasting case studies.

9.2 Network Sublayers

The network layer has to provide a common service across a variety of interconnected subnets ranging from a broadcast LAN to a circuit-switched network. The services offered by these subnets may be very different and so the network layer has been divided into three sublayers [Callon, 1983; Lenzini 1984; IEEE Computer, 1983] as shown in Figs. 9.2 and 9.3.

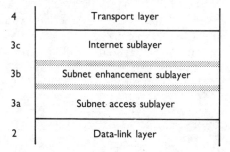

Figure 9.2 Sublayers in network layer

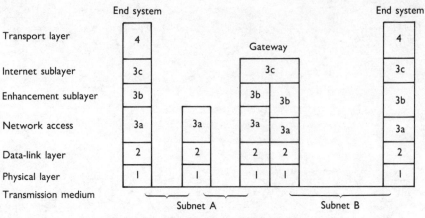

Figure 9.3 Layers in interconnected subnets

1. **Subnet-access sublayer**
   This includes all the functions required to access a particular subnet and is specific to that type of subnet, i.e. the subnet access sublayer for a connectionless LAN and connection-oriented public network are very different. This sublayer merely accesses the service offered by the subnet and does not modify that service.

2. **Subnet-enhancement sublayer**
   This performs a mapping of the service provided by a particular subnet into that required for the interconnections of the subnets. The subnets are 'wrapped' by a functional shell which matches them to a common level of service. This could involve enhancement of the service offered by the subnet, for example providing a connection service over a connectionless subnet. It may be necessary to 'de-enhance' or reduce the functionality of the subnet service, for example when including a connection-oriented subnet within an overall connectionless internetwork service.

3. **Internet sublayer**
   This provides the global network service to the transport layer and includes functions such as routing and switching between subnets.

There have been some suggestions to include an additional sublayer above the internet sublayer [Lenzini, 1984]. This is called a global enhancement or internet interface sublayer and maps the service provided by the internet layer into that required by the transport layer. It is considered an end-to-end network sublayer and in our view should really be considered part of the transport layer. Note that if the subnet service is compatible with the internet service, some of the above sublayers may be null.

9.3 Network Layer Service

One of the most controversial issues relating to the design of communication systems has been whether the network layer should provide a connectionless (datagram) or connection-oriented (virtual circuit) service [Pouzin, 1976]. There has been general agreement that a connection service is needed by many applications and so should be provided by the transport layer. The controversy is whether the transport connection service should be based on a network-layer connection or connectionless service.

Connectionless or datagram service

This is the simplest approach in that each message is treated as an independent entity so a destination address must be provided for each message transaction. Minimal functionality is assumed from the network or individual subnets. There is no enhancement of the reliability offered by the underlying service so messages may be lost or delivered out of sequence. It is assumed that higher layers will provide error- and flow-control mechanisms on an endstation to end-station basis to enhance the reliability of the internet service.

This type of service is analogous to that offered by the postal system. Each letter is an independent unit of information which may be lost (hopefully infrequently) without informing the sender or receiver. Letters do not always arrive in the order in which they were posted.

Most of the early research networks such as Arpanet in USA [McQuillan, 1977], Cigale/Cyclades in France [Pouzin, 1973], and EIN in Europe [Poncet, 1976] were based on switching datagrams between store-and-forward nodes. The DARPA Internet Protocol [Hinden, 1983] provides a datagram service across heterogeneous LANs and WANs. Many LAN-based distributed systems assume a datagram-based network layer, e.g. Xerox Internet [Xerox, 1981], Apollo Domain [Leach, 1983], Lawrence Livermore LINCS [Fletcher, 1982] and CONIC [Sloman, 1986].

Reliable connection or virtual circuit (VC) service

A virtual circuit (VC) is a logical point-to-point path between two end stations which may traverse a number of intermediate nodes and provides a reliable message stream service. This has many of the features of a circuit-switched network – hence its name. The connection is established before data transfer and released afterwards. This type of service is analogous to the telephone system, where a call must be dialled before a conversation can take place. Most VC implementations allow bidirectional information transfer but some do require one VC for each direction of transfer.

Abbreviated addresses (VC numbers) can be used once the connection is set up. This type of service ensures in-sequence delivery and no loss of messages without notification to the users. In theory, the transport layer can be simpler because the network layer provides a reliable service. These advantages come at the expense of increased internet protocol complexity and decreased performance. This increase in complexity is particularly acute where a large number of connections may be needed in a gateway which interconnects two high-speed LANs.

The connection approach to network service and internetworking has been favored by CCITT for public networks, e.g. X.25 and X.75 standards [Rybczynski, 1980] and is used by IBM within SNA [Tanenbaum, 1981]. The main argument against it is that users do not rely on the network-layer service, particularly if provided by a third party such as a public network. The transport layer thus often duplicates the functions performed in the network layer and so it is better to provide connection services at the transport layer above a datagram network layer. Some applications require a request–reply transport layer service. Basing this above a connection network service results in a performance penalty as the overhead of setting up a VC on a per transaction basis is very high. In addition many applications, such as packetised voice, do not require the reliability of a VC service. These arguments have resulted in the extension of the X.25 standard to provide an optional datagram service [Folts, 1980].

9.4 Internet Protocols

The internet protocols also fall into two classes—virtual circuit and datagram:

1. **Datagram protocol**
   Datagram internet protocols maintain no state information. The full source and destination address is inserted into a message. Intermediate nodes use the destination address to choose a route on a per message basis. The choice of route can be based on current delay and so messages to the same destination do not necessarily follow the same route. Also the routing mechanism can easily adapt to component failures. This adaptive routing may result in some messages in a sequence being delayed and arriving at the destination much later than others. There are no acknowledgements or retransmissions of a message at the network level and a node may discard a message, e.g. for lack of buffers. If the data-link layer performs retransmission, duplicates may be generated. An internet datagram protocol may occasionally result in lost, duplicate or out-of-sequence messages, but it is much simpler to implement than a virtual-circuit protocol.
   The fact that no information is maintained to relate messages within a sequence makes flow and congestion control more difficult.

2. **Virtual-circuit (VC) protocols**
   These protocols have the three phases discussed in Chapter 6 – establishment, data and termination. A VC is set up by means of a connect message containing full source and destination addresses. The VC is assigned a number (VC number) and the network maintains tables to map the VC number onto the source or destination address. Once the VC is established, messages use VC numbers rather than addresses. The number of active virtual circuits is likely to be far less than the number of possible pairs of source–destination conversations. A VC number is assigned only when a connection is set up and can be reused after termination. Thus the VC

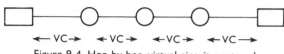

Figure 9.4 Hop-by-hop virtual-circuit protocol

number requires far less bits than the full source and destination address, and so reduces the control information overhead in packets. Usually the path to a destination is chosen when a VC is set up and thereafter all messages follow the same route. The failure of a component means a new VC must be set up. To prevent this many VC networks use highly reliable switching nodes with redundant data links to interconnect them.

The VC protocol usually performs flow control and may perform error control. This may be on a hop-by-hop basis between all switching nodes as in many X.25 implementations (see Fig. 9.4). The concatenation of these hop-by-hop controls provide end-to-end flow and error control. The problem with this approach is that setting up and clearing down the VC always has end-to-end connotations and involves some form of source to destination protocol.

Some X.25 networks and Arpanet implement a VC protocol between the source and destination access nodes and use datagrams for internal switching (see Fig. 9.5). These access nodes maintain tables to translate VC numbers into source and destination addresses, which are put into the messages for routing within the network. Alternate routing techniques can then be used to bypass component failures without the need to reset the VC interface.

As discussed in Chapter 5 there need not be a direct correspondence between class of service and the protocol used to provide that service. A network which provides a VC service may use datagram protocols internally, as is the case with Arpanet. IBM's SNA and most X.25 networks use VC protocols to provide a VC service. The X.25 specification does allow for an optional datagram service which may be provided using VC protocols. The most common approach is to use datagram protocols to provide a datagram service, e.g. CONIC, Xerox Internet, Lawrence Livermore Lincs, Decnet.

Table 9.1 summarizes the main differences between datagrams and virtual circuits in the network layer. The choice between the two for a communication service is really application dependent. In our view the decision should be left to the higher layers, with the network layer providing the simplest possible service. Provision of a VC service in the transport layer seems more natural and leads to much simpler network implementations.

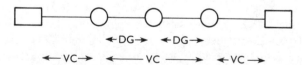

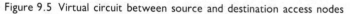

Figure 9.5 Virtual circuit between source and destination access nodes

Table 9.1   A comparison of datagrams and virtual circuits

Datagrams	Virtual circuits (VC)
Each message is an independent entity.	VC set up before information transfer and closed afterwards.
Provides a simple service without any form of end-to-end error control or sequencing, as this is assumed to be provided at a higher level. It is inefficient to implement a datagram service above a VC service.	Provides in-sequence reliable delivery of messages with error and flow control. Users are notified of errors. May still need transport-layer error and flow control to provide necessary quality of service, i.e. duplication of function and increased complexity.
Usually rely on discarding messages for congestion control.	Back pressure effect of hop-by-hop flow control can be used to control congestion.
Each message must contain the full source and destination address, which may entail high overheads in large public networks.	Messages contain VC numbers rather than addresses, so less overheads in header. Network maps these onto source and destination.
Adaptive routing techniques may be used to optimize network resources and so message sequencing is not guaranteed.	Usually fixed routing is used after a VC is set up as messages must arrive at the destination in the order in which they were transmitted.
Adaptive routing techniques applied to each message can give high reliability with comparatively little redundancy in a mesh network.	Redundant transmission lines and switching nodes may be required to provide high-reliability service. Otherwise a new VC will have to be set up if a failure occurs.
When an end-to-end connection based on datagrams must be reset as a result of an error, it is not easy to ensure that messages are flushed out of the network. This implies all messages should have a maximum lifetime, but this leads to problems of deciding when to discard messages.	The sequential message transmission and fixed routing makes it easy to flush messages out of the network if a VC is reset.
The unit of information for switching is a variable-length message.	A VC can be considered an infinite length sequence of messages which is the unit of information for switching.
Most suited to applications which require short transactions, e.g. query reply.	Most suited to applications requiring long sessions due to the overheads of VC set-up and clearing.

9.5 Addressing

The network layer is concerned with identifying subnets, stations and virtual circuits. At this level, identifiers are generally machine-readable binary numbers. In a datagram network, every message contains source and destination station address. In a VC network, station addresses are needed to set up the VC and thereafter VC numbers can be used as addresses in messages. The network maps VC numbers to stations. Many network-layer protocols have socket or port address fields. These are used to identify a service or process within a station so really should be considered transport-layer addresses.

9.5.1 Network and Station Addresses

There are two choices for station addresses in an internetwork environment. Each station has a **unique global address**. This implies the need for very large routing tables which would be indexed by station address to determine the subnet and the gateways to be used to reach the station. Alternatively a **network-specific address** can be used. The station address is of the form *subnet.station*. The station component need only be unique within the subnet, although the combined address is globally unique. The network component is used for routing to get to the final subnet; thereafter the station address is used. This is used in both CONIC and Xerox PUP networks, each component being 8 bits long. The 8-bit station component was found to be inadequate in the PUP system as some subnets used 24-bit internal station addresses so station address translation had to be performed by gateways.

There are a number of disadvantages of station addresses being network specific [Dalal, 1981]. Stations with connections to multiple subnets may have different addresses. Administrative procedures are needed to assign station addresses within a subnet. This can lead to problems in a dynamic environment where stations are constantly being added or removed from the network. Mistakes or lack of cooperation in the organizations sharing a subnet can result in duplication of addresses. The current Xerox Internet Architecture assumes 32-bit network component and 48-bit station component, the latter being an Ethernet station address. The network component is used as a hint for routing but the station component is also globally (world-wide) unique and is built in when a station is manufactured. Xerox administer these addresses and assign blocks of them to manufacturers who purchase Ethernet licences. There is no possibility of address clashes and a station can have the same address on each subnet to which it is connected. The station identifiers can also be used within the operating system to generate unique numbers for the file system or for resource management. The address space is large enough to allow **logical addresses** to be assigned to groups of stations for multi-destination addressing (called multicast). The filtering of unwanted messages can then be performed by the Ethernet interface circuits. The Darpa IP also uses a *subnet.station* address but the station component is only 24 bits, which means address translation is needed within gateways to Ethernets.

Ethernets are unusual in that the station address component actually identifies a station object, and so can be considered the name of a station. In most subnets the station address identifies the subnet attachment point [Saltzer, 1982]. Stations with multiple attachment points usually have different identifiers for each one and the routing algorithms used in most networks cannot map different attachment point identifiers to a single station.

The CCITT X.121 recommendation provides an addressing scheme for public networks which is similar to that used in the telephone network. The network address consists of 14 decimal (4-bit) digits, providing a hierarchical address of the form *country.network.station*. The first 3 digits specify the country, digit 4 the network and the final 10 digits specify the station but some of the station digits could be used to specify a port within a station. Some countries have been assigned multiple-country identifiers, e.g. 200 country numbers have been assigned to the USA. This is clearly inadequate for the number of possible LANs within the USA and is a typical example of the lack of foresight in CCITT standards.

It is possible that a future international network addressing scheme will allow variable-length fields or components within a hierarchic scheme similar to that of X.121.

9.5.2 VC Identifiers

A VC provides an end-to-end addressing function in that it identifies a particular source and destination, but it is not practical to use a network-wide set of VC numbers. It is impractical to maintain a global distributed database of VC numbers as connections are dynamically set up and cleared by individual stations. Instead VC numbers are allocated on a hop-by-hop basis. Each pair of switching nodes or switching nodes and host computers has

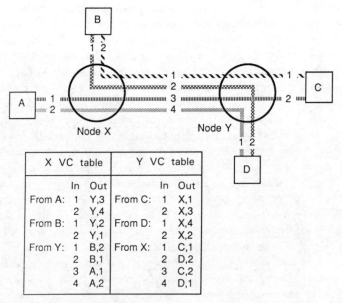

Figure 9.6 Example of virtual circuit numbers

a different set of VC numbers. Thus a particular connection between a source and destination will be known by different VC numbers as it traverses the switching nodes through the network. For example, consider the network of four host computers (A, B, C, D) and two switching nodes (X,Y) shown in Figure 9.6. Four VCs are shown in the diagram (AXYD, AXYC, BXYC, BXYD). Nodes X and Y have tables to map incoming VCs onto the next node and VC number.

In this example the VCs are assumed to be full duplex and so messages sent between A and C will contain the VC number 1 on the AX hop. As both sides of a hop use the same VC number there may be a clash in choice of numbers if both sides are trying to set up VCs simultaneously. For example, A may choose the number 3 for a VC to another host F while X also chooses the number 3 for an incoming VC for A from host G. This can be avoided in most cases by one side choosing numbers from the top end of the range while the other side chooses numbers from the bottom end of the range. Unless the range is big enough there may still be a clash in the middle of the range and the VC set-up protocol must cater for this, e.g. by one side having priority over choice of numbers. This is the mechanism used in X.25, but it means that the protocol entities on each side of a hop are not symmetrical.

An alternative strategy for the allocation of VC numbers is for each side to assign their own number to the connection (Fig. 9.7). A chooses a number when setting up a connection via X. When X confirms the connection set-up, it assigns its own (possibly different) number to the connection which is notified to A. A uses X's number when sending messages via X and X uses A's number when sending messages to A. This simplifies the tables needed in the stations as the VC number can be an index into a table which gives

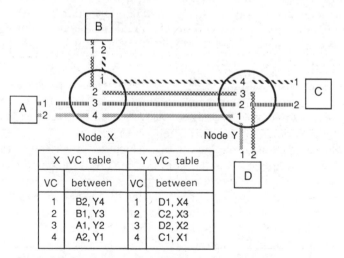

X VC table		Y VC table	
VC	between	VC	between
1	B2, Y4	1	D1, X4
2	B1, Y3	2	C2, X3
3	A1, Y2	3	D2, X2
4	A2, Y1	4	C1, X1

Figure 9.7 Symmetric virtual circuit number assignments

the two adjacent stations interconnected by the VC. There is also no problem of VC number clashes and the protocol is symmetrical.

9.6 Routing

Routing is the collection of algorithms used to determine the path along which messages are exchanged between source and destination where switching is involved. It is necessary in store-and-forward networks and in interconnected subnetworks. A LAN such as a ring or serial highway, provides only a single path for all communication and so does not require any routing. However, if redundant transmission lines are provided the source will have to decide which to use.

9.6.1 Routing Mechanisms

There are two main aspects to routing:

1. **Routing decision**
   This is the choice of a particular path to a destination. This is usually based on a cost factor such as delay, number of hops or tariff. The time at which such a decision is made could be at connection set up in a virtual circuit network or on a per message basis in a datagram network. A routing decision could be made at the source station, in which case routing information is sent with the message or it could be distributed in inter-mediate switching nodes and gateways. They use the destination address to choose a route.
2. **Routing updates**
   This is maintaining and updating the information on which the routing decision is based. Update strategies range from distributed (in which switching nodes or gateways exchange routing information and generate new routing tables locally) to centralized (in which a network routing center collects information and generates routing tables which are then distributed).

With **fixed** routing, all messages between a particular source destination pair (or on a particular connection) follow the same path through the network. This does not take advantage of alternative paths to recover from component failures or to bypass congestion.

An **adaptive** routing technique is one which adapts either to topology changes (e.g. component failures) or to changing traffic conditions (e.g. loading or delays). The latter may attempt to optimize the use of network resources and increase throughput by splitting the load along parallel paths. Adaptive routing may result in messages arriving out of sequence at the destination. It takes time for information about changing conditions to reach all nodes in a network. During this period messages may loop back and forth between nodes, unless specific mechanisms are included to prevent this.

There is obviously a compromise between the benefits of a complex routing policy and the costs in terms of computational time, table space and bandwidth for the transfer of state information between nodes. In the following we describe a few routing mechanisms relevant to distributed systems. A more exhaustive discussion is available elsewhere [Davies 1979; Schwartz, 1980, Tanenbaum, 1981].

9.6.2 Source Routing

The source station inserts the route to be followed by a message into the header [Saltzer, 1981]. The route takes the form of a list of gateway (or switching node) addresses along the path from the source to the destination. Each intermediate node merely takes the relevant address out of the message header to use as the next station address, and updates the next address pointer, before forwarding the message (see Fig. 9.8).

Source routing is often used for interconnected networks where it is impractical to maintain network-wide routing information within gateways; for example, interconnection of Campus or office LANs via WANs. It is also used for interconnecting very high-speed LANs by hardware gateways. The gateways are not responsible for updating routing tables so can be very simple. Switching of messages can even be achieved 'on the fly', i.e. the first bytes of the message are forwarded on the next hop before the complete message is received. Messages only need contain a single address as the source address can be obtained by reversing the order of the address list in the header. The disadvantages are that stations have to deal with variable-length fields in the headers which complicates protocol implementation. It is difficult to make use of alternative routes to adapt to failures. Addresses can only be interpreted in the context of the sender so monitoring of traffic is more difficult.

Each station could maintain information on topology to be used in working out a route to be used as an address. This is done in the Usenet Mail Service for interconnected Unix Systems. Alternatively a name/route server can provide addresses in the form of source routes.

9.6.3 CONIC Routing Algorithm for Interconnected LANs

The CONIC routing is a good example of a distributed algorithm. It is implemented in the gateways which interconnect broadcast LANs. The gateways exchange information on delays (in terms of hops). This allows them to automatically build up routing tables which adapt to component failures [Sloman, 1985]. Very similar algorithms are used in Decnet (for point-to-point links) and Xerox Internet.

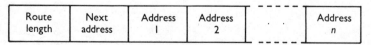

Figure 9.8 Source routing header

The routing decision involves using the subnet address to choose the next subnet on which to send the message and the next station (i.e. gateway or final destination) to which it should be addressed. This decision is based on the minimum distance in hops to a destination subnet. This is a good estimate of delay for interconnected high-speed LANs.

Gateways update routing information by broadcasting **routing vectors** on all adjacent subnets. These vectors contain an entry for every subnet giving the minimum distance to that subnet via the source gateway. Other gateways receiving the vector know that their distance to a remote subnet via the source of the vector must be one hop more than the distance in the vector. Distances in received vectors can be compared to find the best route to a subnet.

Each gateway maintains two routing data structures:

1. **Distance table**
   This is an array which holds the latest routing information received from each adjacent gateway as well as the data link (subnet) by which it can be reached. It is a two-dimensional table with a column for each neighboring gateway on adjacent subnets. A row of the table gives the alternative distances (in hops) to a particular subnet via each neighboring gateway.

2. **Routing table**
   This is used to perform the switching of messages and holds the routing vector sent to adjacent gateways. It is accessed using the destination subnet address in the message as an index and is derived from the minimum distance entry in a row of the distance table. The table entries contain the address of the next gateway to which the message must be forwarded, the link (subnet) on which the message must be transmitted and the

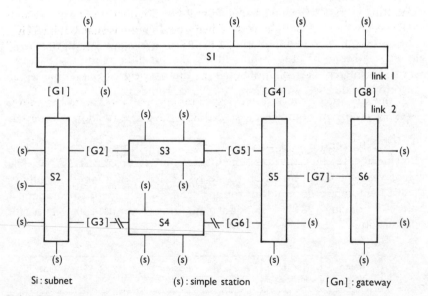

Si : subnet   (s) : simple station   [Gn] : gateway

Figure 9.9 An example network. Used with permission of Elsevier Science Publishers BV.

shortest distance in hops to the subnet. However, an entry corresponding to an adjacent subnet has a distance of 1 and a null value for the address of the next gateway.

Gateways must know which subnets they are connected to so that distances to these subnets can be set to 1. Figure 9.9 shows a typical network configuration with subnet S4 unreachable and Fig. 9.10 shows the stable data structures in gateway G8.

The maximum distance in hops between any two stations in a network is called the **diameter**. A linear network of N subnets with no redundant paths has a diameter of N. A network with redundant paths has a diameter less than the number of subnets. For example in Fig. 9.9 the maximum distance between two stations (on subnets S2 and S6) is three hops, but there are six subnets. This maximum distance (*maxhops*) is a threshold for testing for unreachable subnets. When a gateway receives a routing vector it increments the distances to give the distance via the source of the vector. If a distance is > *maxhops* the network is considered unreachable. Any suitable value > *maxhops* can be used to indicate unreachable subnets (indicated by U in Fig. 9.10).

A gateway broadcasts a vector in the following cases:

● When it detects a change in the status of a link or one of its neighboring gateways.
● When it receives a routing vector which results in a change to a minimum distance in its routing table.
● Periodically, for example, every 30 seconds.

Routing vectors will be exchanged until they no longer result in a change in the routing table of any gateway. When a new station is enabled, it receives routing information via the periodic brodcast of vectors carried out by all the gateways in the subnet.

A gateway performs the following actions when it receives a vector:

1. If there is no column in the distance table corresponding to the source gateway, a new column is assigned and the gateway address inserted.

Distance table

Subnet	Gateway and link		
	G1, 1	G4, 1	G7, 2
S1	2	2	3
S2	2	3	4
S3	3	3	3
S4	U	U	U
S5	3	2	2
S6	3	3	2

Routing table

Subnet	Next gateway	Link	Distance
S1	—	1	1
S2	G1	1	2
S3	G4	1	3
S4	—	—	U
S5	G7	2	2
S6	—	2	1

Figure 9.10 Tables of gateway G8. Used with permission of Elsevier Science Publishers BV.

2. Each distance entry of the received vector is incremented by 1. If the resulting distance is greater than *maxhops* then it will be set unreachable.
3. This incremented routing vector is copied to the column of the distance table corresponding to the source gateway.
4. For all non-adjacent subnets, the minimum distance for each row of the distance table is found. If it differs from the entry in the relevant row of the routing table, the routing table is updated with the new minimum distance, the next gateway address and the link to use. Adjacent subnets are left with a routing table distance of 1.
5. If there have been any changes in the minimum distances recorded in the routing table, then a routing vector is broadcast on all active adjacent subnets.

It must be emphasized that the termination condition for the propagation of routing vectors is no change in the **distance** entries of the routing table rather than no change in the distance table. This is because a change in the distance table may simply imply a change in the status of a route which was not being used by the gateway. Thus, a new routing vector will be transmitted only if it differs from the last one which had been transmitted.

Ordinary non-gateway stations on the same subnet use identical routing tables, which are generated and periodically broadcast by the gateways. This consists of an array with the next gateway address for each reachable subnet, a null (zero) entry for the subnet on which the array is broadcast and an indication of unreachable subnets. For example the arrays broadcast on S1 will be (– ,G1,G4,G4,G4,G8) and on S6 will be (G8,G8,G7,G7,G7, –). Whenever a new array is received it replaces the old one. There is no reliability problem in generating these updates only in gateways, since if all gateways fail the remote subnets are unreachable.

It takes time for knowledge of a component failure to propagate through the network to all gateways. During this period loops can occur in gateway routing tables while they stabilize. This can be prevented by a gateway never offering routes on a subnet via other gateways on that subnet. The processing of vectors and updating of tables is as before, but different vectors must be derived for each adjacent subnet. The routing vector distance to a subnet is set to unreachable if the route is via the subnet on which the vector is to be broadcast. Other improvements on the basic algorithm are discussed in Sloman [1985].

Most internet protocols include a hop count in each message header to prevent indefinite looping of messages during the routing table instability period. The *hopcount* is incremented by the gateways and when the value is greater than *maxhops* the message is discarded.

9.6.4 Problems with Routing Based on Subnets

If a subnet is not broadcast but is itself a store-and-forward network then it may make a difference by which gateway a packet enters the subnet. One gateway may be adjacent to the destination station whereas another is many hops away. Also if a station is connected to two different subnets, i.e. it effectively has two different addresses, one address may be a better one to use than the other. If both addresses are known to the source, then it can access routing tables and choose the best to use, but that is not usually the case. The use of a unique global station address for routing is thus necessary to guarantee optimal routing. In the DARPA IP protocol the network address is used as a hint. If a gateway receives a message which is better routed via another gateway it forwards the message but generates a notification to the source giving the best route to the destination. This can be used to update routing tables.

9.7 Error Control

Most networks do not perform recovery from information corruption in the network layer, but rather in the data link and/or transport layers. This type of error control is sometimes needed across interconnected subnets to improve the error rate of a particular one. In that case techniques similar to those used in the transport layer will be used end-to-end across the subnet by gateways as part of the enhancement sublayer. If the subnet provides a VC service it will detect and correct lost or out-of-sequence packets.

9.8 Flow and Congestion Control

Flow and congestion control are often confused. Flow control relates to the control of the flow of information between a sender and receiver to prevent the sender flooding the receiver, i.e. it is control between a pair of entities. A congestion-control mechanism prevents more messages entering a network than can be handled, i.e. it is really a global mechanism. The confusion arises because the information needed to implement global strategies is distributed throughout the network. Propagation delays make it impossible to obtain completely up-to-date state information on the whole network. Thus flow control is often used to attempt to prevent congestion and deadlock. Flow control is also used to manage the fair allocation of shared resources amongst competing users.

Deadlock prevention
Deadlock can occur in store-and-forward networks when stations are unable to exchange messages because of lack of buffers.

Direct store-and-forward lockup occurs when two neighboring nodes connected by a direct data link are deadlocked. All the buffers in the first node contain messages bound for the second node and all the buffers in the second node contain messages bound for the first. Neither node can receive a message due to lack of buffer space and no buffers can be freed until a message has been successfully transmitted. The situation can only be resolved by one node discarding a message. This can be prevented by not allowing all buffers to be assigned to a single output queue and reserving buffers for input lines.

Indirect store-and-forward lockup involves a 'loop' of nodes each filled with messages destined for the next node in the loop. This type of traffic pattern is unlikely to occur in a store-and-forward network but it is theoretically possible. It can be prevented by reserving two buffers in each node for use as overflow buffers if deadlock is detected. Thus at least one overflow message at a time can be delivered.

Reassembly lockup occurs in a network in which long messages are fragmented into smaller messages for transmission. The messages must be reassembled into a complete message for delivery to destination host or process. Deadlock arises if the destination node has a number of partially assembled messages but runs out of buffers and so cannot receive any of the messages which would complete a message and allow it to be delivered. This can be prevented by reserving the required reassembly storage at the destination before a multipacket message can be transmitted by the source.

The following types of flow control are found in the network layer:

1 . **Network access** – between the host processor and access node of a store-and-foward network (e.g. X.25 level 3).
2. **End access node to end access node** – this is needed in a datagram network which provides a virtual circuit network interface (e.g. Arpanet). The objective is to prevent buffer overflow in the end access node, but there may also be error control, in that the flow-control messages can act as acknowledgements and so detect lost messages.
3. **Stepwise** – between adjacent switching nodes which implement hop-by-hop virtual circuits or between gateways across a subnet.

We will now discuss typical mechanisms used to perform flow and congestion control [Kleinrock, 1980; Tanenbaum, 1981].

Discarding messages

If a switching node or gateway receives more messages than it has buffer space to handle, it discards incoming messages on the assumption that the sender will retransmit. Obviously if the incoming message contains an acknowledgement for a previously transmitted message then it should not be discarded as it will free a buffer. If acknowledgements are piggybacked with data the node may act on the acknowledgement but still discard the data part of the message. This implies that at least one receive buffer must always be reserved for each data link so that the node can always receive a message to examine it before discarding.

An extension of the above technique is to have a maximum outgoing queue length for each data link. This prevents all buffers being used while waiting for acknowledgements on a data link. Also incoming messages from the network should be given priority over new messages being generated by a host computer attached to the node, i.e. the node should switch messages already in the network in preference to allowing access of new messages.

Some internet protocols (e.g. Xerox, DARPA and ISO) generate an error notification to the sender when a message is discarded. This can be used to delay further transmissions and hopefully cure some of the congestion.

After receiving a message, there is a certain amount of processing time involved in resetting the receiver with a new buffer, etc. This 'dead time' may result in implicit discarding of incoming messages, particularly in high-speed LANs.

Delayed acknowledgements

Delay in acknowledgements of received messages can reduce the amount of traffic entering the network. When transit delays and response times become intolerable, humans tend to give up and stop using the network, which decreases the offered traffic. This obviously does not apply to computer sources which are more likely to time out and retransmit, thus merely increasing the amount of traffic and congestion.

The use of delay as a throttling technique is not recommended as it means information is stored within the network for a longer time, tying up resources. Eventually the network may saturate, with no useful traffic movement taking place, i.e. congestion occurs.

Window flow control

This technique is used to control the flow across the network interface for each virtual circuit in level 3 of X.25. Similar schemes are used in transport-layer end-to-end controls. Also the acknowledgement error-control mechanism of data-link protocols such as HDLC, SDLC and DDCMP is a form of window flow control.

A number (modulo N, where N is often 8) is sequentially assigned to every message transmitted. At the transmitting end the window corresponds to the allowed number of unacknowledged outstanding messages, as shown in Fig. 9.11. At the receiving end the window corresponds to the allowed range of sequence numbers which will be accepted, i.e. for which buffers are available. Some window mechanisms such as in X.25 insist that messages arrive sequentially, whereas others will accept any message within the window. A received message whose sequence number is outside the window usually means an error and is discarded or results in a reset.

A sequence number range of N allows a maximum window size of $N - 1$ if out of sequence messages are discarded at the receiver. For example, a 3-bit sequence number gives a range of 8 numbers (0–7), but a maximum window of 7. The reason is that if all 8 numbers were used, and the acknowledgements

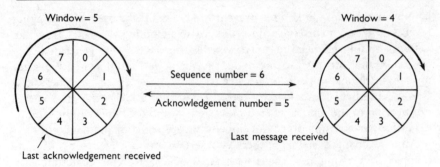

Figure 9.11 Window flow control (modulo 8)

were lost, the receiver would not be able to distinguish between retransmissions and a new series of messages.

If the receiver accepts out of sequence packets, then the maximum window size must be limited to $N/2$ for a sequence number range of N. This can be shown by assuming the sender transmits 7 packets in the above example before waiting for an acknowledgement. The acknowledgement for packet number 1 is lost even though the packer was received by the destination, which is now expecting packets, 7, 0, 1 ..., 6. So when the retransmitted packet number 1 is received, it is treated as a new one which has arrived out of sequence. If the allowed window had been limited to only 4 packets, then the sender would stop after transmitting packets 0–3. Once these have been acknowledged by the receiver, its window is now packets 4–7, and so retransmissions from the previous window can be detected.

The receiving and transmitting windows should initially be the same size but may have different instantaneous values due to packets in transit. The sender's transmit window may be moved implicitly whenever it receives an acknowledgement. For example with a window size of 3, the senders window is initially 0–2. When message 0 is acknowledged the window becomes 1–3, i.e. the transmit window is always 3 more than the last acknowledgement received. This mechanism is used in X.25 and for many data-link layer protocols, e.g. DDCMP and HDLC.

Stepwise control

Many of the X.25 public packet switched networks make use of stepwise flow control without any end-to-end control. The network then acts as a first-in-first-out queue with the source and destination each having independent access. If flow is stopped along one hop, then a 'back pressure' effect will eventually stop the flow from the source station into the network.

Store-and-forward deadlocks are avoided by assigning a particular source-to-destination VC to different buffer classes in each node. Thus two adjacent nodes or even a loop of nodes do not compete for buffers from the same class. Reassembly deadlock is prevented by assigning one buffer to the ap-

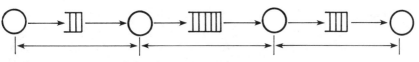

Figure 9.12 Stepwise flow control

propriate VC at each intermediate node for a multipacket message. The destination node assigns as many buffers as is required for reassembly. Dynamic assignment of buffers to virtual circuits is used to dynamically adjust window sizes and this is claimed to avoid congestion.

Buffer reservation

Arpanet uses the packet reservation scheme for the transmission of multi-packet messages. The source node, upon receiving the first packet of a multipacket message from a host, sends a control message to the destination node requesting the allocation of eight reassembly buffers. If the buffers are available the destination node returns a reservation confirmation to the source node, which can then transmit the packets. If no buffers are available the source must repeat the request until it succeeds. When all the packets have arrived and been reassembled at the destination node, the message is delivered to the destination host. The destination node then reserves eight more buffers and sends a request for next message (RFNM) to the source node. This acknowledges delivery of the complete message and confirms a credit of a further eight buffers. The source node either sends the next message or cancels the reservation if it has nothing to send.

A single packet message is transmitted to the destination node immediately without need for a reservation. If there is space at the destination it is accepted and delivered to the host, and an RFNM is returned. If there is no space available at the destination node the message is discarded and a request for buffer allocation is queued. When buffers are available the source node is informed and it retransmits the message.

Messages are sequentially numbered. At most eight messages can be outstanding between any source and destination nodes. Not more than eight messages can be queued at each node output queue.

9.9 Priority

In general, a high-priority message should be able to overtake another message, from the same source, which was transmitted at an earlier time. Thus multiple priority levels are incompatible with maintaining message sequence. A priority scheme could be applied to a datagram service where every message is independent and sequence checking is not implemented.

In a virtual circuit service a general priority structure can only be implemented if priority is assigned to a virtual circuit rather than on a per message basis. If two communicating partners require multiple levels of priority they must set up multiple VCs to maintain sequencing for each priority level.

Expedited data. A common technique used in virtual circuit systems is to allow a single very short message at a time on each virtual circuit to bypass the flow-control procedure. These are called interrupt messages and are limited to one or two bytes of user information. An interrupt may overtake normal user messages on the same virtual circuit, and can be transmitted, even if the flow-control mechanism is preventing the transmission of normal user messages. This implies special buffers must be available in intermediate nodes or end stations to receive interrupt messages.

Within the network priority is indicated by a special field in the packet header. The number of priority levels will depend on the number of bits available in the field. The priority field is used within the network for **queue jumping**. This could be used at any level, not only network layer. Messages are inserted into queues according to priority. These queues may occur within protocol entities or at interfaces.

9.10 Segmentation and Reassembly

Segmentation and reassembly is sometimes provided in the network layer as in Arpanet. The host processor is able to send 1000 byte messages across the network interface, although internally the maximum packet length is 128 bytes. Experience has shown that in most cases it is better to perform segmentation and reassembly within the host processor which generally has more memory available for buffering and so reassembly deadlock problems are less likely.

An X.25 implementation option allows different size packets at the source and destination ends of a virtual circuit. For example, 256-byte messages are put in at one end of the network, but are received as 128-byte packets at the other end.

In general the following fields are needed in the protocol header to support segmentation and reassembly:

1. **More bit**
   This indicates whether the packet is part of a segmented service data unit (higher-level message). The last packet of the sequence has the bit cleared.
2. **Data unit identifier**
   This identifies to which message the segment belongs.
3. **Segment offset**
   This provides the sequence number of the segment within the original message to enable reassembly and detect lost segments.
4. **Total length**
   This is needed in the first message to allow reservation of buffer space.

A VC service guarantees in-sequence delivery so only needs the more bit.

Two types of fragmentation can be used for internetworking. **Intranet segmentation** implies a message is fragmented on entry to a subnet and reassembled afterwards. This occurs in the subnet access or enhancement sublayer and so is transparent to the internet protocol. With **transnet segmentation** a gateway segments a message but it is only reassembled at the destination and so is part of the internet sublayer. This simplifies the buffer management in gateways.

9.11 Network Interconnection Approaches

The interconnection of networks exacerbates all the problems of networking computers. Incompatibilities between the communication systems used in different networks have to be overcome in addition to the incompatibilities of the stations connected to the networks [IEEE Computer, 1983]. Examples of network incompatibilities include:

- type of service provided – datagram, VC, etc;
- protocols – message formats, acknowledgement methods, error and flow control techniques used, etc;
- message lengths – requiring fragmentation and reassembly;
- security and accounting, particularly with respect to public networks.

9.11.1 Subnet Independence

There is a very large investment in the hardware and software of existing networks, both in terms of the switching nodes and the hosts connected to the networks. The cost of rewriting this communication software would be prohibitive and disrupt the present users. If possible, internet protocols should preserve the independence of existing subnets, and be superimposed on top of them. To achieve this, internet messages are embedded within the subnet message as user information (Fig. 9.13), just as network layer messages are embedded in data-link layer messages. The internet header contains the final destination subnet and station addresses. The subnet header contains the address of the next gateway. The gateway strips off the first subnet header and trailer and adds new ones before routing the message to the next gateway, and so on. The internet message is thus completely transparent to the local network, but this technique does have the disadvantage of increased overhead of the local as well as internet headers and trailers.

If the network layer of the subnets is designed with internetworking in mind, then the network header can be made compatible with the internet header as in CONIC and Xerox Internets. It may be possible to alter the

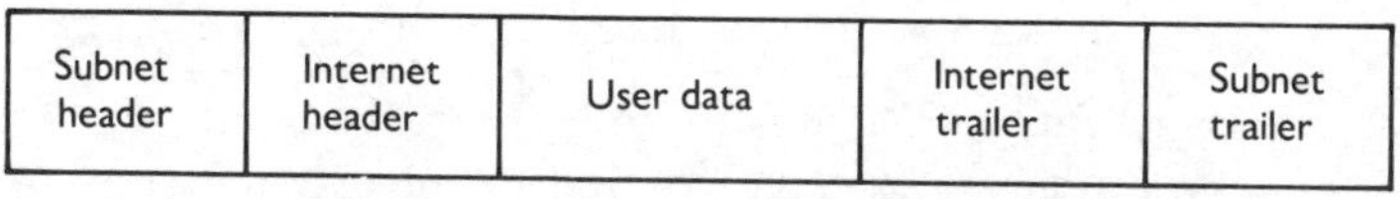

Subnet header	Internet header	User data	Internet trailer	Subnet trailer

Figure 9.13 Imbedded internet messages

Internet/subnet header	User data	Internet/subnet trailer

Figure 9.14 Compatible internet/subnet network layer

network layer of some existing subnets to achieve compatibility, e.g. by adding additional type or escape fields to existing protocols and formats (see Fig. 9.14). This minimizes changes but allows local and internet packets to be differentiated. Each subnet has to be able to interpret an internet address and route the internet message to an appropriate gateway. If there is more than one gateway (which is desirable for reliability) the subnet switching nodes are unlikely to be able to make optimal routing decisions as that would require knowledge of conditions or topology of the other subnets.

9.11.2 Gateway Implementation

The gateway need not be implemented in a single physical station but could be split into two or more stations. The implementation choices, shown in Fig. 9.15 are:

- software in a pair of packet switches;
- a single station connected as a host computer to 2 or more networks;
- half a gateway in each network. The gateway half could be a switching node or a host computer. This has the advantage that each half falls under the administration of its own network.

9.11.3 Case Studies

There are two sets of constraints to be considered in designing an internet architecture. The first is the type of service provided by the subnets, i.e. the subnet-access service level. These may have to be harmonized by the enhancement sublayer. The second is the overall service to be provided by the global internet sublayer. The following case studies are examples of different approaches to the problems of network interconnection.

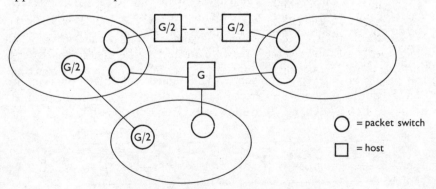

Figure 9.15 Gateway implementation alternatives

Datagram internet protocol (e.g. Xerox internet) [Xerox, 1981]
Xerox internet provides a datagram service on top of a datagram subnet enhancement sublayer. The gateways are connected as host computers to the subnets. The subnet access and enhancement sublayers within hosts and intermediate gateways are responsible for encapsulating an internet message within a subnet message. The Internet message can be up to 576 bytes in length, so these layers must perform segmentation and reassembly across a subnet if necessary. Transnet segmentation is not supported. There is no need for a subnet enhancement layer for an Ethernet or a datagram subnet which supports messages of 576 bytes. A virtual circuit subnet will require the subnet enhancement layer to set up connections between hosts and gateways. These connections will be transparent to the internet sublayer. The strategy for establishing and clearing these connections is not defined and depends on the particular subnet. The following strategies may be used:

1. Permanent connections are established between gateways and from hosts to gateways. This is feasible if only a few hosts set up connections to the gateways. In public networks there is a time element in charging for communications so this may prove costly if there is not much internet traffic.
2. Connections are established and cleared for each message. This will result in considerable delay for each message.
3. Connections are set up when needed but are only cleared when they have not been used for a period of time.

Addresses. These are of the form *network.station.socket*. The socket component is really a transport layer address as it identifies a service or process within the station. It will be discussed in the next chapter. The station address can be specific (i.e. the message is addressed to a single station within a subnet), multicast (i.e. the message is addressed to a group of stations in a subnet) or broadcast (i.e. the message is addressed to all the stations in the subnet). The broadcast and multicast addressing may not be supported by some subnets. Broadcast or multicast addressing of subnets is not supported. An 'unknown' network address value can be used by hosts for sending a message on the subnet to which they are connected, e.g. for the host to discover its network address.

The **checksum** is a 1s complement add and left-cycle rotate over the whole message. It is easily generated by software and can be used for error detection. It can be incrementally updated in intermediate gateways which update fields (e.g. hop count) in a message.

The **length** field indicates the length of the message including header.

The **control** field includes a 4-bit hop count which is incremented by a gateway. The message is discarded when the hop count reaches 16 and an error notification is sent to the source. Packets are also discarded if they remain on a queue within any station for more than 6 s, so as to provide an upper bound on the maximum packet lifetime.

The **type** field identifies the format of the message within the data field.

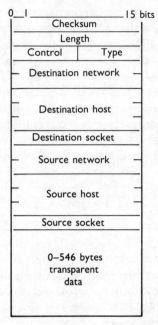

Figure 9.16 Internet message format

It is really transport-layer information but it can be used to direct the received message to the relevant protocol module as multiple transport protocols are supported.

Many distributed systems based on LANs (e.g. CONIC, Lincs, Appollo Domain [Fletcher, 1982; Leach, 1983]) use very similar Network Layer protocols. The DARPA IP [DOD, 1980] and new ISO Internetwork Protocols [International Standards Organization, 1984; Callon 1983] are also datagram based, but are more complex in that they support transnet segmentation and a variety of quality of service parameters (e.g. priority, security level and reliability). The ISO protocol has variable-length address fields. Many internet protocol messages contain an explicit time to live field which is decremented to take account of transmission and queuing times. The message is discarded when the value reaches zero. This gives a more accurate maximum packet lifetime than a hop count.

Common network access interface – X.25/X.75

The current standard interface for accessing public packet-switched networks is the CCITT X.25 recommendations, which defines a virtual circuit protocol between the data terminal equipment (DTE) and the data circuit terminating equipment (DCE) [Rybczynski, 1980; Tanenbaum, 1981]. The DTE corresponds to a host computer and the DCE is strictly speaking a modem, but really corresponds to the network or access node (Fig. 9.17). X.25 also

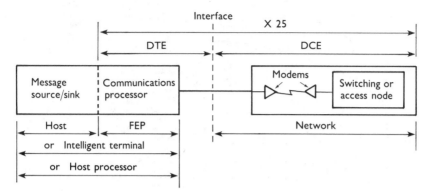

Figure 9.17 X.25 interface to a public packet-switched network

specifies HDLC as the data-link protocol across the interface and X.21 as the physical layer (Fig. 9.18).

X.25 networks may internally use hop-by-hop VCs or datagrams, but they all present the same external interface to the host computers. A VC is established by a host computer sending a call request packet which specifies the destination address (in X.121 format). The source address is optional as it can be inserted by the access node. Various facilities can be negotiated at call set-up time, e.g. flow-control windows, line speeds, etc. Data packets specify a VC number and use window flow control. Each message contains a sequence number and the sequence number of the next message the sender is expecting. The latter can be a form of end-to-end acknowledgement if a bit in the header is set to say these numbers have end-to-end significance. Otherwise they have only hop-by-hop significance.

The protocol is rather complex and the number of options available make it difficult to ensure compatibility between different implementations.

Interconnection of X.25 subnets is via the X.75 protocol which is very similar to X.25, but includes additional subnet to subnet information, e.g. routing and accounting. The end-to-end internet service is a virtual circuit and is based on concatenated VCs across each subnet. The subnet access

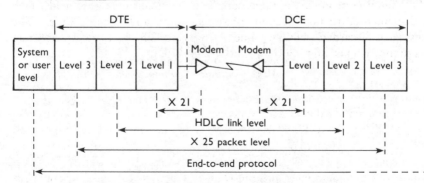

Figure 9.18 Protocol levels in the X.25 standard

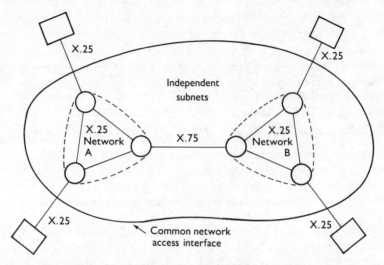

Figure 9.19 X.25/X.75 network interconnection

layer is VC based, so the enhancement sublayer is minimal. The gateway must maintain the sequence of packets on a particular VC and so fixed routing between gateways must be used. Gateway halves are implemented in switching nodes in each subnet (Fig. 9.19).

High-level interconnection

Interconnection can also be achieved at the application level. The gateways need knowledge of, and are involved in, protocols at all lower layers. The application protocol of one subnet is transformed into the application protocol of another subnet. It is very difficult to perform this type of translation for individual messages 'on the fly'. It is commonly used for transferring files across interconnected networks where the files are stored at intermediate host computers which act as gateways.

References

Callon, R., 'Internetwork protocol', *Proc. IEEE*, Special Issue on Open Systems Interconnection, Vol. 71, no. 12, December 1983, pp. 1388–1393.

Dalal, Y.K., Printis, R.S., '48 bit absolute Internet and Ethernet host numbers' *Proc. 7th. Data Comms. Symp. ACM Computer Comms. Review*, Vol. 11, no. 4, October 1981, pp. 240–247.

Davies, D., Barber, D., Price, W., Solominides, C., *Computer Networks and Their Protocols*, Wiley 1979.

'DOD standard internet protocol', *ACM Computer Comms. Review*, Vol. 10, no. 4, October 1980, pp. 12–51.

Fletcher, J., Watson, R., 'An overview of LINCS architecture' UCID 19294, Lawrence Livermore Laboratory, Livermore, California, November 1982.

Folts, H., 'X.25 Transaction Oriented Features – Datagram and Fast Select', in IEEE Trans [1980], pp. 496–499.

Hinden, R., Haverty, J., Sheltzer, A., 'The DARPA internet: interconnecting heterogeneous networks with gateways', in IEEE Computer [1983], pp. 38–49.

IEEE Computer Special Issue on Network Interconnection, Vol. 16, no. 9, September 1983.

IEEE Trans. Comms., Special Issue on Computer Network Architectures and Protocols, Vol. 28, no. 4, April 1980.

International Standards Organization, *Basic Reference Model for Open Systems Interconnection, ISO* 7498, 1983. See also *ACM Computer Comms. Review*, April 1981, pp. 15–65.

'ISO Internetwork Protocol Standard', *ACM Computer Comms. Review*, Vol. 13, no. 5, January 1984, pp. 10–58.

Kleinrock, L., Gerla, M., 'Flow control: a comparative survey', in IEEE Trans. [1980], pp. 553–574.

Leach, P., Levine, P., Dorous, B., Hamilton, J., Nelson, D., Stumpf, B., 'The architecture of an integrated-services local area network', *IEEE Journal on Selected Areas in Comms.*, Vol. 1, no. 5, November 1983, pp. 842–856.

Lenzini, L. (ed.), *Network Interconnection: Principles, Architecture and Protocol Implications, Part I of Final Report of COST 11 BIS LAN Group*, November, 1984. Available from Imperial College London.

McQuillan, J., Walden, D., 'The ARPA network design decision', *Computer Networks*, Vol. 1, no. 3, August 1977, pp. 243–289.

Poncet, F., Repton, C., 'The EIN communication subnetwork principles and practice', *Proc. ICCC*, Toronto 1976, pp. 523–531.

Pouzin, L., 'Presentation and major design aspects of Cyclades Computer Network', *Proc. 3rd Data Comms. Symp.*, St. Petersburg, November 1973.

Pouzin, L., 'Virtual circuits vs. datagrams – technical and political problems', *Proc. AFIPS NCC*, Vol. 45, 1976, pp. 483–494.

Rybczynski, A., 'X.25 interface and end-to-end virtual circuit service characteristics', in IEEE Trans. [1980], pp. 500–509.

Saltzer, J., Reed, D., Clark, D., 'Source routing for campus wide internet transport', *Local Networks for Computer Communications*, North-Holland 1981, pp. 1–23.

Saltzer, J., 'On the naming and binding of network destinations', *Proc. IFIP TC6 Conf. on LANs*, Florence, Italy, 1982, North-Holland, pp. 311–318.

Schwartz, M., Stern, T., 'Routing techniques used in computer communications networks', in IEEE Trans. [1980], pp. 539–552.

Sloman, M., Kramer, J., Magee, J., 'A Flexible Communication Structure for Distributed Embedded Systems'. *IEEE Proc.-E 'Computers and Digital Techniques'* Vol. 133, no. 4, July 1986, pp. 201–211.

Sloman, M., Andriopoulos, X., 'The CONIC routing algorithm for interconnected LANs', *Computer Networks*, Vol. 9, no. 2, February 1985, pp. 109–130.

Tanenbaum, A., *Computer Networks*, Prentice-Hall, 1981.

Xerox Corporation: *Internet Transport Protocols*, XSIS 028112, Xerox OPD, Network Systems Administration Office, 3333 Coyote Hill Road, Palo Alto, Calif. 94304, December 1981.

Ten

TRANSPORT AND SESSION LAYERS

The transport layer is concerned with providing end-to-end communications across one or more networks. It performs all the functions necessary for making the most efficient use of the network services provided. It isolates the higher layers from any knowledge of the type of network being used, i.e. whether LAN, WAN or interconnected networks. The actual functions performed by a particular transport-layer protocol depends on the type of service offered and the service available from the network layer.

The session layer provides access to the transport-layer services, such as connection set-up and data transfer. It allows users to manage their interaction in terms of assigning permission to send a message. Synchronization points within a session can be established to recover from failures. Additional services include name to address binding and exception reporting.

In many implementations of distributed systems there is no separate session layer. Often the functions are incorporated into higher-layer protocols. File transfer and virtual terminal protocols often include session-layer functions. Those systems which provide a connectionless service (datagram or remote procedure call) often incorporate some session-layer functions into the transport layer. For this reason we cover both layers in this chapter.

In this chapter we review the services provided by a transport layer and concentrate on features, such as connection management, which distinguish a transport protocol from lower layer ones. In distributed systems, the distinction between transport and session layers is rather vague, so the latter is covered rather briefly. The case studies on the CONIC Communication System, Cedar Remote Procedure Call Implementation and the V Kernel IPC elaborate this combined session and transport layer which implements the IPC primitives described in Chapter 4.

10.1 Transport Services

Examples of the various connection and connectionless services described in Chapter 5 can be found in transport-layer implementations. However, most of the standardization work has concentrated on connection services for WANs. The main use of these services is for remote terminal sessions and file transfers rather than distributed processing. The connection service may be provided as an enhancement of an underlying network datagram service as in DECNET [Wecker, 1980], Xerox Packet Stream Service [Xerox, 1981], and TCP [DOD, 1980]. Alternatively transport connections may map directly onto network ones, as is the case when X.25 networks are used.

The **service primitives** define how a user interacts with the provider of a service. We now describe typical transport-connection service primitives as these are usually a superset of those for the other types of service. Figure 10.1 is an example of the use of these primitives.

Connect request: Requests a connection to be set up to a remote transport entity. Parameters passed are source and destination transport addresses, quality of service required and possibly some user data.

Connect indication: An incoming connection request containing an identifier (VC number) allocated to the connection, source transport address and user data if any.

Connect response: The user's response to the connect indication – accept or refuse. The parameters passed include connection identifier, reasons if refused, and optional user data.

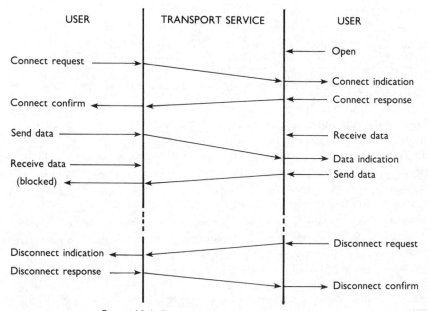

Figure 10.1 Example use of service primitives

Connect confirm: The response given to the originator of a connect request. The parameters passed include the reason if refused, connection identifier to be used for subsequent data requests used, and optional user data.

Open for connections: This allows a server to inform the transport service that it is willing to accept connection indications.

Some services allow connection requests and indications to include a limited amount of user data. This data could be a password or higher-level address. If this is not provided this user data must be passed as a normal data request once the connection has been set up.

Disconnect request: The user requesting to clear a connection. Parameters include connection identifier and reasons.

Disconnect indication: The service indicating to the user that the connection is to be cleared. This could be instigated by a remote user or by the service provider (to both users) after a communication failure. Parameters include connection identifier and reason.

Send data: A request to transmit user data. Some implementations block the user until the data is transmitted while others allow the user to continue immediately (cf. synchronous or asynchronous sends). The parameters passed include a connection identifier and a point to the data buffer to be transmitted.

Receive data: The user informs the transport service that it is willing to receive a message from a particular connection or any connection. The user may be blocked waiting for a message to arrive or may continue immediately if no message is available. Parameters include a connection identifier and a point to a buffer in which the message is to be received.

Data indication: If the user is not blocked on the receive, but can continue, then this primitive is used to indicate that a message has arrived and has been copied into the buffer indicated in the above receive primitive.

The application level IPC primitives described in Chapter 4 could be implemented by a transport connection service providing primitives such as those outlined above. However, this can be very inefficient for a distributed system in a LAN environment. Optimized special-purpose transport services are often used. Special access procedures which map directly onto the above service primitives can be used to allow communication using sequential languages such as FORTRAN, COBOL or Pascal [Andreoni, 1984; Langsford, 1984]. However, the communication is not part of the language syntax, whereas in CSP, CONIC and ARGUS (see Chapter 4) the communication primitives are part of the language and so parameters can be checked by the compiler for type compatibility. An alternative approach is to map the sequential language's input/output facilities onto transport communication primitives. This does not give access to the full power and flexibility of the communication system, which has characteristics very different from I/O devices.

10.2 Connection Management

Store-and-forward datagram networks have variable delays, may deliver out-of-sequence packets and even duplicate packets. This means delayed data packets, from a previous connection, could have sequence numbers which are valid for a current connection, as sequence numbers are generally reused. The transport layer must make sure that sequence numbers are not reused within the expected packet lifetime. Another problem that must be prevented is the setting up of invalid connections. A delayed connection request may arrive followed by delayed data packets with valid sequence numbers for that connection. If the transport entity accepts the delayed connection request as valid, the following data will also be accepted and sequence errors will go undetected.

Most protocols use sequence numbers for ensuring reliable packet delivery, and when the connection is established the initial sequence number (ISN) is zero. This can lead to old packets being accepted if connections are opened and closed rapidly. Stations could wait for all old packets to die out by waiting for a time longer than the maximum packet lifetime (MPL), but this could be in the order of 1 minute in some WANs. A solution is to choose an ISN which distinguishes sequence numbers from different connections. This could be done by mapping a monotonically increasing timer (i.e. a real-time clock) into the sequence number (usually the high-order bits). If the clock wraps around and 'catches up' with the sequence numbers then they must be resynchronized [Sunshine, 1978]. Alternatively each connection could be given a unique identifier from a monotonic clock. Each message must contain the connection identifier.

Simple two-way handshakes are adequate at the data-link level and can be used at the transport level above a connection network service, as no delayed out-of-sequence messages will arise. There are two mechanisms used for reliably opening and closing transport connections above a datagram network service — three-way handshakes and timer-based protocols.

10.2.1 Three-way Handshakes

The two-way connection request handshake always assumes a connection request must be valid, whereas the three-way handshake requires the initiator to confirm that the connect request is valid before the connection can be used [Sunshine, 1978; Watson, 1981]. This prevents data being passed to the higher level until three packets have been successfully exchanged. The three-way handshake works as follows (Fig. 10.2):

1. Station A sends a connect packet which indicates its initial sequence number (ISN) NA_0.
2. Station B returns a connect-acknowledgement which contains its initial sequence number NB_0 and NA_0. This enables A to check that it has an

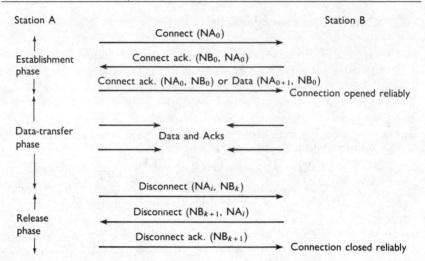

Figure 10.2 Three-way handshake. Based on Watson [1981] reprinted with permission of Springer-Verlag.

outstanding connect request with that sequence number and if not to send an error or reset.

3. Station A sends a packet to B which acknowledges receipt of B's ISN, NB_0, and either the next valid sequence number if it contains data, else NA_0. B will only accept data packets after receiving this confirmation that A was trying to set up a connection.

Note that the ISN used to set up a connection must not be repeated within the maximum packet lifetime.

A three-way handshake is also required to reliably determine that both ends have finished sending data and that all data has been received by the other end. These end-of-data indications must also be sequence numbered. Assume that a full duplex connection is in progress and A wishes to disconnect the connection after sending all its data.

1. Station A sends an indication to B that it has no more data to send and is ready to disconnect. Note A must not disconnect until all its outstanding data has been acknowledged.

2. When Station B receives this disconnect indication it can use the sequence number to check that it has received all data sent by A. Assuming B has no more data to send it also sends a sequence-numbered disconnect indication to A.

3. When A receives B's disconnect packet it can also check there are no outstanding packets in transit from A and so it acknowledges receipt.

If the receiver of a disconnect indication still has data to send it can refuse to release the connection or acknowledge it but delay sending its own disconnect indication. This type of decision is really application dependent. Hence the simplest way of closing a connection is for the user level protocol to decide that there is no more data to send and for each user to inform its local transport entity that the connection can now be closed. The transport entities can then delete the connection records without worrying about the other side. This considerably simplifies the Transport protocol [Xerox, 1981]. The Xerox packet sequence protocol does not provide disconnect primitives.

10.2.2 Timer-based Connection Management

In a timer-based protocol, connection records are maintained at both ends long enough for all duplicates to die out [Watson, 1981]. The receiver maintains its connection record long enough to detect duplicates and only accepts packets with sequence numbers in its acceptance window. The sender must maintain its connection record for a slightly longer time in order to recognize all acknowledgements. The mechanism requires a bound on the time for which a sender retransmits (R), maximum packet lifetime (MPL) and the receiver's time to acknowledge a packet (A). The times for holding the connection records given below are derived in [Fletcher, 1978].

Receiver's hold time $> 2(MPL + R + A)$
Sender's hold time $> 3(MPL + R + A)$.

The sender's timer is reinitialized whenever a new sequence number (SN) is transmitted. The receiver's timer is reinitialized whenever a new SN is acknowledged. A data run flag (DRF) is set to indicate an initial ('connection open') packet or when all previously sent SN have been acknowledged. When a valid connection record exists at the receiver, only packets with SNs within a receive window will be accepted. When the receiver does not have a valid connection record for the source, only a packet with the DRF flag on will be accepted. If the sender has a valid connection record to a destination, then the next contiguous SN must be used for an outgoing packet. If

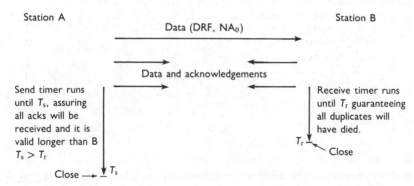

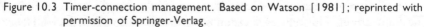

Figure 10.3 Timer-connection management. Based on Watson [1981]; reprinted with permission of Springer-Verlag.

the connection record has been deleted, the sender can choose any ISN but it puts the DRF flag on.

No exchanges of packets are required to open or disconnect a connection reliably. Connection records are held only for as long as is needed, but it is necessary to guarantee that packets are discarded by the network when their maximum lifetime expires. Each packet has a field initialized at the source with the MPL. This is decremented to take into account link delays and hold times in switching nodes and the packet is discarded when the count is reduced to zero. Other mechanisms for enforcing bounds on packet lifetime are described in Sloan [1983].

10.3 Addressing

The transport-layer address used for both connection set-up and datagrams generally identifies a 'socket' or 'port' within a particular station. A socket is assigned to a process within the station, but a process may have more than one socket. Transport-layer addresses should map onto processes whereas network-layer addresses should refer to stations. In practice the distinction between the two layers is not as clear. For example, the X.121 addressing scheme allows network addresses of the form *country.network.station.port*. This is because X.25 connections may map directly onto transport connections. The port or socket gives a network-wide standard means of identifying a process or an entry in a process. It is independent of the process identifiers used within the local operating systems of the computers connected to the network. The socket could map onto a mailbox, entryport, process name, etc.

A transport address may be obtained by asking a name server to translate a process or resource name into a transport address, cf. telephone directory service. This is really considered a session layer service. The address of the name server has to be fixed and known to all users. Another use of a well-known address is the log-in server on a time-sharing computer system. A connection request is sent to its well-known socket. The log-in server assigns a socket number for use by the client, possibly creating a process to handle the connection. The client may request the use of a particular resource (e.g. editor) and so the socket will be mapped onto the editor process. Thus some socket numbers are global and uniquely identify a transport entity, whereas others are assigned dynamically and may eventually be reused. Socket numbers must not be reused if there is any possibility of delayed packets arriving containing a socket number from a previous connection.

In CONIC a transport address is of the form *subnet.station.module.port*. The modules which implement executive functions (such as module creation/deletion and read or write memory block for debugging) are identical in every station. They are assigned the same module number and obviously have the same ports and so are examples of the use of well-known addresses.

10.4 Multiplexing

The transport layer is likely to perform multiplexing under the following circumstances:

1. Upward multiplexing of transport connections (process to process message streams) onto a datagram network service access point, i.e. the transport layer provides end-to-end VCs on top of a datagram network layer. This is the most logical way to implement transport connections and is often used across interconnected networks.
2. Upward multiplexing of transport connections onto a network layer VC. This might be done to optimize costs in a network which has peculiar tariff structures and has a comparatively high charge for VC duration compared to the data transfer charge.
3. Downward multiplexing (splitting) of transport connections onto multiple network connections in order to improve throughput.

It is unlikely that transport layer protocols for WANs which use public X.25 networks with sensible tariff structures will implement multiplexing, but will simply map a transport layer connection onto an X.25 connection.

10.5 Error and Flow Control

Transport-layer error and flow control is always end-to-end. In a store-and-forward network there is a probability of loss or corruption of a packet in an intermediate switching node. Transport layers generally use a sum check or longitudinal parity check over all the bytes in a message rather than CRC as the error rates are much lower. Also sum checks are much easier to implement in software than CRC checks.

Loss of a packet may occur due to the crash of an intermediate node or the discarding of the packet because a node has insufficient buffers. Thus some transport protocols perform end-to-end acknowledgements and timeouts. Most of the error-control mechanisms described under 'data-link layer' (Section 8.3) apply. The main differences compared to the data-link layer are:

- Delays are longer and more variable.
- Error rates are lower.
- The transport layer has to cater for delayed, out of sequence messages from a datagram network layer service. A data link has no storage so cannot generate out of sequence messages.
- Duplicate messages at the transport layer may be generated by lower layer transmissions. However a data-link layer which does not perform retransmissions does not have to deal with duplicates.
- More complex connection set-up mechanisms are needed.

The flow-control mechanisms described in the previous chapter can also be used in the transport layer but the mechanism usually used is **credit flow control**. The receiver informs the sender of the amount of information that can be sent, i.e. for which buffers have been allocated at the receiver. The amount could be in terms of characters, packets, sequences of packets, etc. A credit packet may be sent when the user issues a receive primitive and passes a buffer to the transport entity. Note that polling is a particular case of a credit scheme with a credit of only one packet.

A flow-control packet should carry a credit indication of the form 'send up to packet 5', or 'send 3 after 27', rather than 'send y more packets'. The former can be repeated with no ambiguity whereas relative credit can be ambiguous, e.g. if duplicated $2y$ packets may be sent. Many protocols piggy-back an explicit credit indication with an acknowledgement for a packet correctly received [DOD, 1980]. Often the unit of flow control is bytes rather than packets, i.e. the receiver requests x bytes.

10.6 Message Segmentation and Reassembly

The reasons for segmenting a large message into smaller packets for transfer across a network were discussed in Chapter 5, and the mechanisms were elaborated in the previous chapter. Segmentation should preferably be performed in the transport layer rather than in a lower layer. The transport layer is implemented within a host computer which is likely to have larger memory than a switching node and so can afford the larger buffers needed for segmentation and reassembly. Some transport layer implementations use application buffer space for reassembly.

10.7 ISO Transport Protocol Classes

The transport layer enhances the quality of service provided by the network layer, and so the functions implemented by a transport protocol depend on the service provided by the network over which it is to be used. Currently ISO appear to be converging on five slightly different classes of a connection-oriented transport service [von Studnitz, 1983; Knightson, 1982; ISO, 1982].

Simple Class 0:   This does not enhance the service provided by the network. It is designed for use over X.25 type networks with low residual error rates and failure rates. Only functions for connection establishment, data transfer with segmenting and error reporting are available. The lifetime of the transport connection is dependent on and is the same as the lifetime of the network connection, i.e. there is no multiplexing.

Basic error recovery class 1:   This provides recovery from network signalled disconnect or resets. It is designed for use over networks with a low residual error rate but an unacceptable rate of connection failures. It provides connection and disconnection, expedited data transfer and flow control based on the underlying network service flow control, but no multiplexing.

Multiplexing class 2: This provides for the multiplexing of several transport connections within a single network connection to minimize costs. It is also designed for use over networks with low error and connection failure rates. It allows an optional window flow-control mechanism and expedited data transfer.

Error recovery class 3: This is similar to class 2 but permits recovery from network-signalled disconnects and resets. It permits more flexible flow control based on credits.

Error detection and recovery class 4: This class provides full error control by means of sequence numbers, checksums, timeouts and retransmissions. It is designed for use over a datagram network service, so will recover from lost or mis-sequenced packets. It uses a three-way handshake connection set-up procedure.

We will not describe the ISO transport layer protocol as it differs in detail rather than fundamental concept from the lower-layer connection protocols covered earlier. A full specification can be found in ISO [1982]. This has been extended to allow a connectionless transport protocol [Stein, 1984].

10.8 Session layer

The session layer functions are not well defined in most network architectures. It has traditionally been incorporated into a higher-level protocol such as a terminal access or file-transfer protocol. It was defined as a layer in the ISO model because there are some common features of these protocols which could be incorporated into a general-purpose protocol and so be shared by different applications. The objective of the session layer is thus to achieve application-oriented functions in a unified way, and it is concerned with the management of interactions between users. It differs from the objectives of the lower layers in that they are concerned with data transportation problems [De Luca, 1982; Schindler, 1983].

Our opinion is that the session layer as defined by ISO is not really required for distributed systems, but is more applicable to networked autonomous systems. Some of the services specified can be identified in other layers of the distributed systems described in the literature. For these reasons we will not cover it in detail.

10.8.1 Session-layer Services [Schindler, 1981; 1983]

Mapping of sessions onto transport connections
The basic service is setting up and releasing session-layer connections and transferring data. There is a one-to-one mapping between a session connec-

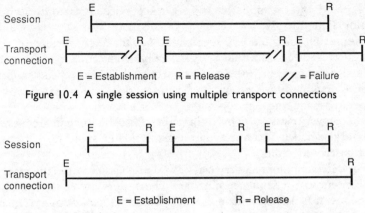

Figure 10.4 A single session using multiple transport connections

Figure 10.5 Multiple sessions using a single transport connection

tion and a transport connection at any given instant. However, the lifetime of a session connection can span multiple transport connections to cater for failures of the latter (Fig. 10.4). Also sequential sessions can use the same transport connection as shown in Fig. 10.5.

Data transfer
The session layer provides for the transfer of normal packets and expedited data. An additional service often provided is **quarantining** – normal messages are collected together into a 'quarantine unit' which corresponds to a user transaction. This is stored within the session layer for delivery as a whole unit or the user can cancel delivery if the quarantine unit is not complete. The user can then ensure that the transaction is processed as a whole or discarded, ensuring consistent state of the application.

Interaction management
The session layer can support two forms of user dialogue:

> **Two-way simultaneous** (full duplex) is the normal mode where either side can transmit at any time.
> **Two-way alternate** (half duplex) where only one side at a time can have permission to transmit. The session layer provides mechanisms for the transfer of a **data transmit token** between the users. Also a user not in possession of the token may request one (a form of interrupt).

It is also feasible to have a unidirectional (simplex) session, e.g. data transmitted via a television channel.

Synchronization
This involves the saving of state information during a session to enable recovery to a known point after a failure. A user requests a synchronization point or checkpoint in the data stream and must not transmit any further

data until the checkpoint has been confirmed. In IBM's SNA these synchronization points are called 'brackets'. Synchronization points are numbered. If an error occurs at a later stage the session can be restored to a previous checkpoint and the transfer of data can be resumed from there. This can be useful for recovery from communication failures during very long file transfers.

The current specification of session-layer synchronization only copes with communication connection failures. If the session is to be made resilient to station failures, then the state information must be saved in stable storage (e.g. on a disk). Many applications require operation to be performed atomically as discussed in Chapter 4. This means that if the operation fails any intermediate side effects must be undone. It is not clear whether provision of atomic action protocols is a session- or application-layer service. Our view is that atomic actions and the type of synchronization described above are really application dependent and so should be provided as an application sublayer.

Exception reporting

This allows the user to report an error or failure to its peer entity during a session. The normal action would be to attempt to resynchronize back to a previous synchronization point.

Name mapping

There is some controversy whether the mapping of an application name to an address by using a directory or name server is a session- or application-layer function. This is one of the few functions which does appear in nearly all distributed systems, as described in the following case studies. However, it is currently not specified as a session-layer service in the ISO Reference Model.

10.8.2 Session Service Primitives

In addition to the normal connection management and data-transfer primitives similar to those described in Section 10.1, the following primitives are required to access the above services. The primitives can take the form of a request for the user to the service or an indication from the service to the user.

Quarantine deliver: Releases the messages being stored as a quarantine unit for delivery to the remote user.
Quarantine cancel: Cancels delivery of a quarantine unit.
Token give: Passes a token (e.g. permission to transmit) to the peer entity.
Token please: Requests a token from the peer entity.
Synch. point: Defines a numbered synchronization point.
Resynchronize: Requests a restart of communication from a specified synchronization point.

Activity: Initiates a new association between two users or reselects a previously unfinished association. This could be used, for example, to switch between updating different windows in a remote terminal.

Further information on the ISO concept of a session layer can be found in Young [1983] and Schindler [1981]. In the remainder of this chapter we will cover a number of case studies of the implementation of the communication system to support distributed systems. These communication systems include both session- and transport-layer functions.

10.9 Case Study: CONIC Communication System

The CONIC communication system supports the transfer of messages between modules in remote stations. An overview of the architecture of the communication system was given in Section 5.7.3. A more detailed description can be found in Sloman [1986], from which Figs. 10.6–10.9 are reprinted with permission from the IEE.

Basic remote communication service
The basic communication system delivers only error-free messages. It includes error-detection mechanisms and discards any messages which are corrupted.

When an exitport is linked to a remote entryport, it is actually connected to a local server entryport provided by the communication system, as shown in Fig. 10.6. The exitport data structure then holds both the local communication entryport address and the address of the remote destination entryport.

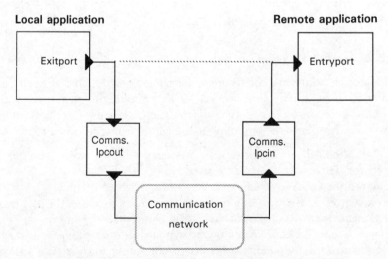

Figure 10.6 Remote links. Reprinted with permission of IEE.

Linking an exitport to an entryport corresponds roughly to an ISO model session connection, but this is the responsibility of a third party (the configuration manager) rather than the application tasks. Linking of port is considered to be an operating-system service rather than a communication-system service.

When a task sends a message to a remote module, the kernel treats it as a standard local IPC call and transfers the message to the communication system module, IPCOUT. This module effectively multiplexes all outgoing exitports onto a single message stream into the network. IPCOUT receives the message via its datagram entryport (Fig. 10.7) into a communication buffer. The source task performing a notify send can continue as soon as the message is copied into the communication buffer. IPCOUT gets the remote entryport address from the local sender's exitport and places both source and destination address in the message header. A pointer to the communication buffer is sent to the data-link driver. Once the frame has been transmitted the communication buffer can be used to send another message, as there are no acknowledgements or retransmissions at this level. IPCOUT processes a single message at a time and waits until it has been transmitted by the hardware.

The remote communication system demultiplexes the incoming messages onto the relevant entryports within the station. At the remote end, the local destination task may not be ready to receive the incoming message and so the communication module could be suspended, waiting to deliver the message. Thus a group of modules (multiple instances of IPCIN) are provided to act as surrogate senders and hold incoming messages (Fig. 10.7). Each

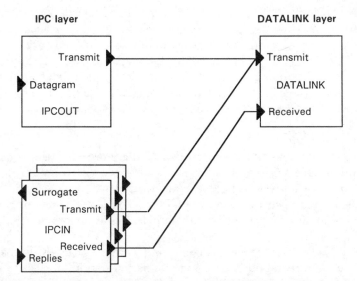

Figure 10.7 Basic communication-system modules in a station. Reprinted with permission of IEE.

free instance of IPCIN offers its services to the DATALINK module by sending a pointer to its buffer, i.e. free modules will queue at the data-link entryport. DATALINK replies when the message has been received into the buffer of the first IPCIN instance in the queue.

When a request message is received, the IPCIN module links its surrogate exitport to the destination task's entryport. It then performs a local send wait (or send for a notify or incoming reply). IPCIN receives the reply into its communication buffer, and swaps the destination and source addresses. It then passes the message to DATALINK for transmission. When the reply has been transmitted that instance of IPCIN is free to deal with a new incoming message.

It is important to make sure that a reply is not received for the wrong request. Every task has a transaction identifier which is incremented when the task times out of a send wait or when a correct reply is received. This identifier is sent in the request and is returned in the reply. The kernel uses it to detect and discard out-of-date replies.

Both IPCIN and IPCOUT are implemented using the CONIC programming language and use the standard IPC primitives. However, they do make use of some special kernel calls to access exitport data structures. Hence they are privileged CONIC modules and should be considered as part of the station executive.

Extension to the basic communication system

Routing
Simple systems will contain a single LAN and will not need to perform routing. They can be expanded to include routing and multiple networks (Fig. 10.8). IPCOUT sends outgoing messages to the router which chooses the data link to which the message should be sent, and forwards it to the relevant driver. IPCIN still receives all incoming messages, and those which are not for the station are sent on to router. The router maintains routing tables and exchanges routing updates with similar modules in other gateways as described in Chapter 9.

Reliable connections
Reliable connections or virtual circuits (VCs) are provided as a configuration option. One VC is provided per exitport-to-entryport link. The VC is set up or cleared at the same time as the exitport-to-entryport link. There is no distinction made between the VCs for request–reply and notify links: all VCs are bidirectional. VC set up and clearing is always initiated from the exitport end.

We take advantage of the configuration facilities of CONIC by creating a module instance in both source and destination station for each VC. The state of the VC is represented implicitly by the program counter. Standard CONIC facilities for creating and deleting modules are used for setting up

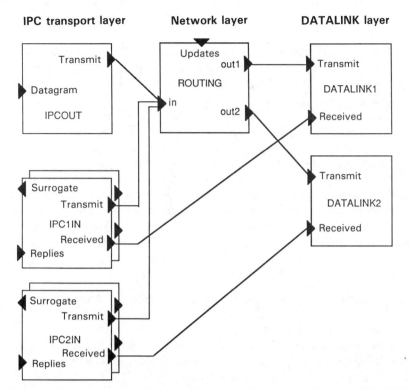

Figure 10.8 Communication system with routing. Reprinted with permission of IEE.

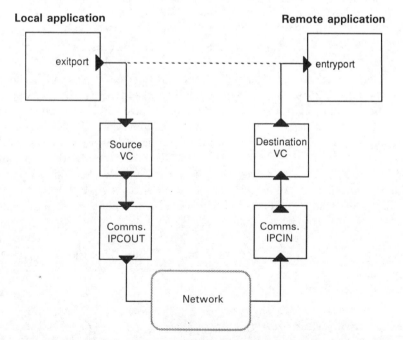

Figure 10.9 Virtual circuit enhancement. Reprinted with permission of IEE.

or clearing a VC resulting in considerable simplification of the code required. The overhead of module creation and deletion is acceptable because VCs are not likely to change frequently. In addition the Kernel automatically discards messages for non-existent modules so the handling of error states is also simplified. VC modules in the same station share code, and so this approach results in much less code. However the data space required for a module is more than the data space per virtual circuit needed by a single module implementing all virtual circuits in a station.

These VC modules reside between the application modules and the rest of the communication system (Fig. 10.9) rather than within the communication system modules. Hence they are completely transparent to the basic communicating service. This results in a much cleaner and simpler approach to providing a VC service.

10.10   Case Study: Cedar Remote Procedure Call (RPC) [Birrell, 1984]

Chapter 4 discussed the RPC as an inter-process communication primitive. The following descriptions of the RPC implementation for the Cedar distributed programming environment developed at Xerox is based on a paper by Birrell and Nelson [Birrell, 1984].

Remote procedure call could be implemented as an application service above a general-purpose message stream transport service, as is the case in the Xerox Courier RPC (see Fig. 5.33). The Cedar RPC implementation includes transport-layer error recovery, which is the reason for describing it under 'transport layer'.

The semantics of the Cedar RPC are that if the call returns to the client, then the remote procedure has been invoked exactly once. Otherwise, an exception is reported to the client and the procedure will have been invoked either once or not at all – the user is not told which. The RPC is designed to cope with the errors which can occur within a datagram internetwork environment and to protect both client and server from each other's station crashes. The RPC does not provide an atomic action, i.e. there is no attempt to undo side effects if a failure occurs between invoking a call and its completion. The Cedar RPC is unusual in that the client cannot specify a timeout. The reason is that local procedure calls do not normally specify a timeout. Instead the languages which use the Cedar RPC support an exception mechanism which aborts an activity in case of failure. There is thus no upper bound on the time it takes to service a call and so the client will wait indefinitely if the server deadlocks or loops.

Implementation structure
Figure 10.10 shows the components used to implement the RPC. In Cedar

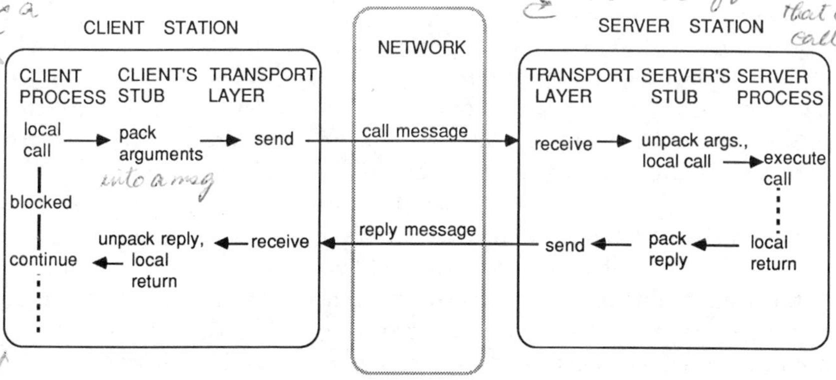

Figure 10.10 Remote procedure call implementation components

the transport and session layers are implemented by a package called *RPCRuntime*. This is responsible for binding particular servers to clients (i.e. setting up sessions) for a call, and for recovering from communication errors. There is an instance of RPCRuntime in each station within the distributed system and it handles all incoming and outgoing calls for that station. The stubs are specific to each application program and correspond roughly to the presentation layer of the ISO model. They perform the packing and unpacking of arguments and could also perform representation transformations for communication between different machines.

The procedures which can be called by other programs must be **exported** by the providing program. The external procedures implemented within other programs must be **imported** by the caller. These **exported** and **imported interfaces** specify the procedure names and their parameters. These interfaces are used to generate an **RPC stub** for each program, which calls remote procedures or provides procedures which are called by remote programs. There is a local stub procedure for each imported or exported procedure.

In order to perform an RPC, the client makes a local call on the corresponding procedure in its stub. This packs the call arguments into one or more messages. Pointers to these messages are passed to the transport layer, which is responsible for transmitting the messages reliably to the server's station. The transport layer in the server's station passes the incoming messages to the callee's stub which unpacks the arguments and makes a normal local procedure call on the server. When the call is completed a similar process is used to pass the return arguments back to the client, which was suspended waiting for the call to return. The procedure calls should not contain arguments which cannot be passed by value (see next chapter). A station's transport layer is implemented as a pool of worker processes, but they can be created and deleted dynamically to adjust to traffic conditions. Alternative implementations based on a monitor or a single multithreaded process are feasible. However, the transport layer in a station must not be blocked waiting for a server to handle an incoming call.

Binding

The binding operation binds an importer of an interface to a particular **instance** of the program which exports the interface. An interface **type** specifies the procedures and parameters of the operations which can be performed on a server. The compiler can use the imported interface type to check that the caller's parameters are type-compatible with the callee's parameters. A system may include multiple instances of programs offering the same service. For example, there can be multiple file servers so a client will have to be bound at run time to the instance of the file server in which its file resides.

A distributed name server is used to locate an appropriate interface exporter. The name server can map a type name of an interface to a list of instance names and can map an instance name to the exporter's station address.

A server wishing to export an interface calls the transport layer via the server stub. The *Exportinterface* procedure is given the interface type name, instance name and the incoming call dispatcher procedure to use in the server stub. The transport layer sends this information together with the station address to the name server which performs some validity checks, e.g. that the instance is of the stated type and that the address is valid. The server's transport layer enters this information about the export in a table. A unique **export ID** generated from a 32-bit clock is associated with each exported interface.

When a client wishes to bind to an imported interface, it makes a call via the client stub on the transport layer's *Importinterface* procedure, giving the required interface type and instance. Transport layer uses the name server to map these names onto the address of the instance and then calls the server's transport layer giving the instance name and type name. If the server is still exporting the interface, the export table index and export ID of interface are returned, else the binding fails. All subsequent calls on the server must contain this index and export ID.

If the exporter crashes and restarts it must re-export its interfaces and they will get new export IDs. This means all bindings are implicitly broken by a server crashing.

An importer can bind to **any** instance of a server by specifying only the type name. The nameserver returns the list of instances and the transport layer tries each in turn to find one that will accept a binding.

Transport protocol

Simple calls

The transport protocol was designed to support the RPC, to optimize performance and provide the semantics specified above. It has some similarity to the timer-based protocol described previously. When a client makes an RPC on a remote server the transport layer sends a call message containing:

- Transaction ID: a unique identifier generated for each call of the client.

It consists of the globally unique client's station identifier, client station incarnation number, client process identifier and a monotonic sequence number. Its use is explained below.

- Called procedure identifier.
- Export ID of the remote interface, obtained during binding.
- Call parameters.

A positive acknowledgement error-control mechanism is used to recover from lost messages. A call or reply is retransmitted after a timeout unless an acknowledgement is received. The reply message can act as the acknowledgement of a call message and a new message from the same client can act as the acknowledgement of a reply mesage. Thus two transport messages can be used for a simple RPC, provided the parameters fit into a single message, the processing time is fairly short and the client makes frequent calls on the same server.

The **transaction ID** is used by the client to check that the reply corresponds to the current call and by the server to detect duplicate calls. The transaction ID must not repeat after a client crashes, hence the inclusion of an incarnation number. The server maintains a table of the last transaction ID for each active client. Duplicate calls are acknowledged and discarded. Calls with an invalid interface export ID are rejected. This can only occur if the server failed and recovered without the client knowing.

A client can only have a single call outstanding at a time. The servers only check that the transaction ID from a client is monotonic, i.e. it does not have to be sequential. Thus the client does not have to maintain a separate sequence counter for each server it calls, as is the case for normal connections. A counter which is incremented when read can be used to generate all client transaction IDs within a station. The station incarnation number is the time at which the station was initialized (obtained from a time server).

The server's transport layer maintains state information about a client (transaction ID) for about 5 minutes, which is long enough to make sure no duplicates will arrive. If no further calls arrive in that time, the information can be discarded. This minimizes state information overheads.

Complicated calls
If the call or result parameters are too long to fit into a single message they have to be sent as a series of messages (packets). Each message is numbered and all but the last request an immediate acknowledgement.

If an acknowledgement is not received within a timeout period a message is retransmitted and a flag requesting an immediate acknowledgement is set. When all acknowledgements are received the client's transport layer waits for the reply. A probe message is sent periodically to detect a communication failure or server crash. Probes are retransmitted if not immediately acknowledged. Figure 10.11 shows the messages needed for an isolated, long-duration call, requiring two messages to send the call parameters and a single message for the reply parameters.

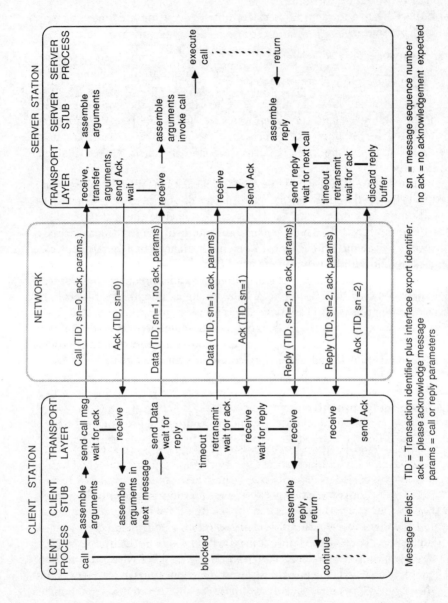

Message Fields: TID = Transaction identifier plus interface export identifier.
                   ack = please acknowledge message
                   params = call or reply parameters

sn = message sequence number
no ack = no acknowledgement expected

Figure 10.11 A complicated remote procedure call

Extensions

The RPC can be made secure by use of private keys and encryption. Each communication partner has a private key known to itself and the **authentication service** (key-distribution center). The two partners wishing to communicate obtain a conversation key from the authentication service. This is used to encrypt the information transferred between the partners. Details of this security service can be found in Birrell [1985].

The Cedar RPC does not deal with 'orphans'. If the client crashes the server will be unaware and will continue to process the call. The client could recover quickly, bind to a new server on the same station and initiate another call. If both servers access common data this could lead to interferences. A mechanism for dealing with orphans is described in Panzieri [1985].

10.11 Case Study: V-Kernel Interprocess Communication
[Cheriton, 1984]

The V-Kernel has been developed at Stanford University to support distributed systems in a LAN environment. It differs from the previous case studies in that the IPC primitives available to the user are operating-system level with no type checking. The primitives provide a request–reply service with some extensions. The same primitives can be used for both local and remote communication. The V-Kernel is unusual in that users pass explicit pointers in messages which can be used by inter address-space copy primitives, as the basic message is fixed length. The V-Kernel supports dynamic process creation and this is used within the communications system.

Communication primitives

Send (message, pid)
Sends a fixed-length 32-byte message to the process specified by *pid*, a 32-bit globally unique process identifier. The sender is blocked until a reply is received. The reply overwrites the original message. The process can also pass read or write access to a single segment of its address space.

(pid, count) = ReceiveWithSegment (message, segptr, segsize)
The process is blocked until a message arrives. The 32-byte message is received into the specified buffer and if the message specifies a segment with read access, the first *segsize* bytes are copied into the buffer specified by *segptr*. The source is returned in *pid* the source and the actual number of bytes received in *count*.

Replywithsegment (message, pid, destptr, segptr, segsize)
A 32-byte reply message is sent to *pid* together with a segment of length *segsize* pointed to by *segptr*. The segment address in the destination

(*destptr*), in which the message will be copied must have been sent to the replying process in a previous message.

CopyFrom (srcpid, destptr, srcptr, size)

Copies *size* bytes from the segment *srcptr* in the source process *srcpid* into *destptr*. The source process must be blocked waiting for a reply from the process invoking the copy, and must have passed the segment with read access. This is used to copy additional segments after a request has been received.

CopyTo (destpid, desptr, srcptr, size)

This is similar to the *CopyFrom* but copies from the invoker to the destination process which must be waiting for a reply.

Forward (message, srcpid, destpid)

Forwards the original message received from *srcpid* to *destpid*, which then replies directly to the source. The forwarder is not blocked.

A server would typically issue a *ReceiveWithSegment* to wait for any calls. If the parameters of the call are too long to fit into a single segment, they would be copied across by means of a *CopyFrom*. Long reply parameters would be copied to the client by means of a *CopyTo* and finally a *ReplyWithSegment* would complete the transaction and allow the client to continue. If the parameters are very short, as is often the case, then they are likely to fit into the 32-byte message and no segments need be transferred.

Addressing

A name server can be used to map names into process identifiers (pid) needed for the IPC primitives. The pids are unique within a domain of a single local area network. The pid consists of two fields, A 16-bit **logical host identifier** and a 16-bit **process index** which is locally unique within the host. At initialization time the kernel chooses a random number as a logical host identifier and broadcasts it to check that it is unique. The host identifier subfield is used to detect whether a process is local or remote.

The logical host identifier has to be mapped into station addresses (e.g. 48-bit Ethernet address), by means of a translation cache of recently used hosts. If there is no entry for the specified host, the message is broadcast over the LAN. Source pids and station addresses are extracted from incoming messages and inserted into the cache on the assumption that they will be used as destination addresses. Note that this mechanism precludes the migration of individual processes between stations, but a complete logical host could be moved to a new station to recover from a failure.

The distributed systems implemented using V-Kernel make extensive use of process groups [Cheriton, 1985]. The V-Kernel provides multicast or group addressing (as well as broadcast) to support this. A groupid is similar to a pid, as shown in Fig. 10.12. The **logical host group identifier** indicates the set of hosts in which members of the group reside and the **specific group identifier** indicates the specific group within the set of hosts. The mapping

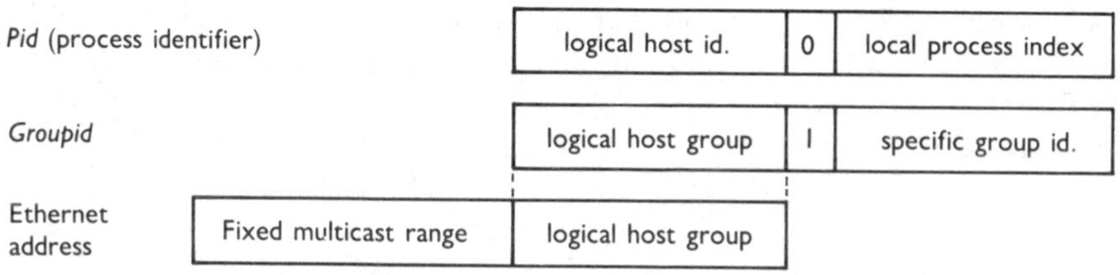

Pid (process identifier)	logical host id.	0	local process index

Groupid	logical host group	1	specific group id.

Ethernet address	Fixed multicast range	logical host group

Figure 10.12 Process group identifiers

to a station address is network dependent but Fig. 10.12 shows the mapping to an Ethernet multicast address.

Note that the first reply received from a messsage sent to a process group unblocks the caller. A get-reply primitive can be used to receive additional replies, which are queued. If a new message transaction is started, subsequent replies to the old transaction are discarded.

Transport protocol

Remote communication for the above primitives is implemented by a request–reply transport protocol which performs timeouts, retransmissions and duplicate filtering. The transport message contains a header, 32-byte fixed-length message field and an optional variable-length data segment. The header contains the following fields:

- Message type: send, reply, forward, copy, acknowledge, etc.
- Transaction ID: monotonic transaction sequence number obtained from station-wide counter.
- Source process ID.
- Destination process ID.
- Forwarder: pid of the process that forwarded the message, if any, else zero.
- Segment address: source or destination address for the segment in the message, depending on the type of message.
- Length: in bytes of the data segment field (may be zero).

An initial send includes the data segment, if any, as an optimization. It can be discarded at the receiver if it is short of buffer space or the receiving process is not waiting for the message.

The Kernel retransmits a packet after a timeout until a valid reply is received, a reply-pending message is received, or a retry count is exceeded. Replies with invalid transaction IDs are discarded and ignored. A forwarder must notify the originator of a message of its new destination. Retransmissions are then addressed to the new destination.

When a message is received at a station, the Kernel creates a buffer process to represent the remote sending process. The transport message header and message fields are copied into the process descriptor, which is then queued off the receiver's process descriptor. The buffer process minimizes the differences in handling local and remote communication within the kernel.

The receiving kernel filters out duplicates by comparing the source pid and transaction ID with those of buffer processes. Duplicates are discarded and either the reply message, if it has been generated, or a reply-pending indication is transmitted. Buffer processes are saved for a time after a reply is transmitted to deal with duplicate requests (cf. timer-based protocol).

A user can indicate that a reply message is idempotent and need not be saved by the kernel. In this case the buffer process is discarded immediately and duplicate requests generate a repeated user-level transaction.

The copy-to and copy-from primitives are implemented by means of a sequence of maximum size transport messages and a single acknowledgement is returned at the end. Retransmissions occur from the last correctly received packet. The assumption is that low LAN error rates mean full retransmission occurs infrequently. The segment address field in the header acts as a sequence number. The 'copy' messages do not have to be queued or buffered in the Kernel, but could be copied directly from the network interface to (or from) the user's space. Thus they could be accepted out of order.

It is interesting to contrast the CONIC and V-Kernel communication systems. The latter has been highly optimized for performance so the communication system has been implemented as part of the Kernel. CONIC has been designed for flexibility and to allow optional configuration time facilities, and so has been implemented as a set of application processes.

10.12 Summary

This chapter has described the transport service primitives for a typical transport-layer connection service. A three-way handshake or timer protocol are needed to set up and clear connections reliably above a datagram network, which can deliver delayed out-of-sequence messages. However, a simple two-way handshake can be used above a network-connection service. In distributed systems session-layer synchronization and interaction management services are usually incorporated into the application layer. However, as indicated in the case studies, distributed systems do include an explicit name-binding or name-mapping service which could be considered a session layer.

The CONIC and Cedar RPC case studies described the communication support for language primitives so they included type checking when binding to the remote communication partner. The V-Kernel provided operating system primitives so no type checking was involved. In all the case studies a local process was used as a representative of the remote application process, and a local call was made between this representative and the application. Both the Cedar and V-Kernel communication systems were optimized for performance, whereas the CONIC communication system was implemented as a set of application processes which could easily be configured to provide a variety of services.

References

Andreoni, G. 'Fortran Interface to X.25 and Transport Service', *Computer Networks*, Vol. 8, no. 1, 1984, pp. 17–22.

Birrell, A., Nelson, B., 'Implementing remote procedure calls', *ACM TOCS*, Vol. 2, no. 1, February 1984, pp. 39–59.

Birrell, A., 'Secure communication using remote procedure calls', *ACM TOCS*, Vol. 3, no. 1, February, 1985, pp. 1–14.

Cheriton, D., 'The V Kernel: a software base for distributed systems', *IEEE Software*, Vol. 1, no., 2, April 1984, pp. 19–43.

Cheriton, D., Zwaenepoel, W., 'Distributed process groups in the V Kernel', *ACM TOCS*, Vol, 3, no. 2, May 1985, pp. 77–107.

De Luca, G., Rietti, G., 'An introduction to the ECMA session layer protocol', *Proc. 6th ICCC*, North-Holland, 1982, pp. 792–797.

'DOD transmission control protocol', *ACM Computer Comms. Review*, Vol. 10, no. 4, October 1980, pp. 52–132.

Fletcher, J., Watson, R., 'Mechanisms for a reliable timer based protocol', *Computer Networks*, Vol. 2, no. 4, September 1978, pp. 271–290.

ISO/TC97/SC16, 'Transport protocol specification', *ACM Computer Comms. Review*, Vol. 12, no. 3, July 1982, pp. 24–64.

Knightson, K.G., 'The transport layer', *Proc. 6th ICCC*, North-Holland, 1982, pp. 787–791.

Langsford, A., 'The open systems user's programming interfaces', *Computer Networks*, Vol. 8, no. 1, 1984, pp. 3–12.

Panzieri, F., Shrivastava, S., *Rajdoot: A Remote Procedure Call Mechanism Supporting Orphan Detection and Killing*, University of Newcastle upon Tyne, Computing Laboratory, NE1 7RU, UK, 1985.

Schindler, S., Schulze, J., 'Open systems interconnection: the session service', *Computer Communications*, Vol. 4, no. 2, April 1981, pp. 43–55.

Schindler, S., Flasche, U., Oranen, J., Widlewski, H., 'Open systems interconnection – the Teletex based session protocol Parts 1 & 2', *Computer Communications*, Vol. 6, nos. 2&3, April & June 1983, pp. 78–79, 126–140.

Sloan, L., 'Mechanisms that enforce bounds on packet lifetimes', *ACM TOCS*, Vol. 1 no. 4, November 1983, pp. 201–211.

Sloman, M., Kramer, J., Magee, J., *A Flexible Communication Structure for Distributed Embedded Systems*, IEE Proc. Part E. Computers and Digital Techniques, Vol. 133, no. 4, July 1986.

Stein, S., 'The ISO connectionless transport standards', *ACM Computer Comms. Review*, Vol. 14, no. 4, October 1984, pp. 18–45.

Sunshine, C.A., Dalal, Y.K., 'Connection management in transport protocols', *Computer Networks*, Vol. 2, no. 6, 1978, pp. 454–473.

von Studnitz, P., 'Transport protocols: their performance and status in international standardisation', *Computer Networks*, Vol. 7, no. 1, February 1983, pp. 27–35.

Watson, R., 'IPC interface and end-to-end protocols', *Distributed Systems Architecture and Implementation*, Springer Verlag Lecture Notes No. 105, pp. 140–174.

Wecker, S., 'DNA: the digital network architecture', *IEEE Trans. on Comms.*, COM Vol. 28, no. 4, April 1980, pp. 510–526.

Xerox Corporation, *Internet Transport Protocols*, XSIS 028112, Xerox OPD, Network Systems Administration Office, 3333 Coyote Hill Road, Palo Alto, California 94304, Dec. 1981.

Young, C.E., 'A standard session protocol for OSI', *AFIPS NCC*, Vol. 32, 1983, pp. 617–622.

Eleven

PRESENTATION LAYER

The lower layers of the communication system which we have covered are concerned with establishing and maintaining an association between two (or more) processes in different stations to allow them to communicate and synchronize their activities. These layers are thus responsible for information transfer and recovery from errors that may occur during communication. The presentation layer is needed to overcome differences of representation of information in non-homogeneous computers and languages.

We will first discuss the need for a presentation layer followed by an overview of data types as these form the basis for specifying representations. The rest of the chapter is devoted to standard external representations and transformations needed for the transfer of information.

11.1 Purpose and Relation to Other Layers

Computers can differ in their representation of primitive data items:

- Character codes can be ASCII, EBCDIC or a graphical character set.
- Integers can vary in length from 8 to 64 bits and use 1s or 2s complement representation.
- Reals can be encoded as fixed or floating-point numbers and the latter can differ in lengths of mantissa and exponent as well as using different bases for the exponent.
- Bytes may be addressed left to right within a word or right to left. This may require byte swapping when words (e.g. integers) are inserted into a message which is transmitted a byte at a time.

Programming languages can also differ in the way they represent numbers or data structures such as arrays, records or lists. It is necessary to transform between these data representations when transferring information between application entities within different computers and/or implemented using different programming languages.

In an open system environment there may be N different computers which potentially can communicate. It is impractical to provide a separate transformation mechanism for every possible pair of computers, as this would lead to $N*(N-1)$ translators for N different computers, without considering language differences. Instead a network-wide **standard representation** is defined for the transfer of information (Fig. 11.1). This requires $2N$ translators (one to and one from the internal representations of each of the computers or language). This is similar to the use of an intermediate language for cross compilers.

Application entities may access shared information stored in a variety of different file systems or communicate with remote terminals or printers. File systems and devices differ in their representation of information and the operations which can be performed on them. The presentation layer should provide the facilities to specify a common representation and set of operations for a class of devices or a generalized file service, i.e. a **virtual device** or a **virtual file service**. The dialogue between an application program and a device, or between two application programs which share information, can be described as a set of operations on typed objects. Devices and shared data can be specified as an abstract data type (ADT). This will be discussed in more detail in Section 11.6 and in the next chapter.

The presentation layer's purpose is thus to represent information to communicating application entities in a way that preserves meaning (values) while resolving syntactic or representation differences. It provides protocols to enhance the session service by providing standard representations for information transfer as well as mechanisms to define or select these representations.

The borderline between the application and presentation layers of the ISO model is very vague. Information being transferred between applications is, in some sense, common information [Schindler, 1981]. Traditionally the definition of common or shared information between application entities was always considered part of the application. However, some of the working

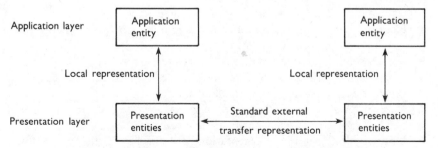

Figure 11.1 Presentation layer representation transformations

papers from the standardization organizations consider file transfer and virtual terminal protocols as part of the presentation layer. In our view these are specific to a subset of applications and so should be considered a sublayer within the application layer but make use of the presentation layer services for the specification of representation and transformations. This is very similar to using the predefined types of a high-level programming language to specify a set of application specific data types.

11.2 Data Types

Data typing is used in most high-level programming languages. A type specifies a template from which named instances (objects) can be created. The type essentially characterizes the set of values which can be assumed by objects of that type as well as the set of operations which can be applied to the objects. For example, objects of type boolean can take the values true or false. The type boolean specifies the set of logical operations such as OR, AND, NOT. Types can be implicitly defined (i.e. predefined) within the language or user defined. User-defined types (e.g. arrays, records, sequences) can be constructed from simpler predefined types. A compiler for a typed language can check the compatibility and legality of various constructs. For example it can detect that an arithmetic operation (e.g. add) is not allowed on a boolean object or that an integer value is not assigned to a boolean object. Similarly a compiler can check that the interfaces used for interprocess communication are type compatible, as is done for CONIC and the Cedar RPC (see Chapter 10).

The presentation layer should define the standard external representation for a set of types which will cater for most of the predefined types found in high-level programming languages.

Primitive Types
A primitive type is an elementary data unit which is not decomposable into smaller elements. Computer systems provide hardware support for the manipulation of most of the following primitive types:

- Boolean (bit) can take only two values, true and false (1 or 0).
- Integer a signed natural number.
- Cardinal an unsigned natural number.
- Floating point a representation for real numbers in which the decimal point is not fixed.
- Fixed point a representation for real numbers in which the decimal point is fixed.
- Character the set of printable characters.
- Octet (byte) an 8-bit unit of data which may be used to represent a character, cardinal or integer.
- Binary coded decimal (bcd) a 4-bit representation of a number in the range 0–9.

- Null   a typeless and valueless placeholder.

Many languages also include a type address or pointer, but it may be meaningless to transfer an address value to another application entity in a different address space or computer system (see Section 11.5.1).

Constructed types

Most high-level languages provide facilities to specify constructed (or structured) types as collections of elements which are of primitive or constructed type. As elements can themselves be constructors, nested data structures can be specified. A constructed object may be manipulated as a complete unit or the individual elements may be manipulated. Note that it is the constructors which are provided by the language, but the actual constructed types are application specific.

Constructed types have a number of attributes. If **bounded**, the number of the elements is predefined and cannot be modified at run-time. The order of elements within the structure may be significant or elements can be specified in any order. The elements may all be of the same type (**homogeneous**) or mixed types (**heterogeneous**). Typical high-level language constructors include:

- Array   bounded and ordered collection of elements of homogeneous types.
- Record   bounded and ordered collection of elements of various types.
- Set   bounded, unordered collection of elements of homogeneous or heterogeneous types.
- Enumerated bounded, ordered set of identifiers denoting values.
- Sequence   unbounded, ordered collection of homogeneous elements.
- Byte string bounded, ordered collection of bytes or characters.
- Bit string bounded, ordered collection of bits.

Some languages allow the element type to be specified at run time from a predefined choice of types, e.g. Pascal *variant record*. An element of type 'unspecified' allows a value of any arbitrary type to be used at run time.

11.3 Presentation-layer Services

We will now give an overview of the services provided by the presentation layer [Schindler 1981; Langsford 1984].

Information transformation

The most important function of the presentation layer is to allow the transfer of arbitrary typed data structures, performing the necessary transformations between representations. The presentation layer provides a standard external representation for both primitive and constructed data types as discussed in

Section 11.4. An implementation of the presentation layer provides the transformations between machine- or language-dependent local representations and the standard external one (see Section 11.5).

The presentation layer may also provide a set of optional syntax transformations. Data compression can be used to reduce the volume of information being transferred. Encryption/decryption may be required to protect information from unauthorized access. These will not be further discussed as they are well described elsewhere [Computer, 1983; Tanenbaum 1981, Ch. 9].

Specifying application-specific abstract data types

Shared data structures, virtual devices, virtual file services can all be modelled as abstract data types (ADTs). In addition ADTs can be used to encapsulate application-specific external representations together with their transformation procedures in a single syntactic unit. It has been suggested that the presentation layers should support the specification of ADTs [Schindler 1981], but as yet none do. We will discuss the use of ADTs in more detail later.

Negotiation

In an open systems environment application entities often have to cater for a wide range of communicating partners with different facilities. It is thus necessary to allow variations, by negotiation, in the local representation of an instance of a type. For example, the number of characters on a line or the number of lines on a page for a page mode virtual terminal. Some presentation-layer implementations allow the negotiation of the representation of primitive data objects, e.g. the number of bits for an integer or real [Moulton, 1982].

Context manipulation

A context is the set of types, objects and constants currently available in a presentation-layer environment. A context may be provided by default when a connection is set up or it could be selected during a connection. Consider, for example, a user accessing a remote file store. The types pertinent to the file service as well as the actual file (i.e. data object) being accessed and its types would constitute a current context. Selecting a new file for access would require modification to the current context to introduce the new file and its associated types.

The presentation layer provides a set of service primitives to manipulate the context, and this can be considered part of the negotiation procedure. Typically these would be to select or delete a named context.

Access to session-layer communication service

The presentation layer must also provide application entities with the means to access the session-layer services for establishing and releasing session-layer connections and transferring information. There is no multiplexing or splitting within the presentation layer, so a presentation-layer connection maps directly on to a session-layer connection. The presentation layer is just providing access, without improving the quality (reliability, performance etc.) of the data-transfer services provided by lower layers. The additional services it provides are those dealing with representation and transformation of data.

The current ISO reference model does not consider the provision of connectionless presentation-layer services. The representation and transformation services apply equally to both connection and connectionless data transfer.

11.4 External Type Representations

11.4.1 Representation Characteristics

There are a number of proprietary and proposed standards for the external representation of primitive and constructed data types. Three examples will be described in the next sections. These presentation-layer protocols differ in the extent to which they are able to represent the types described earlier and the way in which they represent data values. These differences can be characterized as follows.

Variable- or fixed-length data values
Data values can be represented as a **variable**-length string of bytes, usually with an explicit length indicator. In some older protocols the bytes are printable characters from a standard character set such as ASCII or CCITT International Alphabet 5 (IA5). One byte then represents one decimal digit. Nearly all computers provide operating-system procedures for input and output of numbers using such character sets. This representation places no field size limitations on data values, but it is very inefficient. For example, six bytes would be needed to represent a 16-bit integer.

An alternative is to use a variable length string of bytes but treat the group of bytes as a binary integer or cardinal. This is more efficient but the processing overheads of transforming local representations which are usually 16- or 32-bit into these variable-length representations can be quite high.

Some representations pack data values into **fixed** size fields (e.g. 16 or 32 bits). This may occasionally lead to limitations on the maximum value which can be represented; however, the transformations between the local and external representations are simpler.

Explicit or implicit type information
The external representation of a data value may include an **explicit** type identifier or tag. This increases the size of the message to be transferred and hence the communication overhead. However, all the information required

to perform transformation of representation at the receiver is self-contained within the message.

If type identifiers are omitted from the representation then the receiver has to know in advance the format of the messages it will receive. For example an entryport on which a message is received is of a predefined type or the parameters of a remote procedure being called are of a known type. The address (entryport or procedure identifier) contained in the message implicitly identifies a message type descriptor which can be used at the receiver to transform the message. This also applies to nested constructed types.

Explicit type tags result in position independent data values so they do not have to be in a predefined order e.g. the elements of a set. Similarly variant types or optional fields in a data structure must be tagged to allow the receiver to relate values to types. The scope of these tags is limited to the particular data structure whereas in general the scope of explicit tags is global or application specific.

Type tags can be used by the receiver to dynamically verify that information received is of the expected type. This is similar to the compile-time type checking normally performed by some compilers. For example if an element of type integer is expected and a boolean is received there must be a logical fault in the sender program (we assume communication errors are detected at a lower level). This run-time type checking provides another level of error detection in a distributed environment where the communicating entities are not trustworthy. Normal range checks would not detect this error as the value of a boolean (e.g. 0 or 1) is a valid integer.

Conic is good example of the use of static type checking with no type identifiers in messages. The Conic module programming language is strongly typed and so the compiler can check that a message sent to an exitport or received from an entryport corresponds to the type of the port. The configuration language checks for type compatibility when linking an exitport to an entryport. The communication system discards any corrupted messages which might have caused a type mismatch at the receiver. Type descriptors can be included in the exit and entryport data structures to allow the Presentation Layer to perform transformations. However, the Conic Presentation Layer has to be concerned with only hardware differences as Conic is a single language system.

11.4.2 Xerox Courier Representation

Courier [1981] was designed to minimize the processing overheads required to prepare and interpret data in the external representation rather than minimizing the communication bandwidth needed to transport messages. Thus the external representation was chosen to make the transformation as simple as possible. The basic data unit size is 16 bits. All primitive data values are packed into 16- or 32-bit fixed-size fields and **implicit type identifiers** are used. The following primitive data types are supported:

- Boolean   16-bit value of 1 (true) or (false).
- Cardinal   16-bit unsigned binary number.
- Long cardinal 32-bit unsigned binary number.
- Integer   16-bit 2s complement binary value.
- Long integer   32-bit 2s complement binary value.
- Character   8- or 16-bit unsigned binary value. 8-bit characters are used to represent the normal printable characters and 16-bit values for an extended character set which includes graphics, Greek and Japanese characters. Note that there is no standard representation for a single character but only strings (see below).
- Unspecified   16-bit data object of unspecified interpretation.

No representation has been defined for reals and so they would have to be mapped onto two integers in either a fixed- or floating-point format, i.e. the interpretation would have to be programmed into the application.

In the remainder of this chapter hexidecimal notation is used for examples of representations. The following constructors are supported in Courier:

- Strings   a length field followed by the required number of 16-bit words needed to hold the characters of the string. 8-bit characters are packed 2 to a 16-bit word. The length field, which can be specified at run time, is a cardinal number which specifies the number of bytes needed to hold the string. If the number is odd, then the final byte is zero; e.g., 'sum Σ' is encoded as 5 words:

Count	Su	m	Greek	Σ	
0007	5375	6D20	FF01	3200	(hex.)

                    The element Greek indicates the character set of the following string.

- Array   one-dimensional collection of data objects. The number and type of objects are predefined. The elements of an array can be of primitive or constructed type, including arrays. The representation of the array is simply the standard representation of the elements transferred in sequence.
- Record   a heterogeneous collection of elements which can be of primitive or constructed type.
- Sequence   an ordered, one-dimensional collection of homogeneous elements. It is similar to an array, but only the maximum number of elements is predefined. At run time the actual number can be specified. The very first field of a sequence contains a 16-bit cardinal number indicating the number of elements following.
- Enumeration   a quantity that can assume any of a relatively few named

integer values. For example,

$$errorcode\ TYPE = \{ok(0)\ commsfail(1),$$
$$destabsent(2)\};$$

The value *commsfail* is represented as 0001 (hex).

Choice The type of the data object is chosen at run time from a previously specified set of candidate types. Each type in the set must be given a cardinal number (a tag) to identify it. The set of types in the choice can be any primitive or constructed type. For example,

$$Fileidentifier:\ Type = CHOICE\ OF$$
$$\{name(0) = > string$$
$$fileid(1) = > longcardinal\};$$

fileid is represented as: tag   object
                              0001   0FA37DE1

Procedure This identifies a remote procedure and passes parameters to that procedure. It is encoded as a cardinal which identifies the procedure followed by the procedure's parameters. The parameters can be any primitive or constructed type except procedure.

Courier provides a rich set of constructors which is similar to those found in most high-level languages. It is comparatively simple, but has some short-comings in the primitive types it supports.

11.4.3 CCITT X.409 Presentation Transfer Syntax

This proposed standard [CCITT, 1984] has been defined for message-handling systems, but it may be used in other applications as it is more comprehensive than most of the other current proposals. The ISO proposals are also based on X.409 [ISO 1985 a and b]. Data values have **explicit type tags** and are **variable length**. The representation of a data object consists of three fields:

1. A type **identifier** which can be one or more bytes. Every predefined or user-defined type will have a different identifier. There are four classes of identifiers:
   (a) Universal: generally useful, application independent types.
   (b) Application-wide: specific to a particular application (e.g. banking).
   (c) Context-specific: used within a particular context (e.g. a set).
   (d) Private-use: reserved for any application entity's private use.
2. The **length** of the encoded value can be of three forms:
   (a) Short: one byte for lengths < 128.

(b) Long: first byte is the length of the length field (with most significant bit = 1) and the remaining bytes give the length as an unsigned binary number.

(c) Indefinite: first byte = hex (A0) and the end of the contents field is indicated by a special delimiter (EOC) whose type = 0, length = 0 and has no contents.

3. The **contents** – a variable length value for the object. The data values for constructed types may themselves consist of objects of the form identifier, length and contents.

The following primitive types are predefined:

(a) Boolean: length = 1, and contents = 0 (true) or FF_{16} (false).

(b) Integer: length = minimum number of bytes required to represent the number. Contents = 2s complement binary number, with no leading all-zero bytes for positive numbers or bytes with all ones for negative numbers.

(c) Null: length = 0 and no contents field.

(d) Any: a type whose value is unrestricted, i.e. the type of the element is chosen at run time (cf. Courier 'unspecified').

There is no representation for reals, which would have to be mapped onto an application specific sequence of two integers. Cardinals map onto positive integers. Characters are not defined as primitive types but can occur in octet (byte) strings. Enumerated types can be constructed from constants, e.g.

PrimaryColour:: = INTEGER{red(0),yellow(1),blue(2)} .

The following constructors are specified:

- Bitstring   The length indicates the minimum number of bytes required to contain the bitstring. The first byte of the contents contains a number in the range 0–7 which indicates how many bits are unused in the final byte. A single bitstring is actually considered to be a primitive type as it is possible to define a bitstring of bitstrings.

- Octetstring   The contents are characters from a predefined character set or binary 8-bit values. There are a number of predefined types which are refinements of the octet string, i.e. limit the range of values of elements, e.g. international alphabet 5 (IA5), numeric, printable, Teletex (S.61), Videotex (S.100) and generalized time.

- Sequence   This is a collection of homogeneous, unbounded elements. Alternatively it may have a fixed number of heterogeneous elements (cf. record). Components can be optional, i.e. may be omitted by the entity constructing the sequence if all the component types are distinct. Optional elements can have default values. Components can be of any primitive or constructed type. For example,

SEQUENCE {*name IA5string, ok BOOLEAN*}
the value {*name 'Smith', ok FALSE*} is encoded as
sequence   length   contents
   30   0A

                    IA5string   length   contents
                    16   05   536D697468
                    boolean   length   contents
                    01   01   FF

● Set   Three forms of sets are allowed:
1. The members may be variable in number but homogeneous (cf. Pascal sets).
2. There are a predefined number of members each of a distinct type.
3. It contains a variable number of heterogeneous members.
Default values can be associated with optional members. Each component must have a distinct context-specific identifier (see tagged below). For example,

SET {*name*[0] *IA5string, age*[1] *INTEGER*
                                 OPTIONAL}
The value {*name Smith*} would be encoded as
set length contents
31 09

      name length contents
      A0   07

            IA5string length contents
            16   05   536D697468

● Choice   A value whose type is chosen from a set of one or more prespecified alternatives.

● Tagged   An existing type can be tagged to create a new type identifier which reflects semantic or syntactic constraints, e.g. a user name and country name can be distinguished even if both are of type octet string. This is used to construct identifiers for elements of sets or choice types.

Arrays and records are not explicitly defined as constructors; however, they can be mapped onto sequences. The X.409 syntax is very flexible, but rather complex. There are often a number of alternative representations for a particular data structure which means the programs to perform the mappings from local to external representations would be rather complex [Pope, 1984]. The external representation is not particularly efficient, but that is not so important in a high-bandwidth LAN.

11.4.4 GM Standard Message Format

This is the current proposal for the presentation layer of MAP [GM-MAP, 1984] which has been designed for a flexible manufacturing environment. It is based on the use of **explicit type identifiers** and **variable-length** component values, so has some similarity to X.409. The following primitive data types are specified:

- Boolean: single byte with value 0 (true) hex FF (false).
- Bits: a group of 1–8 bits. The type identifier defines the number of bits in the group.
- Integer: 2s complement, variable-length, signed integer.
- Cardinal: binary, variable-length, unsigned integer.
- Signed binary-coded decimal: packed two digits per byte.
- Fixed point: represented as an ASCII string, e.g. 1.5.
- Floating point: represented as an ASCII string, e.g. 3.201.

There is no difference between external representations of fixed and floating point. The distinction is made in the type identifier to determine the mapping to a local internal representation.

There are only two types of constructors specified – strings and groups. The latter is similar to a sequence and can be used to map arrays and records. The elements in a group can be of the same or varying types, and can be of either predefined or undefined length.

The GM standard message format constructors are not as flexible as the CCITT X.409 ones, but a more comprehensive set of primitive types is supported.

11.5 Representation Transformations

11.5.1 The Problem

The transfer of information between two computers or language contexts requires an **encode** operation at the sender to transform internal types (IT) into external types (XT). The destination performs the opposite transformation to **decode** the external type into an internal type, as shown in Fig. 11.2. The internal types used at source and destination may be different.

These transformation operations must overcome a number of problems:

Preservation of value equality
The value of data objects should be unchanged by the encode and decode

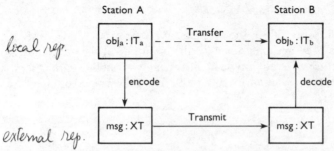

local rep.

external rep.

Figure 11.2 Type transformations for data transfer

operations. This may be difficult to achieve in some cases due to rounding or truncation errors introduced by the transformations. For example, a 32-bit integer may have to be truncated to 16 bits if the latter has been defined as the internal representation of type integer. Transforming real numbers generally produces rounding errors so the transfer of an object may only guarantee that the values differ by very little.

Semantics of representations

Two representations for a particular type can have similar syntax but completely different meaning. For example a complex number can be represented by a pair of coordinates $(x, y : real)$, but the pair of real numbers could represent rectangular or polar coordinates. The choice between rectangular and polar depends on the relative frequency of addition versus multiplication. A simple transformation between representations of real numbers would be syntactically compatible but semantically incompatible. Thus the encode and decode operations would have to be application specific in that they might have to transform between rectangular and polar coordinates as well as between real representations. In Section 11.6 we explain how abstract data types can be used to encapsulate these application-specific external representations and transformations.

Some types such as pointers or file names may have internal representations (cardinal number and character string respectively) which are theoretically transformable into an external representation. However, the values of these data objects may be meaningless outside the context of their own address space or computer system and so should not be sent as values in messages. This restriction on transferring pointers causes problems in transforming some application-specific data structures, as described below.

Some languages allow procedures to be passed as parameters. Obviously these cannot be passed by values, i.e. the code cannot be transferred as it would not be executable in a different machine. However, an identifier for the procedure could be transferred and the receiver can use it to make a remote procedure call to where the code resides.

Maintaining structural information

A constructed type may contain other constructed types, e.g. arrays of records

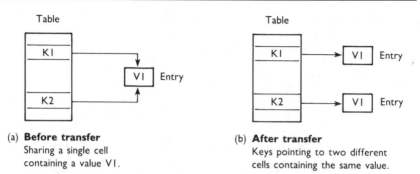

Figure 11.3 Loss of structure during transfer

or tables. Sometimes multiple elements in a data structure share a common sub-element: for example, a symbol table in which a particular item has two different names. This structural relationship is usually represented internally by means of pointers. Many application-specific data structures such as queues, trees or doubly linked lists contain pointers and may be cyclic. As mentioned above, it is not possible to transfer pointers between computer systems or even between different address spaces within the same sytem.

If a shared object is transferred by value (i.e. a copy is taken) each time a reference to it occurs, structural information will be lost. For example, a table of entries accessed by a key could have two different keys for a particular entry, as shown in Fig. 11.3(a). Changing the value of this entry using one key should result in the new value being obtained when accessed using the second key. If the transfer of the table results in a copy of the entry being transferred for K2 and entered in the table as a different entry, the table reconstructed at the remote station would be as shown in Fig. 11.3(b). This is not correct.

Ideally communication mechanisms should allow the transfer of arbitrary data structures as parameters of messages or remote procedure calls. Structural information must be maintained for cyclic or recursive data structures or those with shared sub-elements. Similar problems arise when storing or retrieving structured objects from backing store and so some work has been done in this area [Shu, 1977]. In Section 11.6 we describe transformation mechanisms which do maintain structural information.

11.5.2 Transformation of Simple Data Types

A presentation-layer implementation should provide transformation functions for all the primitive types described previously. These take the form:

function *encodetype (obj:IT):XT*
function *decodetype (msgfield:XT):IT*

where *IT* is the internal type and *XT* the external type representation. If required the encode would generate a type tag, length field and value for the external representation.

Type *rec* = **record**
        a : *integer*;
        b : *boolean*;
    end;
   form = **record**
        x : *integer*;
        y : *real*;
        z : *array* [1..3] **of** rec;
    end;

for CONIC use I, B, R for descriptor
form   I, R, 3(I, B)
in Conic descriptor.

The encoding of an object *obj* of type *form* will result in the following sequence of encode calls:

```
encoderecord (obj,  formdescriptor)
    encodeinteger (obj.x)
    encodereal (obj.y)
    encodearray (obj.z,  1,3,  recdescriptor)
        encoderecord (z[1],  recdescriptor)
            encodeinteger  (z[1].a)
            encodeboolean (z[1].b)
        encoderecord (z[2],  recdescriptor)
            encodeinteger (z[2].a)
            encodeboolean (z[2].b)
        encoderecord (z[3],  recdescriptor)
            encodeinteger (z[3].a)
            encodeboolean (z[3].b)
```

Figure 11.4 Example encoding of a structured type

The encode procedure for a simple constructed object with primitive elements consists of a series of calls on the relevant encode functions for each element until the whole object has been tranformed. It can then be transmitted across the network, as a collection of one or more messages, to the destination where the reverse operation is performed for decode. This mechanism works for constructed elements, provided the objects can be transferred as values and there is no need to maintain structural information (see Fig. 11.4).

Figure 11.4 is a simplification which ignores the updating of pointers to the message buffer used for constructing the external representation. It also assumes *encoderecord* and *encodearray* take parameters of any type. The procedure calls would be driven by a type descriptor generated by the language compiler.

The receiver has to call a similar set of decode procedures. If explicit typing is used the type identifier in the external representation indicates the particular decode procedure to call. The receiver must have a type descriptor similar to that needed at the sender if implicit typing is used in the external representation.

11.6   The Use of Abstract Data Types for Complex Type Transformations

It is not feasible for the presentation layer to include predefined transformations for all conceivable types. It was shown above that some application-specific data structures have to maintain structural information. Also the semantics of the external representation may be application specific, e.g. the complex numbers discussed previously. Thus the presentation layer must allow users to define application-specific external representations together with the appropriate encode and decode procedures. Abstract data types can be used for encapsulating these representations and procedures in a single syntactic unit

11.6.1   Review of Abstract Data Types (ADTs)

An abstract data type [Guttag, 1977] encapsulates both data and operations into a single syntactic unit. It is usually characterized by the operations it provides. It has been suggested as the formalism for specifying virtual device services and for encapsulating standard representations and transformations for application-specific types [Schindler, 1981; Herlihy, 1982; Langsford, 1984]. The ADT specification should permit different local implementations.

There are two approaches to the specification of ADTs: operational and definitional. The **programming-language** or **operational** approach is based on the use of languages such as Simula [Dahl, 1970] or Clu [Liskov, 1974] and may lead to over-specification of both the operations and the representation of the ADT. The **definitional** approach tends to be more formal, for example an algebraic specification of the syntax of the operations (i.e. names, parameters) and a set of axioms which define the meaning of the operations in terms of their relationship to one another. We will concentrate on the less formal programming-language approach, as this is closer to current presentation-layer proposals.

An example of an ADT specification for a table of entries which is accessed by means of a key, and is parametrized by the type of both the key and the entry stored in the table, is given in Fig. 11.5.

Ideally, the definition of an ADT should not specify the implementation of its operations or data structures. For example, there are at least two implementations for the above ADT table. The first uses an array of entries indexed by *key* and the second performs a hashing function on *key* to access a table of pointers to the associated *entry*. It is quite feasible to have different compatible implementations of such an ADT where nothing is known about their internal data structures. It is only necessary to know the types of *key* (e.g. *integer*) and *entry* (e.g. *real*) and the operations which can be performed.

Most programming-language based ADT specifications do specify the implementation of the data structures. This is in terms of predefined primitive types and type constructors. The operations are specified as procedures which define how the operations are to be performed in terms of the basic primitives supported by the language, e.g. assignment, arithmetic operations, iterations or selection. A compiler translates the ADT into a particular internal representation which will depend both on the langauge and on the target computer. The internal representation is in terms of primitive data types supported by the hardware of the computer and the operations map onto machine instruc-

Data type *table (key, entry: type) =*
{ *the table is parameterized by the types of key and item* }

    Enter   *(k: key, i: entry, t: table)*
           { *Inserts the object pair (k, i) into the table object t. If k is already in t, the entry associated with k is replaced by i* }

    Find   *(k: key, t: table,* **var** *i: entry): boolean*
           { *Returns True if k is in t, in which case i holds the value of the entry associated with k. Returns false if k is not in t, in which case i is undefined.* }

    Delete *(k: key)*
           { *If k is in the table it deletes k and the associated entry, else it has no effect.* }

    Encode *(t: table,* **var** *msg: exttable)*
           { *Converts the internal representation of table into a standard external representation (exttable) which can be transferred.* }

    Decode *(msg: exttable,* **var** *t: table)*
           { *Converts a received message containing the external representation of table into the local internal representation* }
end;

Figure 11.5 An example abstract data type specification

tions. Any changes to the representation require modification to the program and recompilation and so this representation is essentially **static**.

The simplest form of negotiation provided as a presentation-layer service is on the values of parameters passed to an instance of an ADT when it is created. This implies the possible representation variations were known in advance and built into its definition. This is usually the case for a typical virtual device. It would be feasible to **dynamically** define a new representation of an ADT [Schindler, 1981], i.e. an interpreted rather than compilation approach. This may be appropriate where the range and complexity of variation between representations is so great that it is too difficult to specify by parameters. The presentation layer must then provide mechanisms to transfer an algebraic or other very high-level ADT specification and then negotiate on the representation of the instance. So far very little work has been done in this area.

It is necessary to control the concurrency of the operations which can be performed on shared data or virtual device ADTs. This could be done by explicit synchronization operations, e.g. an operation to give access rights to the communicating partner as is the case with virtual terminals used in a two-way alternative mode. Some ADT implementations rely on the queuing of operations so that only one operation is active at a time (cf. monitors). If concurrency of operations is allowed, then internal synchronization must be provided when conflicts can occur.

11.6.2 Transformation of Complex Types

A suitable high-level language which supports ADTs could be used to specify the encode and decode operations for complex types which must maintain structural information. The ADT would include the internal and external representation of the type as well as the operations which can be performed on it. An implementation only requires the compilation of the ADT, provided a compiler for the language is available for a particular machine. The compiler would generate the calls to the local presentation layer for the encode and decode operations for simple types.

We will now describe a transformation mechanism which maintains structural information. It is based on that described by Herlihy and Liskov [Herlihy, 1982].

An arbitrary graph structure (the object) must be transformed into a stream of linear messages, i.e. it must be 'flattened' in order to transfer it between stations. This is accomplished by traversing the object and converting its elements into external representation tokens which contain a sequence number and values or structural information. Any representation using explicit tags could be extended to include a new external type called a reference. These tokens are assembled into messages for transfer to the destination. At the receiving end the tokens are extracted and used to reconstruct the object. Multiple messages may be required to transfer a structured object. There are three kinds of tokens:

1. **Primitive tokens**
   These are used to transmit the values of primitive types directly supported by the presentation layer, e.g. integers, booleans.
2. **Constructor tokens**
   These mark the start of the stream of tokens of a constructed object. The token contains type-dependent information such as the low bound of an array and number of elements in the array.
3. **Reference tokens**
   These denote shared elements and contain the constructor token stream address (i.e. sequence number) of the element to which they refer.

A constructed object is thus transformed into a stream of sequentially numbered tokens. A reference map is created for each object over which structural information is to be preserved. The map is a table for transforming internal references to elements (addresses) into external references (token sequence numbers). At the sending station, when a constructed component is reduced to tokens, its internal address and constructor token sequence number are entered into the map. If another reference to the same element is encountered (i.e. the object's address is already in the map) its token sequence number is extracted from the map and placed in the stream in a reference token.

The map can be reconstructed at the receiving end and need not be transmitted. The receiving station decodes (reconstructs) a constructed element and enters its local address and token sequence number in the map. When a

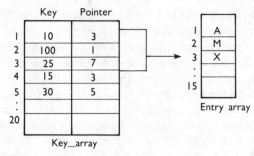

Figure 11.6 Example table object

reference token is received, the reference sequence number is used to extract the address of the element from the map.

Figure 11.6 represents a table in which an integer key is used to access an entry object. It is implemented as a key array in which each item is a record containing the key value and a pointer to an item in the entry array. More than one key can point to the same entry. Table 11.1 shows the external representation (i.e. token stream) generated by the encode operation for the table object. The first pointer to an entry is transformed into the value of the entry, but subsequent pointers to that entry are transformed into references to the first occurrence.

A slight modification at the receiving end is needed to deal with cyclic structures such as circular lists and doubly linked lists. The receiver will get reference tokens to sub-objects that have not been fully reconstructed and so are not in the reference map. A technique similar to that used in compiler symbol tables for dealing with forward references can be used. The sequence

Table 11.1 External representation of table

Token no.	Token type	Token value	Explanation
1	Constructor		Constructor for table
2	Constructor	1,20	Constructor for array (20 elements, low bound = 1)
3	Constructor		Constructor for key_array record 1 (2 elements, key and entry or reference)
4	Primitive	10	Key value
5	Primitive	X	Entry value
6	Constructor		Constructor for key_array record 2
7	Primitive	100	Key value
8	Primitive	A	Entry value
⋮	⋮	⋮	⋮
12	Constructor		Constructor for key_array record 4
13	Primitive	15	Value of 4th key
15	Reference	5	Reference to token 5 (shared entry)

number in the reference token is placed in the map, but no object address is available. Instead the entry acts as a start of a chain of unresolved references to the object. When the object is finally created, this chain of references can be followed, substituting the address of the object for the next link in the chain.

11.7 Summary

We have covered the problems arising from representation differences in computers and languages and how these can be overcome by transforming local representations into a single standard external representation. Not many external representations have been specified. The three case studies presented were Courier, CCITT X.409 and GM MAP. These representations differ in whether they support fixed- or variable-length data values and whether type information is explicit or implicit. None of the representations directly support all the primitive types and constructors found in common high-level languages. X.409 provides very flexible constructor mechanisms but the processing overheads needed to transform between the external and internal representations are quite high.

Complex data structures often represent structural information in the form of addresses or pointers. It is necessary to transform these pointers into token stream references in order to transfer these structures from one address space to another and still maintain structural information. Abstract data types are a suitable mechanism for encapsulating application specific encode and decode procedures with the external representation specification.

In the next chapter we described the use of ADTs for virtual devices and virtual file stores.

References

CCITT Draft Recommendation X.409, *Presentation Transfer and Syntax Notation*, 1984.

'Computer security technology', Special Issue *IEEE Computer*, vol. 17, no. 7, July 1983.

Dahl, O., Myhrhaug, B., Nygaard, K., *The Simula 67 Common Base Language*, Publ. No. S-22, Norwegian Computing Centre, Oslo, 1970.

General Motors, *Manufacturing Automation Protocol: GM Standard Message Format*, APMES A/MD-39, GM Technical Centre, Warren, MI 48090-9040, USA.

Guttag, J. 'Abstract data types and the development of data structures, *CACM*, vol 20, no. 6, June 1977, pp. 396–404.

Herlihy, M., Liskov, B., 'A value transmission method for abstract data types', *ACM TOPLAS*, vol 4, no. 4, October 1982, pp. 527–551.

ISO TC97 (a) *Specification of Abstract Syntax Notation One (ASN.1)*, Draft International Standard ISO/DIS 8824, 6 June, 1985.

ISO TC97 (b) *Specification of Basic Encoding Rules for Abstract Syntax Notation One (ASN.1)*, Draft International Standard ISO/DIS 8825, 6 June 1985.

Langsford, A., 'The open systems user programming interfaces', *Computer Networks*, Vol. 8, no. 1, January 1984, pp. 3–12.

Liskov, B., Zilles, S., 'Programming with abstract data types', *Proc. Symp. on Very High Level Languages, ACM Sigplan Notices*, Vol. 9, no. 4, 1974, pp. 50–59.

Moulton, J., 'Description of a planned federal information processing standard for data presentation protocol', *6th ICCC*, London, North-Holland, September 1982, pp. 896–901.

Pope, A., 'Encoding CCITT X.409 presentation transfer syntax', *ACM Computer Comms. Review*, Vol. 14, no. 4, October, 1984, pp. 4–10.

Schindler, S., Flasche, U., Borman C., 'Open systems interconnection – the presentation service model', *Computer Communications*, Vol. 4, no. 5, October 1981 pp. 227–241.

Shu, N., Housel, B., Taylor, R., Ghosh, S., Lum, V., 'EXPRESS: a data extraction, processing and restructuring system', *ACM TODS*, Vol. 2, no. 2, June 1977, pp. 134–174.

Tanenbaum A., *Computer Networks*, Prentice-Hall, 1981.

Xerox Corporation, *Courier: The Remote Procedure Call Protocol*, XSIS 038112, Xerox OPD, 3333 Coyote Hill Rd., Palo Alto, Ca 94304, 1981.

Twelve

APPLICATION-ORIENTED SERVICES

There are a number of standard services which are specific to a set of applications, and so are considered part of the application layer. For example, many distributed processing applications require access to a file service which may be on a remote station or interact with humans via terminals which may be remote from the application entities with which they are communicating. There is thus the need for services and protocols which are specific to particular applications, but nevertheless are still candidates for standardization. Typical examples are virtual-file service, virtual-terminal service, job manipulation and transfer, electronic funds transfer, document manipulation and transfer. These application-oriented services form a sublayer of the application layer of the ISO model as they provide a service to users which are themselves within the application layer. We will discuss the first two in this section as they are the most widely applicable.

File protocols, terminal protocols and remote job submission protocols have existed for longer than the ISO reference model, and so most current implementations of these protocols do not correspond exactly to the application layer of the model. They often include session management functions and information representation and transformation, i.e. they effectively interface directly with the transport layer. To some extent it was the design and implementation of these protocols which led to the realization that they contained common features which could be separated out into session and presentation layers.

12.1 Virtual-File Service (VFS)

12.1.1 Motivation

Many networks include a variety of computer systems each with their own file service. Users need to transfer files between systems. For instance to submit a job for execution on a remote computer or to print a file from a work-station which does not have an attached printer. There is also the need to access files remotely to update shared information or because it is impractical to transfer the whole file in order to access it.

The problem is that file systems differ greatly with respect to file structure, information representation, access methods, file-management information maintained and naming conventions.

The objective of the virtual-file service (VFS) [Linington, 1984] is to provide a single uniform user interface to all network-accessible file systems. This assumes all real file systems can be described in terms of a common representation and common operations. Each local system then provides a mapping between the VFS and its real file service.

As yet, there is no single standard virtual file service, but ISO are defining a standard. We will now examine the attributes of the various proposals and implementations for a VFS. A more detailed survey is available in Hale [1982].

12.1.2 Virtual File Store Model

A virtual file store [Popescu-Zeletin, 1981; Bucciarelli, 1982] defines the types of structured data a file may contain, the management information maintained about the file (e.g. size and date of creation), as well as the operations which can be performed on the file store.

The advantage of the virtual file store approach is that the user only sees a single interface to the file service irrespective of where the information to be accessed is stored. Any proprietary file system can be incorporated into the virtual file service by providing a suitable mapping between representations. This is particularly important for interaction between computer stations with different operating systems. Note that the various file systems are not integrated into a single virtual file store. There may be a number of independent virtual file stores within the virtual file service.

Structure
This defines the organization of the information within a file in the file store. There are three types of structure:

Unstructured: There is no internal structure visible to the user. A file is seen as a sequence of characters or transparent octets (cf. Unix).

Flat: The file is divided into records which are the units of access as seen by the user. There is no relationship between records other than sequencing. The record may be a fixed- or variable-length sequence of octets or may be structured into fields. The ECMA model [Bucciarelli, 1982] defines fixed-length fields, which implies fixed-length records. Record descriptors will contain a list of record fields, their data types and lengths. There are thus three levels of structure – a file, a record and a field within a record.

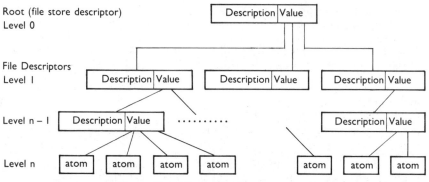

Figure 12.1 Hierarchical file structure

Hierarchical: The three-level structure of the flat file can be extended to a tree in which nodes correspond to typed structural units [Popescu-Zeletin, 1981]. For example a file can be structured into records, which consist of fields, which consist of subfields which hold a number of data items, etc. (see Fig. 12.1). This tree structure indicates the relationship between the structural unit types and should not be confused with the tree-structured directory found in many modern file stores. Each structural unit contains a description of the unit which includes information such as a unique name, length of the unit, types of the data within the unit. The value stored in the unit is a list of lower-level structural units or actual data values.

Most implementations support only unstructured flat files. The HMI filestore [Popescu-Zeletin, 1981] and the ISO proposal both support hierarchical structures. The hierarchical structure increases the overheads in defining the structure, e.g. 10 bytes per record compared with about 3 for a flat structure.

Naming
Most virtual file services do not define a standard naming convention, but use the name structure provided by the real file store. This can range from a simple two-level name (e.g. *fred.obj*) to variable-length multilevel names (e.g. *project1/Jones/net/pascal/obj*). However, the syntax of multilevel names should be standardized. For instance character strings with standard delimiters between the components of a multilevel name.

The structural unit of a hierarchical file may also be named. For example a field name rather than position is used to access information (see below).

Means of access
The structural units of a file can be accessed in the following ways:

sequential;
random by position or key;
indexed sequential;

by structural unit name for hierarchical files

e.g. *personnel-file.person-record.salary-value.*

Most implementations support only sequential access, but some also support random access. The ISO proposal is for access by name.

Data types

Data-type information is needed to allow transformation of representations between the network standard and those of the particular real file store. Presentation-layer services do not currently exist, so most virtual file stores allow the use of a few primitive types in order to minimize translation problems. Future VFS will use predefined types from the presentation layer and others will be specific to the VFS.

File security

There are two methods used to protect files from unauthorized access:

- Passwords, together with a distinction between access permission for the file owner (creator) and others.
- Access-control lists which specify users and the type of access allowed.

The virtual file store may provide different security from that provided by the real file store and could also support encryption both for transfer across the network and for storage. Encrypted storage would have to be supported by the real file store.

History

Typical history attributes which are maintained are dates and times of creation, last modification and last read access, identity of creator, last modifier and later reader. These attributes can be maintained only if the real file store supports them.

Accounting

This is information on current size and allowed maximum size, account number of owner etc.

12.1.3 Types of Service

The three types of service [Hale, 1982] which constitute the VFS are file transfer, remote file access and remote file management. Most VFS support only complete file copy as a single user transaction. The HMI VFS supports limited access operations.

File transfer

File transfer is similar to the copy facility in most file systems. The transfer can be between the user's station and a remote one (Fig. 12.3) or between two remote stations (Fig. 12.2). The following information must be specified:

Source and destination file descriptions: File store and file names. The file-store name will be mapped onto a station address if remote.
Mode: This indicates the effect of the transfer on each file. For example:
   Delete or leave source on transfer completion.
   Create new file at destination and fail if name already exists.
   Overwrite existing file.
   Append to end of existing file.   ↗ *error recovery action*
Quality of service: This specifies recovery options (see protocols below).
Security information: Password, etc.

Either side must be able to suspend the transfer to provide some form of flow control at the application level, e.g. while waiting for transfer to a disk. It must be possible to abort the transfer with any partially transferred files being discarded.

Remote file access

This allows the contents of a remote file to be examined or altered. The unit of transaction is typically a record or a block of data. This requires an association with a particular file to be maintained over several data-transfer transactions.

The typical remote file-access operations are:

Open or close a named file: This essentially sets up an application layer connection to a particular file. The file store and file name must be specified together with mode of use and security information.
Read or write a named data unit (record, block or smaller unit).
Append or update of a data unit: These can be provided as composite read and write operations.
Lock and unlock a named data unit: This is to allow the synchronization of multiple accesses to a shared file. *eg airline reservation*

The data unit named in the transaction is identified in terms of a key, index, address or name. To maintain consistency in distributed systems, the above transactions have to be atomic, i.e. they complete successfully or they have no effect. Thus a failure during a transaction must not be allowed to leave a partially updated data unit. In practice not many real file services support atomic transactions.

Remote file management

The management operations query or change the properties of a file rather than its contents. Examples are:

- Create or delete a file
- Rename a file
- Examine the properties of a file e.g. size or history.

- Change file attributes e.g. access rights or password.
- List a directory – returns a list of filenames in the directory together with some properties.

12.1.4 Example File Store ADT

The following is an example of an ADT for a simple file store which supports sequential access to data elements of a type provided by the user when the file is created. The notation used is not based on a particular language but is roughly Pascal-like, with extensions.

```
ABSTRACT TYPE file (datatype:type)
    {file is parameterized with the type of data stored in the file}
BEGIN
    TYPE accesscontrol = SET OF [rd, wr, del]; {read, write, delete}
         fileattributes = RECORD
                        name:string;
                        datatype:type;
                        owner:string;
                        owneraccess, useraccess:accesscontrol;
                        currentsize:integer;
                        maxsize:integer
                  END;
    VAR:
        attr: fileattributes;
        content: LIST OF datatype;
    PROCEDURE query (fid:fileid, VAR attributes:fileattributes)
    PROCEDURE change (fid:fileid, attributes:fileattributes)
    PROCEDURE read (fid:fileid, VAR data:datatype)
    PROCEDURE write (fid:fileid, data:datatype)
        {appends to end of file}
END {file};

ABSTRACT TYPE filestore
BEGIN
    TYPE modetype = (read, write)
    VAR:
        name:string;
        filecatalogue : LIST OF file {could map onto tree structure or
                                   flat directory}
    PROCEDURE create (filename:string, filetype:type, ownerid:string)
        {creates a new file and enters it into the file catalog with default values
        for the file attributes (see below)}
    PROCEDURE delete (filename:string, userid:string)
    PROCEDURE open (filename:string, userid:string, mode:modetype,
                 VAR fid:fileid)
        {returns a file identifier to be used in subsequent access to
        the file}
```

PROCEDURE *close (fid:fileid)*
PROCEDURE *select (filename:string, userid:string, VAR fid:fileid)*
   {*enables a file to be selected for querying or changing file attributes*}
END;

12.1.5 File-service Connections

In general there are three processes involved in providing a VFS. A controller acts on behalf of the user and a server at both the source- and destination-file systems (see Fig. 12.2). The server processes access the file store at each site involved in a transaction and map the virtual file store onto the local real file store. A management connection is required between the controller and each of the servers. A file transfer connection is needed between the source

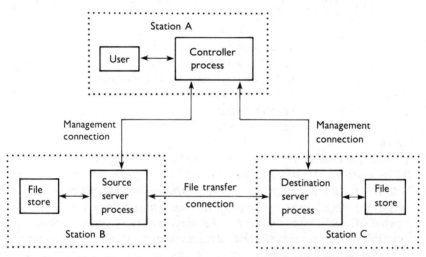

Figure 12.2 Generalized application layer connections for file transfers

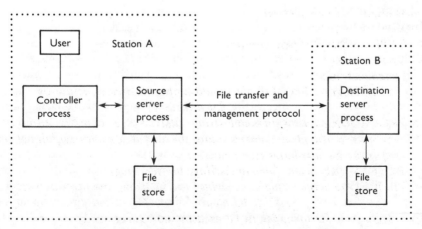

Figure 12.3 Simplified structure for file transactions

and destination. The source and destination processes are not symmetric. Often, the transfer is between the user's station and a remote file store, and so a single connection which is used for both management and file transfer is adequate (Fig. 12.3). The file-transfer protocol must then carry both control information and data.

12.1.6 Protocols

If only file transfer is required, it is possible, and more efficient, to identify and open the remote file in a single protocol exchange. If file-management operations are to be supported, then it is necessary to maintain a connection with the same file during a succession of management and transfer operations in order to ensure the integrity of the entire sequence of operations. Similarly it should not be necessary to close and reopen a file between a succession of file accesses.

The following phases can be identified in a generalized VFS protocol:

Connected: A user is connected with a particular virtual file store.

File selected: An association has been set up with a particular file within the file store.

File-open phase: The selected file has been opened for read or write access, i.e. an association exists with the contents of the file. Note that most protocols combine the file-selected and -open phases.

Data-access phase: The file contents are being transferred or manipulated. Most file-transfer protocols allow checkpoints to be defined during the transfer of data (see below). Some protocols allow multiple commands to be grouped together into a single application message, e.g. select a file and open it. A single 'handshake' can then be used to improve efficiency. Data compression is sometimes included in the data-transfer phase although this is considered a presentation service by ISO.

Many file-transfer protocols perform error recovery by means of a 'checkpoint rollback' mechanism. This returns the transfer to a point of known synchronization to recover from errors such as device errors or even loss of communication connection. This is particularly important for transfer of long files over low-speed connections. The file transfer service must then allow the capability of resuming a partially completed transfer. The checkpoint consists of an identifier inserted as a special message in the data stream. When acknowledged it means that both servers have saved sufficient state information (e.g. addresses, parameter values, checkpoint identifiers, position in file) to be able to restart the transfer if either station or the transport connection fails. This implies that state information must be saved in non-volatile memory (e.g. on disk) in order to be able to restart after a station failure. It is not really feasible to rely on session-layer synchronization for this sort of recovery, although session-layer synchronization might be able to recover from loss of a transport connection.

12.2 Virtual-terminal Service

Human interaction with distributed systems is usually via a terminal, which consists of a presentation unit such as a printer or display for output and a keyboard for input. In this section we will examine the problems encountered in communication between application programs and remote terminals and how remote terminal handling has evolved into the virtual-terminal service.

12.2.1 Problems of Remote Terminal Handling

One of the major advantages of networking is that a terminal user can potentially communicate with any computer attached to the network. Conversely, each computer must be capable of handling every kind of terminal that can access the network. Most of the problems encountered in communicating with remote terminals are due to the differences in characteristics of the many types of terminals on the market. Terminals can range from old electromechanical devices to sophisticated, intelligent terminals with a variety of devices such as touch-sensitive screens, light pens, local storage etc. It is thus very difficult to make the application program independent of the type of terminal used.

Although terminals exhibit broadly similar characteristics, the unit of information manipulation or transfer can be a single bit on a graphics terminal, a single character, a line of characters or even a complete screenful of data. The typical amount of information which can be displayed at a time can vary. Typical screen sizes are 12 to 60 lines with 40 to 130 characters per line. Some terminals allow control of the presentation of data in terms of color, intensity, character fonts, etc. and there are many different codes used for transfer of information between computers and terminals, e.g. ASCII, CCITT International Alphabet No 5, EBCDIC. Some electromechanical devices take longer to perform functions, such as carriage return, than to print a normal character, so the terminal handler program may have to allow for this by delaying the next printable character after a carriage return.

Some terminals automatically display a character when a key is pressed, whereas others send the character to the computer and it is only displayed when the computer echoes it back to the terminal. Remote echoing becomes unacceptable to human operators when delays become greater than 200 ms. Remote echoing can be very inefficient in that it may result in packets of only 1 or 2 characters being sent backwards and forwards across the network.

Most terminals provide a means of interrupting or demanding attention from the remote application program, e.g. via a break key. Treating these consistently can be complicated due to the inherent delays and storage of messages within the network, as will be discussed in Section 12.2.9.

The diversity in terminal characteristics and in application requirements for terminal communication has resulted in a categorization of remote terminal handling for particular classes of terminals:

Scroll mode: These are simple display or printing terminals which are able to present a single line at a time to the user. After printing a line the display or paper is scrolled up and it is not possible to modify or change characters from previous lines. The basic unit of manipulation and transfer is a character.

Page mode: These are able to display y lines, each of x characters. The unit of manipulation and transfer is also a character but the cursor can be moved to any position on the screen in order to write or change a character. They usually provide some means of emphasizing characters by changing intensity or reverse video. Most modern display terminals fit into this category.

Data entry mode: This is known as a **forms mode** terminal as it is used for applications such as airline reservation or banking where the operator is essentially filling in a predefined form consisting of various fields. Fields can be protected to prevent the user writing in them or to allow only numeric data to be entered. Often the terminal has considerable local intelligence and is capable of storing a number of pages of information. It may be possible to perform local editing and transfer a complete block of information to the remote computer.

Graphics mode: These can range from a comparatively simple bit-mapped display (where each bit sent to the terminal corresponds to a point on the screen) to a sophisticated graphics terminal capable of receiving commands to draw lines or circles.

Videotex or teletex mode: This is a mixed graphics and text mode of display where the presentation image is optimized for display on a commercial color television. These terminals are generally used to access information stored in a data base. Videotex uses the telephone system to access the data base and provides a very limited form of input. Teletext is broadcast via a television channel and so there is no input from the terminal.

We will be discussing only the handling of scroll, page and data entry type terminals in this chapter.

12.2.2 Evolution of Remote Terminal Handling

One of the earliest uses of networks has been for terminal access to remote computers. We will now examine how remote terminal handling has evolved from being embedded within application programs to the device and communication system independence provided by a virtual-terminal service.

Within the application
The earliest approach was to incorporate terminal-handling functions within the application which also handled communication functions (Fig. 12.4(a)).

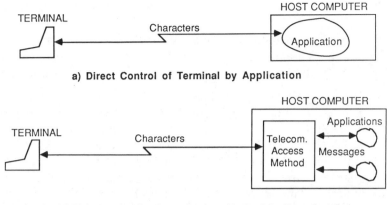

a) Direct Control of Terminal by Application

b) Telecommunications Access Method in Host Computer

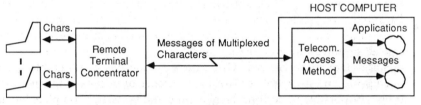

Each message transferred between concentrator and host computer
may contain characters from different terminals

c) Remote Concentrator

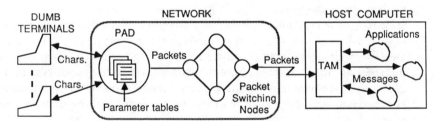

Packets contain characters from a single terminal

d) Packet Assembler Disassembler (PAD)

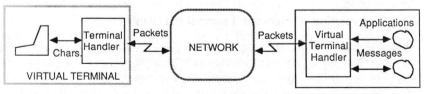

e) Virtual Terminal Approach

Figure 12.4 Evolution of remote terminal handling: (a) direct control of terminal by application; (b) telecommunications access method in host computer; (c) remote concentrator; (d) packet assembler disassembler (PAD); (e) virtual terminal approach

The unit of information transfer was generally a character at a time. The application programs then had to be changed to accommodate new or different terminals.

Telecommunication access method
The next stage in the development of terminal handling was to include a telecommunication access method (TAM) in the host computer's operating system. The application program could then communicate with the TAM using messages, but the TAM still communicated with terminals on a character basis (see Fig. 12.4(b)). This removed the device dependency from the application and also allowed application programs to be tested using sequential local devices (e.g. disk files) to simulate terminals. The TAM was responsible for both communications and terminal handling (including remote echoing), and hence was complicated and difficult to change to accomodate new terminal types.

Remote concentrator
A remote processor is used as a concentrator to handle a cluster of terminals connected to a **single** host computer. The concentrator usually multiplexes characters from different terminals into blocks for transmission, i.e. a block contains characters from, or for, a number of different terminals. A local terminal handler in the host computer then demultiplexes the blocks into separate character streams. The remote concentrator performs local echoing. The terminal characteristics were still usually embedded into the programs of the concentrator, thus limiting the type of terminals which could be handled.

Packet assembler disassembler (PAD)
This is the approach whereby terminals can be directly connected to the network itself, and is favored by the PTTs. The remote terminal handler is part of the switching network and caters for a variety of simple scroll-mode terminals. It allows the terminals to set up sessions with many different remote host computers over a public packet-switched network. The terminal handler assembles the characters from a terminal into packets which are sent over the network to a destination computer. The PAD receives packets from the remote computer and disassembles them into individual characters which are sent to the terminal. A set of parameters is maintained by the PAD to identify the characteristics of each terminal it is handling. These parameters can be changed by the terminal or by the host computer. The terminal access method or application program in the host computer is still aware of the characteristics of the terminals it communicates with (see Fig. 12.4(d))

Virtual terminal service
A virtual terminal is an abstract generalized model of a class of terminals [Magnee, 1979; Day, 1980]. Its characteristics are a superset of those of a number of different terminals. The host computer then communicates with

a single type of terminal – the virtual terminal. The remote terminal handler maps the characteristics of the virtual terminal onto the characteristics of the physical terminal it controls (Fig. 12.4(e)). Once the virtual terminal has been standardized it is hoped that manufacturers will build real terminals which correspond to it.

12.2.3 PAD Protocols

A parametric approach to handling terminals has been taken by CCITT [CCITT, 1981]. They have defined protocols to be used for connecting simple terminals to a packet assembler–disassembler (PAD) in a packet-switched network, via dial-up or leased lines. The PAD is part of the network and can handle a number of different scroll-mode terminals. Parameters in the PAD are set to define the characteristics of each connected terminal. The remote host and PAD communicate over the network using X.25 connections. The protocols defined for a PAD are shown in Fig. 12.5 and are discussed below.

X.3   this specifies the functions performed by the PAD and the set of terminal characteristics which can be controlled by the PAD parameters (see Table 12.1). The parameters take default initial values, but can be changed by the host computer or optionally by the terminal operator.

X.28   this defines the protocol between asynchronous (stop–start) terminals and the PAD. It specifies the procedure for setting PAD parameters, establishing a connection with a remote host, and exchanging data with the PAD, i.e. it specifies the commands typed in to the terminals and the responses from the PAD. Sessions between a terminal and a particular host computer are mapped onto X.25 connections, so characters from the terminal are assembled into X.25 packets and sent to the remote host. The data field of the X.25 packets received from the host is disassembled into characters which are transmitted one at a time to the terminal.

X.29   this defines the protocol for the exchange of control information and user data between a host computer and PAD. It defines how X.25 is used for the exchange of information. The host computer

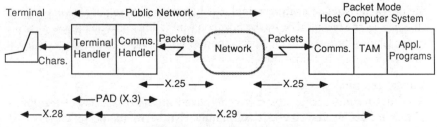

Figure 12.5 CCITT packet assembler–disassembler protocols

Table 12.1 PAD parameters

Mode-switch signals	The mechanism used to switch between data transfer and command mode, and specifies whether the terminal can change PAD parameters.
Data forwarding signals	Specifies when buffered characters are transmitted to the host computer e.g. after a carriage return.
Idle timer	The time interval after which buffered characters will be sent to the host even if no forwarding signal has been received.
Break signal semantics	The action to be taken after the terminal generates a break signal e.g. no action, send interrupt packet to host, reset, change of mode, discard output.
Echo	Whether the PAD should echo characters received from the terminal.
Carriage return padding	The number of padding characters to be inserted after a carriage return sent to the terminal.
Lind folding	The line length after which automatic line folding should take place.
Flow control	The flow control mechanism to be used e.g. X-ON and X-OFF characters.
Bit rate	The bit rate between PAD and terminal.

can initiate, clear and reset connections to a terminal, inspect and modify PAD parameters. Messages are also provided for indicating errors.

The parametric approach to handling terminals is a simple technique for existing asynchronous terminals, but it has a number of disadvantages;

- The terminal handler in the host computer must still be aware of the characteristics of each terminal it communicates with.
- The PADs can only handle a limited class of scroll-mode terminals and do not provide the generic functions found in virtual terminal protocols, as discussed below. They cannot handle the functionality of page mode or data-entry intelligent terminals.
- The PAD protocols are very dependent on X.25.
- They are not end-to-end as the PAD is part of the network, nor are they symmetric, so it is not possible to have direct terminal to terminal communication.

The main objective of the PAD protocols is to allow direct connection of many existing terminals to a network. Many of the problems it presents for use with intelligent terminals can be overcome by the more generalized approach of virtual terminal protocols.

12.2.4 Virtual-terminal Protocols (VTP)

The VTP defines the rules for communication between an application program or terminal handler in the host computer and a hypothetical remote terminal. The user composes input at a terminal. Before this is transferred across the network it is transformed into the virtual terminal (VT) format. Similarly any output received from the host is mapped from VT format onto the characteristics of the real terminal. The host terminal handler either handles VT format data directly or there must be conversion between the VT format and the format expected by the host terminal handler software. The major advantages of this approach are that the host has to handle only a single type of remote terminal, i.e. the virtual terminal, and it can handle sophisticated intelligent terminals. Many modern operating systems use a similar approach to dealing with different terminals.

Most existing VTPs have been designed to fit on top of an end-to-end transport service which provides a connection service for the transfer of sequential blocks of data, and an interrupt service for the transfer of attention or break signals. These VTPs include session-layer and presentation-layer functions. ISO is currently working on a VTP which uses presentation-layer services, although ECMA considers a VTP to be part of the presentation layer [ECMA, 1983].

In many cases a VTP will be used for terminal access to a remote application program. However, it can also be used to support direct terminal-to-terminal communication for teleconferencing or message exchange. In addition it could be used for interconnecting two application programs that were originally intended for use by a user at a terminal. For example, an algebraic manipulation package could be used to simplify equations before passing them on to an interactive graphics package to generate graphical output.

12.2.5 Virtual-terminal Model

Most virtual terminal protocols model the interaction between application and terminal by means of a common data structure which has certain properties and parameters depending on the class of terminals being modelled. The application must then conceptually map its internal data structures onto the common one and similarly the terminal process must map the common data structure onto the presentation unit (Fig. 12.6). This data structure represents the virtual terminal and can be treated as a shared abstract data object. The terminal's presentation unit does not necessarily correspond exactly to the data structure. For example, the screen of a terminal could display several data structures (lines), exactly one data structure, or part of a data structure (one page of a multi-page data structure).

The virtual-terminal service corresponds to the specification of an abstract data type that includes a data store to hold shared data, definitions of the structure of the store (e.g. in terms of pages and fields), the attributes of the data held in the store (e.g. color and intensity), device control and status information. Operations are provided to modify the contents of the data store, define or change the data structure, change attributes, synchronize the dialogue (i.e. access to the data structure), control devices, as well as to

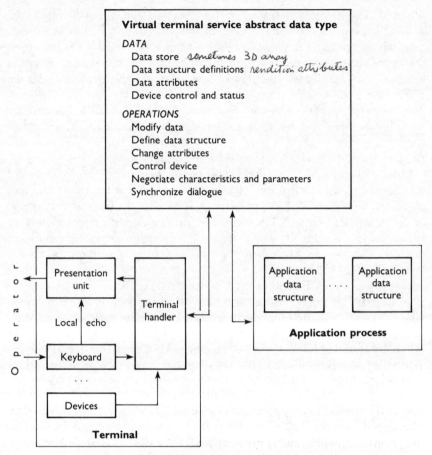

Figure 12.6 Virtual terminal model

negotiate on the selection of primitives and parameters to be used for a particular terminal session [Dhondy, 1984].

The implementation of a VTS need not be in terms of a single shared data store, but could be distributed. Copies of the (conceptually) shared store could be held at both the terminal and application and it would be the responsibility of the virtual terminal protocol to maintain consistency.

12.2.6 Data Structure and Data Attributes

The data store consists of a set of cells, which are the smallest individually addressable elements. The relationship between cells is defined by the data-structure information. Each cell contains a **value object**, e.g. a bit, a character or a vector graphic picture element. In addition there is a set of **attributes** associated with each cell, which define how the data is presented and accessed, as discussed below. The structure of the data store and the items held within it depend on the class of virtual terminal.

A scroll-mode VT data store consists of a single-dimensional array in which the value object consists of characters. A page mode VT's data store is structured as a two-dimensional array of characters with the x dimension corresponding to characters in a line and the y dimension corresponding to lines on a screen. A data entry VT's store consists of one or more two-dimensional pages which are divided into fields. A line may contain more than one field or a field may cover multiple lines. A field is a set of contiguous characters which have a common set of attributes which define how the field is to be displayed or used by the terminal operator or application. The following typical attributes apply to the more sophisticated data entry VT, and the others have simple attribute subsets. There is also a set of parameters to define maximum dimension of the data structure.

Rendition attributes define the visual display of object values:
    intensity, e.g. normal, high, low;
    blink, e.g. steady, fast, slow;
    image, e.g. reverse video, normal;
    underline;
    character color;
    background color;
    whether overprinting erases or not.
Typographic attributes:
    character set, e.g. ASCII, APL, EBCDIC;
    character size, e.g. height and width;
    font, e.g. italic, pica, courier.
Protection attributes define how the data is accessed:
    non-displayable, e.g. for passwords;
    write-protected to prevent the terminal user writing into the field;
    selectable by light pen or touch-sensitive screen;
    data must be read from a specific device, e.g. badge reader.
Validation attributes specify constraints on the values of data stored in the fields:
    alphabetic characters only;
    numeric characters only.

12.2.7 Virtual-terminal Operations

The basic operations which can be performed on a data store are to read or write the data at a specified cell or field, or to change its attributes. This implies an ability to specify a position (cell or field) within the data store, as described below. In addition, operations are provided to interrupt the communicating partner and to operate ancillary devices.

Addressing
    Next character (this may be implicit, e.g. when reading or writing a string);

next line, field, or unprotected field;

absolute address, i.e. x, y and z coordinates for character, line and page;

differential addresses, i.e. the dx, dy displacements from the current pointer position;

home address, i.e. moving the pointer to a defined position in the data structure, e.g. top left or first character in the first unprotected field.

Initialization

This is a reset operation whereby the existing data structure is abandoned and replaced by a new one consisting of just null characters. It generally sets the pointer to the first character position in the data structure. Clearing erases the contents of the complete data structure, but leaves the defined fields. A field can also be cleared. In a scroll-mode VT, initialization is equivalent to a carriage return/line feed.

Data structure definition

Selecting a class of VT effectively defines the overall data structure, e.g. whether one, two- or three-dimensional. Also the parameters which define the dimensions of the axes can be set dynamically. A data entry mode VT also allows forms to be defined dynamically. This is usually the responsibility of the application process, for example when one form is completed and the data structure is initialized and a new form is loaded for display. Some VT allow the user to specify form structures.

Device control

Devices such as light pen, touch-sensitive screen and mouse interact with the data store and act as alternatives to the keyboard for input. More sophisticated devices such as local disk store can be considered a separate data store within the virtual terminal with a set of commands to control it.

12.2.8   Example Virtual-terminal ADT

The following is a description of a simple page-mode virtual terminal. The notation used is similar to that in Section 12.1.4.

```
ABSTRACT TYPE pageterminal (xmax, ymax:integer)
   {when an object of type pageterminal is created, the maximum x and y
   dimensions of the data store are passed as parameters.}
BEGIN
   TYPE cellattribute = (normal, highlight, reverse);
      position = RECORD
                  xpos:integer;
                  ypos:integer
               END;
      cell = RECORD
         c:char;
         attr:cellattribute
         END;
```

```
    stringlength: 1..xmax
VAR:
    cursor:position;
    datastore: ARRAY [1..xmax,1..ymax] OF cell;
    PROCEDURE clear
        {clears datastore, i.e. screen}
    PROCEDURE setcursor (pos:position)
    PROCEDURE readcursor (VAR pos:position)
    PROCEDURE read (VAR pos:position; VAR leng:stringlength;
                    VAR data:string)
```
{*Reads any data already written into the data structure, from current cursor position to end of line. If the data store contains a null string at this position the read blocks, waiting for something to be written. If anything new is written into the data store, the procedure returns with the position and string which had been written*}
```
    PROCEDURE write (pos:position; ca:cellattribute; len:stringlength;
                    data:string)
```
{*writes the characters from the string into the data store. The attributes apply to the whole string.*}
```
    PROCEDURE changeattribute (start,end:position; ca:cellattribute)
```
{*changes the attributes of any data in the store between the given positions.*}
```
END;
```

12.2.9 Elements of a Virtual-terminal Protocol

The virtual terminal protocol (VTP) implements the communication between the users of the virtual terminal service. There is not necessarily a one-to-one correspondence between service primitives and the protocol elements or actions.

The following phases of operation can be determined in most VTPs:

Session establishment: All protocols provide a means for setting up sessions between host computers and terminals. These may map directly onto connection establishment at the session or even transport layer.

Negotiation phase: The application and terminal must negotiate a set of primitives, parameters or class of protocol, which will apply for a virtual terminal session. This negotiation could be controlled by one side. For example the application process requests the terminal to send its set of parameters. It then selects a suitable set which it sends back to the terminal which can agree or disagree. Alternatively some protocols define a symmetric negotiation procedure, whereby both sides send their parameters. They then use a suitable algorithm for reaching a compromise on a suitable set of parameters for the session. Typical parameters which are negotiated are the terminal class, data structure dimensions, character set and local or remote echo.

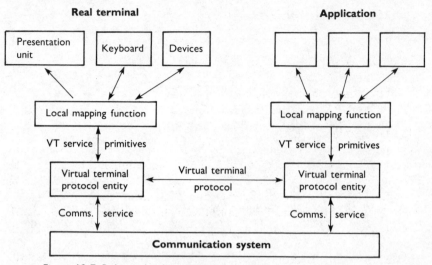

Figure 12.7 Relationship between virtual terminal service and protocol

Form definition phase: This phase applies only to data entry terminals and allows the modification of the shared data structure by defining or changing fields.

Data exchange phase: This involves exchanging messages which could be text, data-structure parameters defining attributes of a field, or control information such as actions on a field, interrupt, your-turn indication (see synchronization below), initialize data structure, etc.

The message format consists of a header indicating:
address – terminal process or auxiliary device etc.;
message type – text, control, parameter list;
your-turn indicator;
end-of-message-sequence indicator;
message-sequence number.

The header is followed by a number of variable-length items. Each item indicates its length and type in the first byte. Typical types of items are:
text – data to or from the display unit;
new-line indicator;
pointer address;
an attribute value – for setting attributes;
field control – erase a particular field or erase all unprotected fields, etc;
mark indication (see below);

Interrupts or expedited data are a particular type of limited-length (one byte) message used for attention requests.

Termination phase: This closes a virtual terminal session and may result in the transport-layer connection being terminated if there is a direct mapping.

12.2.10 Dialogue Synchronization

As with any shared data structure it is necessary to synchronize access by the terminal and application processes to the common data structure. This could be accomplished by assigning the right to transmit. There are two modes of operation, and the choice of the best one for a standard VTP is still a subject of controversy.

Alternating mode

Each partner alternatively receives the right to access the data structure, i.e. to transmit data to the other partner. This is accomplished by a flag in the message which indicates if it is the receiving partner's turn. The operator may be able to type ahead, if the terminal has local storage even when it is not his turn, but the data will not be sent. If there is no local storage the operator will only be allowed to press attention keys which will eventually signal to the application that the operator wishes to type something.

The alternating mode implies that the VTP maintains a single conceptual data structure which is always consistent as only one side can write to it at a time.

Free-running mode ∽ UNIX

Each partner can send data at any time. This implies that each side has its own copy of the common data structure and the two copies can be temporarily inconsistent due to concurrency and network delays. The VTP will eventually sort out consistency problems. This may be more suitable for the use of a VTP in symmetrical configurations, e.g. between terminals or between application processes.

Attention handling

The attention is a mechanism by which one communicating partner can interrupt the other to stop the flow of incoming information permanently or temporarily or to obtain permission to transmit from the other partner. It is also used by a terminal to return to the host operating system.

The attention should take effect immediately so is usually transmitted by an out-of-band signalling mechanism such as an interrupt service within the session connection. In some networks, interrupt messages can overtake ordinary messages transmitted earlier. Because of network delays, messages already in transit will arrive at the source of the attention before the response to the attention request has been received. These messages will have to be discarded or queued depending on the meaning of the attention request. For example, when the terminal operator presses an attention key requesting control be returned to the host operating system, all output should be aborted and in-transit messages discarded, but the prompt from the operating system must be displayed. Figure 12.8 shows a generalized attention-handling mechanism which allows the remote end to decide whether to abort or resume

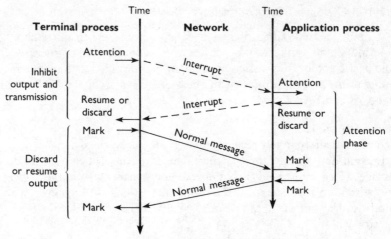

Figure 12.8 Attention handling

Interrupt eg. ^c, ^o

output at the terminal. The terminal sends an attention, which travels as an interrupt to the application process. The terminal process inhibits any further output of data from the application and does not send any further data messages to the application. The application process sends an interrupt back indicating whether output should be resumed or aborted. This depends on the type of attention received. The application process needs to know where in the incoming data stream the attention was generated and so the terminal process sends a mark as an ordinary message. Similarly, the application must inform the terminal when the attention was received with respect to the outgoing data stream from the application and so it also sends a mark message. A more detailed discussion on attention handling can be found in Bauwens [1979].

12.3 Other Application Services

In this chapter we have covered two basic application-oriented services, the virtual file and terminal services which can be used to build other application-specific services. An example is a job-transfer and manipulation service [Larmouth, 1982] which allows a job to migrate around a distributed computing service using various resources at different sites. For example suppose that a user at station A submits a job to be run at station B. The job collects data files from stations C and D and spawns a sub-job to be run at station E, where there is a suitable graphics package. Output is generated at a printer at station A and on a microfilm plotter at station E. This type of service needs the VFS to transfer data and jobs and a VTS to interact with the user or with operators.

Other application protocols that are emerging are electronic funds transfers allowing funds to be transferred between banks and possibly other financial institutions, airline reservation protocols allowing travel agents and airlines to automatically book seats on each other's reservation systems, electronic mail and document transfer between communicating word processors.

References

Bauwens E., Magnee F., 'Remarks on negotiating mechanism and attention handling'. *ACM Computer Comms. Review*, Vol. 9, no. 4, October 1979, pp. 40–61.

Bucciarelli P., Poubian A., Schumacher J., Thiele W., 'ECMA virtual file protocol – an overview', *Proc. 6th ICCC*, London, September 1982, North-Holland, pp. 859–864.

CCITT X.3, X.28, X.29, Character Terminal Access to Public Packet Switched Data Networks, 1981, available from International Telecommunications Union, Place des Nations, 1211 Geneva, Switzerland.

Day J., 'Terminal protocols' *IEEE Trans. Comms.*, Vol. 28, no 4, April 1984, pp. 585–593.

Dhondy R., Elie M., Touzin F., 'Accessing OSI Virtual Terminal Services From Cobol Application Programs', *Computer Networks*, Vol. 8, 1984, pp. 23–29.

Eliassen F., Jensen W., 'OSI Application Dialogues Expressed As Operations on Typed Data' *Euteco Conf.*, Varese, Italy, North-Holland, 1983, pp. 303–314.

Generic Virtual Terminal Service and Protocol Description: Standard ECMA-87, March 1983, ECMA 114 Rue du Rhone, 1204 Geneva, Switzerland.

Hale R., 'File transfer protocols – a comparison and critique' *Proc. 6th ICCC*, London, September 1982, North–Holland, pp. 889–895.

Larmouth J., 'The 'Red Book' JTM Protocol and its Application to Distributed Processing'. *Proc 6th ICCC*, 1982, pp. 902–905.

Linington P., 'The virtual filestore concept', *Computer Networks*, Vol 8, no. 1, 1984 pp. 13–16.

Magnee F., Endrizzi A., Day J., 'A survey of terminal protocols', *Computer Networks*, Vol. 3, 1979, pp. 299–314.

Popescu-Zeletin R., Henckel L., Heinze W., Jacobsen K., Maiss G., 'Network data management for heterogeneous computer networks: the virtual file concept', *Computer Communications*, Vol. 4, no. 3, June 1981, pp. 132–137.

Popescu-Zeletin R., Henckel L., Eliassen F., Jensen W., 'The virtual fileservice', *Euteco Conf. Proc.*, Varese, Italy, North-Holland, 1983, pp. 291–301.

Appendices

A Abbreviations

ACK	Acknowledgement
ARPA	Advanced Research Projects Agency – a USA defense-related research funding agency
ASCII	American Standard Code for Information Interchange – a 7-bit set of character codes used by many computers, and peripherals
BSC	Binary synchronous communication – a character-oriented data-link protocol
CCITT	Consultative Committee for International Telegraph and Telephones – standards organization for national telecommunications authorities
CRC	Cylic redundancy check
CSP	Communicating Sequential Processes
d.c.	Direct current
DCE	Data circuit terminating equipment, i.e. a modem
DDCMP	Digital Data Communication Message Protocol – Digital's character oriented data-link protocol
DMA	Direct memory access
DNA	Digital's network architecture
DTE	Data terminal equipment – the data-processing equipment connection to a data circuit, e.g. a computer or terminal
FCS	Frame check sequence (usually CRC)
FDM	Frequency-division multiplexing
FSK	Frequency-shift keying – frequency modulation
FTP	File transfer protocol
HDLC	High-level data-link control – a synchronous, bit-oriented, data-link protocol standardized by ISO
Hz	Hertz – a unit of frequency (cycle per second)
IA5	International alphabet number 5 – character codes standarized by CCITT
IEEE	Institute of Electrical and Electronic Engineers
I/O	Input and/or output
IPC	Interprocess communication
ISO	International Standards Organization
LAN	Local area network
LSI	Large-scale integration
IP	Internal protocol – an American Department of Defense network layer, datagram protocol
MAC	Medium-access control

MAP	Manufacturing automation protocol – a set of protocols developed by General Motors for factory automation
NAK	Negative acknowledgement or reject message
OS	Operating system
OSI	Open systems interconnection (reference model)
PSK	Phase-shift keying – phase modulation
PTT	Postal telegraph and telephone authority, e.g. British Telecom in Great Britain
RJE	Remote job entry
RPC	Remote procedure call
SDLC	Synchronous data-link control – IBM's bit-oriented data-link protocol
SNA	Systems network architecture – IBM's network architecture
TCP	Transmission control protocol – an American Development of Defense transport layer protocol
TDM	Time-division multiplexing
VC	Virtual circuit
VFS	Virtual-file service
VLSI	Very large-scale integration
VTP	Virtual terminal protocol
VTS	Virtual terminal service
WAN	Wide area network
X.25	A CCITT network-layer standard for interfacing to public networks.

B   Problems and Selected Solutions

The following problems are arranged according to chapters. Some problems cover material in a number of chapters: the problem is then placed in the highest chapter to which they refer. Solutions are included for selected problems. Note that many of the questions involving design choices do not have a single correct answer. A well-reasoned argument, stating assumptions made and justifying a choice different from the one given in the solution would be equally acceptable.

Chapter 1

1.1   Prepare a case for and against an automated office for a large firm of accountants with branches throughout the country and in major cities throughout the world. Assume the firm already uses computers for traditional data-processing applications such as their payroll, and billing of accounts. The automated office would consist of computerized workstations for most office workers together with networking facilities. Consider the functions which could be performed by the workstations and then argue the benefits of this type of distributed processing.

Chapter 2

2.1   Given the environment described in Problem 1.1, identify the main issues that must be faced in the design and construction of a suitable distributed system.

Chapter 3

3.1   Describe and compare the use of mailboxes with the use of entry and exit ports

in interprocess communication with respect to
(a)   naming,
(b)   source and destination connection and connection patterns, and
(c)   system modification and extension.

3.2   Patient monitoring system
The intensive-care ward in a hospital consists of 16 beds. Patients in each bed
are continuously monitored for a number of factors, such as pulse, temperature
and blood pressure. The rate of monitoring for each patient can be set at a
central nurse station. For each patient the current readings are displayed both
at the bedside and at the nurse station.
(a)   given the system described above, outline a design indicating your break-
      down into software components (processes). Outline the function of each
      component, its interface in terms of the message types it sends and receives,
      and the interconnection patterns.
(b)   For each main process component, outline the code you would provide
      to perform its function. The communication primitives available are:

      SEND *message* TO *destination(s)*
         (send message and continue processing: asynchronous)
      RECEIVE *message* FROM *source(s)*
         (receive message if available, otherwise wait)

      You may assume any other communication primitives that you feel are
      appropriate, but you must then explicitly define their assumed behavior.

   [Advice:
   1 . You should provide a process component to handle each device (e.g.
       interrupts). This then provides a message-passing interface to the rest of
       the system. Do not try to minimize the number of processes; this can
       always be done later if necessary.
   2. The coordination of the system is dictated by the design decisions as to
       which process initiates message transactions (e.g. a reading may be
       requested from a device handler process or periodically sent).]

3.3   Define what is meant by direct and indirect naming in interprocess communica-
      tion. 'The Ada rendezvous provides a mixture of direct and indirect naming.'
      Explain what is meant by this statement and briefly indicate how this affects
      system modification.
3.4   Using examples from Ada, CSP and CONIC, identify the differences in the
      process interfaces and naming used in their message-passing primitives. What
      are the advantages and disadvantages of each of the approaches?

Chapter 4

4.1   The following CSP example of a bounded buffer process, X, is not correct.
      Can you correct it? Also, what is the protocol that the consumer must use
      in order to get a portion from the buffer? (Give the message passing code.)

      X:: [*buffer*: (0..9) *portion*;
           in, out: *integer*; *in*:= 0; *out*:= 0;
           * [*in* < *out* + 10; *producer*?*buffer*(*in* mod 10) → *in*:= *in* + 1
           ☐*out* < *in* → *consumer*!*buffer*(*out* mod 10); *out*:= *out* + 1
           ]
        ]

4.2   Each of the types of communication primitives given below can be considered
      as primitive. Given three systems, each of which provides one of the com-

munication types as primitive, show how the other two types could be implemented using the primitive type (i.e. each could be used to provide the other two types):

(a) asynchronous send;

(b) synchronous send;

(c) request reply (rendezvous).

4.3 Mailboxes are sometimes used as a means of **indirectly naming** the processes to or from which messages are sent or received. Describe the role of the mailbox in the implementation of

(a) synchronous and

(b) asynchronous interprocess communication.

Given a number of user processes and a number of identical printer processes in a distributed system, outline a scheme for providing a general printer service *without spooling* (i.e. user output must be sent line by line to a printer process). You should also outline the relevant code that would be used in the processes. Describe your solution for *either* synchronous *or* asynchronous communication. That is,

i.e.   **SEND** *message* **TO** *mailbox-id*
            RECEIVE *message* **FROM** *mailbox-id*.

You may assume that mailbox names may be included in messages and that *mailbox-id* can be a variable.

4.4 (a) What is the behavior of

(i) a source process which uses synchronous, bidirectional communication:

SEND *expression* **TO** *destination-process* **WAIT** *variable*

(ii) a destination process using a selective receive:

SELECT RECEIVE *variable-1* **FROM** *source-1* **REPLY** *expression*
                                                    ⇒ . . .
OR RECEIVE *variable-2* **FROM** *source-2* **REPLY** *expression* ⇒ . . .
OR . . .
END

(b) Each of the rooms in a building has a control station for monitoring and controlling the environment. Each control station measures and displays the current temperature and humidity. For each room, the desired temperature and humidity is set by a pair of dials. If the current readings are outside the desired setting by more than some percentage, then the station can control the heating / ventilation in the room. A central operator station is able to request the current readings from any control station.

Outline the overall software structure and behavior of the process(es) you would use in a *control station* assuming a language which provides processes and the bidirectional message-passing primitives as given in part (a).

4.5 (a) What is the behavior of

(i) a source process which uses an asynchronous send:
     SEND expression TO destination-process

(ii) a destination process using a selective receive:
     SELECT RECEIVE *variable-1* **FROM** *source-process-1* ⇒ . . .
     OR RECEIVE *variable-2* **FROM** *source-process-2* ⇒ . . .
     OR . . .
     END

(a)   A pipeline has a number of control outstations distributed along its length. Each outstation measures and displays the current fluid flow, pressure and temperature. If the current *readings* are outside some set *limits* then the outstation displays and issues an *alarm*. An operator station is able to request the current readings from an outstation, to set the safe limits on any outstation, and also to receive an alarm if the readings at any outstation exceed the set limits.

   Outline the overall software structure and behavior of the process(es) you would use in an *outstation* assuming a language which provides processes and asynchronous message passing. For the operator station, merely indicate the messages which can be sent to or received from an outstation.

4.6 (a) (i) In the Ada rendezvous the caller can use a delay part to limit the time spent waiting for the receiver task to accept the call. This delay is cancelled on acceptance of the call by the receiver.

    (ii) In the CONIC request–reply the source task can use a timeout to limit the time spent waiting for the reply. This timeout is cancelled when the reply message is received by the source.

   What are the advantages and disadvantages of each approach?

  (b) Given a **reliable asynchronous** communication service, describe the protocols you would use to implement

   (i) the Ada rendezvous, and

   (ii) the CONIC request–reply.

4.7 (a) Given the following message-passing primitives:

source process:
 SEND *request-message* **TO** *process-id.entry-id* **WAIT** *reply-message*
destination process:
 RECEIVE *request-message* **FROM** *entry-id*;
  process message
 REPLY *reply-message*

  (i) identify the form of naming used,

  (ii) identify the connection and transaction patterns usually used with these primitives.

  As an alternative to replying, a destination process can forward the request to another process:

 FORWARD *request-message* **TO** *process-id.entry-id*

 What are the advantages of this primitive?

  (b) A database is partitioned and access is provided by a number of different server processes, each holding a part of the information. A manager process holds the main directory indicating which server holds which information. Using the primitives given above in (a), outline a scheme for providing a data enquiry service to user processes, giving the relevant code that would be used in the processes.

  (c) Rather than using the forward primitive, *name passing* can be used to provide dynamic connections. Outline the relevant code for the processes in (b) using name passing instead.

   Briefly compare the two solutions, indicating the conditions which make each scheme preferable.

4.8 A 'reliable send' primitive in interprocess communication can be described as a message-send primitive in which the sending process is blocked until the message is delivered at the receiver's station, though not necessarily accepted by the receiver process itself. This is a compromise between the traditional asynchronous and synchronous send primitives. What do you think the advantages of this approach are when compared with asynchronous and synchronous communication?

4.9 In synchronous communication, why is the combination of a guarded (selective) send and a selective receive difficult to provide?

Chapter 5

5.1 A general-purpose distributed computing system is based on a local area network which interconnects intelligent workstations, file servers, printer servers, name server, etc. A gateway provides access to the public packet-switched network for access to specialized resources on remote mainframe computers, such as microfilm plotters or particular software packages.
 (a) Discuss the types of names that would be used by the human user. When and how would these be mapped to the addresses of specific resources?
 (b) How can broadcast addressing at the data-link layer be used in such an environment?
 (c) Discuss the advantages of using indirect names for interprocess communication when programming servers.

5.2 Discuss the tradeoffs which have to be considered in fixing the maximum message length within a communication system.

5.3 Two processes in remote computers communicate over a single point-to-point link. Discuss the types of synchronization which have to occur to allow the processes to communicate.

5.4 Why must there be upward multiplexing somewhere within the communication layers within a station?

5.5 Justify the choice of a suitable network configuration for interconnecting databases at various factories, throughout the country, of a large manufacturing company.

5.6 Consider two host computers A, D connected via two switching nodes B, C in a store-and-forward network.

[A]———————(B)———————(C)———————[D]

Ignoring processing times in the hosts and switching nodes, and assuming transmission rates of 10 k.bit/s, calculate the time to send a 3 k.bit message from A to D:
 (a) if the whole message is transmitted as a single block;
 (b) if the message is segmented into three 1 k.bit packets which are transmitted one after the other.
 Explain the differences in the times in the above two cases.

5.7 The boss of company X asks his secretary to obtain Joe Bloggs, who is director of another company, on the telephone. Identify the various layers of peer-to-peer protocols involved.

5.8 Explain the ISO terms 'service data unit', 'interface data unit', and 'protocol data unit'. Describe a situation in which the protocol data unit differs in size from the interface data unit and the service data unit.

5.9 Identify the layers of the ISO Open Systems Interconnection Reference Model and identify the main functions performed by each layer.

5.10 Discuss the merits of connection (virtual circuit) and connectionless services in a LAN for implementing a request–reply language primitive.

5.11 (a) What state information must be held by a typical connection protocol?
 (b) Why is it not possible to implement a connection-oriented reliable message stream service using a datagram protocol?

Chapter 6

6.1 What is the difference between bandwidth, baud rate, and channel capacity?

6.2 Define simplex, half-duplex and full-duplex transmission modes.

6.3 Compare asynchronous (start–stop) and synchronous data transmission methods.

6.4 A 2400 baud rate data link uses four-level amplitude modulation for asynchronous data transmission with 1 start bit, 2 stop bits, 1 parity and 8 data bits. Calculate the user data rate.

Chapter 7

7.1 Explain how 'lost' messages are detected in a ring LAN.

7.2 Explain the operation of a CSMA/CD bus and a token-passing bus. Compare the advantages and disadvantages of each. Why is the latter favored for real-time applications such as process control?

7.3 Explain the differences between **broadcast** and **multicast** addressing in a local area network (LAN).

Explain why broadcast addressing cannot be easily achieved on the Cambridge Ring.

A LAN provides hardware support for only broadcast addressing. Describe how multicast addressing can be supported by software within the communication system. Comment on the efficiency of this approach.

7.4 Two minicomputers, running multitasking operating systems, are connected via a token ring local area network, with a 10 M.bit/s capacity. A task in one computer performs a request–reply message transaction on a server task in the remote computer.

(a) Discuss what factors *at all levels in the system* affect the **transaction response time**.

(b) Discuss what overheads affect **data throughput** between the remote tasks.

7.5 Discuss the main differences between a ring and a serial highway (bus) as a local area network topology.

7.6 A typical university computing department has microcomputers and terminals in staff members' offices, clusters of terminals and microcomputers for student use and a number of multi-user computers. Prepare a case for the installation of a local area network, justifying your choice of topology and access method.

Chapter 8

8.1 Describe two methods of determining the start and end of a data-link message.

8.2 Describe the main message errors which typically occur at the data-link layer. Explain how each error occurs and a method of correction.

8.3 Explain why both messages and acknowledgements need to carry sequence numbers for a reliable data-link protocol.

8.4 Under what circumstances would you expect pipelining to improve data-link layer protocol throughput.

8.5 Why are protocol supervisory (or control) messages not subject to sequence checks?

8.6 A serial bus local area network interconnects a number of computers to form a resource-sharing network. Each computer has a hardware network interface which performs the following functions:

bit, byte and block synchronization;
generation and checking of CRC codes (at end of frame);

access control;
DMA access to memory for transmitting or receiving messages;
station address recognition.

The interface thus sends or receives messages and detects corrupt ones.
Design a simple connection-oriented data-link protocol which uses the service
provided by the above media access layer, and provides in-sequence delivery
and error correction. Your solution must identify:

when a connection should be set up, or reset;
the formats of the control and data messages needed, justifying the required
fields in each message;
what state information must be maintained for the connection;
a description of the protocol operation of both a sender and receiver.

Chapter 9

9.1   Describe the sublayers found in the network layer and explain the need for
      them.
9.2   Describe the characteristics of connectionless (datagram) and connection (vir-
      tual circuit) network layer service for a wide area network.
9.3   Compare the use of a symmetric independent assignment of virtual circuit
      numbers by both ends of a connection, with the use of a single identifier which
      is common to both ends of the connection.
9.4   Work out the routing tables for gateway G2 in Fig. 9.10.
9.5   Explain the difference between flow control and congestion control.
9.6   Define **transmit and receive windows**.
      A connection protocol for a wide area network provides a transmission win-
      dow size of N messages. Derive the **minimum** message sequence number range
      for the protocol in the following cases:
      (i)   The receiver accepts out-of-sequence messages and lost or corrupted
            messages are selectively retransmitted.
      (ii) Only in-sequence messages are accepted and if a message is lost all subse-
            quent messages must be retransmitted.

Chapter 10

10.1 Describe how a **connectionless transport layer** service could be provided over
      a **virtual circuit network layer**. Suggest when connections should be set up
      and cleared and discuss the efficiency of your approach.
10.2 Discuss the problems of implementing message priorities in a virtual circuit
      transport service. Describe how high-priority message transfer service could
      be offered in a virtual circuit network.
10.3 A transport layer protocol provides a reliable packet stream connection ser-
      vice between workstations connected by a **single** local area network. The net-
      work interface hardware performs a cyclic redundancy check over messages
      and discards any corrupted messages, i.e. they are not seen by the transport
      protocol.
      (a) What entities are addressed by the transport-layer protocol?
           Outline a suitable connection establishment procedure and justify your
           choice.
      (b) Describe what errors are likely to be seen by the transport layer and why
           they occur.

(c) Suggest suitable error-control mechanisms for each type of error described in (b).

10.4 Many data-link layer protocols initialize a connection with a 'two-way hand-shake' as shown below, where ISN_i is the initial sequence number to be used by station i for the transfer of data.

8 4.

STATION a   STATION b

           Connect (ISN_a)

        ————————————————▶   Expected sequence
                                      no. $= ISN_a$

           Connect back (ISN_a, ISN_b)
        ◀————————————————

enter data transfer mode   enter data transfer mode

Explain why this cannot be used to initialize **transport**-layer connections across a store-and-forward datagram network. Describe a suitable alternative connection set-up procedure.

10.5 Explain the need for segmentation of long messages into small packets within the communication system.

86

A transport layer over an unreliable, datagram wide area network implements segmentation. Identify the transport-layer fields required in the header of a data message to perform segmentation and reassembly.

Chapter 11

11.1 Data structures and their representations are very application specific. Justify the need for a standard presentation layer for communication between different computers rather than performing information transformations within the application layer.

85

11.2 Compare the use of

86

(a) variable- or fixed-length number values
(b) explicit or implicit type tags
within an external representation syntax.

An external representation syntax does not support the primitive type **real**, but does support most other common primitive and constructor types. Suggest a suitable representation for a **real** in terms of other constructor and/or primitive types. Assume variable-length data values and explicit type tags are used for the external representation.

11.3 Write down the primitive and constructed types for a high-level language with which you are familiar. Describe a suitable representation for each type in that language using:
(a) Courier types
(b) CCITT X.409 types.

11.4 Discuss the problems of transferring structured information such as doubly linked lists between two computers. Describe a solution to the problem.

Chapter 12

12.1 Explain why there is a controversy as to whether virtual file and virtual terminal protocols should be considered presentation or application layer.

12.2 Describe the characteristics of the communication traffic generated by a file transfer protocol and hence justify the choice of a suitable inter-process communication primitive for the implementation of the file transfer protocol when the maximum length of a message is limited (e.g. 256 bytes).

12.3   What is a virtual file store? Discuss the three main services provided by a virtual file store.

12.4   Compare the CCITT packet assembler–disassembler standards with the concepts of a virtual terminal service.

12.5   Discuss the attributes of data which can be represented on a terminal.

12.6   Design a forms mode virtual terminal as an abstract data type. Define a data structure to represent the display and define a set of operations which could be performed on that display.

12.7   Define downward multiplexing (splitting) and upward multiplexing. A minicomputer is used to connect 10 visual display terminals to a datagram-based network to allow terminal access to remote computers. Only 2.4 k.bit/s leased lines are available to connect the minicomputer to the nearest switching node. All lines go to the same switching node. The communication software in the minicomputer conforms to the ISO Reference model. What multiplexing functions would you expect in each layer?

12.8   Assume the terminals in Problem 12.7 are supplied by a number of different manufacturers and differ in character and control codes as well as screen size. Give the reasons for using a virtual terminal protocol for communication between the terminals and the remote computers. Outline the main functions to be performed by the minicomputer to allow the terminals to communicate with the remote computers over a network. Assume the terminals are connected to the computer via asynchronous V.24 (RS232) type interfaces.

12.9   A terminal is connected via a network to a remote computer. Describe a mechanism in a virtual terminal protocol, whereby the terminal operator can temporarily stop the terminal displaying output from the remote application. Assume:
   (a)   Any input typed by the operator, prior to the stop command, must reach the remote process.
   (b)   There must be no loss or duplication of output, when it is resumed.
   (c)   The terminal has no spare capacity for buffering undisplayed output.
   (d)   The stop command must be obeyed immediately.
   (e)   The prompt from the remote process, in response to the stop command, must be displayed.

C Solutions

Chapter 3

3.1

Mailboxes	*Entry and Exit Ports*
Separate entities from the processes which send to and receive from them.	Local entities to which messages are sent and from which messages are received.
Naming	
Processes name the mailbox directly but not each other.	Processes name their local ports and not each other.
Global naming of mailboxes.	Processes have global names, not ports.
Connection	
Name the same mailbox.	Linkage of exitport to entryport(s).
Connection Patterns	
Includes many-to-many.	Many-to-many only possible in conjunction with multidestination.

Modification

Linkage (connection) changes may require recompilation of processes as they name the mailboxes in the process code.

Linkages may be easily changed even at run time.

Extension

Process compilation requires mailbox names and types.

Process compilation requires only message types.

New processes communicate with existing system via existing mailboxes.

New processes linked to existing system ports (as with modification).

3.3 **Direct naming**

The sender (receiver) names the destination (source) process in the send (receive) statement. The connection between sender and receiver is specified in the process code.

Indirect naming

The sender (receiver) names a local or intermediate entity rather than the destination (source) itself. The connection between sender and receiver is not specified in the process code but provided by a separate operation (linking) or entity (mailbox).

ADA has direct rendezvous calls

– *task.entry* (. . .) names the destination,

and indirect call acceptance

– *accept entry* (. . .) is from an anonymous caller.

New or modified tasks which make calls (users or clients) can be introduced into a system without difficulty since they call existing entries (servers); but the introduction of modified or new servers will require that users' code is also modified to call the appropriate tasks and entries.

Chapter 4

4.1 (See Section 4.7.2)

4.3 Mailboxes provide a separate name and storage component to/from which messages are sent/received.

Synchronous: Queue the sender until the message is received *or* queue the receiver until the message is sent. (The message may be queued with the sender.)

The mailbox therefore consists of *either* a queue of senders *or* a queue of receivers, never both.

Asynchronous: Copy and queue the message when sent and not received *or* queue the receiver if no messages available.

The mailbox therefore consists of *either* a queue of messages sent *or* a queue of receivers, never both.

Open (Fig. P4.1):

- User i requests printer service (i.e. opens the print stream) by sending its mailbox identity UMB$_i$ to a general printer service mailbox GPS.
- A free printer server j accepts a print request and responds by sending its local print mailbox PMB$_j$ to the user at UMB$_i$.

Use:

- User repeatedly sends records to be printed to the mailbox of the printer server PMB$_j$.
- Printer server repeatedly accepts records, formats and prints them.

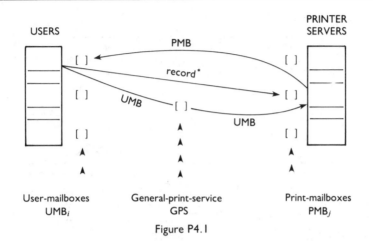

Figure P4.1

Close:
- User ends the session (i.e. closes the print stream) by sending an end-of-file message.
- Printer server completes printing and again awaits a print request at the general printer service mailbox GPS.

Synchronous communication: The user and printer are tightly coupled with each waiting for the other at the points of communication.

Asynchronous communication: Identical logical behavior except that during use, the user can run ahead of the server since records can be queued at the server's print mailbox.

User: Printer: *loop*
  SEND *UMB* **TO** *GPS*;   **RECEIVE** *UMB* **FROM** *GPS*;
  RECEIVE *PMB* **FROM** *UMB*;   **SEND** *PMB* **TO** *UMB*;
  repeat   *repeat*
    process record   **RECEIVE** *rec* **FROM** *PMB*
    SEND *record* **TO** *PMB*;   *print rec*
  until no more records;   *until rec = eof*
  SEND *eof* **TO** *PMB*;   *end*

Alternatives:
1. The users' mailboxes can be eliminated by a different open protocol:
   - when free, a printer process sends its local print mailbox, PMB_j, to GPS;
   - a user requests service by receiving the mailbox of a free printer from GPS.
2. The printer mailboxes can be eliminated by designing the printer processes such that they receive records for printing directly from the user's mailbox. After sending its mailbox to GPS for receipt by a free printer, a user merely sends records for printing to its mailbox.

With asynchronous communication, both 1 and 2 allow the user to run ahead of the printer, with possible buffer exhaustion as a result. Solution 2 is worse in this respect. (Why?)
3. A printer manager process can receive user requests and assign a printer server according to some policy (rather than let the servers allocate themselves).

Station

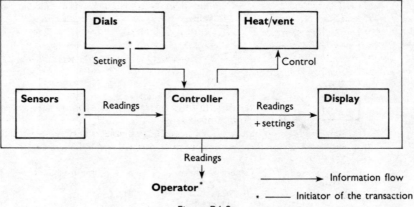

Figure P4.2

4.4   (a)   (i) *Source*: blocked, until the reply message is received from the destination.

          (ii) *Destination*: blocked if no messages available, otherwise selects from those available (nondeterministic/arrival order/lexical order...), sends a reply message and continues processing.

    (b) See Fig. P.4.2.

Sensors process:
LOOP
   read local sensors
   IF *different from before* **THEN**
      SEND *readings* **TO** *Controller* **WAIT** *signal*;
   delay (period)
END
Dials process:
LOOP
   read local settings
   IF *different from before* **THEN**
      SEND *settings* **TO** *Controller* **WAIT** *signal*;
   delay (period)
END
Heat/vent process:
LOOP
   RECEIVE *control* **FROM** *Controller* **REPLY** *signal*;
   actuate heater/ventilator according to control setting
END
Controller Process:
LOOP
   SELECT
      RECEIVE *readings* **FROM** *Sensors* **REPLY** *signal* ⇒
         SEND *(readings + settings)* **TO** *Display* **WAIT** *signal*;
   OR
      RECEIVE *settings* **FROM** *Dials* **REPLY** *signal* ⇒
   OR
      RECEIVE *request* **FROM** *Operator* **REPLY** *readings* ⇒
   END

IF *readings outside setting range* **THEN**
    SEND *control* **TO** *Heat/Vent* **WAIT** *signal*;
END
Display process:
LOOP
    RECEIVE *(readings + settings)* **FROM** *Controller* **REPLY** *signal*
    display readings
END

4.5   (a)   (i) *Source*: unblocked, continues processing as soon as the message
                 copied out of source process.
             (ii) *Destination*: blocked if no messages available, otherwise selects from
                 those available (nondeterministic/arrival order/lexical order...)
         (b)   See Fig. P4.3.

Sensors Process:
LOOP
    read local sensors
    SEND *readings* **TO Controller**;
    delay (period)
END
Controller Process:
LOOP
    SELECT
        RECEIVE *limits* **FROM** *Operator*;
    OR
        RECEIVE *readings* **FROM** *Sensors* ⇒
            SEND *readings* **TO** *display*;
            IF *outside limits* **THEN SEND** *alarm* **TO** *Operator, Display*;
    OR
        RECEIVE *request* **FROM** *Operator* ⇒
            SEND *readings* **TO** *Operator*
    END
END
Display Process:
LOOP
    SELECT
        RECEIVE *readings* **FROM** *Controller* ⇒ *display readings*
    OR
        RECEIVE *alarm* **FROM** *Controller* ⇒ *display alarm*
    END
END

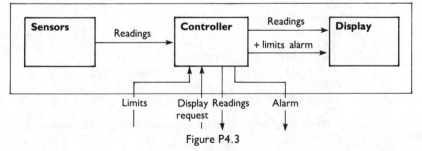

Figure P4.3

4.6   (a)
Ada   *CONIC*
+   −
Timeout of the caller can be trans-   Receiver may process the request even
parent to the receiver.   though the source timed out.
−   +
Delay specified by caller is not ab-   Timeout specified by source is
solute. Receiver can prevent com-   absolute.
pletion of the rendezvous.
−   +
Implementation is complex, par-   Implementation easier.
ticularly in a distributed environment.
(b)   (see section 4.6.4)

4.7   (a)   Naming is asymmetric, partially indirect.
1–1 and *m*–1 connections, 1–1 transactions.
Forward permits third party replies direct to the source, thereby freeing
the intermediaries (switches) for other transactions.
(b)   See Fig. P4.4.

User:	*Manager*:	*Server*:
	entry req;	*entry req*;
	:	:
SEND *enq* **TO**	**LOOP**	**LOOP**
Manager.req **WAIT** *info*	**RECEIVE** *enq* **FROM**	**RECEIVE** *enq* **FROM**
	req;	*req*;
	identify server;	*process enq*;
	FORWARD *enq* **TO**	**REPLY** *info*;
	server.req;	**END**
	END	

The reply information is returned direct to the user. The manager is
free to answer other queries after forwarding the enquiry to the server.

(c)

User:	*Manager*:	*Server*:
SEND *enq* **TO**	**LOOP**	**LOOP**
Manager.req	**RECEIVE** *enq* **FROM**	**RECEIVE** *enq* **FROM**
WAIT *server*;	*req*;	*req*;
SEND *enq* **TO** *server.req*	*identify server*;	*process enq*;
WAIT *info*;	**REPLY** *server*;	**REPLY** *info*;
	END	**END**

(b)   is a much easier and more efficient protocol for single enquiries.
(c)   is more efficient if a user is to make a number of enquiries to the same
server.

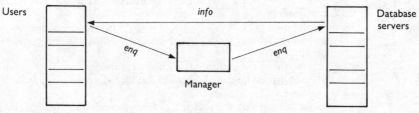

Figure P4.4

4.8   More reliable than asynchronous send – allows confirmation of delivery or the opportunity to report communication errors to the sender.
Comparison with asynchronous send:
Sender and receiver still loosely coupled.
Still suffers from buffering problems of the asynchronous send.
Poorer time behavior as no longer unblocked.
Same ordering semantics as asynchronous send.
More difficult to implement than asynchronous send.
Comparison with synchronous send:
Better time behavior than synchronous send.
Ordering semantics rather than strict point of synchronization of synchronous send.
No indication of the state of the receiver as given by synchronous send (i.e. receive statement or failed receiver).
Easier to implement than synchronous send.

Chapter 5

5.1   (a)   The human user would use symbolic names to identify objects. These could specify a particular object (e.g. a file name) or could be generic (e.g. a printer). The user should not have to specify the address of a **local** resource location, but might indicate that a **remote** resource is located on a particular host, e.g. *microplotter. Rutherfordlab.IBM*. The name server would be used to translate symbolic user names into numeric addresses for use in the network. The name-to-address translation takes place when a session is set up to use the resource, e.g. when the user connects his output stream to a printer. There will have to be an interaction by the user with a resource manager for a generic resource like a printer to find the address of a free one. Thus the name server returns the address of the resource manager and not the actual resource.
      (b)   Broadcasting means a message is sent in a single transaction to all stations on a network. It can be used to optimize the transmission of a single message to multiple destinations. A broadcast message can be used to find where a particular resource is located in the network or to find a free resource, e.g. 'is there a free printer?' It can be used to address by name. A message contains a higher-level (process) name. The broadcast message is only accepted by the station which holds that process and discarded by all other stations. This allows dynamic migration of processes between stations as the source does not have to know the address of the destination process, only its name.
      (c)   Servers do not know where requests will come from, so cannot name their communicating partner, i.e. they must use a 'receive any' primitive or use indirect naming such as a port or mailbox. It is possible to provide multiple communication channels via ports or mailboxes to reflect different functions – channels can be typechecked.
            Indirect naming provides more flexibility for clients. The name can be mapped to a particular service at run time or configuration time without recompiling.
5.2   Internal buffers within the communication system have to be large enough to hold the longest messages. This requires additional memory space in the switching nodes etc.
Long messages monopolize the use of a shared transmission medium, thus increasing access delays for other users.

Some processing overheads within a protocol layer are independent of message length; thus longer messages increase throughput.

If the error rate is high, improved efficiency can be obtained with shorter messages, as a long message is more likely to be corrupted and the whole message will have to be retransmitted.

5.3   See Section 5.2.

5.4   See Section 5.2.

5.6   (a)   3 k.bit message transmitted over 3 hops @ 10 k.bits/s.
Time = 3×3 k.bits$/(10$ k.bits/s$) = 0.9$ s.

     (b)   Message divided into 1 k.bit packets.
Time to transmit packet over each hop = 0.1 s, but packet 1 can be transmitted over hop BC while packet 2 is transmitted over hop AB.
Time to receive first packet at D = 0.3 s.
Last packet arrives 0.2 s after first.
Total time = 0.5 s.
The overall delay for packet switching is reduced because it makes use of the inherent parallelism of multiple switching nodes and multiple transmission lines.

5.8   See Section 5.4.2.

5.9   See Section 2.6.2.

5.11   (a)   A connection protocol state information includes:
Address of remote station
Local and remote connection identifiers.
Sequence number of last message sent.
Sequence number of last message received.
Local and remote flow control information (i.e. credits).
List of unacknowledged messages.

     (b)   A datagram protocol maintains no state information so it cannot detect duplicates, lost or out-of-sequence messages. It does not perform acknowledgements or retransmissions so cannot recover from errors. Hence it cannot provide a reliable message sequence service.

Chapter 6

6.1   See Section 6.2.

6.2   See Section 6.3.

6.3   *Asynchronous transmission*
Start and stop bits reduce efficiency.
A character can be transmitted at random times.
Variable idle time between characters.
Constant bit rate within a character.
No limit on block length.
Low-speed communication (< 19.2k.bits/s).
Synchronization errors results in loss of only a single character.
Synchronous transmission
More efficient use of bandwidth.
Characters buffered into blocks for transmission.
No idle time between characters.
Constant bit rate over a block.
Higher-speed communication.
Synchronization errors result in a loss of a complete block.

Chapter 7

7.1 See Section 7.2.

7.2 See Section 7.5.

7.3 In broadcast addressing a single message is sent to *all* stations on the network as a single transaction. Stations recognize and receive messages addressed to the broadcast address (e.g. all 1s) as well as their normal station address.

In multicast addressing a single message is sent to a *group* (not all) of stations on the network. The network interface has to be explicitly set up to receive a particular multicast address. An interface could be set up to receive several multicast addresses.

When a station on the Cambridge Ring is receiving the multiple minipackets which form a typical data-link layer message, it sets up the ring interface to receive minipackets only from a single source. It would not accept minipackets from another station trying to broadcast a message. Broadcasting can be implemented only by multiple sends at the data-link level.

Multicast using LAN broadcast:

Broadcast message to all stations, i.e. use broadcast address at data-link layer. Message must contain multicast address as well. The communication system will have to maintain a list of multicast addresses applicable to the station and discard messages for which there is no multicast address (software filtering).

This is inefficient for two reasons:

- All stations have to process every multicast message.
- Searching a list of multicast addresses is slower than identifying the address by means of an associative memory in a hardware interface, thus increasing delays.

7.4 (a) The transaction response time consists of the message delay in transferring the request to the server task, the processing time in the server task and the delay in transferring the reply. The following factors contribute to overall message transfer delays:

- Queuing time in source processor due to multiple tasks simultaneously sending messages.
- Local operating system time to get message into communication system tasks.
- Processing time within various layers of the communication software in both source and destination processor.
- Access delay to ring while waiting for token to be received at the source station.
- Transmission time = length of message (in bits)/10 M.bits/s. This is probably negligible compared to other times.
- Possible retransmission times due to errors. This will include the time to send a NAK from the receiver or the expiry of a timeout at the source.
- Operating system overhead at the destination required to a copy a received message into the destination task and schedule it to run.

(b) Application data throughput is limited by the following:

- Protocol headers and trailers containing sequence numbers, addresses, CRC checks, etc., often amounting to more than 50 bytes on each message.
- Protocol supervisory frames such as connection initialization and termination, or acknowledgements.
- Errors resulting in retransmission of messages.

- Reinitializing the destination's network interface after receiving one message involves providing a new receive buffer and resetting the hardware. This results in a 'dead' time within which no messages can be received.
- Processing overheads in the operating system and communication system of both the sender and receiver reduce the message-transfer rate.

7.5   A comparison of serial bus and ring.

Serial bus	*Rings*
Broadcast transmission.	Not true broadcast if message is removed by destination.
Passive couplers onto transmission medium, so power failure at a station does not affect communication on the highway.	Ring interface regenerates the signal so power failure at a station would stop communication on the ring. It is possible to use bypass relays or double rings to circumvent station failure.
A single coupler onto transmission medium is sufficient.	Two couplers needed, which can be expensive if armored cable is used.
A break in transmission medium stops all communication.	Full duplex or double rings can recover from break in medium.
Redundant bus needed to overcome failures.	Double ring also needed to overcome failures.
Minimum length of cable needed to interconnect stations.	Up to double length of cable needed to interconnect stations.
There are limitations on highway length unless signal regenerators are included.	Signal regenerated at each station, so ring length can be longer.
Transmitters drive multiple receiver loads, so more power is required.	Transmitters drive single receiver loads.
Propagation delays independent of number of stations on bus.	Delays proportional to number of stations on ring.
Usually coaxial cable. Difficult to use fiber optics.	Can use any transmission medium, and can mix media in a single ring.

Chapter 8

8.1   See Section 8.1.
8.2   See Section 8.3.
8.4   Pipelining means more than one message is sent before an acknowledgement is sent. It is effective only if there is normally more than one message waiting to be sent to the particular destination. It is particularly used when the round-trip delay is long compared to the transmission time of a message.

8.6   Connections are set up between stations at the data-link layer, and not between processes. Two strategies for setting up connections are:

(a) Connections are set up to every other station on the network when a station is switched on. This is feasible only if the maximum number of stations is fairly small. The connection could last for the whole time the station is powered up and need never be terminated.

(b) Establish a connection whenever a session is required to another station, e.g. logging into a mainframe or for a file transfer. The connection is cleared when the session is cleared. A finite number of connections (e.g. 10 or 20) is adequate for most applications.

Frame format:

Dest.	Source	Type	Seq. No.	Data

Dest   Destination address needed to identify which station the message is being sent to.

Source   Source address needed to identify from which station the message came.

Type   Needed to distinguish the message types.

Seq. No.   Message sequence number of message being sent or message being acknowledged.

Data   User data (not in control messages).

(Length field is not essential)
Virtual circuit numbers are not really necessary as there can be only one connection between any pair of stations so that the remote station's address can be used to identify the connection. If the addresses are very long it may be convenient to use virtual circuit numbers as an index into a connection table.

Message types:

Connect   Needed to initialize connection and can also be used to reset a connection after a sequence error. Sequence numbers set to zero.

Connect Ack

Connect Nack   Reason (e.g. no connection space) in sequence number field (not essential, could do without it).

Disconnect }
Disconnect Ack }   not needed in (a) above.

No data field in all the above and sequence number field set to zero if not being used.

Data   Specifies message sequence number.

Data ACK   Specifies sequence number of message being acknowledged.

Data NAK   Not really necessary. It can only be used to indicate temporary lack of buffers etc., but cannot be used to indicate CRC failure. A message received with CRC error *must* be discarded as the source or destination addresses may be corrupted.

State information
If connections are set up to all stations the remote station's address may be implicit (e.g. index number into array of connection records), otherwise address must be stored as part of state information. Other state information includes sequence number of next data to be sent and sequence number of last data message received.

Operation

Connection set up

Sender transmits connect, sets timeout and waits for connect ACK. Repeat up to n (e.g. $n = 10$) times if not successful, then signal failure. If the ACK to the connect is lost and the station which sent the ACK immediately starts sending data, it will arrive at the initiating station on a connection which has not been fully set up. The connection should then be reset. If the station which initiates the connection always uses it first, this situation will not arise.

A connection request on an existing connection is always treated as a reset and a connect ACK sent.

If connections are being set up to all stations at power up, then the best method is to repeatedly broadcast the connect message and not use connect acks or nacks. The connection can last until the station is switched off and so a disconnect is not needed but a connection reset would be needed to recover from sequence errors.

Disconnection

Send disconnect and set timeout, repeat up to 5 times and then clear connection anyway.

Receiver should always return disconnect ACK even if no connection existed, as it may be a duplicate disconnect request.

Data transfer

Send data message with current send sequence number and set timeout. If timeout expires retry up to a retry limit. When ACK received for data message, increment sequence number modulo n. After a retry limit has been exceeded the connection must be reset before being used again as the sender cannot know if the last message did get through and all ACKS were lost.

When station receives data message check sequence number.

If < last received, then ACK and discard.

If = (last received + 1) then ACK, increment last received and pass message up.

If > last received, then sequence error so reset connection.

Chapter 9

9.1 See Section 9.2.
9.2 See Fig. 9.6.
9.3 See Section 9.5.2.
9.5 See Section 9.8.
9.6 A transmit window is the number of messages the sender can transmit before waiting for an acknowledgement. A receive window is the range of sequence numbers acceptable by the receiver.

(i) Assume the sender transmits N messages (0 to $N-1$) all of which are received and acknowledged, but the acks are all lost. The sender will timeout and retransmit all packets 0 to $N-1$.

The receiver must be able to distinguish retransmitted messages (0 to $N-1$) from the next window of N i.e. (N to $2N-1$) new messages which may arrive in any order. A sequence number range of 0 to $2N-1$ is needed.

(ii) Assume the sender transmits N messages (0 to $N-1$) all of which are received and acknowledged, but the ack for packet 0 is lost. The sender will timeout and retransmit all packets 0 to $N-1$.

The receiver must be able to distinguish retransmissions (0 to $N-1$) from the next in-sequence message (N) so message sequence number range is window size + 1 (0 to N).

Chapter 10

10.1 If a connection request can contain user data, then the datagram message can be sent within a connection request. The destination transport entity immediately returns a disconnect request (without data). The initiator will have to reply with a disconnect confirm. This results in three messages for each datagram, i.e. efficiency could be as low 33% for short messages.
or:
If no user data can be sent in the connection the following message sequence is needed.

Connect ⟶
⟵ Connect confirm
Datagram ⟶
⟵ Disconnect
Disconnect confirm ⟶

This results in at least five messages for each user message (six if the datagram has to be acked before the connection is closed).

The efficiency of the transaction is improved if the destination holds the connection open for a time, on the assumption that more messages will be generated by the user, rather than closing it immediately, i.e. subsequent datagrams do not have to wait for the connection to be opened. The connection can then be closed by the initiator after a period of inactivity.

10.3 (a) Entities addressed – sockets or ports within a station. These map onto processes, or processes are addressed directly.
Connection set up needed to initialize sequence numbers.
No delayed or out-of-sequence messages possible in LAN, so two-way handshake adequate.

Connect (my VC number, my socketID, your socketID,) ⟶

⟵ Connectack (my VC number, your VC number,) or disconnect (your VC number, reason)

(b) Could be some data corruption due to noise when transferring data between workstation memory and LAN hardware interface (probability quite low).
Main errors – lost messages due to:
Discarding of messages by LAN hardware, e.g. CRC failure.
Receiver not set up quickly enough after a previous message so misses a following message addressed to the station.
Duplicates arising out of transport-protocol retransmissions.
No reordering of messages can occur in LAN.

(c) Sum check over message contents could be used to detect corruption.
Receiver discards corrupted message.
Sequence numbers needed to detect lost messages and duplicates – incremented for each new message transmitted.
Separate sequence numbers for each socket-to-socket connection.
Sender   Transmit message start timeout.
If timeout expires retransmit up to a retry limit.
When acknowledgement received for message cancel timeout.
If retry limit exceeded notify error to user.
Receiver   Discard messages with incorrect sumcheck – could send NAK.

Check sequence number

next expected – pass to user:

> expected – send NAK and discard

< expected – duplicate so discard and send ACK.

10.4   A store-and-forward datagram network has variable delays, may deliver out-of-sequence packets and duplicate packets. This means data packets with valid sequence numbers from old connections can arrive after a new connection has been set up. If an old connection request arrived at b it would be acknowledged. a merely discards the connectack as it was not expecting it, or the connectack may get lost. Old packets with valid sequence numbers are now accepted by b.

An alternative mechanism is to use a three-way handshake (see Section 10.2.1) or a timer-based protocol (see Section 10.2.2).

10.5   Need for segmentation:

- Buffers within the communication system have finite size. Longer messages must be segmented to fit.
- Long messages monopolize shared resources, e.g. transmission medium, increasing delays for other messages.
- A long message can be segmented into small packets which are transmitted over multiple data links, i.e. making use of parallelism to decrease delay or increase throughput.
- Smaller unit of retransmission increases efficiency for high error rates.
- A network may impose an inherent limitation on message length, e.g. Cambridge Ring minislot is only 16 bits of data.
- Interconnected networks may have different maximum message lengths so gateways must perform segmentation.

Fields required:

- Message ID: (unsegmented) message sequence number so receiver can identify which message a segment belongs to (may be a delayed or duplicate packet from a previous message)
- Segment ID: segment number within the message – so segments can be reassembled in the correct order.
- Total number of segments in message: allows reservation of buffer space and the receiver can tell when the last segment has been received.

Chapter 11

11.1   Representation of basic information units (reals, integers etc.) differ between different computers. Transformations of information representations is needed to allow applications to communicate. This need is common to many applications so is best placed within a shared communication layer (see Section 11.1).

11.2   Variable-length number values

No field size limitations ⇒ any degree of accuracy.

Need length or end-of-field indicator – increase overheads.

Could be represented as string of characters – one per digit or as a variable-length bit string which represents an integer (more efficient)

Fixed-length field

Typically 16- or 32-bit fields for integers.

Maximum value limitations – may need to truncate and scale ⇒ loss of accuracy.

Simpler transformations.

Communication buffers have predefined sizes.

Explicit tag
   Each constructed or primitive data value is preceded by a tag indicating
   its type.
   Increased overheads of transferring tags.
   Self-contained type information.
   Can be used for dynamic type checking – extra level of error detection.
   Parameters can be in any order.
Implicit type information
   No explicit indication of type of data values so receiver must know in
   advance the type of data values in a message.
   Address of a port or procedure can implicitly define type of message.
   Fields must be in predefined order.
Representation of real:
Printable character string:
   e.g. string, length, 'xxxxx.xxxxx'
or mantissa and exponent as integers:
record, length,
   integer, length, value, {mantissa}
   integer, length, value, {exponent}
   integer, length, value, {base – could be implicit}

11.4   Implementations of complex data structures generally use pointers (addresses)
to represent structural relationships. It is necessary to maintain structural
relationships between subcomponents when transferring complex data structures between computers. However, address values cannot be transferred
between computers as they are meaningless in different address space. The
solution is to name subcomponents and convert pointers into substructure
identifiers which can be transferred (see Sections 11.5.1 and 11.6.2)

Chapter 12

12.1   See Section 11.1 and introduction to Chapter 12.
12.2   File transfers require a few request – reply type transactions to open the file
and initiate the transfer. Thereafter a large number of messages are sent with
occasional checkpointing. In order to optimize throughput the sending process
should not have to wait for receiving process to receive each message,
(asynchronous send). If the system runs out of buffers, the sender could be
blocked as it is not performing a time-critical function.
12.3   See Sections 12.1.2 and 12.1.3.
12.4   A PAD is a special access node in a public packet-switched network. Simple,
unintelligent, character mode terminals are connected to the PAD to enable
them to communicate via the network with the remote computer.
   A virtual terminal (VT) is an abstract generalized model of a class of
terminals. Its characteristics are a superset of those of a number of different
terminals. A host computer communicates with a single type of terminal, the
VT.
   The terminal's physical characteristics are controlled by parameters set in
the PAD. These can be default or set by the application process, which is
thus aware of the terminal's characteristics. Application processes thus do
not communicate with a single type of terminal.
   Standardization of virtual terminals could lead manufacturers to build terminals which correspond to the standard. The PAD concept does not lead
towards a standardized terminal.

VT protocols can be used for host-to-host communication, but PAD protocols cannot.

PAD protocols are not upward compatible with more sophisticated intelligent terminals, whereas VT protocols are defined as upward compatible classes of protocols.

12.7   Upward multiplexing – combining multiple $n + 1$ connections onto a single n connection or service-access point (see Section 5.2, p. 122).

Downward multiplexing – splitting traffic on a single $n + 1$ connection amongst multiple n connections.

Multiplexing with respect to the ISO Model:

● Application sessions map directly onto session layer connections.
● No multiplexing in session or presentation layers.
● One transport layer connection per session.
● Upward multiplexing in transport layer of sessions onto single network SAP to allow multiple simultaneous user sessions over the network.
● Network layer – no multiplexing.
● Data-link layer – downward multiplexing to increase throughput as 2.4 K line would be too slow to support 15 users.

12.8   A virtual terminal is a superset of the features found in most terminals. Programs on the host computer communicate with this virtual terminal. This simplifies the programs as they only have to communicate with a single virtual terminal. The remote minicomputer is responsible for mapping the characteristics of the virtual terminal onto those of the real terminals connected to it.

The minicomputer must perform the following functions:

● It acts as a packet assembler and disassembler converting characters into packets for transfer across the network. Similarly, it must receive packets and send individual characters to the terminals.
● It implements the communication protocols.
● Performs character translation and control code (cursor addressing) translation.
● Line folding.
● Local flow control to terminals, e.g. XON, XOFF.

Index

329